Party System Institutionalization in Asia

This book provides a comprehensive empirical and theoretical analysis of the development of parties and party systems in Asia. The studies included advance a unique perspective in the literature by focusing on the concept of institutionalization and by analyzing parties in democratic settings as well as in authoritarian settings. The countries covered in the book range from Northeast Asia to Southeast Asia to South Asia.

Allen Hicken is Associate Professor of Political Science, Research Associate Professor at the Center for Political Studies, and Faculty Associate at the Center for Southeast Asian Studies at the University of Michigan. He is the author of *Building Party Systems in Developing Democracies* (2009) and the editor of *Politics of Modern Southeast Asia: Critical Issues in Modern Politics* (2010). His articles have appeared in the *American Journal of Political Science*, the *Journal of Politics*, *Comparative Political Studies*, the *Journal of East Asian Studies*, *Asian Survey*, and *Electoral Studies*.

Erik Martinez Kuhonta is Associate Professor of Political Science and Member of the Institute for the Study of International Development at McGill University. He is the author of *The Institutional Imperative: The Politics of Equitable Development in Southeast Asia* (2011), which was short-listed for the 2012 Canadian Political Science Association Prize in Comparative Politics. He is also coeditor of *Southeast Asia in Political Science: Theory, Region, and Qualitative Analysis* (2008). His articles have appeared in *Comparative Political Studies*, *Contemporary Southeast Asi ˹·····ℓℴ˒* and *Pacific Review*.

CW01497116

Party System Institutionalization in Asia

Democracies, Autocracies, and the Shadows of the Past

Edited by

ALLEN HICKEN
University of Michigan, Ann Arbor

ERIK MARTINEZ KUHONTA
McGill University

CAMBRIDGE
UNIVERSITY PRESS

CAMBRIDGE
UNIVERSITY PRESS

32 Avenue of the Americas, New York, NY 10013-2473, USA

Cambridge University Press is part of the University of Cambridge.

It furthers the University's mission by disseminating knowledge in the pursuit of education, learning, and research at the highest international levels of excellence.

www.cambridge.org
Information on this title: www.cambridge.org/9781107614239

© Cambridge University Press 2015

First published 2015

Printed in the United States of America

A catalog record for this publication is available from the British Library.

Library of Congress Cataloging in Publication Data
Party system institutionalization in Asia : democracies, autocracies, and the shadows of the past / [edited by] Allen Hicken University of Michigan, Ann Arbor, Erik Martinez Kuhonta, McGill University.
    pages   cm
Includes bibliographical references.
ISBN 978-1-107-04157-8
1. Political parties – Asia. 2. Asia – Politics and government – 21st century. I. Hicken, Allen, 1969– editor. II. Kuhonta, Erik Martinez, 1973– editor. III. Weiss, Meredith L. (Meredith Leigh), 1972– Antidemocratic potential of party system institutionalization. Container of (work)
JQ39.P37   2014
324.2095–dc23   2014027897

ISBN 978-1-107-04157-8 Hardback
ISBN 978-1-107-61423-9 Paperback

To Neric Acosta and Andrew MacIntyre

Contents

Figures

Tables

Contributors

Tun-Jen Cheng is Class of 1935 Professor in the Department of Government, College of William and Mary. He received his B.A. from National Taiwan University, his M.A. from the University of Waterloo, and his Ph.D. from the University of California–Berkeley. He has written extensively on political and economic change in East Asia. Among his recent publications are two coedited volumes, *China under Hu Jintao* (2005) and *Religious Organizations and Democratic Transition in East Asia* (2006). He was editor-in-chief of the *American Asian Review*, is editor of *Taiwan Journal of Democracy*, and is on the editorial board of a number of leading journals on China and Asian studies.

Allen Hicken is Associate Professor of Political Science, Research Associate Professor at the Center for Political Studies, and Faculty Associate at the Center for Southeast Asian Studies at the University of Michigan. He studies political parties, institutions, political economy, and policy making in developing countries, with a focus on Southeast Asia. He has carried out research in Thailand, the Philippines, Singapore, Malaysia, Indonesia, and Cambodia and is the author of a book on parties and elections in Thailand and the Philippines, entitled *Building Party Systems in Developing Democracies* (2009). He is the editor of *Politics of Modern Southeast Asia: Critical Issues in Modern Politics* (2010). His articles have appeared in *American Journal of Political Science*, *Journal of Politics*, *Comparative Political Studies*, *Journal of East Asian Studies*, *Asian Survey*, and *Electoral Studies*.

Yung-ming Hsu is Associate Professor of Political Science at Soochow University. His research analyzes issues such as political learning, party realignment, and ethnic politics in Taiwan. He received his Ph.D. from the University of Michigan.

Erik Martinez Kuhonta is Associate Professor in the Department of Political Science and Member of the Institute for the Study of International Development at McGill University. He is the author of *The Institutional Imperative: The Politics of Equitable Development in Southeast Asia* (2011), which was short-listed for the Canadian Political Science Association Prize in Comparative Politics, and coeditor of *Southeast Asia in Political Science: Theory, Region, and Qualitative Analysis* (2008). Kuhonta has published articles in *Contemporary Southeast Asia, Comparative Political Studies, Asian Survey,* and *Pacific Review.* He received his Ph.D. from Princeton University and has held visiting fellowships at Stanford University, the National University of Singapore, the East-West Center, and Kyoto University.

Scott Mainwaring is the Eugene and Helen Conley Professor of Political Science at the University of Notre Dame. He is the coeditor of *Building Democratic Institutions: Party Systems in Latin America* (1995) and the author of *Rethinking Party Systems in the Third Wave of Democratization: The Case of Brazil* (1999), among many other books. His latest book is *Democracies and Dictatorships in Latin America: Emergence, Survival, and Fall,* coauthored with Aníbal Pérez-Liñán (2013). He was elected to the American Academy of Arts and Sciences in 2010.

Kenneth Mori McElwain is Assistant Professor of Political Science at the University of Michigan–Ann Arbor. His research focuses on the politics of institutional design, including the manipulation of electoral rules and the democratization of political parties. His current project examines the evolution and survival of national constitutions. He received his Ph.D. in Political Science from Stanford University and a B.A. in Public Policy and International Affairs from Princeton University. He is a coeditor of *Political Change in Japan: Electoral Behavior, Party Realignment, and the Koizumi Reforms* (2009). His research has been published in the *American Journal of Political Science, Journal of East Asian Studies, Journal of Social Science,* and numerous edited volumes.

Csaba Nikolenyi received his Ph.D. from the University of British Columbia and has taught at Concordia University since 2000. He has held visiting fellowships at the Hebrew University of Jerusalem and the Australian National University. A former English coeditor of the *Canadian Journal of Political Science* (2006–2011), he is currently co-directing the Azrieli Institute of Israel Studies. His recent publications include a number of articles on the politics of governing coalitions, book chapters on the selection and de-selection of cabinet ministers, the volume *Minority Governments in India* (2010), and the forthcoming book *Institutional Design and Party Government in Post-Communist Europe.* His current research looks at the causes and consequences of anti-defection and electoral integrity legislation in democratic states.

Sorpong Peou received his Ph.D. from York University. He is Professor and Chair of the Department of Politics and Public Administration at Ryerson University (Toronto). Prior to this appointment, he was Chair of the Department of Political Science at the University of Winnipeg, Professor of International Security at

Sophia University (Tokyo), and Canada-ASEAN Fellow at the Institute of Southeast Asian Studies (Singapore). His major publications include *Human Security Studies* (2014), *Peace and Security in the Asia-Pacific* (2010), *Human Security in East Asia*, ed. (2008), *International Democracy Assistance for Peacebuilding: Cambodia and Beyond* (2007), *Intervention and Change in Cambodia: Toward Democracy* (2001), and *Conflict Neutralization in the Cambodia War: From Battlefield to Ballot-Box* (1997).

Netina Tan is Assistant Professor of Political Science at McMaster University. Her dissertation, *Access to Power: Hegemonic Party Rule in Singapore and Taiwan*, from the University of British Columbia, was awarded the 2011 Canadian Political Science Association Vincent Lemieux Prize for the best Ph.D. thesis submitted at a Canadian institution. Her research interests include democratization, electoral authoritarianism, party and electoral politics, and gender and governance in East and Southeast Asia. Her work has appeared in *Electoral Studies*, *International Political Science Review*, and other edited volumes.

Paige Johnson Tan is Professor and Chair of the Department of Political Science at Radford University, Virginia. Her research focuses on political parties and their role in democratization. Tan has contributed articles on Asian topics to *Current History*, *Indonesia*, *Contemporary Southeast Asia*, *Asian Journal of Political Science*, *Inside Indonesia*, *Education about Asia*, and *Asian Perspective*. She has consulted on Asian governance topics with Sea-Change Partners (Singapore), the Drug Enforcement Administration and the State Department (Washington, DC), and the World Bank (Jakarta, Indonesia), as well as the U.S. military (Fort Bragg and Camp Lejeune, NC). Her Ph.D. is from the University of Virginia.

Tuong Vu is Associate Professor of Political Science at the University of Oregon. He has held visiting fellowships at the National University of Singapore and Princeton University. His recent publications include "Socialism and Underdevelopment in Southeast Asia," in *Handbook of Southeast Asian History*, ed. Norman Owen (2013) and "Workers under Communism: Romance and Reality," in *Oxford Handbook on the History of Communism*, ed. S. A. Smith (2014). Currently he is completing a book about the Vietnamese revolution as a case of radical movements in international politics.

Meredith L. Weiss is Associate Professor of Political Science at the University at Albany, State University of New York. She received her Ph.D. from Yale University in 2001. Weiss has held visiting fellowships or professorships at universities and institutes in Australia, Malaysia, the Philippines, Singapore, and the United States. Weiss is the author of *Student Activism in Malaysia: Crucible, Mirror, Sideshow* (2011) and *Protest and Possibilities: Civil Society and Coalitions for Political Change in Malaysia* (2006), as well as numerous journal articles and book chapters. She is editor or coeditor of six books – most recently, *Handbook of Contemporary Malaysia* (forthcoming); *Electoral Dynamics in Malaysia: Findings from the Grassroots* (2013); and *Global*

Homophobia: States, Movements, and the Politics of Oppression (2013). Her research addresses political mobilization and contention, the politics of development, civil society, nationalism and ethnicity, and electoral change in Southeast Asia. Weiss has previously served as Chair of the Southeast Asia Council of the Association for Asian Studies and has served in several positions in the American Political Science Association and component sections.

Joseph Wong is the Ralph and Roz Halbert Professor of Innovation at the Munk School of Global Affairs, University of Toronto. He is also Professor and Canada Research Chair in the Department of Political Science and the Director of the University of Toronto's Asian Institute. He is the author of *Healthy Democracies: Welfare Politics in Taiwan and South Korea* (2004) and *Betting on Biotech: Innovation and the Limits of Asia's Developmental State* (2011). Wong is also coeditor (with Edward Friedman) of *Political Transitions in Dominant Party Systems: Learning to Lose* (2008) and (with Dilip Soman and Janice Stein) *Innovating for the Global South: Towards an Inclusive Innovation Agenda* (2014).

Yongnian Zheng is Professor and Director of the East Asian Institute, National University of Singapore. He is the editor of the *Series on Contemporary China* and editor of *China Policy Series*. He is also the editor of *China: An International Journal* and of *East Asian Policy*. He has studied both China's transformation and its external relations. He is the author of numerous books, including *The Chinese Communist Party as Organizational Emperor* (2009) and *Globalization and State Transformation in China* (2004). Zheng has also been an academic activist. He served as a consultant to the United Nations Development Programme on China's rural development and democracy. In addition, he has been a columnist for *Xinbao* (Hong Kong) and *Zaobao* (Singapore) for many years, writing numerous commentaries on China's domestic and international affairs.

Acknowledgments

This project began in the corridors of academic conferences when the two editors of this book began discussing their common interest in the concept of party system institutionalization. Our goal was to bring the concept more directly in conversation with the study of Asian politics. A workshop held at McGill University on August 27–28, 2009, was crucial in getting this project off the ground and bringing together a wonderful group of scholars to write papers on party system institutionalization in Asia. The workshop was generously supported by the Social Sciences and Humanities Research Council of Canada, the Institute of Southeast Asian Studies (Singapore), the University of Michigan, and McGill's Institute for the Study of International Development. Discussants at the workshop included Jim Glassman, Christopher Goscha, Manuel Litalien, Kimberley Manning, Mariam Mufti, Illan Nam, Phil Oxhorn, Ben Reilly, Wolfgang Sachsenroeder, Richard Stubbs, and Suranjan Weeraratne. A big thanks to all the discussants for helping make the papers stronger.

We would like to express our gratitude to one anonymous reviewer and one not-so-anonymous reviewer – Ben Smith – who provided very helpful and constructive comments on the whole manuscript. Many thanks also to Lew Bateman at Cambridge University Press for his support of this project.

Parts of the introductory chapter are from Allen Hicken and Erik Martinez Kuhonta, "Shadows from the Past: Party System Institutionalization in Asia," *Comparative Political Studies* 44, no. 5 (May): 572–597. We acknowledge permission from Sage Publications to use parts of this article.

Finally, we thank all of our contributors for their patience and willingness to revise their papers for the sake of the collective enterprise. It was a real pleasure working with all of the chapter writers.

This book is dedicated to two individuals who have committed much of their careers to institution building: Neric Acosta, Philippine Presidential Adviser for Environmental Protection and General Manager of the Laguna Lake

Development Authority; and Andrew MacIntyre, Deputy Vice-Chancellor, International and Vice-President of the Royal Melbourne Institute of Technology (RMIT) University.

Allen Hicken
Erik Martinez Kuhonta

I

Introduction: Rethinking Party System Institutionalization in Asia

Allen Hicken and Erik Martinez Kuhonta

Political parties are often the weakest link in democracies, both young and old. This is the conclusion of a large number of scholars, policy consultants, and political practitioners. From Peru to the Philippines, these lynchpins of modern democracy are struggling to carry out the fundamental tasks of representing citizen interests and enabling voters to hold government officials accountable.[1] In some parts of the world, the traditional connections between parties and their constituents are eroding (see the extensive literature on dealignment); in other parts of the world, meaningful links between parties and voters have yet to develop. Some systems present voters with a dizzying number of political parties, distinguishable more by the personalities at their helm than the policies in their platforms. In others, a single party so dominates elections that one can justifiably call into question the credibility of competition.

For scholars trying to make sense of the role parties play in supporting (or undermining) effective and robust democracies, *party system institutionalization* has emerged as an important concept. The literature on party system institutionalization suggests that a democracy with a more institutionalized party system is more likely to survive than one without. Institutionalized parties, defined as coherent, adaptable, and complex institutions, provide a stable means for channeling the interests of social groups and a mechanism for citizens to hold government accountable. Without parties acting as a bridge between state and society, demands from society will overwhelm government institutions and may lead to the weakening of democracy. Institutionalized parties thus serve as a crucial bulwark for sustaining democracy and maintaining its representative quality.

But institutionalization does not only matter for democratic stability. The literature on institutionalization suggests that party system institutionalization

---

[1] Powell 2000.

can affect the longevity and stability of *nondemocratic* regimes as well. Precisely because institutionalized parties are more stable, complex, and adaptable, they may help nondemocratic regimes withstand opposition, understand and adapt to changes in citizen preferences, and successfully manage factional conflicts from within the ranks of the ruling party.

Institutionalized parties, regardless of regime-type, are furthermore often better equipped to advance public goods, such as social reforms or economic growth, in part because they tend to be more programmatic and thus have stronger incentives to provide public goods and in part because they tend to have greater levels of party discipline and cohesion.[2] The study of party systems thus helps us clarify why democratic regimes – and certain authoritarian regimes – may persist, and how effective they are at translating citizen demands into needed public policies.

The literature on party system institutionalization has to date focused primarily on Latin America, and more recently on Western and Eastern Europe, with Scott Mainwaring and Timothy Scully's edited book, *Building Democratic Institutions: Party Systems in Latin America* (Stanford University Press, 1995) as a seminal example. The rich cases in Asia have generally, and regrettably in our view, been ignored.[3] One implication of this neglect is that the literature has been heavily focused on understanding party system institutionalization only in the context of democratization.

This project shifts the lenses of party institutionalization toward Asia. This geographical shift leads to distinct analytical questions and enables us to make at least three distinct contributions to the literature, as laid out in this introductory chapter. First, we find that historical legacies are a crucial variable affecting current levels of party system institutionalization across Asia. In particular, the immediate postwar period was the crucible from which institutionalized party systems in Asia developed. Second, we claim that for a significant number of institutionalized party systems, historical legacies are rooted in some element of authoritarianism, either as former authoritarian parties or as semi-democratic regimes. Third, precisely because authoritarianism has played an important role in the origins of institutionalized party systems, we argue that the concept of institutionalization needs to be decoupled from the concept of democracy.

The rest of this chapter proceeds as follows. In the next section, we discuss the concept of institutionalization and the various ways in which it has been defined and measured in the literature, after which we identify some of the primary hypotheses about the causes of institutionalization. We then turn our attention to Asian polities and provide a simple overview of party system institutionalization vis-à-vis the rest of the world and across Asia. Drawing on the chapters in this volume, we note that many of the conventional explanations for why institutionalization emerges in some contexts but not others do not find much

---

[2] Kohli 1987; Kuhonta 2011.
[3] See Croissant and Völkel's (2012) review for a notable exception.

empirical support in Asia. Instead, we highlight the role that institutional legacies have played, particularly the shadow of authoritarianism, on the development of Asian party systems. The final section of the chapter presents an overview of the rest of the volume.

PARTY SYSTEM INSTITUTIONALIZATION AS A CONCEPT

A voluminous literature in comparative politics has now emerged on party and party system institutionalization.[4] Tracing its roots to Samuel Huntington, this literature was spurred by an attempt to explain why party institutionalization was necessary for establishing political stability. Without institutionalized parties, polities in the developing world would be unable to temper and channel social demands. Institutionalized parties therefore provided the organizational structure within which to incorporate and stabilize social demands and thereby ensure effective governance. Since Huntington's pioneering work, the study of party institutionalization has centered more on its effect on democratic consolidation. When parties are institutionalized, these later studies argue, there is more accountability, greater stability of interests, and more broadly targeted policy programs – all of which augur well for democracy. By contrast, in democracies lacking institutionalized parties, party politics is often simply an arena for charismatic or clientelistic politicians to gain power without any real advancement of the public good. Institutionalized parties therefore are a crucial pillar in the functioning and consolidation of emerging democracies.

The substantive move away from Huntington's emphasis on party institutionalization as a basis for order also entailed an important analytical shift away from a focus on parties qua organizations to party *systems*. In a context in which democracies tend to be prevalent and researchers are concerned with the relationship between parties and democracies, institutionalization is necessarily analyzed through the party system, as it is within the party system that democratic competition occurs.[5] When analyzing party systems in terms of institutionalization, we are looking in particular at the stability of patterned interactions among parties, rather than primarily at parties as organizational behemoths. Institutionalized parties nonetheless still play an important role in party system institutionalization, as the stability of interparty competition must necessarily depend on the presence of cohesive and ideological organizations

---

[4] Huntington 1968; Welfling 1973; Panebianco 1988; Dix 1992a, 1992b; Coppedge 1994; Mainwaring and Scully 1995; Bruhn 1997; McGuire 1997; Levitsky 1998; Roberts 1998; Mainwaring 1999; Kuenzi and Lambright 2001; Moser 2001; Stoner-Weiss 2001; Randall and Svasand 2002; Mainwaring and Torcal 2006; Mainwaring and Zoco 2007; Riedl 2014.

[5] Sartori (1976: 44) provides a useful conceptual description of a party system qua system: "a party system is precisely the *system of interactions* resulting from inter-party competition. That is, the system in question bears on the relatedness of parties to each other, on how each party is a function (in the mathematical sense) of the other parties and reacts, competitively or otherwise, to the other parties" (emphasis in original).

creating a setting for patterned electoral contests. In fact, as our research will show, not only are institutionalized parties crucial for explaining party system institutionalization; semi-democratic or authoritarian parties are particularly important in shaping party system institutionalization.

Most of the early literature on institutionalization has concentrated on explaining the characteristics of political parties, party systems, democracies, political stability, and general patterns of political development. More recently, a vibrant debate has also emerged to explain the factors that *cause* party system institutionalization. Although this literature has made some valuable contributions, it has largely been focused on materials from Western regions. Our goal in this volume is to reexamine the causes of party system institutionalization through Asian empirics. We believe that this is an important analytical exercise not only because of our interest in testing theory but also because the Asian political landscape presents a notably contrasting picture to Western polities. Not only has the Third Wave of democracy come just partly ashore in Asia; institutions in Asia have also developed in distinct ways. Therefore, an exercise in testing some general hypotheses of party system institutionalization will be of broad analytical use precisely because Asia provides a sharp contrast.

It is important to first lay out our concepts clearly. In defining *institutionalization*, we return to Huntington's (1968: 12) concise statement: "the process by which organizations and procedures acquire value and stability."[6] Huntington argued that four factors were particularly important for explaining the level of institutionalization: adaptability, coherence, complexity, and autonomy. In their groundbreaking work on Latin America, Mainwaring and Scully build on Huntington's definition, although their focus is on party systems. For them, the four factors that define an institutionalized party system include stability in the rules and nature of interparty competition; parties having stable roots in society; legitimacy of the electoral process and parties; and cohesive, disciplined, and autonomous parties (Mainwaring and Scully 1995: 5–6). The difference between Huntington's and Mainwaring and Scully's definitions hinges on the latter's focus on the party system. In effect, Mainwaring and Scully have subsumed Huntington's factors, which were all concerned with party institutionalization within their fourth variable: cohesive, disciplined, and autonomous parties.

We focus in this volume on party system institutionalization in part because it is easier to quantify and measure institutionalization across competitive and semi-competitive party systems. In doing so, we build directly on Mainwaring and Scully's study of party system institutionalization in Latin America. However, we diverge from their analytical framework in two important ways. More broadly, the shifts we make signal our own differences with the general trend in the literature. First, we analyze institutionalization in the context not

---

[6] For other conceptual definitions, see Welfling 1973; Panebianco 1988; Levitsky 1998; Randall and Svasand 2002.

just of democratic regimes, but nondemocratic regimes as well. Mainwaring and Scully's focus was squarely on the relationship between party system institutionalization and democracy, precisely because they were assessing the extent to which party system institutionalization strengthened democratic consolidation.

When we look at party systems in Asia, it becomes strikingly apparent why party system institutionalization should be assessed in the context of both democratic and nondemocratic regimes. Many Asian party systems, such as those in Singapore and Malaysia, as well as until recently, Taiwan, are not fully democratic, although they are *competitive* – and increasingly so. These party systems, as we will see, are also the most institutionalized in the region. It is therefore of paramount importance to be able to identify the institutional characteristics of the party system separate from a normative concern for, or an analytical interest in, democratic consolidation. Furthermore, it also bears emphasizing that we should not assume that the process of institutionalization necessarily leads to democratic consolidation. Institutionalized party systems may or may not be consolidated democracies.

A second and related point that differentiates work in this volume from Mainwaring and Scully's analytical framework is our argument (to be detailed later) that traces current highly institutionalized party systems in Asia to the presence, historically, of authoritarian institutionalized parties. It is these authoritarian, institutionalized parties that are now democratic or maintain some aspects of democracy, that often serve as the anchor for emerging democratic, institutionalized party systems or semi-democratic systems. Therefore, whereas our analysis focuses on the party system, in contrast to Mainwaring and Scully, we give much greater weight to the role of authoritarian (or semi-authoritarian) parties. In this sense, although our study concerns competitive parties in a party system, we still take seriously Huntington's claim that dominant, institutionalized parties are critical for establishing institutionalized polities.

PARTY SYSTEM INSTITUTIONALIZATION AS A CONSEQUENT

Scholars have proposed a variety of hypotheses for explaining the causes of party system institutionalization: (1) passage of time, (2) timing or a period effect, (3) characteristics of the prior regime, (4) political institutions, and (5) political cleavages.[7] We review each of these categories in this section. However, from the outset it is important to note that despite the recent flurry of work on institutionalization in authoritarian settings, most of this work focuses on the causes of party system institutionalization in new and developing democracies. The literature we build on is therefore concentrated on democracies, but it is

---

[7] An additional factor discussed in much of the literature is the state of the economy. Economic downturns are associated with higher levels of volatility (lower levels of institutionalization).

precisely our intention in this volume to move this literature toward a greater appreciation of nondemocratic variables and settings.

The Passage of Time

A number of scholars claim that institutionalization is largely a function of time. Voters' attachment to parties, information about the relative strength and position of various political parties, party organizational structures, and knowledge about institutional incentives all take time to develop.[8] Although it is plausible to believe that this hypothesis applies equally to democratic and nondemocratic settings, the empirical evaluations have exclusively relied on data from democracies. The evidence for this hypothesis is thus far mixed. Tavits (2005) and Lupu and Stokes (2007) find that volatility declines and party identities strengthen the more time a country spends under democracy. Likewise, Roussias (2007) and Tavits and Annus (2006) find evidence for better strategic coordination by voters and candidates over time in new democracies.[9] By contrast, Mainwaring and Torcal (2006), Mainwaring and Zoco (2007), Reich (2001, 2004), and Roberts and Wibbels (1999) find no evidence of a decline in volatility and the number of parties over time.

Timing or Period Effect

The second hypothesis focuses on the timing of elections relative to expansion of suffrage and citizenship. The key distinction is between countries that transitioned to democracy in the First and Second Waves versus those that transitioned later. In early democracies, political parties played a lead role as a mobilizing institution by for example incorporating new citizens into the political system and pushing for an expansion of suffrage and other rights for those citizens.[10] This forged strong links between parties and the citizens they helped mobilize. By contrast, in later democracies, the switch to competitive elections and new party formation was preceded by or occurred in conjunction with the adoption of universal suffrage. As a result, the kinds of links and networks that characterized early democratizers never developed. What is more, with the advent of mass communication, specifically television, parties and candidates had a means of mobilizing large numbers of voters without the costly investment in party organization or grassroots networks.[11] In short, given the structural differences of late democratizers, party institutionalization is less likely to occur than in earlier periods, *ceteris paribus*.[12]

---

[8] Converse 1969; Bartolini and Mair 1990.
[9] See also Dalton, McAllister, and Wattenberg 2000.
[10] Colomer 2001; Mainwaring and Zoco 2007.
[11] Mainwaring and Zoco 2007.
[12] In a similar manner, Hutchcroft and Rocamora (2003) trace the origins of weak parties in the Philippines to initiation of early elections in a political environment in which the central government was relatively weak.

In support of this argument, a number of scholars demonstrate that parties, voters, and party systems in Third Wave democracies are qualitatively different from those in advanced industrial democracies.[13]

The Nature of the Prior Regime

A number of scholars argue that the characteristics of the pre-transition authoritarian/semi-authoritarian regime help shape the party system in democratic periods. Some authors explore the relationship between the length of authoritarian interludes, voter attachment to party labels, and the stability of the party system. Some find that the longer the authoritarian interludes the more destabilizing the effects on the party system.[14] Others argue that there is no straightforward link between the duration of authoritarian regimes and party system instability.[15] Geddes and Franz (2007), for example, examine the effect of authoritarian interludes on the evolution of party systems in Latin America. They find that the types of strategies employed by dictators cast a long shadow. Where authoritarian leaders simply repress or outlaw parties, voter loyalties remain intact (even over many years), and those same parties reemerge when democratic elections return.[16] However, if, in addition to outlawing existing parties, dictators create one or more new parties, then the new parties tend to attract candidates and supporters at the expense of the traditional parties.[17] When democratic elections return, these new parties initially dominate, but the party system then tends to fragment as the artificially created new parties fall apart.[18]

One question not explored in the existing literature is the link between institutionalization under electoral authoritarian regimes and the nature of the party system after a democratic transition. As we noted in the introduction to this chapter, institutionalization can occur under either authoritarian or democratic regimes. We hypothesize that party system institutionalization is more

---

[13] Coppedge 1998; Mainwaring and Torcal 2006; Mainwaring and Zoco 2007.

[14] Remmer 1985; Lupu and Stokes 2007.

[15] Wittenberg 2006.

[16] Notice for example the rebirth of the Socialist Party in Chile following Pinochet's departure.

[17] Between these two extremes is the case where the dictator allies with a preexisting party.

[18] Whereas existing work has mostly a unidirectional focus – looking at transitions from autocracy to democracy – it may be fruitful to reverse the arrow and consider how the characteristics of the party system in democratic periods shape the party systems (and dictator strategies) in succeeding authoritarian periods. For example, where there are strong ties between parties and voters, authoritarian elites may find it necessary to suppress existing parties and promote a new party. However, where strong attachments are absent, leaders may be able to secure sufficient support for a new party without resorting to direct suppression and intimidation of existing parties. The creation of Golkar in Indonesia in the wake of the 1965 coup is a good example of the former, whereas the 1991 coup and subsequent creation of a military-backed party in Thailand seems to be a case of the latter.

likely where there was a high degree of institutionalization under the previous electoral authoritarian or semi-democratic government.

Political Institutions

The electoral system has a substantial impact on the nature of the party system. Permissive rules, such as proportional representation with large district magnitude, tend to produce more parties and hence a greater correspondence between party positions and voter preferences than restrictive electoral rules. If we assume that voters' attachment to a particular party is some function of the distance between the voter's ideal point and what he or she perceives as a party's position, permissive rules should be more likely to produce party systems with strong voter-party links. On the other hand, if electoral rules are too permissive, they will produce party fragmentation, which itself is associated with higher electoral volatility.

Other features of the electoral system may also hinder or encourage party institutionalization. For example, branch and membership requirements may encourage parties to develop stronger roots. Electoral rules that place a premium on party-based electoral strategies (as opposed to a personal vote) may help promote the development of party label differentiation. Likewise, restrictions on party switching can increase the incentives for politicians to invest in the party label.

Some authors hypothesize that presidentialism hinders the emergence of strong, cohesive parties,[19] and by extension we might expect the same for party system institutionalization. However, evidence from studies of cross-country differences on some dimensions of institutionalization (i.e., volatility) has not revealed a significant empirical connection between presidentialism and institutionalization.[20]

Political Cleavages

A number of studies trace the origins of strong party-society links to characteristics of the social structure.[21] Lipset and Rokkan (1967) argue that Western European party systems reflect the shared preferences among subsets of voters (social cleavages). Politicized cleavages – whether based on class, religion, or urban/rural differences – gave rise to political parties that (1) had deep roots within cleavage groups and (2) had distinct, collective identities.[22] In more recent work, Birnir (2007) finds that strong parties and stable party systems are more

---

[19] Lijphart et al. 1993.
[20] For example, Mainwaring and Zoco 2007.
[21] Lipset and Rokkan 1967; Sartori 1969; Prezworski and Sprague 1986; Bartolini and Mair 1990; Dix 1992a, 1992b; Kitschelt 1994; Kalyvas 1996; Chhibber 2001, 2002; Ufen 2012.
[22] As noted earlier, these parties often were the key mobilizers of underrepresented cleavages.

likely to emerge in ethnically divided societies. In short, this literature suggests that where the party system is not built on societal cleavages, whether in democratic or nondemocratic settings, party system institutionalization should be slower to develop, and we should expect a lower level of institutionalization, *ceteris paribus*.

Party systems often may not be rooted in societal cleavages for a number of reasons. To the extent countries are relatively homogenous, there may be a lack of deep-seated cleavages around which to organize. This of course is relatively rare, particularly in the developing world. A more likely situation is one in which there are a variety of cleavages, but those cleavages are crosscutting.[23] Crosscutting cleavages diminish the opportunity for forming viable parties rooted in particular cleavage groups. Instead, multi-group, catchall parties become a more appealing option. These crosscutting catchall parties are the goal of some party system engineers because of their potential for moderation and conflict amelioration. However, the cost of moderation is perhaps greater distance and weaker links between political parties and some voters.

Party systems may also be divorced from societal cleavages not because of any feature of the social structure but because of the political system. For example, governments may explicitly or implicitly ban certain types of cleavage-based parties.[24] Restrictive electoral rules may make certain cleavage-based political parties unviable.[25] Ethnically based parties may be forced by law to enter into alliance with other parties.[26] Such engineering attempts are common in Asia.[27]

PARTY SYSTEM INSTITUTIONALIZATION IN ASIA IN COMPARATIVE PERSPECTIVE

Turning our attention toward Asia, what can we learn about the factors that shaped party system institutionalization in this region of the world? As an estimate of the degree of institutionalization, we use one of the most commonly used indicators – electoral volatility. Electoral volatility is a measure of the stability or volatility of the party system from election to election – the degree

---

[23] Selway 2010.
[24] For example, regional parties are effectively banned in Indonesia, and class-based political parties have been excluded in much of Northeast and Southeast Asia. Although class-based parties have emerged throughout the postwar period in Southeast Asia, they have been routinely repressed through a combination of authoritarian repression and external support driven by the Cold War. In the late 1940s in Thailand, leading members of the leftist party based in the northeast, Sahachip, were systematically eliminated; in the Philippines, the six elected members of the leftist Democratic Alliance were prevented from taking their seats in Congress. The Indonesian Communist Party, the largest outside mainland China, was annihilated following the 1965 coup.
[25] Amorim-Neto and Cox 1997; Clark and Golder 2006.
[26] In Singapore's Group Representative Constituencies, party teams must be multiethnic, which effectively eliminates challenges from ethnically based opposition parties.
[27] Hicken 2006a, 2006b, 2008; Reilly 2007; Kuhonta 2008.

to which there is variation in aggregate party vote shares from one election to another. Where there is a stable pattern of interparty competition and where parties have strong links with voters, we expect to see the same sets of parties receiving consistent levels of support from election to election, reflected in a low volatility score. High levels of electoral volatility, on the other hand, can reflect both instability in voters' party preferences from election to election and elite-driven changes to the party system such as the creation of new parties, the death of existing parties, party switching, party mergers, and party splits.[28] Electoral volatility is not without its problems – tracing party vote shares can prove extremely complicated where there are lots of party mergers or splits. Where possible, we follow Mainwaring and Zoco's (2007) rules about how to treat such events. More fundamentally, electoral volatility does not allow us to differentiate the sources of instability – fickle voters or ephemeral parties.

Electoral volatility is calculated by taking the sum of the net change in the percentage of votes gained or lost by each party from one election to the next, divided by two ($\Sigma\ |v_{it} - v_{it+1}|)\ /\ 2$). A score of 100 signifies that the set of parties winning votes is completely different from one election to the next. A score of 0 means the same parties receive exactly the same percentage of votes across two elections. The higher the volatility score, the less institutionalized the party system is.

It bears emphasizing that by focusing on electoral volatility, we are using only one of potentially four or five indicators to measure institutionalization. We should recall that beyond electoral volatility of the party system, we could also conceivably measure other variables, such as the cohesiveness, adaptability, complexity, social rootedness, and autonomy of political parties. In this chapter, we follow the literature's convention and focus on electoral volatility because we are interested in party *system* institutionalization and because it is simpler to operationalize and measure quantitatively compared to other possible variables. We note that the authors of the chapters in this volume employ a variety of empirical strategies to estimate and trace the degree of institutionalization within their country of focus. This includes electoral volatility, but also historical analyses, use of public opinion polls, and information about party creation and durations. We should note that because of the solidly authoritarian character of the Vietnamese and Chinese regimes, these two chapters focus specifically on historical analyses of the party, rather than volatility within the party system.

Table 1.1 compares the average electoral volatility of Asian states compared to states in other regions. We include in our calculations states in Northeast Asia, South Asia, and Southeast Asia that have experienced relatively free and fair elections as well as those countries where opposition parties are allowed to compete and win seats in regular elections, but the electoral playing field is tilted heavily against the opposition (i.e., Singapore, Malaysia, and Cambodia). We do not include those polities where elections are not regularly held or where

---

[28] Mainwaring and Zoco 2007.

TABLE 1.1. *Electoral Volatility across the Globe*

	Electoral Volatility
Asia I	24.5
Asia II (w/out Cambodia, Singapore, and post-1971 Malaysia)	27
Western Democracies (including Aust. and NZ)	10.4
Eastern Europe and Former Soviet States	44.1
Latin America	25.6
Africa	N.A.

Sources: Authors' calculations; Hicken 2008; Mainwaring and Zoco 2007.

autonomous opposition parties are banned outright (e.g., Vietnam, Myanmar, China). Although by Huntington's definition, the Communist parties in China and Vietnam are institutionalized parties, for the purposes of measuring electoral volatility, which must include at the very least semi-competitive elections, we cannot include them. For informational purposes, we also include an estimate for all of Asia excluding the semi-democratic cases (Asia II). A full list of the countries we include is displayed in Table 1.2.

Viewed through the prism of electoral volatility, Asian party systems are on par with those in Latin America – both regions have volatility scores between 24 and 26. By contrast, Asian states appear more institutionalized than their counterparts in Eastern Europe and Africa. Not surprisingly, Western democracies exhibit the lowest level of electoral volatility.

As useful as comparing across regions may be, Asia's regional average masks a high degree of variation among Asian states. Table 1.2 displays the electoral volatility scores for each of the countries in our sample. For countries that experienced an authoritarian interlude (i.e., Malaysia, Philippines, and Thailand), we estimate separate volatility scores for the periods before and after such interludes. The countries with the most stable party system/highest degree of institutionalization are the dominant party regimes in the region – Malaysia post interregnum and Singapore. If we exclude these two states, average volatility ranges from a low of 16.5 in Taiwan to a high of 41.1 in Thailand II.[29]

What light do these Asian cases shed on the causes of institutionalization? In earlier work,[30] we find that many of the traditional explanations provide little leverage when applied to Asian cases. First, in terms of the passage of time, the experiences of the countries explored in this volume do not allow us to conclude

[29] If we treat all three parties affiliated with former Thai prime minister Thaksin Shinawatra as the same party (Thai Rak Thai, Palang Prachachon, and Phua Thai), then Thailand II falls to 34.2. Cambodia post-1997 should also be viewed as a polity with circumscribed political competition.
[30] Hicken and Kuhonta 2011.

TABLE 1.2. *Electoral Volatility in Asia*

	Years	Number of Elections	Volatility: 1st and 2nd Elections	Volatility: Last Election	Average Volatility
Malaysia II	1974–2013	10	8.6	4	10.1
Singapore	1968–2011	11	24.6	20.4	15.4
Taiwan	1992–2012	7	8.6	11.5	16.5
Sri Lanka	1947–2010	14	27.7	9.0	16.6
Japan	1947–2012	24	27.4	16.3	16.8
Philippines I	1946–1969	7	20.4	43.6	18.5
India	1951–2009	15	25.1	11.3	19.2
Cambodia	1993–2013	5	27.9	22.9	24
Indonesia	1999–2009	3	25.2	29.8	27.5
Malaysia I	1955–1968	4	38.8	36.4	30.6
Timor Leste	2001–2012	3	49.0	22.5	35.8
South Korea	1988–2012	7	41.9	35.2	36.5
Philippines II	1992–2013	8	57.0	42.9	38.3
Thailand I	1979–1991	4	40.8	32.1	38.4
Thailand II	1992–2011	8	48.7	58.2	42.0

Note: If the political parties linked to former prime minister Thaksin Shinawtra (Thai Rak Thai, Palang Prachachon, and Phua Thai) are treated as the same party, then the average volatility score for Thailand II falls to 32.6.
Sources: Authors' calculations; Hicken 2008.

decisively that more elections necessarily lead to greater institutionalization. In some cases, institutionalization does appear to improve over time; in others, it appears to worsen as more elections accumulate (e.g., India); in many states, there is no clear pattern. At the very least, the greater experience with elections does not appear to be inexorably linked with greater institutionalization, consistent with the findings of Mainwaring and Torcal (2006) and Reich (2001, 2004).

Second, the chapters in this volume fail to demonstrate a straightforward general relationship of macro political institutions, such as electoral systems and government type, with institutionalization. This is not to say that institutions are unimportant. As the chapters demonstrate, institutional arrangements had profound effects on the development of the party system in many cases (see, e.g., the chapters by Nikolenyi and Hicken), but these institutions or, more precisely, their configuration was unique to each case and hence difficult to generalize from. By themselves, macro institutions, such as presidentialism v. parliamentarism or plurality v. proportional representation (PR), are not good predictors of the level of institutionalization in Asia.

Third, some of the literature suggests that higher levels of fractionalization should be correlated with less volatility, but this simple version of the cleavage argument is not supported by the data presented in these chapters. Ethnic fractionalization does not appear to be systematically associated with less (or more) volatility.[31] There is some support however for the argument that where cleavages crosscut each other (and where non-ethnic, catchall parties are thus more likely), the attachment to party label is less strong. The two least crosscut societies in this volume[32] – Malaysia and Singapore – have among the highest levels of institutionalization in the region.

The first conclusion that emerges most clearly from the chapters in this volume has to do with institutional legacies.[33] Under both democratic and authoritarian regimes, parties that were institutionalized at an earlier point of time generally tend to maintain a high level of institutionalization relative to those parties that emerged later. The countries with the highest level of party system institutionalization are Malaysia, Singapore, Taiwan, Japan, and Sri Lanka. Except for Taiwan, these parties were all born in the postwar period.[34] The argument that a prior period of institutional development affects current levels of party system institutionalization is in line with other studies on the causes of party system institutionalization.[35] What this points to then from a theoretical perspective is the importance of path dependence in the study of party institutionalization. Historical developments during a critical juncture may have long-term effects on institutional form.[36] We stress however that our claim is probabilistic rather than deterministic. Our evidence is based on a sample of cases in which prior levels of institutionalization can be linked to current levels of institutionalization. We are open to the possibility that some cases may track differently than those based on path dependence.

Important scholarship on the development of political parties – both past and recent – buttresses our argument concerning institutional legacies. In his classic study on the relationship between patronage and political parties, Martin Shefter argues that "the circumstances under which a party first mobilizes a mass following has enduring implications for its subsequent behavior."[37] Emphasizing the idea of a "critical" experience in defining the trajectory of political parties, Shefter argues that externally mobilized parties are more likely to rely on programs and mass organization compared to internally mobilized parties. Yet, not all internally mobilized parties are patronage oriented. In countries such as Germany and England, where bureaucratic constituencies

---

[31] See also ibid.
[32] As measured using Selway's cross-cuttingness score 2010.
[33] See also Croissant and Volkel 2012.
[34] One can argue, however, that the KMT was reborn during this period as it gained new direction after it fled mainland China.
[35] Mainwaring and Zoco 2007.
[36] The recent methodological advances that have been made in thinking of politics through time should be useful for theorizing about theses issue. See Collier and Collier 1991; Thelen 1999; Mahoney and Rueschemeyer 2003; Pierson 2004; George and Bennett 2005.
[37] Shefter 1977: 417.

coalesced prior to the emergence of a mass electorate, patronage was blocked; in countries such as Italy, where such coalitions did not develop prior to party formation, patronage consumed the party system. In his work on states and regimes, as well as on single-party rule, Benjamin Smith (2005, 2007) shows that the durability of states, regimes, and single parties can be explained in terms of earlier processes of institutional formation and coalition building. Where a party, regime, or state faced significant opposition and lack of easy access to rents prior to the initiation of economic development, the institution was more likely to become durable and institutionalized precisely because structural constraints necessitated greater institutional capacity. On the other hand, where political institutions were not faced with significant opposition and had easy access to rents, they were less likely to expend their resources on institution building and were therefore more vulnerable to collapse when a crisis struck. A sophisticated study by Dan Slater (2010) on state, regime, and party formation in Southeast Asia also gives significant emphasis to historical timing. Slater argues that the period between World War II and the onset of bureaucratic-authoritarian regimes was the critical juncture in which current patterns of state and party formation were molded. Our analysis of party system institutionalization in Southeast Asia therefore confirms what other researchers are finding: institutional capacities, whether of parties, states, regimes, or party systems, can be explained through long-term historical processes.

Our second conclusion concerns the specific character of these institutional legacies. It is here where we diverge from some major studies of party system institutionalization. Whereas Mainwaring and Zoco emphasize that "the critical determinant of electoral competition is when democracy was born, not how old it is,"[38] we argue that the relationship between parties and democratization is not the only key to explaining the relevance of specific time periods. The evidence from Asia indicates that the three most highly institutionalized party systems were not shaped under particularly democratic conditions. All three party systems carry with them significant authoritarian legacies. Singapore's party system developed through sharp repression of the left even though some degree of electoral competition was still allowed. Malaysia's party system was initially more democratic in its incipient stage in the late 1950s, but after 1969, it became decisively more closed. It was after 1969 that the party system became more institutionalized. Both of these party systems, although competitive, are rooted in highly illiberal structures and processes that undermine the opposition's ability to defeat the incumbent. Taiwan, the country with the third-highest level of party system institutionalization, was for much of its modern history ruled by a deeply coercive party-state apparatus, the Kumointang (KMT). The electoral volatility scores for two other party systems in which hegemonic parties were dominant in the past, Cambodia and Indonesia, are also relatively lower than the average for Asia. These two party systems are not highly

---

[38] Mainwaring and Zoco 2007: 171.

institutionalized, but they are also not highly fragmented and volatile. What this suggests then is that party systems in Asia are institutionalized because of some constraints on competition, whether these constraints were forged in the past or continue to structure the party system.[39]

It is easy to downplay seemingly high levels of institutionalization in authoritarian settings as artifacts of constrained competition. Indeed, Mainwaring in the concluding chapter makes a strong case for doing so. However, if we were to do so, we would assume that elections in authoritarian regimes have no substantive merit. The cases of Malaysia and Singapore indicate otherwise. The increasing competitiveness of elections in the past few years in these two semi-authoritarian countries necessitates a more complex view of elections in authoritarian regimes. The odds of the opposition winning in Malaysia and Singapore are surely slim; yet, the forcefulness with which the dominant parties campaign, seek to maintain voter support, and continue to deepen their roots in society suggests that institutionalization and electoral patterns in these authoritarian regimes are not unrelated. Furthermore, the patterns of organization and competition forged in less-than-fully competitive systems can and do cast important shadows on party organization and patterns of competition even after competitive strictures have been loosened. This argument is elaborated further by Weiss in her chapter on Malaysia, Tan in her chapter on Singapore, and Vu in his chapter on Vietnam. Therefore, in contrast to Mainwaring and Zoco, the Asian cases point not to mobilizing effects of parties during the early stages of democracy, but to the capacity of dominant parties to assert themselves and constrain the opposition while in power. We thus argue that structural constraints at an early point in time have a long-term impact on institutional configurations and capacities.[40]

To elaborate, in contrast to authors who claim that the persistence of authoritarian regimes is a function of strong states and parties, we argue that it is authoritarian or semi-democratic regimes that have a causal effect on the characteristics of party systems, even after a transition to democracy.[41] In other words, we reverse the causal argument relating institutions to authoritarianism, positing that coercive structures tend to reinforce party systems. At least for the three most institutionalized party systems in Asia, authoritarian or semi-democratic parties play a fundamental role in structuring and solidifying the party system. Our research then provides somewhat of a troubling conclusion: to

---

[39] A parallel argument is made by Riedl 2014 regarding party system institutionalization in Africa. Riedl argues that where strong authoritarian parties constrained the level of competition in the subsequent democratic transition, the party system was more institutionalized. However, where weak authoritarian parties allowed competition to flourish, the party system became less institutionalized. Thus, authoritarian constraints have had a significant effect on the level of party system institutionalization in democratic regimes in Africa.

[40] Smith's work 2005, 2007 is again relevant here – this time, less in terms of historical processes as much as in terms of structural constraints. As Smith notes, it is the pressures from strong oppositions and lack of resources that compels elites to build institutions.

[41] Brownlee 2007; Levitsky and Way 2010; Slater 2010.

get highly institutionalized party systems in democratic contexts, it is useful to have had some form of an authoritarian party in power at an earlier point in time. A highly institutionalized party system – an institutional arrangement that analysts consider valuable for democratic consolidation and policy continuity – may emerge from the shell of undemocratic politics. We should emphasize that this is not the case for all five of the highly institutionalized party systems in this volume, but it is the case for the three with the highest scores. It is also worth pointing out that several chapters in this volume disagree with this conclusion, notably those of Nikolenyi on India and Tan on Indonesia, as well as Mainwaring in the conclusion.

Furthermore, where some degree of competition is allowed, hegemonic institutionalized parties can push the oppositional forces to also become more institutionalized. Although Smith emphasizes the causal impact of a strong opposition on regime durability, it is also possible that the dominant institution may help solidify the opposition, thereby in effect creating the foundations for an institutionalized party system *once party competition is permitted*. To compete effectively against hegemonic institutionalized parties, the opposition must also establish cohesive and disciplined organizations. In Taiwan and Mexico, two newly democratizing countries that have long been characterized by dominant parties, the opposition parties are strong organizations, the Democratic Progressive Party (DPP), and the National Action Party (PAN) and the Party of the Democratic Revolution (PRD), respectively. The opposition parties are able to mobilize voters through cohesive organizational structures, consistent ideologies, and regular linkages between party and society. In Malaysia, the opposition to the United Malays National Organisation (UMNO) and the Barisan Nasional (BN) also tends to be relatively institutionalized. For example, the Islamic party, Parti Islam-se Malaysia (PAS), competes with UMNO toe-to-toe in the state of Kelantan in terms of organizational depth. It maintains numerous branches throughout the state and controls the vast majority of mosques as mobilizing sites. Throughout the state, the party's offices are extremely visible. In Taiwan and Malaysia, the largest opposition parties have historically had a more stable vote share from election to election than the ruling party.[42] Voters in these countries can clearly make a choice among parties with distinct political agendas. This is not the case in some democratic countries, such as the Philippines and Thailand, where hegemonic parties have never played a role in the polity.[43]

---

[42] Over the five elections between 1992 and 2012, the average change in vote share from elections is actually less for the opposition DPP than for the KMT (2.9 vs. 8.1 percentage points). Between 1974 and 2008, the average change in the vote share for PAS and the DAP is 2.3 and 4.1, compared to 8.1 for Barisan Nasional.

[43] There are clearly other potential explanations for the strength of opposition parties within hegemonic or former hegemonic party systems. For example, social polarization may create sharp divisions among parties while solidifying the relationship between parties and their supporters. But it is also theoretically plausible that the struggle against a powerful institutionalized force may serve as a catalyst for invigorating the opposition and its supporters.

Our final conclusion is that precisely because of the importance of authoritarianism in shaping the party system, either historically or in the contemporary polity, institutionalization must be analyzed as a separate category from democracy. The problem with analyzing institutionalized party systems only through democratic lenses is that we occlude the possibility that authoritarianism in some guise may contribute to institutionalization. This was, after all, the implicit claim that underlay Huntington's seminal work – and that made it so contentious. By shifting the geographical emphasis toward Asia and away from Western party systems, where parties largely operate under a democratic framework, it becomes evident that party systems can possess distinct institutional characteristics and legacies.

This final section summarizes the chapters that will follow. The chapters are arranged roughly from the more institutionalized to the less institutionalized party systems.

The volume begins with Malaysia's highly institutionalized party system – perhaps the best example of the complex intertwining of institutionalization and semi-democracy or semi-authoritarianism. Meredith Weiss writes that Malaysia's party system is characterized by patterns of routinized and predictable competition. Party organizations have long histories, are rooted in society, and are representative of societal interests. Yet, such institutionalization has occurred within a coercive framework that has benefited the hegemonic party. The closing of political space in the postwar period was particularly crucial in institutionalizing the party system. But like other party systems distinguished by authoritarianism and institutionalization such as Vietnam, the Malaysian party system has shown some vulnerability to change. Party system deinstitutionalization in recent years along with the surge of alternative media and new ideas among the middle class portends the possibility for some democratization.

Netina Tan argues forcefully that in Singapore, as in Malaysia, one of Southeast Asia's most highly institutionalized party systems has emerged out of a deeply autocratic setting. The People's Action Party, Singapore's dominant party, has become highly institutionalized through an extremely effective leadership selection process that allows it to reinvigorate the party by bringing in new talent while ushering out the less accomplished. The organizational structures and procedures of the party have therefore been at the core of the party system's high level of institutionalization. Tan's chapter analyzes in detail the procedural structure through which the party selects its leadership, providing an in-depth view of one Asia's most organized and cohesive institutions.

Japan – a more democratic regime than Malaysia or Singapore – has remained a highly institutionalized party system but through two institutional equilibria. Initially, Kenneth Mori McElwain argues, the party system was institutionalized through an electoral system that led to the dominance of the Liberal Democratic Party, or a "1.5-party system." This system was characterized by low levels of partisan identification and battles over pork rather than program. Yet, its level of electoral volatility was remarkably low. With a change in the electoral system toward a mixed member majoritarian system, parties now compete over policy programs, but electoral volatility has also spiked because linkages between voters and politicians – held together previously by pork – have now loosened.

Taiwan is one of the most institutionalized party systems in Asia. This, T. J. Cheng and Y. M. Hsu argue, has resulted from early efforts by the Kumointang to allow some competition at the local level. This competitive system eventually became institutionalized once the country moved toward a more democratic regime, allowing parties to challenge the government. Besides these early competitive structures gaining hold, what also helped institutionalize the party system in Taiwan was its peculiar electoral system and the fact that the democratic transition occurred during a period of economic prosperity and stability. An interesting contrast emerges in South Korea, where democratic transition during prosperity in South Korea did not aid the institutionalization of the party system.

Within Southeast Asia, Vietnam remains one of the most institutionalized parties, and like Malaysia and Singapore reflects again the intertwining of authoritarianism and institutionalization. But as Tuong Vu charts in his chapter, the Vietnamese Communist Party's level of institutionalization has fluctuated through time. Initially institutionalized in the process of war making and nationalism, by the 1970s the party became significantly less institutionalized. After 1986, it embarked on a gradual process of reinstitutionalization but has not reached the levels of its earlier strength. Vietnam's highly institutionalized party and party system were deeply linked to its totalitarian regime, but – as in Malaysia – as institutionalization declines, the polity becomes more vulnerable to liberalization.

In China, authoritarianism has remained an intimate bedfellow of institutionalization. The Chinese Communist Party, Yongnian Zheng argues, has consistently sought to remain relevant, and in doing so it has institutionalized the party, institutionalized state-party ties, and institutionalized the bond between state and society. This institutionalization has in turn helped the party remain in power. In the process of institutionalization, the Communist Party has accommodated some democratic elements within the party and between the party and state and society, but these have not been motivated by any larger democratic agenda. Rather, Zheng claims that one has to distinguish clearly between democratic accommodation and democracy. Democratic accommodation as dictated by the Communist Party has enabled it to ensure its continued domination over the polity.

Our lone case from South Asia – the moderately institutionalized party system of India – presents some interesting and contrasting findings from our own argument. Contrary to what we have found in Asia, Csaba Nikolenyi posits that the advent of authoritarianism under Indira Gandhi weakened party system institutionalization in India. This is an important claim that opens up room for more debate about the relationship between regime-type and institutionalization. Nikolenyi furthermore argues that two other hypotheses we have given less priority do indeed matter. The passage of time and institutional rules – in this case, an anti-defection rule – have helped reduce electoral volatility and strengthen institutionalization in the long-run. Nikolenyi's forceful response to our own hypotheses, particularly the argument about institutionalization and authoritarianism, thus effectively extends theoretical debate on the importance of authoritarianism for institutionalization.

Cambodia remains a weakly institutionalized party system, but one that is becoming increasingly institutionalized. This institutionalization, Sorpong Peou shows, has moved in an authoritarian direction, driven by the dominance of the Cambodian People's Party (CPP). Peou posits that historical factors as well as international and domestic variables have institutionalized the party system. The CPP has become the most institutionalized party because it was institutionalized earlier than opposition forces, but also because it was more strategically effective at consolidating political and military power. Furthermore, international actors, including donors and the United Nations Transitional Authority in Cambodia have intentionally or unintentionally helped strengthen the CPP. Worth noting in Peou's chapter is the question of whether authoritarian *personalism* – a crucial factor in facilitating electoral stability in the party system – should be considered a component of institutionalization.

One of Asia's newest democracies – Indonesia – lies somewhere on the middle to low level of institutionalization. Paige Johnson Tan shows that there are some elements of Indonesia's party system that strengthen institutionalization, including geographic rootedness of parties and the presence of a few parties with strong organizational structures. But overall, Tan concludes that institutionalization is weak because vote shares are very much in flux, parties remain factionalized and personalistic, and legitimacy of the party system is low. Tan argues that electoral rules have shaped the nature of the system's institutionalization and contrary to our findings, that authoritarianism under Sukarno and Suharto undermined party system institutionalization. In addition, Tan notes that economic performance, international intervention, and elite choice matter in explaining patterns of party system institutionalization.

Compared to the general pattern in Northeast Asia, where parties and party systems have been highly institutionalized, South Korea presents a stark contrast. Joe Wong shows in his chapter that the party system in South Korea is characterized by parties without strong identities and programmatic agendas and voters lacking in partisan affiliations. Most significantly, Wong argues that democratization has not led to the institutionalization of the party system. Contrary to Cheng's argument regarding Taiwan, "transitioning in good times" helped the authoritarian government split the opposition and crucially create a fluid ideological environment that prevented the establishment of partisan cleavages that might have helped order the party system. Strategic maneuvering by the ruling party along with missed opportunities from the fragmented opposition thus created a deeply volatile party system.

Thailand is notorious for having one of the weakest institutionalized party systems in Asia. Erik Martinez Kuhonta argues that one can trace the roots of this to failed efforts at party and democracy building in 1932 and 1946. During these periods, significant efforts were made to develop parties within constitutional settings. The failure to pursue these developments to their furthest extent set Thailand on a trajectory of weak party system institutionalization. Parties today are extremely shallow, fluid, and short lived. Rather than party organizations setting the agenda, it is factions based on friends, family, or financial ties that dominate. However, the current crisis that has deeply divided Thailand has led to some linkages between parties and social forces and to parties advancing programmatic policies. The closer ties between parties and social groups began under Thaksin Shinawatra and his Thai Rak Thai Party. These developments may potentially lead to some greater degree of party system institutionalization. It remains nonetheless too early to tell how significant the effect of the current polarization in society will be on the party system.

Like Thailand, the Philippines remains stuck in a groove of weak institutionalization. Allen Hicken argues that the historical nature of Philippine political development had a strong impact on party system institutionalization. The advent of elections in the early American colonial period prior to the building of parties had a long-term impact on the party system, in effect allowing oligarchs to dominate incipient institutions. Furthermore, the choice of electoral systems and strategic interventions, such as the ban on presidential reelection, and the particular character of the party list also further weakened the party system.

The concluding chapter by Scott Mainwaring addresses four key themes of the book. It explains why the concept of party system institutionalization is value added in the literature on political parties; it argues for a clear distinction of party systems based on regime-type, specifically competitive party systems, hegemonic party systems, and party-state systems; it then defines institutionalization across four dimensions and argues that these dimensions do not track equally across the three regime-types; and finally, it calls for distinguishing institutionalization from democracy. Mainwaring's chapter reflects skepticism of the book's move toward analyzing party system institutionalization as a uniform category across regime-types. In doing so, it highlights a central axis of debate over the concept of institutionalization – whether it should be analyzed strictly in relation to regime-type or whether it should cut across regime-type.[44]

---

[44] This debate has its origins in Huntington's landmark study, *Political Order in Changing Societies*, where institutionalization trumped regime-type.

REFERENCES

Amorim-Neto, Octavio, and Gary C. Cox. 1997. Electoral Institutions, Cleavage Structures, and the Number of Parties. *American Journal of Political Science* 41(1): 149–174.

Bartolini, Stefano, and Peter Mair. 1990. *Identity, Competition and Electoral Availability: The Stabilisation of European Electorates, 1885–1985*. Cambridge: Cambridge University Press.

Birnir, Johanna Kristin. 2007. *Ethnicity and Electoral Politics*. Cambridge: Cambridge University Press.

Brownlee, Jason. 2007. *Authoritarianism in an Age of Democratization*. Cambridge: Cambridge University Press.

Bruhn, Kathleen. 1997. *Taking on Goliath: The Emergence of a New Left Party and the Struggle for Democracy in Mexico*. University Park: The Pennsylvania State University Press.

Chhibber, Pradeep K. 2001. *Democracy without Associations: Transformation of the Party System and Social Cleavages in India*. Ann Arbor: University of Michigan Press.

Clark, Willam Roberts, and Matt Golder. 2006. Rehabilitating Duverger's Theory: Testing the Mechanic and Strategic Modifying Effects of Electoral Laws. *Comparative Political Studies* 39(6): 679–708.

Collier, Ruth B., and David Collier. 1991. *Shaping the Political Arena*. Princeton: Princeton University Press.

Colomer, Josep. 2001. *Political Institutions: Democracy and Social Choice*. New York: Oxford University Press.

Converse, Philip. E. 1969. Of Time and Stability. *Comparative Political Studies* 2(2): 139–171.

Coppedge, Michael. 1994. *Strong Parties and Lame Ducks: Presidential Partyarchy and Factionalism in Venezuela*. Stanford: Stanford University Press.

Coppedge, Michael. 1998. The Dynamic Diversity of Latin American Party Systems. *Party Politics* 4(4): 547–568.

Croissant, Aurel, and Philip Völkel. 2012. "Party System Types and Party System Institutionalization. Comparing New Democracies in East and Southeast Asia." *Party Politics* 18(2): 235–262.

Dalton, Robert J., Ian McAllister, and Martin Wattenberg. 2000. The Consequences of Partisan Dealignment. In R. J. Dalton and M. Wattenberg (Eds.), *Parties without Partisans: Political Change in Advanced Industrial Democracies*, pp. 37–63. Oxford: Oxford University Press.

Desai, Manali. 2002. The Relative Autonomy of Party Practices: A Counterfactual Analysis of Left Party Ascendancy in Kerala, India, 1934–1940. *American Journal of Sociology* 108(3): 616–657.

Dix, Robert H. 1992a. Cleavage Structures and Party Systems in Latin America. *Comparative Politics* 22(1): 23–37.

Dix, Robert H. 1992b. Democratization and the Institutionalization of Latin American Political Parties. *Comparative Political Studies* 24(4): 488–511.

Fearon, James. 2003. Ethnic and Cultural Diversity by Country. *Journal of Economic Growth* 8(2): 195–222.

George, Alexander L., and Andrew Bennett. 2005. *Case Studies and Theory Development in the Social Sciences*. Cambridge, MA: MIT Press.

Hicken, Allen. 2006a. Stuck in the Mud: Parties and Party Systems in Democratic Southeast Asia. *Taiwan Journal of Democracy* 2(2): 23–46.

Hicken, Allen. Party Fabrication: Constitutional Reform and the Rise of Thai Rak Thai. *Journal of East Asian Studies* 6(3): 381–408.

Hicken, Allen. 2008. Political Engineering and Party Regulation in Southeast Asia. In B. Reilly et al. (Eds.), *Political Parties in Conflict-Prone Societies: Regulation, Engineering and Democratic Development*. Tokyo: United Nations University Press.

Hutchcroft, Paul, and Joel Rocamora. 2003. Strong Demands and Weak Institutions: The Origins and Evolution of the Democratic Deficit in the Philippines. *Journal of East Asian Studies* 3(2): 259–292.

Huntington, Samuel P. 1968. *Political Order in Changing Societies*. New Haven: Yale University Press.

Kalyvas, Stathis N. 1996. *The Rise of Christian Democracy in Europe*. Ithaca: Cornell University Press.

King, Dwight. 2003. *Half-Hearted Reform: Electoral Institutions and the Struggle for Democracy in Indonesia*. Westport: Praeger.

Kitschelt, Herbert. 1994. *The Transformation of European Social Democracy*. Cambridge: Cambridge University Press.

Kohli, Atul. 1987. *The State and Poverty in India: The Politics of Reform*. Cambridge: Cambridge University Press.

Kuenzi, Michelle, and Gina Lambright. 2001. Party System Institutionalization in 30 African Countries. *Party Politics* 7(4): 437–468.

Kuhonta, Erik Martinez. 2008. The Paradox of Thailand's 1997 "People's Constitution": Be Careful What You Wish For. *Asian Survey* 48(3): 373–392.

Kuhonta, Erik Martinez. 2011. *The Institutional Imperative: The Politics of Equitable Development in Southeast Asia*. Stanford: Stanford University Press.

Levitsky, Steven. 1998. Institutionalization and Peronism. *Party Politics* 4(1): 77–92.

Levitsky, Steven, and Lucan Way. 2010. *Competitive Authoritarianism: The Emergence and Dynamics of Hybrid Regimes in the Post-Cold War Era*. Cambridge: Cambridge University Press.

Lijphart, Arend, Ronald Rogowski, and Kent Weaver. 1993. Separation of Powers and Cleavage Management. In R. K. Weaver and B. A. Rockman (Eds.), *Do Institutions Matter: Government in the United States and Abroad Abroad*, pp. 302–344. Washington, DC: Brookings Institution.

Lipset, Seymour Martin, and Stein Rokkan. 1967. Cleavage Structures, Party Systems, and Voter Alignments. In S. M. Lipset and S. Rokkan (Eds.), *Party Systems and Voter Alignments: Cross-National Perspectives*, pp. 1–64. New York: Free Press, 1967.

Lupu, Noam, and Susan Stokes. 2007. Democracy Interrupted: Regime Change and Partisan Stability in Twentieth Century Argentina. Unpublished manuscript, Yale University.

McGuire, James W. 1997. *Peronism without Peron: Unions, Parties, and Democracy in Argentina*. Stanford: Stanford University Press.

Mahoney, James, and Dietrich Rueschemeyer (Eds.). 2003. *Comparative Historical Analysis in the Social Sciences*. Princeton: Princeton University Press.

Mainwaring, Scott. 1999. *Rethinking Party Systems in the Third Wave of Democratization: The Case of Brazil.* Stanford: Stanford University Press.

Mainwaring, Scott, and Timothy Scully (Eds.). 1995. *Building Democratic Institutions: Party Systems in Latin America.* Stanford: Stanford University Press.

Mainwaring, Scott, and Mariano Torcal. 2006. Party System Institutionalization and Party System Theory after the Third Wave of Democratization. In R. S. Katz and W. Crotty (Eds.), *Handbook of Political Parties,* pp. 204–227. London: Sage.

Mainwaring, Scott, and Edurne Zoco. 2007. Political Sequences and the Stabilization of Interparty Competition: Electoral Volatility in Old and New Democracies. *Party Politics* 13(2): 155–178.

Moser, Robert. 2001. *Unexpected Outcomes: Electoral Systems, Political Parties, and Representation in Russia.* Pittsburgh: University of Pittsburgh Press.

Panebianco, Angelo. 1988. *Political Parties: Organization and Power.* Cambridge: Cambridge University Press.

Pierson, Paul. 2004. *Politics in Time.* Princeton: Princeton University Press.

Powell, G. Bingham. 2000. *Elections as Instruments of Democracy.* New Haven: Yale University Press.

Przeworski, Adam, and John Sprague. 1986. *Paper Stones: A History of Electoral Socialism.* Chicago: University of Chicago Press.

Randall, Vicky, and Lars Svasand. 2002. Party Institutionalization in New Democracies. *Party Politics* 8(1): 5–29.

Riedl, Rachel B. 2014. *Authoritarian Origins of Democratic Party Systems in Africa.* Cambridge: Cambridge University Press.

Reich, Gary. 2001. Coordinating Party Choice in Founding Elections. *Comparative Political Studies* 34(10): 1237–1263.

Reich, Gary. 2004. The Evolution of New Party Systems: Are Early Elections Exceptional? *Electoral Studies* 23(2): 232–250.

Reilly, Benjamin. 2007. *Democracy and Diversity: Political Engineering in the Asia-Pacific.* Oxford: Oxford University Press.

Remmer, Karen. 1985. Redemocratization and the Impact of Authoritarian Rule in Latin America. *Comparative Politics* 17(3): 253–275.

Roberts, Kenneth M. 1998. *Deepening Democracy? The Modern Left and Social Movements in Chile and Peru.* Stanford: Stanford University Press.

Roberts, Kenneth M., and Erik Wibbels. 1999. Party Volatility and Electoral Systems in Latin America: A Test of Economic, Institutional, and Structural Explanations. *American Political Science Review* 93(3): 575–590.

Roussias, Nasos. 2007. Electoral Coordination in New Democracies. Unpublished manuscript, Yale University.

Sartori, Giovanni. 1969. From the Sociology of Politics to Political Sociology. In S. M. Lipset (Ed.), *Politics and the Social Sciences,* pp. 65–100. New York: Oxford University Press.

Sartori, Giovanni. 1976. *Parties and Party Systems: A Framework for Analysis.* Cambridge: Cambridge University Press.

Selway, Joel. S. 2010. Cross-cuttingness, Cleavage Structures, and Civil War Onset. *British Journal of Political Science.*

Shefter, Martin. 1977. Party and Patronage: Germany, England, and Italy. *Politics and Society* 7(4): 403–451.

Slater, Dan. 2010. *Ordering Power: Contentious Politics and Authoritarian Leviathans in Southeast Asia*. Cambridge: Cambridge University Press.

Smith, Benjamin. 2005. Life of the Party: The Origins of Regime Breakdown and Persistence under Single-Party Rule. *World Politics* 57 (April): 421–451.

Smith, Benjamin. 2007. *Hard Times in the Land of Plenty*. Ithaca: Cornell University Press.

Stoner-Weiss, Kathryn. 2001. The Limited Reach of Russia's Party System: Underinstitutionalization in Dual Transitions. *Politics and Society* 29(3): 385–414.

Tavits, Margit. 2005. The Development of Stable Party Support: Electoral Dynamics in Post-Communist Europe. *American Journal of Political Science* 49(2): 183–198.

Tavits, Margit, and Taavi Annus. 2006. Learning to Make Votes Count: The Role of Democratic Experience. *Electoral Studies*, 25(1): 72–90.

Thelen, Kathleen. 1999. Historical Institutionalism in Comparative Politics. *Annual Review of Political Science* 2: 369–404.

Ufen, Andreas. 2012. Party Systems, Critical Junctures, and Cleavages in Southeast Asia. *Asian Survey* 52(3): 441–464.

Welfling, Mary B. 1973. *Political Institutionalization: Comparative Analyses of African Party Systems*. Beverly Hills: Sage Publications.

Wittenberg, Jason. 2006. *Crucibles of Political Loyalty: Church Institutions and Electoral Continuity in Hungary*. Cambridge: Cambridge University Press.

The Antidemocratic Potential of Party System Institutionalization: Malaysia as Morality Tale?

Meredith L. Weiss

To an extent unusual for Southeast Asia, parties structure Malaysian political life. These parties perform all the functions they are supposed to: they represent and organize groups in society, channel and express interests, and significantly structure social and economic as well as political life. Nearly all those parties most active and supported now are long-standing and organizationally solid; all claim a reasonably high degree of institutionalization. Moreover, by the terms of the literature engaged here, Malaysia has a strongly institutionalized party system, or "set of patterned interactions in the competition among parties."[1] Malaysian parties at least officially accept and follow established rules in electoral contests; the ranks of primary contenders are reasonably stable, rooted in society and organizational life, and ideologically consistent; and the same set of parties tends to hold its niche in government.[2] Though parties themselves suffer crises, the systems holds – and generally, the same party or a dominant faction regenerates post-crisis and returns to the fray within the span of a single election cycle. Based solely on its lattice of parties, the Malaysian polity seems well positioned to support a democratic government: although party system institution need not yield democratization in any teleological way, party strengthening

---

[1] Mainwaring and Scully (1995: 4). Alternate criteria offer a different reading. Randall and Svåsand 2002: 7–8, for instance, suggest that what marks an institutionalized, *competitive* party system are accountability-boosting continuity among party alternatives; parties that "accept each other as legitimate competitors"; "a sufficient degree of autonomy from the state," notwithstanding some necessary degree of state regulation and support; and public "trust in parties as institutions and commitment to the electoral process." Any nondemocratic system would fare less well if held to these standards. In Malaysia, not only have competition and interparty respect always been limited, but party and state are substantially fused; especially in the 1980s–1990s, the regime drifted increasingly toward authoritarian statism (Saravanamuttu 1989; Tan 1990: 33–35).

[2] Mainwaring and Scully (1995: 5). Malaysia less clearly meets the criterion for democratic party systems that party organizations not be subordinated to party leaders' interests (Mainwaring and Scully 1995: 25), given the iconic role of particular long-serving leaders.

is commonly presumed to be a path toward developing and buttressing representative, accountable institutions.

And yet Malaysia could hardly be considered a liberal democracy. Malaysia and Singapore "are the dogs that haven't barked": their dominant party systems have not yielded to more competitive alternatives, as their ruling parties have remained unified overall, and their regimes highly resilient.[3] Parties in Malaysia observe established rules for electoral competition to an extent, but not only are these rules arguably skewed (e.g., by limits on free speech and assembly) but also breaches by the dominant coalition go unchecked. Few of those opposition parties so active in society have historically had a real shot at office through elections and hence of realizing the goals of their well-organized constituents, although they routinely win more than 40 percent of the popular vote and have moved incrementally toward increasing their clout by working in coalitions.[4] Rather, Malaysia is a hegemonic party system, centered on the strongly dominant Barisan Nasional (National Front, BN) coalition, although the system does allow greater space for competition at the state level than would a comparable framework in a unitary state. In addition, democratic legitimacy is higher for specific parties than for the competitive electoral authoritarian state as a whole, as contention is more vibrant and determinative within certain parties than between them.

Overall, though, autonomous state institutions and democratic praxis remain tenuous: the strength, reach, and stability of a subset of Malaysian parties have stunted the development not only of their competitors but also of a democratic political system as a whole. Counterintuitively, then, but echoing the process Netina Tan describes here for Singapore's one dominant party, elections may undermine Malaysian democracy: skewed rules of the game work to sustain and seemingly validate an illiberal status quo. Likewise, much as Tuong Vu details here for Vietnam, it is the *deinstitutionalization* of core parties or of the party system that seems most likely to open space for political change, including liberalization.

The semi-authoritarian trajectory of Malaysian political development has directed political activity and accountability to political parties, blurred the lines between party and state, and undercut the space available for democratic political discourse and engagement. At a basic level, formalization of parties before and beyond that of other structures of the polity has fostered a party-centric order with an autocratic partisan slant, which other trends and factors have only exacerbated. Under the circumstances, it is remarkable that Malaysians remain so attached to their parties – not just the oligarchic parties that consistently form the federal government but also to more- and

---

[3] Hicken 2008: 90.
[4] Not that campaigns and elections are just about voters' rational weighing of options and the winners' legitimate ascent to office (Chua 2007).

less-empowered opposition parties. To understand how this condition has come to be, we first sketch out the parameters and extent of institutionalization of Malaysia's party system and parties, including how these patterns have varied over time and across parties; then consider why the system has developed in this way; and finally, ponder the implications of Malaysia's party system for politics and policy.

PARAMETERS AND INSTITUTIONALIZATION

Although the key political parties in Malaysia are themselves well institutionalized – enduring, stable, and distinct[5] – what sets the polity apart is the institutionalization of its party system. Malaysia probably comes closest to satisfying Mainwaring and Scully's criteria for party institutionalization of all the states in Southeast Asia.[6] Levels of institutionalization have fluctuated over time, but not dramatically; the authoritarian interregnum of 1969–1971 left in its wake an even more consolidated and resilient system than the one before, such that even much-touted recent fluctuations will be hard to sustain. And it is worth noting that whereas Hicken and Kuhonta contest the relevance of legitimacy, Mainwaring and Scully's third criterion, as being more germane to evaluating the quality of democracy than that of a party system, Malaysia does arguably meet even this standard – but with antidemocratic implications, to which we shall return.

Mainwaring and Scully offer four scored criteria for situating party systems on the continuum from inchoate to institutionalized:[7]

1. *Volatility*, or the degree of regularity in parties' share of votes and seats across elections;
2. The *stability* of parties' roots in society, including with organized interests, as indicated by party longevity;
3. The *legitimacy* citizens accord parties and elections as the main way of determining who governs, indicated by survey data or rough estimates; and
4. The *solidity* of party organizations, as indicated by party discipline and the loyalty of political elites.

We consider each of these criteria in turn.

In terms of volatility, as Hicken and Kuhonta document (see Table 1.2), post-authoritarian Malaysia has the least volatile party system in the region.

---

[5] Even disallowed parties – which Mainwaring and Scully still "count" because they would put forth candidates if permitted to do so (Mainwaring and Scully 1995: 2) – have proved well institutionalized. Hence, Parti Sosialis Malaysia, for instance, was able to hit the ground running when finally permitted to compete.

[6] Mainwaring and Scully (1995: 1), or see Hicken and Kuhonta's Introduction.

[7] Mainwaring and Scully 1995: 6–16.

Parliamentary democracy has been suspended only once in Malaysia since independence in 1957, for a 21-month period following the 1969 elections. During that time, a National Operations Council, headed by soon-to-be prime minister Tun Abdul Razak governed the country by decree. That trend of low volatility seems to be buckling somewhat, but it still holds. The opposition did reasonably well in 1999, for instance, and posted its best showing ever in 2008, yet the intervening 2004 elections saw the BN's strongest result to date: the incumbent coalition garnered 64 percent of the popular vote and more than 90 percent of parliamentary seats.[8] What complicates our reading of volatility, however, is the subnational level. Our comparative data on volatility – and indeed, the literature broadly – focuses on the national level. Malaysia's much-touted safety valve, in contrast, and the "proof" of Malaysian democracy for many observers, is the ability of opposition parties to win control of state governments, even if they make sparse inroads at the federal level. That said, most of Malaysia's 13 state governments are and always have been firmly in the grip of the BN; the two states in which the Malaysian Islamic Party (PAS) traditionally does well tend to fluctuate relatively little from election to election, as well. Overall, volatility at the state level is higher than at the federal level, but still not markedly high. It is worth noting, though, that the 2008 elections, in which opposition parties secured control of five states as well as more than one-third of parliamentary seats, could mark the start of a trend toward increasing volatility.

In terms of whether Malaysian parties have stable roots in society, including with organized interests, the picture is less equivocal. Not only individual parties but also the dominant coalition of parties and the general pattern of support for parties are remarkably stable. Taking longevity as an indicator, the three leading parties in the BN – the United Malays National Organisation (UMNO), Malaysian Chinese Association (MCA), and Malaysian Indian Congress (MIC) – all took shape before independence and have persisted since.[9] The two long-dominant peninsular opposition parties are nearly as old: PAS formed out of a faction from UMNO in the 1950s, whereas the Democratic Action Party (DAP) formed in the 1960s as the successor to the Singapore-based People's Action Party (PAP) after Singapore left the federation in 1965. Two other peninsular parties bear mention for their relevance (in Sartori's sense of

---

[8] Part of the issue is the discussion of results in terms of coalitions rather than component parties, especially for the BN. For instance, in 1999, it was really UMNO that fared poorly and PAS that posted serious gains; a change in leadership, plus a more Islamic focus, helped UMNO turn the tide for the BN in 2004 (Funston 2006).

[9] Today's UMNO is technically "UMNO Baru" (New UMNO), formed from Prime Minister Mahathir's faction after the party split in 1987. UMNO Baru's constitution emphasized leadership and party unity more than democracy, to preclude further such crises (Means 1991: 283–288). The bulk of the rival faction – temporarily reconstituted as Semangat '46 (Spirit of '46, year of UMNO's founding) – has since been reabsorbed into UMNO.

parliamentary representation).[10] On the government side is Parti Gerakan Rakyat Malaysia (Malaysian People's Movement Party, Gerakan), launched in 1968, so also reasonably venerable; on the opposition is the newer Parti Keadilan Rakyat (People's Justice Party, Keadilan). Keadilan dates only to 1999, but it includes the much older Parti Rakyat Malaysia (Malaysian People's Party, PRM), with which the original Keadilan (Parti Keadilan Nasional, National Justice Party) merged in 2003. Moreover, to some extent, Keadilan might be seen as occupying a long-standing niche for the chief rival to the UMNO leader and his entourage, previously filled by Semangat' 46, a late-1980s splinter party from UMNO, which likewise anchored a more coordinated opposition challenge.[11]

Seen from a different angle, the stability not just of individual parties but also of the set of alignments the system as a whole represents is even clearer. Different parties appeal to particular ethnic (and for PAS, also religious) constituencies. The three cornerstone parties of the BN (which formed the earlier, tripartite Alliance) define themselves explicitly as communal, as do some relevant East Malaysian parties, such as the Parti Bansa Dayak Sarawak (Sarawak Dayak People's Party, PBDS), a splinter party from the Sarawak National Party (SNAP) that advocated multi-racialism but still explicitly championed ethnic Dayak leadership.[12] Parties in the opposition typically claim not to be communal, specifically to distinguish themselves from the BN – and, of course, to broaden their base in the process. And yet voters still recognize the DAP as a party of and for Chinese Malaysians (including the powerful Chinese education movement), PAS as of and for Muslims (including a network of *dakwah*, Muslim proselytization and strengthening, organizations), and so on. The stability of these alignments has stymied collective action across the opposition, generally limiting the challenge these parties can pose to the BN even when the latter is weak,[13] and hence helping to keep volatility in check.

Our third criterion is whether the public and political leaders accord parties and elections legitimacy. Here again, the evidence from Malaysia is surprisingly straightforward. Even though elections empirically offer little prospect for holding elites truly accountable, they remain the primary mode of political engagement among the public. Furthermore, survey data[14] show Malaysians to be among Asia's strongest supporters of political parties: almost 20 percent state that they are members of parties, whereas another 22 percent think they

---

[10] I focus here primarily on peninsular politics. For more on Sabah and Sarawak, Loh 1997 and the other contributions to that journal issue are a good place to start, as well as the chapters by Loh and Aeria in Puthucheary and Norani 2005.

[11] See Hari 1991 for details.

[12] Chin 1996. Parties in Sarawak and Sabah may have an ethnic identity, but politics there does not fit the same sort of communal model as in West Malaysia.

[13] For instance, Case 2004.

[14] Loh cites cross-national data gathered in 2000.

might join one – levels unusually high for the region. In addition, Malaysians lag behind only Filipinos and Japanese among Asians (and then only slightly) in their inclination to help a party or candidate during an election, and they have the highest propensity in the region to contribute financially.[15] Beyond helping out parties, Malaysians do turn out voluntarily to vote. More than 70 percent of those surveyed claimed to have voted in at least some, if not all, recent elections; turnout rates back up those claims.[16] Nearly all those surveyed agreed that citizens have a duty to vote in elections, and few consider that vote merely a formality: just fewer than 80 percent agreed that the way people vote determines how the country is run.[17]

On the converse, Malaysians display less interest in other forms of participation. Those with party ties were less likely than counterparts elsewhere in Asia to engage in extra-electoral political activities such as protests or petition signings. Not surprisingly, BN leaders encourage the idea that democratic participation *is* voting and discourage extra-electoral engagement.[18] More than one-third of Malaysian survey respondents have apparently fully internalized this message, to the extent of believing that citizens should not be allowed to organize public meetings – the highest level in Asia.[19] Although a spate of mass protests since 2007, most notably over electoral reform, suggests increasing popular belief in both the right to engage and the unevenness of the current playing field, those protest events have still been both intermittent and concentrated among the urban middle class. Yet, Malaysians are, on the whole, happy with democracy. If we take being proud "of the way Malaysia's democracy works" as an indicator for system legitimacy, the country fares well; only 16 percent claimed to be less than proud.[20]

Carlson and Turner support these findings, with more recent (2006–2007) AsiaBarometer data: Malaysians are second only to Singaporeans among the Southeast Asian nations surveyed in their overall trust in government institutions,[21] are near-unanimous in satisfaction with their right to vote (more than 96 percent), and rank second in satisfaction with their right to participate in organizations (88 percent). Citizens report far less satisfaction with their rights to freedom of speech (62 percent), to criticize the government (52 percent), or to gather and demonstrate (53 percent), ranking Malaysia fifth out of sixth in terms of civil liberties. They also were the least satisfied with their government's

---

[15] Loh 2007: 117.
[16] All citizens older than age 21 are eligible to vote, but it is not compulsory and requires pre-registration.
[17] Loh 2007: 116.
[18] Jomo 1996.
[19] Loh 2007: 117.
[20] Ibid.
[21] Malaysia's overall "trust" score is 79 percent, albeit lower (69 percent) for the police than for the central government, parliament, and the legal system (all more than 80 percent) (Carlson and Turner 2008: 229).

accountability and responsiveness – and yet lagged behind only Singapore in approving the central government's performance on a range of specific issues.[22] Loh helps puts such contradictory data in context:

> Malaysians have a narrow definition of democracy which is defined by involvement in legally registered political parties and participation in multi-party elections conducted regularly and rejecting participation which extends into the extra-electoral realms … unlike elsewhere in Southeast Asia (Singapore excepted), elections and party politics are the stuff of contemporary politics in Malaysia, at least for a majority.[23]

Carlson and Turner, too, note that in hybrid regimes such as Malaysia, we might expect to find "conceptual fuzziness" in citizens' understanding of what democracy means.[24]

Last, we consider the solidity of party organizations themselves. Although resources are spread unevenly across parties, party leaders and politicians share both commitment and common strategies. Party organizations are relatively solid and party discipline high, particularly among peninsular parties. The occasional politician does hop parties,[25] but once elected, most follow their whip's lead consistently. In the meantime, what keeps the leading parties, especially UMNO and PAS, strong is a deep, thick network among supporters, detailed later. Not only do such networks keep party leaders informed of sentiments and priorities at the grass roots, but they also offer a conduit for communicating party messages and organizing members to vote – and specifically to vote for the party – on election day. Most Malaysian parties define themselves primarily on particularistic grounds, clarifying their niche among the grass roots; ideological or policy orientations offer a second-order rubric for differentiation. For instance, both UMNO and PAS appeal first to Malay-Muslims, then stress aspects of Malay rights and Islam respectively to distinguish themselves, ultimately converging on the same increasingly Islamist ground in contest for the same voters. That said, Malaysian parties tend to have thick, often highly personalized ties to their constituents, offering points of access for grievance articulation, a range of social services, civic education, and more, however closed and cliquish actual decision making within parties is. Given their varied functions, out of office (opposition) parties look much like social movement organizations for their continual mobilization, consciousness raising, collective action, and service provision.

Indeed, to some extent, as elsewhere in Southeast Asia, elections in Malaysia serve more to legitimate the existing government's continued rule than to offer a chance to change the government;[26] although voters still turn out, many leave

---

[22] Ibid.: 229–233.
[23] Loh 2007: 117.
[24] Carlson and Turner 2008: 227.
[25] Opposition parties in Sabah, for instance, were devastated by a plague of *katak* (party-hopping "frogs") in the 1990s, as the BN allegedly bought off newly elected legislators.
[26] Taylor 1996.

frustrated (as the increasing availability of alternative media and channels for voice makes ever more clear). Still, the BN's quest always to retain a two-thirds majority in parliament (needed to amend the constitution, and lost for the first time only in 2008) ensures at least some responsiveness to voters' demands – part of a complex carrot-and-stick (or repressive/responsive) approach.[27] And yet the Malaysian case serves as a sort of morality tale of the potential incompatibility of a strongly institutionalized party system with democracy, if that system is institutionalized prior to democratic consolidation.

The Place of Parties and Elections

Not surprisingly, one of the primary contributions of the Malaysian case to the literature thus far has been on how party systems manifest in non-liberal democratic regimes.[28] Conventional arguments for why elections remain germane even where their outcome is largely predetermined and accountability, therefore, limited apply well to Malaysia (as partly derived from the case): elections provide a legitimating function for local and international audiences, as well as a mandate to rule; even small changes in patterns and levels of support update leaders' information on public sentiment, contenders, and sources of opposition, and elections assist in social control by pacifying the public, proving the strength of incumbents, and sanctioning only certain avenues for participation.[29] (See Netina Tan's chapter here on Singapore for a cognate argument on the electoral function in institutionalizing and maintaining autocracy.)

Elections are held regularly in Malaysia, the results are honored, and extra-electoral political participation is almost always civil, if not necessarily fruitful or well received. Yet, the regime has been variously labeled pseudo-democratic,[30] illiberal democratic,[31] statist democratic,[32] dominant-party democratic,[33] soft authoritarian,[34] capitalist authoritarian statist,[35] and competitive electoral authoritarian.[36] Freedom House consistently labels the state "partly free." Malaysia has the trappings of Westminster-style parliamentary democracy, a legacy of comparatively benign British colonial rule. As a constitutional monarchy in which the position of (largely disempowered) king rotates among

---

[27] Crouch 1996.
[28] Its other main contribution has been on whether and when democracy mitigates or exacerbates social conflict (Hicken 2008: 89, 92–93).
[29] Also Case 2002: 7–8; Hicken 2008: 90.
[30] Case 2001.
[31] Jones, Bell, and Brown 1995.
[32] Jesudason 1995.
[33] Alagappa 1995.
[34] Means 1996.
[35] Tan 1990.
[36] Levitsky and Way 2002.

the hereditary state-level sultans,[37] executive authority in Malaysia lies chiefly with the prime minister. Legislative power at the federal level rests in a bicameral parliament, with an elected lower house and appointed upper house; similar structures are replicated in each of the 13 states. Voting is majoritarian (first-past-the-post), with single-member districts at both the federal and state levels and elections called by the prime minister within a five-year window. Rural votes carry more weight than urban ones (in terms of voters per constituency), enhancing Malay representation. Local elections were suspended for political reasons – specifically, the too-strong performance of non-Malay-based opposition parties – in the 1960s and have yet to be restored.[38] Only from 1969 to 1971 has parliamentary rule been suspended on the national level since independence in 1957. Civil society is hardly negligible and social activism has at times influenced policies and political attitudes,[39] but elections remain the primary mode of mass engagement.

The BN coalition (organized as the Alliance until 1974) has won every election at the federal level, although it sometimes loses to the left-wing or Islamist opposition at the state level; the losses in 2008 marked the BN's worst result to date. The BN (which is itself registered as a party) is composed of three core parties representing Malaysia's major ethnic groups – UMNO, the MCA, and the MIC; when the Alliance became the BN in 1974, six auxiliary parties were added, then several others, for a current total of fourteen.

UMNO dominates the BN, usually in terms of votes/seats, and always in terms of power and status. Moreover, it is with UMNO's internal elections and factional struggles that Malaysia's real political battles are often said to be fought.[40] The leader of UMNO traditionally leads the government, and the party wields considerable influence on the internal politics of its BN partners. Clientelist or entourage networks are critical to intraparty machinations, and not just in the BN (although it is the BN that controls the most resources for patronage). Other parties vie for dominance in particular states – PAS especially in Kelantan and Trengganu and the DAP in Penang, for instance.

The Malaysian government has been commonly styled as consociational,[41] and that label may have applied reasonably well in the Alliance days.[42] However, political affiliations have never been purely ethnic, despite the

---

[37] Hari 1995.

[38] Saravanamuttu 2000; Goh 2005.

[39] Weiss 2004.

[40] Hari 1991; Case 1997.

[41] Lijphart's definition: "government by elite cartel designed to turn a democracy with a fragmented political culture into a stable democracy" (1969: 216).

[42] For instance, see Funston 1980: 11–17 on the limits to Malay dominance in the Alliance, the result of the MCA's clout, the character of then prime minister Tunku Abdul Rahman, and the bureaucracy's independent authority.

availability of communal parties; Malaysia has never really approached the sort of order of which Horowitz, for instance, warns, in which all voters are essentially committed to their designated ethnic party, and these parties' claims are incompatible.[43] Some parties even within the BN (especially in the non-peninsular states of Sabah and Sarawak) cross ethnic lines; parties or factions compete within as well as across communal groups;[44] and, *contra* Lijphart, Malay dominance within the BN has grown stronger over time. Lustick's control model fits the case better, given its "focus on effective group control over rival group(s)"[45] and maintenance of stability through (even coercive) domination of the strongest group rather than compromise and cooperation.

Importantly, issues that elsewhere may be decided on more functional or pragmatic grounds (e.g., policies on education or pioneer industries) tend to be decided largely on communal, partisan grounds in Malaysia. In fact, von Vorys suggests that what really forced the breakdown of cordial consociationalism in 1969 was that the difficult, especially racial, issues then ascendant had not really featured in the two previous elections since *Merdeka* (independence): in 1959, Malaysia was still basking in independence and in 1964, Indonesian *Konfrontasi* (confrontation, its armed assault on the newly expanded Federation of Malaysia) distracted the electorate. When democracy was put to the test, the system proved inadequate to withstand particularistic pressures, forcing Alliance leaders to reconsolidate their control under the National Operations Council.[46] Apart from the long-enduring PAS and the DAP, opposition parties have come and gone, have been absorbed into the BN, or have sustained only small, if loyal, niches. Subsets of these parties have negotiated electoral pacts and more substantial coalitions for some elections, but these are seldom effective or enduring: the playing field is slanted clearly in the incumbent BN's favor and the natural rifts between opposition parties are deep. Patterns of party politics in the 11 states of peninsular Malaysia have historically differed from those of Sabah and Sarawak, but BN/UMNO dominance is settling in there, as well – especially because UMNO coopted a range of indigenous (non-Malay, and some non-Muslim) Sabahans into the party in 1990.[47] Although our focus here is primarily on party systems as a whole rather than their discrete parts, it would be helpful to supplement that discussion with a brief overview of the institutionalization of the component parties within that system.

---

[43] Horowitz 1985.
[44] Musolf and Springer 1977: 116.
[45] Lustick 1979: 326.
[46] von Vorys 1976: 249.
[47] Hari 1998: 249.

Institutionalization of Political Parties

The criteria for party (rather than party system) institutionalization outlined by Vicky Randall and Lars Svåsand present a useful starting point for interrogating the nature of political parties in Malaysia.[48] Their criteria follow:

1. *Systemness*: scope, density, and regularity of interactions within the party;
2. *Value infusion*: the extent to which party actors and supporters identify with and are committed to the party for more than instrumental reasons;
3. *Decisional autonomy*: the party's ability to set its own policies without interference; and
4. *Reification*: presence in the public imagination.

By Randall and Svåsand's metrics, the primary parties in Malaysia –UMNO, the MCA, and the MIC in the ruling coalition, and PAS and the DAP in the opposition – are reasonably well institutionalized, as are several other parties.[49] All are complex, coherent organizations, even if marked to varying degrees by factionalism, clientelism, corruption, and over-reliance on individual leaders.[50] What complicates matters is that the governing BN is officially registered as a single party; candidates from member parties technically contest under the coalition flag rather than that of their own party. The opposition has likewise organized since 2008 as the Pakatan Rakyat (People's Alliance, successor to the short-lived Barisan Alternatif, Alternative Front, which formed for the 1999 elections, as well as earlier pacts), though not legally registered as a party. Indeed, the fact that relevant opposition parties are so well institutionalized makes collaboration against the BN harder: these parties have real, distinct identities and constituencies, reflecting important divisions within the electorate.[51]

First, in terms of systemness, all these parties have clearly defined, elaborate internal leadership structures stretching down to the grass roots, effective and varied means of communicating with members, and a committed mass base. UMNO, for instance, is known for its *kepala sepuluh* system: one member is responsible for mobilizing and monitoring ten others; that pattern repeats up the pyramid. PAS relies not just on similar networks but also on small prayer and discussion groups (whether under the aegis of the party or of feeder *dakwah* organizations). Most Malaysian political parties have newsletters, often

---

[48] Randall and Svåsand 2002: 12–15.
[49] Exceptions include the People's Progressive Party, formed in 1953, which was really the vehicle of the charismatic Seenivasagam brothers until their deaths and remains a poorly institutionalized junior partner in the BN (Vasil 1971: 222–251) and the (better-known in recent years) Keadilan, which developed around the personality of Anwar Ibrahim.
[50] The very notion that factional struggles present threats to party leadership even in UMNO, though, hints at the extent of party institutionalization: structures are in place through which to lodge a challenge.
[51] Barraclough 1985.

circulating well beyond party membership; PAS has gotten in trouble in the past, for instance, for selling its paper, *Harakah*, to nonmembers,[52] whereas the DAP's *The Rocket* has long been a source of leftist news in Malaysia. Web-based communications have grown increasingly important to all parties, as well, from e-newsletters to online repositories of press statements to blogs.[53] Perhaps most importantly, political parties, especially UMNO and the MCA, dominate the mainstream print media by way of party-linked holding companies[54] – although these media may be compelled to temper their enthusiasm lest they turn off undecided voters or make supporters think their vote is not needed.[55]

Second, the bases of Malaysian political parties tend to strengthen value infusion. As Randall and Svåsand suggest is common,[56] the major Malaysian parties' roots in particular ethnoreligious communities and the social movement pedigree of several smaller (especially opposition) parties foster distinctive party values, priorities, and cultures. For instance, given both the resources UMNO commands and the veins of patronage weaving throughout the organization, self-interest clearly motivates many in the party. At the same time, most of UMNO's mass supporters garner little in concrete rewards. Although UMNO champions far-reaching preferential policies to benefit Malays and other *bumiputera* (indigenes), for example, critics blast those policies for disproportionately benefiting only a privileged, narrow segment of the Malay community. At the same time, UMNO's calls of *hidup Melayu* ("long live the Malays") carry real resonance among the party's sprawling base, and its identity as the community's long-term protector inspires real loyalty and confidence. Moreover, as the party's fiery general assemblies attest,[57] party culture is slow to change: despite nods toward multiculturalism and a more "Malaysian Malaysia" (currently branded as "1Malaysia") over the years, old-style *keris* (ceremonial knife) waving communalism still rouses the crowds and reassures Malay voters of the party's priorities.

Part of what allows this sort of consistency and commitment is that the leading parties, at least, enjoy a reasonably high degree of Randall and Svåsand's third factor, decisional autonomy, yet they also have fruitful linkages with other organizations and constituencies. The exceptions seem to prove the rule: within the BN, only UMNO enjoys true decisional autonomy; the MCA, MIC, and other component parties are subject to UMNO dictates to some extent. Their relatively lower autonomy has kept these parties less coherent and weaker than UMNO. Chinese voters, for instance, tend to be less party-loyal

[52] *Asia Times Online*, May 19, 1999. Available from http://atimes.com/se-asia/AE19Ae01.html.
[53] See Weiss 2009.
[54] See Zaharom 2002.
[55] Loh 2007: 121.
[56] Randall and Svåsand 2002: 21–22.
[57] For instance, *Malaysiakini*, Nov. 16, 2006. Available from http://www.malaysiakini.com/news/59631.

than Malay voters and to vote more based on rational calculations.[58] The MCA's apparent subservience to UMNO within the BN leaves the party unable to articulate the community's interests as firmly as it may prefer to cement party culture, values, and loyalty, leaving the party (along with Gerakan, which also attracts Chinese support, though via a somewhat different message) less well institutionalized than it might otherwise be.

All these parties, though, fare well in terms of Randall and Svåsand's fourth and final factor, reification. Politicians, parties, and voters do shape their behavior in large part with an eye to a basically stable array of parties. UMNO pursues Islamization not least because it sees PAS as a continuing and threatening presence; left-wing activists know that the DAP and its peers in the opposition are likely to be sympathetic to their interests and provide at least minimal policy access; young *dakwah* activists groom themselves from their early years to enter PAS after university. In fact, so firm is the public's concept of the leading parties that meaningful reform of party objectives or bases is difficult. PRM (now merged with Keadilan) was still commonly dismissed as socialist years after dropping the term from its name and declaring itself only for progressive social change. The DAP cannot shed its Chinese image no matter how earnestly it seeks and showcases non-Chinese leaders and members. The public and BN-linked media scoff at PAS's attempts to collaborate with non-Malay-based parties in the name of non-communal Islamism;[59] popular imagination holds PAS as first and foremost a party of Malays, whatever ideological or programmatic gloss the party may offer. In short, where increasing systemness and decisional autonomy might boost flexibility in an institutionalizing political party, reification can add rigidity, especially where a strongly institutionalized party system leaves limited space for maneuver.

KEY FACTORS IN MALAYSIA'S PATTERN OF INSTITUTIONALIZATION

Although a host of factors contribute to the pattern of party and party system institutionalization we find in Malaysia, historical legacies and the regime's illiberal character are most critical. Malaysia fits the pattern Hicken and Kuhonta describe well: born in the postwar period,[60] its party system, like those of Singapore, Taiwan, Indonesia, and Cambodia, "institutionalized because of some constraints on competition";[61] in all these states, "coercive

---

[58] For instance, Lai 1997.
[59] Non-communal refers to "attitudes, orientations and actions motivated by a concern for the common good rather than by a preoccupation with the interests of a single ethnic group (or combination of ethnic groups)" (Barraclough 1985: 34 n3).
[60] Hicken and Kuhonta, this volume, 10–12.
[61] Ibid.: 12.

structures tend to reinforce stable party systems."[62] The Malaysian state tightened the applicable constraints – which remain in effect today – after the 1969–1971 authoritarian interregnum by coopting most parties into an expanded ruling coalition, removing contentious issues from public discourse, ending local elections, further whittling back rights of expression and association, and more. Prior to that point, the system was at least somewhat more volatile and vulnerable, even if the incumbent coalition still always won at the federal level, and negotiations within the BN were relatively more democratic; since 1971, a blatantly skewed playing field has molded the "set of patterned interactions in the competition among parties" (i.e., the party system).[63] An assertive coalition of dominant parties effectively controls the discursive and physical space available to contenders, forcing opposition parties to fit themselves into available – even if ultimately debilitating – corners. All the same, the regime is not truly hegemonic. The chance to compete keeps opposition parties continually searching for new messages and niches, as well as ways to institutionalize not just their own organizations but also coordinated appeals that could plausibly challenge the encompassing BN.[64]

Two primary factors help explain the specific pattern of party development and party system institutionalization in Malaysia. First and foremost is the sequencing of the institutionalization of parties before that of state structures, and specifically before meaningful democratization. Complementing those effects has been a legacy of skewed rules of the game that deny representation to particular interests and shift citizens' calculus in deciding whether and how to engage. The concatenation of these factors has yielded a polity in which elections are more honored than honorable and a well-institutionalized system is inimical rather than essential to democratic stability. Malaysian experience, thus, suggests important trade-offs that institutionalization may entail, particularly in terms of system rigidity and responsiveness. Mainwaring and Scully do not address these implications directly, but the effects mirror those they note may apply to less polarized, and hence more stable and governable, democracies.[65]

Sequence of Stages of Political Development

The majority of the parties most significant in contemporary Malaysia formed in advance of independence, starting with UMNO in 1946. Both the Alliance and the PAP (progenitor of the DAP) won their first elections for semi-sovereign legislative councils under colonial rule. These parties developed personalities, structures, and programs for outreach and mobilization before the structures they aimed to control had fully formed and when Cold War threats and

---

[62] Ibid.: 13.
[63] Mainwaring and Scully 1995: 4.
[64] Hicken and Kuhonta, this volume, 13–14.
[65] Mainwaring and Scully 1995: 32.

responses – particularly the hard-edged anti-communist campaign of 1948 to 1960 called the Emergency – tempered calls for *too* free an order. Once the Alliance and the PAP in Singapore controlled something more akin to a state, they molded it to their advantage: party and state have never been fully disentangled. Malaysia's post-1969 restructuring, which bolstered the ruling coalition and dismantled a class-based challenge, reinforced that fusion, and processes of executive centralization (and assaults on overly independent institutions such as the judiciary and the monarchy) under Prime Minister Mahathir in the 1980s took it to a new level.[66] At the same time, as Jesudason describes, unlike in less statist regimes, Malaysian civil society has not been positioned to provide a real check:

The timing of franchise extension in relation to the development of the administrative apparatus, the state's economic managerialism, and its ability to link itself to fundamental cultural orientations of the population, have left civil society unable to provide an alternative political vision or to develop an alternative political coalition to that of the dominant party.[67]

The result today in Malaysia is a party-centric order with an autocratic partisan slant.

More fundamentally, as von Vorys explains in his classic work on Malaysian democracy, as in other states that gained independence in the postwar period, elites installed democracy before the conditions that make it work well elsewhere were in place: normative consensus, opportunities for social advancement and mobility, circulation of elites, sense of belonging to an overarching heterogeneous nation, predisposition to settle issues through the political process, and so forth. Malaysia failed to address these tensions seriously – especially that between majority rule and zero-sum ascriptive solidarities – as these elites themselves were communal leaders yet found democracy useful for getting along with the British as well as resolving domestic conflicts. These elites never intended the democracy they designed to be crosscutting or transparent: it was intended to be "democracy without consensus."[68]

Skewed Rules of Engagement

Although the standard narrative in which British officials carefully handed power to a close-knit set of Western-educated, Anglophone, capitalist Malay, Chinese, and Indian successors is not without some truth, the story does not end there. The ethnic-based parties of that Alliance did enjoy real advantages as incumbents and as respected elites in their own rights. Yet, through the 1960s, Malaysia supported a much broader set of political possibilities, including

---

[66] Khoo 1997; Hwang 2004.
[67] Jesudason 1995: 353.
[68] von Vorys 1976: 4–9, 13–14.

genuinely popular class-based left-wing parties and other non-communal alternatives.[69] The authoritarian National Operations Council, then the BN government that succeeded the Alliance, put in place new, strong curbs on civil liberties, as well as dissolving most organizations of the left. Meanwhile, the BN itself absorbed most of its challengers and left little legitimate space for alternative parties. The combination of these processes not only denied representation to particular interests but also shifted citizens' calculus in deciding whether and how to engage: elections became and remain the only safe, acknowledged channel for active participation, but that engagement carries less transformative potential than before – notwithstanding the euphoric expectations the 2008 results in particular fostered for opposition parties.

This narrowing of political space in Malaysia occurs on two dimensions. On the one hand, opposition parties are hard pressed to find a niche. Settlement, education, and occupational patterns dating back to the colonial era, as well as real differences in language, ritual, and more have encouraged vertical segmentation along racial and religious lines.[70] Pre-independence, communally organized interest groups morphed into communally organized political parties, especially to champion communally structured issues (e.g., highly contentious issues related to education and language or, more recently, the place of Islam in the public sphere). The fundamentally racialized BN encourages these patterns.

First, opposition parties preferring not to identify on ethnic or religious lines face challengers who do identify thus; convincing Malay voters, for instance, that their interests are not best served by a party focused only on them, when so much of their lived experience is ethnically stratified, is a hard sell. Second, among the most convincing and successful non-communal parties earlier in Malaysia's history were parties of the left, organized around horizontal class-based identities. Not only were the most threatening of these parties banned or demobilized, beginning even well before independence, but the societal organizations that fed into them – left-wing student groups, for instance – were also broken up as of the early 1970s. Trade unions and supportive labor organizations, too, lost clout and options or were deregistered, especially as aggressive export-oriented development plans gained steam through the 1970s and 1980s. The state's continued reluctance to register the Parti Sosialis Malaysia suggests how much the BN still fears a class-based challenge, while to be called a "communist" remains a slur, long after the term is even germane to Malaysia. By now, opposition parties crowd the margins – but different, hard-to-reconcile margins, while the incumbent sits massively in the middle.

On the other hand, even when parties do find a platform and even grounds for collaboration, they face real hurdles in communicating with and mobilizing supporters; semi-democratic Malaysia allows parties to compete regularly, but

---

[69] Vasil 1971; Weiss 2006: chs. 3–4.
[70] Among many others: Lee 1986; Abraham 1997.

not effectively.[71] Malaysia's constitution grants the usual raft of civil liberties: freedoms of speech, press, assembly, religion. Yet all these are curbed in practice. The Police Act precludes meetings of more than a handful of people without a permit. College and university students are forbidden even to support a candidate, let alone join a political party. Overly provocative media tend to lose their publishing permits, and so on. The BN communicates its messages with ease through the media it controls or through mass gatherings for which securing a permit simply is not a problem. Its opponents, on the other hand, are hamstrung. Elections themselves are of dubious fairness; the Election Commission comes under fire with each general election for being overly sympathetic to the incumbent regime, for instance in (non-)enforcement of campaign spending limits,[72] or in (not) purging "phantom voters" from electoral rolls.[73] In addition, a web of protections ensures Malay as well as BN dominance: gerrymandering and skewed constituency sizes, registration requirements, provisions for postal votes, and so on. And in the steps leading up to those elections – blocked from many campaign events, poorly covered by media, and liable to charges of sedition for raising especially sensitive issues – opposition parties face a sharply tilted playing field. Although protests for electoral reform organized by the Coalition for Clean and Fair Elections (a.k.a. Bersih) secured minor reforms for the 2013 elections – for instance, the expansion of postal voting for expatriate Malaysian citizens – larger processual complaints escaped redress. The unsurprising outcome is usually low volatility, even as the various parties further refine their organizational structures and messages and persuade their followers that they still should vote – in other words, ever-greater institutionalization, even as democratic pretensions wilt.

IMPLICATIONS

That a nominally democratic, but at least aspirationally hegemonic, system would have a strongly institutionalized party system makes sense: that combination of hegemony and relatively meaningful elections requires at least one genuinely strong party and some number of reasonably plausible competitors. However, this version of illiberalism offers real benefits over the alternatives (e.g., authoritarian populism or military rule). An institutionalized but only

---

[71] Case 2002: 6–7.

[72] Welsh 2004: 125–127 notes a shift toward increasingly steep campaign expenditures through the Mahathir years – a trend with both ethical implications, for the misuse of state funds and machinery at its heart, and practical ones, because opposition candidates command far less lavish resources.

[73] For instance on the especially mismanaged 2004 elections: Funston 2006: 149–151. Lim Hong Hai 2005 carefully assesses the Election Commission: what it does, how the public perceives its efforts, and how it (and the electoral system it supervises) could be improved. In the same volume, Ong Kian Ming 2005 homes in specifically on the much-maligned (but improved) electoral roll.

mildly competitive party system ensures a degree of predictability – much as an institutionalized party system offers in a democracy. We find, therefore, semi-democracy[74] to be more a stable, long-lasting, if not ultimately permanent, endpoint than a temporary way station in Malaysia: we can be reasonably confident that the BN will win at the federal level, though its precise margins are harder to predict, even if it is driven under pressure to more crassly authoritarian controls than in the past.[75]

Moreover, the specific process by which this system has developed and matured – particularly the implications of limited civil liberties – has meant that even if elections are less than fully meaningful, they are the only game in town for all but the boldest of citizens. What Malaysia loses in democratic legitimacy it gains in governability: its highly institutionalized party system channels political participation and conflict so they will not overwhelm the system.[76] In an illiberal system, that process amounts more to a safety valve function precluding disruptive outbursts than a mechanism for bringing public sentiment to bear on political and policy outcomes, as in a more open regime. In addition, the fact that the BN has devoured enough of its would-be contenders to occupy so much of the middle ground forces opposition parties to both appeal across multiple marginal positions (i.e., presses the opposition, too, to converge on the center) and build as strong coalitions as possible. This moderation and consolidation further facilitate governance.

Most importantly, Malaysia's dominant-party, institutionalized system limits prospects for real democratization, even if it also limits the space available for populists and personalistic appeals. Whereas Mainwaring and Scully see it as an asset that institutionalization means parties play a key role in structuring the political system, rendering politics more predictable,[77] that assessment reflects their focus on democratic systems. In a nondemocratic system, that role readily translates into parties' turning the rules to their own advantage – an argument against institutionalization, if democracy is the ultimate aim. Hence, in a democratic system, for instance, elections grant a mechanism for account-ability and peaceful removal of an unpopular leader, but unfair rules make such an outcome unlikely in Malaysia. Moreover, the fact that all parties do play by the rules may in fact sanction those rules in the eyes of the public,

---

[74] Case 2002: 9 refers to Malaysia sometimes as a semi-democracy and sometimes as a pseudo-democracy; he defines the latter as more coercive and less rooted and stable. In fact, Malaysia seems to hover between the two: in terms of competitiveness, the regime seems more "semi" now than at any point since the 1960s, but without Mahathir as glue, it seems to have lost an element of elite cohesion and mass respect sustained through much of the 1980s–1990s and thus to resort more quickly to coercion.

[75] Case 2001, 2004. It bears reiterating that the Pakatan Rakyat's momentous victory of 2008 still left the BN with clear majority control of the federal parliament (albeit without its usual two-thirds supermajority) and able to form the government in eight states.

[76] Mainwaring and Scully 1995: 25–26.

[77] Ibid.: 22.

complicating mobilization for reform – yet opposition parties are in a bind, as not playing by the rules would bar them from any chance at office, even at the subnational level. Such dilemmas cloud easy assessments of the quality and legitimacy of Malaysian democracy. Tun Razak's statement as he reinstated parliamentary government after the National Operations Council rule seems still germane to today's BN regime: "The view we take is that democratic government is the best and most acceptable form of government. So long as the form is preserved, the substance can be changed to suit conditions of a particular country."[78]

All that said, however stable, the Malaysian system is not static. Elections have developed, in Malaysia as elsewhere in the region, to pacify and depoliticize the population by "limiting the politically possible to formalized campaigns and episodic voting opportunities," yet they still offer the possibility of "prying open and widening the sphere of legitimate political activity by demonstrating the illegitimacy of the old regime," if the latter drifts too far out of touch.[79] Party system institutionalization (though less party institutionalization) seems to be crumbling at the edges, particularly as new media, new ideas, and new influences ease information dissemination and mobilization. The Internet's deep permeation has been a key vector among some communities, for instance, by allowing new means of disseminating unfiltered platforms, news, and viewpoints,[80] while new ideas increasingly circulate among the middle class and intellectuals about the nature of politics and prospects for political change.[81] Taken together, these developments are nipping at the heels of party system institutionalization by encouraging greater volatility as voters question previous alignments and increasing popular frustration with elections as they find newly articulated preferences unmet.

The comparatively extreme fluctuations in margins of support for the BN, PAS, the DAP, and Keadilan over the past four general elections (1999, 2004, 2008, and 2013) represent a measurable uptick in volatility (see Table 2.1).

At the same time, ideological differentiation suffers when UMNO, PAS, and Keadilan compete for Malay votes, as they have with especial keenness since the tumult of 1998's Reformasi and as opposition coalitions to counter the BN gain traction. Even the solidity of the BN parties' bases of support seems diminished today, with high-profile backbenchers' revolts within UMNO, struggles between hard-liners and moderates in PAS, and defections to and from all sides. And the confluence of an increasingly vibrant civil society and those hard-to-block new media has fed ever more elaborate strategies for election monitoring and awareness raising about the frailties of the electoral system. Although turnout

---

[78] Quoted in Zakaria 1989: 349.
[79] Taylor 1996: 8.
[80] Abbott 2004; Weiss 2009.
[81] Derichs 2004.

TABLE 2.1. *Percentage Shares of Votes and Seats for Past Four Malaysian General Elections*

		1999	2004	2008	2013
BN	votes	57	64	51	47
	seats	77	90	63	60
PAS	votes	15	15	14	15
	seats	14	3	10	9
DAP	votes	13	10	14	16
	seats	5	5	13	17
Keadilan	votes	12	9	19	20
	seats	3	1	14	14

Sources: Sun (Malaysia); *Star* (Malaysia); http://www.spr.gov.my.

rates are unlikely to plummet, the legitimacy of parties and elections may decline to an extent.

Whereas predictions are risky at best, this process of deinstitutionalization seems likely to continue over future electoral cycles. In that case, Malaysian parties will remain institutionalized (meaningful, supported, strong), but the party system will become more inchoate as increasing transparency, broader participation in extra-electoral channels (which has been developing since the 1980s),[82] and the more contingent factor of a lack of inspiring leadership in UMNO[83] nudge the regime toward a degree of liberalization incompatible with a dominant party system. (Of course, "party system" and "regime" are not synonymous. Other elements of the regime may remain unchanged, or may transform differently or at a different pace.) What will make this transition easier is the deeply ingrained habit of voting: beyond election day, voting inculcates habits of participation, and general elections themselves tend to see comparatively lax enforcement of controls on extra-electoral participation.[84]

---

[82] For an ultimately optimistic perspective in the wake of a 1987 crackdown, see Saravanamuttu 1989; for a discursively oriented (and also optimistic) take on the implications of the 1998–1999 Reformasi movement, see Farish 1999; for a discussion of the place of civil society and alternative media in the "political tsunami" of 2008, see Weiss 2009.

[83] The enduringly paternalistic quality especially of UMNO (and hence, of the BN-led regime) (Zakaria 1989: 371–372) casts the greatest doubt on the institutionalization of specific parties. UMNO has yet to find a doyen adequate to fill Mahathir's shoes – and that lack of a commanding, quixotic presence could offer a real opportunity for intraparty reform, percolating up to inter-party, systemic reform. Yet, the idea that UMNO needs to lose coherence for reform to be possible is not a new one. Jesudason describes the UMNO-led state's adroit absorption or deflection of sources of challenge particularly well, positing that any change must come from within the party (Jesudason 1996).

[84] Loh 2007: 128.

Overall, though, Malaysia's institutionalized party system will not help move democratization along. It is only as that system wavers that liberalization may be possible, and the process will necessarily entail some amount of at least transitional instability.

CONCLUSIONS

The skewed trajectory of political development in Malaysia, in which parties have been institutionalized ahead of and often apart from the broader party or political systems, compounded by authoritarian constraints on civil liberties, has directed political activity and accountability to political parties, blurred the lines between party and state, and undercut the space available for political discourse and engagement. Analysis of Malaysia reminds us that the rules and characteristics of an electoral system are hardly neutral, and that the institutionalization of a strong party system may work against democratization rather than for it. Regime change is still possible but will most likely be incremental, slow, and difficult to sustain, requiring that party system institutionalization be undone to a degree.

REFERENCES

Abbott, Jason P. 2004. The Internet, Reformasi and Democratisation in Malaysia. In E. T. Gomez (Ed.), *The State of Malaysia: Ethnicity, Equity and Reform*, pp. 79–104. London: RoutledgeCurzon.
Abraham, Collin E. R. 1997. *Divide and Rule: The Roots of Race Relations in Malaysia*. Kuala Lumpur: Institute for Social Analysis (INSAN).
Alagappa, Muthiah. 1995. The Asian Spectrum. *Journal of Democracy* 6(1): 29–36.
Barraclough, Simon. 1985. Barisan Nasional Dominance and Opposition Fragmentation: The Failure of Attempts to Create Opposition Cooperation in the Malaysian Party System. *Asian Profile* 13(1): 33–43.
Carlson, Matthew, and Mark Turner. 2008. Public Support for Democratic Governance in Southeast Asia. *Asian Journal of Political Science* 16(3): 219–239.
Case, William. 1997. The 1996 UMNO Party Election: "Two for the Show." *Pacific Affairs* 70(3): 393–411.
Case, William. 2001. Malaysia's Resilient Pseudodemocracy. *Journal of Democracy* 12(1): 43–57.
Case, William. 2002. *Politics in Southeast Asia: Democracy or Less*. New York: RoutledgeCurzon.
Case, William. 2004. New Uncertainties for an Old Pseudo-Democracy: The Case of Malaysia. *Comparative Politics* 37(1): 83–104.
Chin, James. 1996. PBDS and Ethnicity in Sarawak Politics. *Journal of Contemporary Asia* 26(4): 512–526.
Chua Beng Huat. 2007. Introduction: Political Elections as Popular Culture. In Chua Beng Huat (Ed.), *Elections as Popular Culture in Asia*, pp. 1–21. New York: Routledge.
Crouch, Harold. 1996. Malaysia: Do Elections Make a Difference? In R. H. Taylor (Ed.), *The Politics of Elections in Southeast Asia*, pp. 114–135. Cambridge: Woodrow Wilson Center Press and Cambridge University Press.

Derichs, Claudia. 2004. Political Crisis and Reform in Malaysia. In Edmund Terence Gomez (Ed.), *The State of Malaysia: Ethnicity, Equity and Reform*, pp. 105–129. London: RoutledgeCurzon.

Farish A. Noor. 1999. Looking for *Reformasi*: The Discursive Dynamics of the Reformasi Movement and Its Prospects as a Political Project. *Indonesia and the Malay World* 27(77): 5–18.

Funston, John. 1980. *Malay Politics in Malaysia: A Study of UMNO and PAS*. Kuala Lumpur: Heinemann Educational Books (Asia).

Funston, John. 2006. The Malay Electorate in 2004: Reversing the 1999 Result? In Saw Swee-Hock and K. Kesavapany (Eds.), *Malaysia: Recent Trends and Challenges*, pp. 132–156. Singapore: Institute of Southeast Asian Studies.

Goh Ban Lee. 2005. The Demise of Local Government Elections and Urban Politics. In Mavis Puthucheary and Norani Othman (Eds.), *Elections and Democracy in Malaysia*, pp. 49–70. Bangi: Universiti Kebangsaan Malaysia Press.

Singh, Hari. 1991. Political Change in Malaysia: The Role of Semangat 46. *Asian Survey* 31(8): 712–728.

Singh, Hari. 1995. UMNO Leaders and Malay Rulers: The Erosion of a Special Relationship. *Pacific Affairs* 68(2): 187–205.

Singh, Hari. 1998. Tradition, UMNO and Political Succession in Malaysia. *Third World Quarterly* 19(2): 241–254.

Hicken, Allen. 2008. Developing Democracies in Southeast Asia: Theorizing the Role of Parties and Elections. In Erik Kuhonta, Dan Slater, and Tuong Vu (Eds.), *Southeast Asia in Political Science: Theory, Region, and Qualitative Analysis*, pp. 80–101. Stanford: Stanford University Press.

Horowitz, Donald L. 1985. *Ethnic Groups in Conflict*. Berkeley: University of California Press.

Hwang In-Won. 2004. Malaysia's "Presidential Premier": Explaining Mahathir's Dominance. In Bridget Welsh (Ed.), *Reflections: The Mahathir Years*, pp. 67–76. Washington, DC: Southeast Asia Program, Paul H. Nitze School of Advanced International Studies.

Jesudason, James V. 1995. Statist Democracy and the Limits to Civil Society in Malaysia. *Journal of Commonwealth and Comparative Politics* 33: 335–356.

Jesudason, James V. 1996. The Syncretic State and the Structuring of Oppositional Politics in Malaysia. In Garry Rodan (Ed.), *Political Oppositions in Industrialising Asia*, pp. 128–160. London: Routledge.

Jomo K. S. 1996. Elections' Janus Face: Limitations and Potential in Malaysia. In R. H. Taylor (Ed.), *The Politics of Elections in Southeast Asia*, pp. 90–113. Cambridge: Woodrow Wilson Center Press and Cambridge University Press.

Jones, David Martin, Daniel Bell, and David Brown. 1995. Towards a Model of Illiberal Democracy. In Daniel Bell et al. (Eds.), *Towards Illiberal Democracy in Pacific Asia*, pp. 163–167. New York: St. Martin's Press.

Khoo Boo Teik. 1997. Democracy and Authoritarianism in Malaysia since 1957: Class, Ethnicity and Changing Capitalism. In Anek Laothamatas (Ed.), *Democratization in Southeast and East Asia*, pp. 46–76. Singapore: Institute of Southeast Asian Studies.

Lai Seck Ling. 1997. *Corak Pengundian di Kalangan Pengundi Cina di Kawasan Dewan Undangan Negeri (DUN) Seri Kembangan: Di antara Straight-ticket Voting dan Split-ticket Voting.* Academic Exercise, Jabatan Sains Politik, Fakulti Sains Kemasyarakatan dan Kemanusiaan, Universiti Kebangsaan Malaysia, Bangi.

Lee, Raymond L. M. 1986. Symbols of Separatism: Ethnicity and Status Politics in Contemporary Malaysia. In Raymond Lee (Ed.), *Ethnicity and Ethnic Relations in Malaysia,* pp. 28–46. DeKalb: Center for Southeast Asian Studies, Northern Illinois University.

Levitsky, Steven, and Lucan A. Way. 2002. The Rise of Competitive Authoritarianism. *Journal of Democracy* 13(2): 51–65.

Lijphart, Arend. 1969. Consociational Democracy. *World Politics* 21(2): 207–225.

Lim Hong Hai. 2005. Making the System Work: The Election Commission. In Mavis Puthucheary and Norani Othman (Eds.), *Elections and Democracy in Malaysia,* pp. 249–291. Bangi: Universiti Kebangsaan Malaysia Press.

Loh Kok Wah, Francis. 1997. Understanding Politics in Sabah and Sarawak: An Overview. *Kajian Malaysia* 15(12): 1–14.

Loh Kok Wah, Francis. 2007. Engaging the 2004 General Election in Malaysia: Contrasting Roles and Goals. In Chua Beng Huat (Ed.), *Elections as Popular Culture in Asia,* pp. 115–138. New York: Routledge.

Lustick, Ian. 1979. Stability in Deeply Divided Societies: Consociationalism versus Control. *World Politics* 31(3): 325–344.

Mainwaring, Scott, and Timothy R. Scully. 1995. Introduction: Party Systems in Latin America. In Scott Mainwaring and Timothy R. Scully (Eds.), *Building Democratic Institutions: Party Systems in Latin America,* pp. 1–34. Stanford: Stanford University Press.

Means, Gordon P. 1991. *Malaysian Politics: The Second Generation.* Singapore: Oxford University Press.

Means, Gordon P. 1996. Soft Authoritarianism in Malaysia and Singapore. *Journal of Democracy* 7(4): 103–117.

Musolf, Lloyd, and J. Fred Springer. 1977. Legislatures and Divided Societies: The Malaysian Parliament and Multi-Ethnicity. *Legislative Studies Quarterly* 2(2): 113–136.

Ong Kian Ming. 2005. Examining the Electoral Roll. In Mavis Puthucheary and Norani Othman (Eds.), *Elections and Democracy in Malaysia,* pp. 292–315. Bangi: Universiti Kebangsaan Malaysia Press.

Puthucheary, Mavis, and Norani Othman. 2005. *Elections and Democracy in Malaysia.* Bangi: Universiti Kebangsaan Malaysia Press.

Randall, Vicky, and Lars Svåsand. 2002. Party Institutionalization in New Democracies. *Party Politics* 8(1): 5–29.

Saravanamuttu, Johan. 1989. Authoritarian Statism and Strategies for Democratisation: Malaysia in the 1980s. In Peter Limqueco (Ed.), *Partisan Scholarship: Essays in Honour of Renato Constantino,* pp. 233–251. Manila: Journal of Contemporary Asia Publishers.

Saravanamuttu, Johan. 2000. *Act of Betrayal: The Snuffing Out of Local Democracy in Malaysia.* Aliran Monthly 20(4): 23–25.

Tan, Simon. 1990. The Rise of State Authoritarianism in Malaysia. *Bulletin of Concerned Asian Scholars* 22(3): 32–42.

Taylor, R. H. (Ed.). 1996. Introduction: Elections and Politics in Southeast Asia. In *The Politics of Elections in Southeast Asia,* pp. 1–11. Cambridge: Woodrow Wilson Center Press and Cambridge University Press.

Vasil, R. K. 1971. *Politics in a Plural Society: A Study of Non-Communal Political Parties in West Malaysia*. Kuala Lumpur: Oxford University Press.

von Vorys, Karl. 1976. *Democracy without Consensus: Communalism and Political Stability in Malaysia*. Kuala Lumpur: Oxford University Press. Original edition, Princeton University Press, 1975.

Weiss, Meredith L. 2004. Malaysia: Construction of Counterhegemonic Narratives and Agendas. In Muthiah Alagappa (Ed.), *Civil Society and Political Change in Asia: Expanding and Contracting Democratic Space*, pp. 259–291. Stanford: Stanford University Press.

Weiss, Meredith L. 2006. *Protest and Possibilities: Civil Society and Coalitions for Political Change in Malaysia*. Stanford: Stanford University Press.

Weiss, Meredith L. 2009. Edging toward a New Politics in Malaysia: Civil Society at the Gate? *Asian Survey* 49(5): 741–758.

Welsh, Bridget. 2004. Shifting Terrain: Elections in the Mahathir Era. In Bridget Welsh (Ed.), *Reflections: The Mahathir Years*, pp. 119–133. Washington, DC: Southeast Asia Program, Paul H. Nitze School of Advanced International Studies.

Zaharom Nain. 2002. The Structure of the Media Industry: Implications for Democracy. In Francis Loh Kok Wah and Khoo Boo Teik (Eds.), *Democracy in Malaysia: Discourses and Practices*, pp. 111–137. Richmond, Surrey: Curzon.

Zakaria Haji Ahmad. 1989. Malaysia: Quasi Democracy in a Divided Society. In Larry Diamond, Juan J. Linz, and Seymour Martin Lipset (Eds.), *Democracy in Developing Countries*, Vol. 3: *Asia*, pp. 347–381. Boulder: Lynne Rienner Publishers.

3

Institutionalized Succession and Hegemonic Party Cohesion in Singapore

Netina Tan*

INTRODUCTION

The regime transition literature has found that apart from exogenous shocks, internal splits and leadership succession are the two most likely causes of single-party breakdown.[1] Unlike hegemonic party systems in Mexico and Taiwan that experienced party alternation, Singapore has been governed by one party uninterruptedly for more than five decades. Under the People's Action Party's (PAP) rule, export-oriented Singapore has weathered a series of global financial crises. Even when the country posted a negative growth rate in 2001, the PAP government was able to garner an exceptional 75 percent vote share in the general election (GE) the same year. Now, apart from tackling rising inflation and income inequality, what appears to concern most people is the imminent death of the country's strongman, Lee Kuan Yew.[2] Will the PAP continue to rule and maintain order after the passing of its founding leader?

This chapter focuses on the PAP's leadership succession to highlight the key intraparty processes and mechanisms that have kept one of the world's longest-serving political parties together. It argues that the PAP's long-term survival will depend more on institutions than coercion, charisma, or ideological commitment. Indeed, the PAP's incumbency advantage, coupled with an institutionalized leadership succession system, has facilitated self-renewal and kept the party together. Specifically, the elitist leadership selection model, based nominally on meritocracy, is well institutionalized and serves as an incentive distribution system that builds party loyalty and elite cohesion.

* The author would like to thank Scott Mainwaring, Ben Reilly, Craig Townsend, and the editors for their thoughtful comments on an earlier version of this chapter.
[1] O'Donnell and Schmitter 1986; Geddes 2003.
[2] Lee Kuan Yew turned 90 in 2013. He had two heart operations in 1996 and was hospitalized in 2008 for abnormal heart rhythm. A conference was held in 2009 to discuss the possible consequences of Lee's death.

As Hicken and Kuhonta suggest in the introductory chapter, party institutionalization ought to be distinguished from party democratization. This chapter's focus on Singapore's leadership succession model intends to offer evidence that party institutionalization can occur in semi-authoritarian regimes and that party system institutionalization need not necessarily lead to democratic consolidation. As Mainwaring notes in the concluding chapter, comparative studies of party system institutionalization need to make distinctions between the different types of democratic and nondemocratic systems to avoid conceptual confusion and measurement problems. This study on Singapore's hegemonic party system based on a two-level theoretical framework of party and party system institutionalization is an effort to this end.

A small island with population less than 4.6 million, Singapore is the wealthiest non-oil-producing country in the world that is not a democracy. Despite its affluence and ideal socioeconomic preconditions for democratization, no substantial opposition party has existed and electoral competition has been weak until the 2011 watershed GE. Unlike in other East Asian states, the large middle class in Singapore has been deemed "passive, deferential, acquiescent, and lacking political mobilization."[3] While political participation has increased in recent years, the regime's persistent refusal to embrace truly competitive multiparty politics has confounded observers, leaving some to exclude it as a deviant case that permits no meaningful comparison.[4] As Huntington once said, "the anomaly remains Singapore."[5]

To explain Singapore's exceptionalism, this chapter begins by proposing a two-level theoretical framework to examine the degree of party and party system institutionalization in the country. Specifically, it considers the degree of its institutionalization based on the following dimensions: autonomy, systemness, rootedness, and stability of interparty competition. It then examines the rules of the game and institutional obstacles opposition parties and candidates face in elections. As leadership succession is one of the gravest threats to single-party stability, this chapter pays special attention on how the PAP's candidate and leadership selection model builds elite cohesion. It concludes with some cautionary remarks on its elitist method and considers the potential problems that could undermine its cohesion and electoral dominance.

PARTY AND PARTY SYSTEM INSTITUTIONALIZATION

Scholars disagree on the definition and measurement of institutionalization.[6] For example, Huntington defines institutionalization as the "process by which

---

[3] Public opinion data from Asian Barometer (2004) and Asian Values Survey (2008) have found Singaporeans to have no strong demand for more democracy or greater civil society, compared to the regional states. See Sinnott 2006: 45.

[4] Neher 2002: 172.

[5] Huntington 1993: 38.

[6] See Levitsky 1998; Randall and Svasand 2002; Meleshevich 2007 for a critique of the concept.

organizations and procedures acquire value and stability" and measures institutionalization by its "adaptability, complexity, autonomy and coherence of its
organizations and procedures."[7] On the other hand, Mainwaring and Scully
identify stability, stable roots in society, legitimacy, and party organization as
four key criteria for the institutionalization of democratic party systems.[8] To
complicate matters, the same dimension of institutionalization is sometimes
analyzed under different labels. For example, Huntington's "complexity" is
similar to Mainwaring and Scully's "party organization."

Despite these disagreements and inconsistencies, the general consensus is that
the concept retains its utility as long as its definition, level of analysis, and
dimensions are clearly laid out. As Levitsky has argued, the challenge is to
"unpack" the concept and demonstrate that the outcome to be explained is
not treated as an aspect of institutionalization.[9] Following North, institutions
are defined as the rules of the game that shape interaction and "reduce uncertainty by providing a structure to everyday life."[10] And a political party is
viewed as an organization and not an institution. It is only through time that a
party as an organization becomes an institution or becomes institutionalized.[11]

In the study of single party or hegemonic party regimes, it is often assumed
that the institutionalization of the hegemonic party leads to the institutionalization of the party system.[12] This is so because a hegemonic party system, by
definition, is a two-tier system in which opposition parties are "second class,
licensed," inferior parties and cannot compete with a hegemonic party on equal
terms.[13] Thus, the institutionalization of the hegemonic party also implies the
institutionalization of a semi-competitive party system in which the opposition
parties are permanently disadvantaged and weak. However, to avoid conflating
party organization and party-system levels of analyses, it may be necessary to
distinguish between the two, so as to better understand the processes and
possible unevenness of institutionalization.

Based on seminal work by Mainwaring and Scully and also Panebianco, the
two-level theoretical framework is proposed to include the following four
dimensions of institutionalization: (1) autonomy, (2) systemness, (3) rootedness,
and (4) stability of interparty competition.[14] The first two dimensions are used to
assess the degree of the party institutionalization; the latter two are used to
measure the institutionalization of the party system. Essentially, autonomy

---

[7] Huntington 1965: 394.
[8] Mainwaring and Scully 1995: 4.
[9] Levitsky 1998: 85.
[10] North 1990: 3–4.
[11] Randall and Svasand 2002: 12.
[12] Ibid: 7.
[13] Sartori 1976: 230.
[14] Panebianco 1988; Mainwaring and Scully 1995. Adaptability is excluded as a dimension of party
institutionalization, as it is considered an effect rather than a feature of institutionalization. See
Randall and Svasand 2002: 17.

refers to the party's control and freedom from external interference (trade unions or religious organizations) in determining its own policies and strategies; system-ness refers to the regularity of interactions that constitute the party and is defined as "regularization of patterns of social interaction, or the entrenchment of the formal and informal rules of the game."[15] A party displays high degree of systemness when rules, procedures, or behavior are routinized, stabilized, and predictable, and a stable set of expectations forms around them. On the other hand, rootedness refers to the party's longevity and average length of electoral experience. The longer the party has been in existence or competed in elections, the more it is rooted in society. Finally, the stability of interparty competition or the strength of the party-voter link will be measured based on Pedersen's electoral volatility index, as Hicken and Kuhonta suggest in the introductory chapter.

SINGAPORE'S HEGEMONIC PARTY SYSTEM

Singapore inherited a Westminster, unicameral parliamentary system from its colonial masters. When it attained self-rule in 1959, it instituted a compulsory voting system and held its full Legislative Assembly election. Then, the PAP won 43 out of all 51 seats and was swept into government. Elections were competitive in the 1950s and 1960s. But by 1968, the PAP had emerged as the hegemonic party and won every seat in that year's election after the Barisan Sosialis party boycotted the election. Since then, the PAP has won every election and had complete legislative hegemony until 1981, when a by-election broke the monopoly. There are now about 24 registered parties in Singapore. However, only about six or seven are active today. See Table 3.1 for the list of key political parties in Singapore.

Singapore's polity is best described as a hegemonic party system or an electoral authoritarian regime that combines both democratic and authoritarian institutions to govern.[16] According to Sartori, a hegemonic party system is one in which opposition parties are "second class, licensed parties" that cannot com-pete with the ruling party on equal terms; the ruling party outdistances the other parties with more than a two-thirds majority of legislative seats; and alternation of power is not envisaged.[17] As a result of the PAP's long-term incumbency and use of state funds for partisan gains, the opposition parties have to compete on a highly uneven playing field. As opposition Reform Party (RP) leader Kenneth Jeyaretnam succinctly puts it,

The control of grassroots organizations by the PAP is just one of the ways the PAP uses state resources to affect and influence voters. Some of the others are state control of the

---

[15] See Levitsky 1998: 80; see also Panebianco 1988: 53.
[16] Electoral authoritarianism is also known as competitive authoritarianism, a form of hybrid regime whereby one party wins again and again under free but unfair conditions. See Levitsky and Way 2002; Schedler 2002; Lindberg 2009; Bunce and Wolchik 2010.
[17] Sartori 1976: 230.

TABLE 3.1. *Key Political Parties in Singapore*

Key Political Parties	Acronyms	Date of Registration	Chrono- logical years	Contested in First GE in 1968	Percentage of Valid Votes in 2011 GE
1. Worker's Party	WP	Jan. 30, 1961	50	Yes	12.8
2. People's Action Party	PAP	Feb. 18, 1961	50	Yes	60.1
3. Pertubohan Kebangsaan Melayu Singapura (Singapore National Malay Organization)	PKMS	Feb. 20, 1961	50	No	–
4. Singapore Democratic Party	SDP	Sept. 8, 1980	31	No	4.8
5. National Solidarity Party	NSP	March 6, 1987	24	No	12.0
6. Singapore People's Party	SPP	Nov. 21, 1994	17	No	3.1
7. Reform Party	RP	July 3, 2008	3	No	4.3

Source: Compiled by author based on media sources.

media, obstacles to the growth and funding of alternative parties, the harassment of individuals through defamation suits, the control of the Elections Department by the Prime Minister's office, and threats to withhold upgrading from Opposition wards.[18]

Singapore has all the democratic electoral institutions. However, constraints in civil and political liberties, restrictions in speech and press freedoms,[19] and the use of the rule of law to intimidate the opposition disqualify it as a liberal democracy.[20] While the government does not rig elections[21] or commit electoral

---

[18] Jeyaretnam 2012.

[19] Freedom House 2011 consistently rates Singapore as "Partly Free" with scores of "5" and "4," signifying constraints in political and civil freedoms. All newspapers are owned by the Singapore Press Holdings, a government-linked corporation, controlled by the Ministry of Information and the Arts. Mainstream media is viewed as the government's mouthpiece as editors and journalists have to work within the out-of-bounds (OB) markers, enforced by the Internal Security Act or self-censorship. OB topics that are not permissible for public discourse include race, religion, and charges of nepotism against the PAP leaders. For more, see Rodan 2004; Gomez 2006; Cheong 2012; George 2012.

[20] For critiques on judicial independence and use of the rule of law against the opposition, see Worthington 2001; IBA Report 2008; Rajah 2012.

[21] However, others might consider the media constraint, misuse of state resources for partisan gains, electoral engineering and harassment of opposition as forms of election rigging. See How to Rig an Election 2012.

fraud, the lack of an independent election commission and regular tweaking of rules and boundaries perpetuate the view that elections are free but not fair.[22]

For the past 12 elections, the average total vote share of the opposition parties in all 12 general elections has been around 30 percent. However, this 30 percent vote share does not translate to seat shares. In fact, on average, the opposition has less than 6 percent of seat shares in the Parliament. Despite the PAP's general declining trend of vote shares in the past two decades, it still retains more than a two-thirds majority of legislative seats.[23] Unlike other dominant party regimes in T. J. Pempel's "uncommon democracies,"[24] the PAP government can change the constitution legally and unilaterally, without forging coalitions with the opposition. With a legislative supermajority and a "flexible constitution," it is easy for the government to push through controversial bills.[25] For example, the Group Representative Constituency (GRC) scheme that ensures ethnic minority legislative presence was passed despite deep opposition, even from ethnic minority leaders. Consequently, this electoral reform changed the country's single-member district plurality system to a mixture of single and multimember district plurality party bloc vote system that tends to benefit the larger, incumbent party.[26]

In addition, other schemes such as the Nominated MP (NMP) and Non-Constituency MP (NCMP) that brought non-elected MPs in the House in 1984 and 1991 have also undermined the candidate selection and interest aggregation roles of opposition parties.[27] The rationale for having non-elected MPs was to ensure a wider representation of community views and to improve the quality of legislative debate. However, institutionalizing the NMP scheme neutralizes the opposition because critics of the government who would otherwise join the opposition can now self-nominate[28] or be appointed without having to join a party.[29] Critics argue that the NMP scheme is elitist, as it privileges only "distinguished" persons to join politics without accountability.[30] Indeed, as the NMPs have limited voting rights and do not represent any

---

[22] Also see Mauzy 2002; Fetzer 2008 on the PAP's electoral engineering strategies.

[23] See Tan 2013 on how PAP boosts its seat shares to rescue its declining vote shares.

[24] Pempel 1990.

[25] Thio and Tan 2009.

[26] See Tan 2013 for the effects of GRC on interparty competition.

[27] Unlike the NCMPs who are members of opposition parties, the NMPs are independent, non-partisan, and "distinguished" persons with special expertise or experience appointed by the president for two and a half years based on the recommendation of a Special Select Committee. Thio 1997; Hussin 2002; Tey 2008.

[28] The NMP scheme allows interested individuals to self-nominate or be nominated by the six functional groups representing business, social, media, and labor organizations.

[29] Like the NCMPs, the NMPs have limited voting powers and are allowed to vote on all issues except public funds, amendment of the constitution, a vote of no confidence in the government, and removal of the president from office.

[30] Thio 1997: 46.

constituency, they are essentially detached from the grass roots and do not serve the traditional representative function of a MP.

WEAKLY INSTITUTIONALIZED OPPOSITION PARTIES

Opposition parties are subject to severe institutional disadvantages in Singapore. A combination of factors such as the legal restrictions of public assemblies, biased media coverage, and strict fund-raising and electoral rules have left the parties with limited room to build support. Public opinion surveys from Singapore's Institute of Policy Studies (ISP) after the 2006 and 2011 GEs show that the opposition parties continue to lag behind the PAP in terms of credibility. For example, the 2011 IPS post-election survey showed that 73 percent of Singaporeans thought favorably of the PAP, while the positive ratings for the opposition parties (Worker's Party [WP], National Solidarity Party [NSP], Singapore Democratic Alliance (SDA), and RP) range from 16 to 56 percent.[31]

In general, opposition parties are inactive between elections, personality driven, and under-institutionalized and lack stable roots, autonomy, and systemness. Apart from the WP and the Pertubohan Kebangsaan Melayu Singapura (Singapore National Malay Organization, PKMS), most have short life spans. In fact, only three parties (WP, PAP, and the PKMS) that formed during the pre-independence period are in existence today. Opposition party memberships have remained small, ranging from just 90 to 3,000. And out of the seven parties active today, only the WP and the NSP have functioning committees or Town Councils. In comparison, the PAP has 87 party branches sprawled across the island. Only the PAP and the WP have regular printed party publications to raise funds and public awareness.[32]

Conventionally, the number of independents in Parliament is used as an indicator of party system autonomy.[33] Based on this, Singapore's party system would display high autonomy, as the number of contesting independents has dwindled from 39 in 1959 to nil by 2011. However, as suggested earlier, the NMP scheme has reduced the autonomy of parties to nominate candidates. Since 1990, opposition parties are no longer the exclusive channels for candidate nomination. Hence, the declining number of independents may not be the best indicator of party system autonomy.

On the other hand, Singapore has displayed a stable pattern of interparty competition over time. In fact, the country has one of lowest electoral volatility measures in the region, with a score of 12.7 percent for the past 11 elections (1968–2011) reflecting a stable party-voter link.[34] Comparatively, the regional

---

[31] Koh 2006; IPS 2011.
[32] For a more detailed study of the organizational capacity of political parties in Singapore, see Tan 2013.
[33] Meleshevich 2007: 27.
[34] Tan 2013.

volatility average of 14 party systems in Asia is nearly doubled at an average of 24.1 percent.[35] Based on Sartori's calculation of relevant parties and ideological pluralism, Singapore would have 1.05 relevant parliamentary parties (1968–2011), a moderate level of party pluralism and low party fragmentation.[36] The low electoral volatility and low party fragmentation suggest that the parties in Singapore have retained their support bases and that the hegemonic party system is stable and institutionalized. As Mainwaring reminds us in the concluding chapter, in uncompetitive hegemonic party systems, the measure of low electoral volatility in fact reflects a highly uneven playing field and suppressed opposition that fails to capture a sizeable vote share.

ROLE OF THE INTERNET ON PARTY MOBILIZATION

Since Prime Minister (PM) Lee Hsien Loong came into power in 2004, gradual steps have been taken to liberalize the political arena. For example, the bans on political podcasts and vodcasts during elections have been lifted and previously banned outdoor protests are now allowed within the confines of the Speakers Corner. Since 2008, opposition parties have used the Internet to reach out to their supporters through party and social network websites such as Facebook and Twitter. Many opposition leaders such as Jeyaretnam from the RP and Dr. Chee Soon Juan from the SDP have turned to Facebook to engage directly with younger Singaporeans. More party leaders are increasingly turning to the Internet to organize events, raise funds, and connect with their supporters.

All the key parties now maintain a party website. While the PAP, the WP, and the SDP post their party newsletters online, the more Internet-savvy SDP and PAP also upload regular podcasts and vodcasts. The leading opposition WP, on the other hand, is more conservative, posting online only parliamentary speeches and party activities. While the Internet has emerged as an alternative platform for the opposition parties to reach out and widen their presence, critics argue that the low quality of political blogs, presence of strict rules, the small number of blog readers, voter apathy, and the state of the technology are likely to constrain the role of the Internet in Singapore politics.[37]

The recent heightened policing of the Internet and public prosecutions of bloggers have also hampered the liberalizing effect of the Internet. As the PAP faced growing opposition challenges and saw its popular vote share drop to a historic low of 60 percent in the 2011 GE, the leaders have returned to their old ways of using defamation suits to intimidate vitriolic online critics into silence. In fact, Rajah argues that the use of defamation suits has fostered an environment

---

[35] Hicken and Kuhonta 2011.

[36] According to Sartori, a party must satisfy three criteria: (1) electoral strength or "strength in seats," (2) coalition potential, and (3) "blackmail" potential to be considered a "relevant" party. See Sartori 2005: 122–124.

[37] See Institute of Policy Studies post-2006 GE Forum report by Koh 2006.

of "generalized self-censorship as users anticipate and avoid government back-lash."[38] For example, the PM threatened to sue the well-known commentator Alex Au for blogging about the potential conflict of interest and abuse of power in the sale of Town Council software to a PAP-backed company. In addition, a series of legal warnings made by senior PAP leaders to force bloggers and opposition leaders to apologize and retract postings have had a chilling effect on the burgeoning political sphere.[39]

ELECTIONS, CANDIDATE SELECTION, AND GATEKEEPER

In Singapore, elections are not opportunities for party alternation. Rather, they are opportunities for the ruling party to renew its mandate to govern. Regular elections every four to five years serve as mechanisms of self-renewal as the leaders make use of the electoral cycle to recruit, reward loyal supporters, and remove dissenters from the inner circle of power structure to reenforce elite cohesion.[40] Elections thus provide the PAP the legitimate opportunity to remove nonperforming or noncompliant members and inject new blood into its rank and file. In the 2006 GE, 24 MPs relinquished their positions.[41] Four out of the 24 MPs had served only one term, and no reasons were given for their removal. Likewise in the 2011 GE, 24 MPs voluntarily stepped down or were asked to retire. On average, the turnover rate for the past four GEs has been around 22 MPs, about a quarter of each cohort. See Table 3.2.

TABLE 3.2. *Parliamentary Turnover (1980–2011)*

Year of Election	Total Elected MPs	Number of New PAP candidates	MPs Retired/Gave up Position (percentage)
1980	75	18	11 (14.7)
1984	79	24	20 (25.3)
1988	81	18	14 (22.2)
1991	81	11	9 (11.1)
1997	83	24	18 (21.7)
2001	84	25	23 (27.4)
2006	84	24	24 (28.6)
2011	87	24	24 (27.6)

Source: Compiled based on data from Singapore elections and Singapore Parliament websites.

---

[38] Rajah 2012: 157.
[39] Mahtani 2012.
[40] Magaloni 2006; Gandhi and Przeworski 2007.
[41] Usually, the PM meets the MPs personally to break the news that they are asked to go. Even when some MPs expressed reluctance, they often obliged without public protests (except members of the old guard such as Toh Chin Chye).

Legally, Singapore's restrictions on candidate eligibility are fairly universal with three key legislative provisions that govern elections.[42] Candidates must comply with Article 45 of the Constitution – which states that anyone sentenced by a court of law in Singapore or Malaysia and imprisoned for not less than one year or fined not less than S$2,000 will be ineligible for candidacy or disqualified from the Parliament. As the ruling government, the PAP often turns to the law to perform its gatekeeping role to prevent those deemed undesirable from entering the House. For example, as the result of Article 45, former WP leader J. B. Jeyaretnam or JBJ[43] was disqualified in 1984 for misstating party funds and again as an NCMP in 1997 because of the bankruptcy lawsuits brought by the PAP leaders. Other opposition leaders such as Wong Hong Toy, Tang Liang Hong, R. Murugason, and Dr. Chee Soon Juan have been excluded as a result of defamation lawsuits brought by PAP leaders. In contrast, Deputy Prime Minister Tharman Shanmugaratnam, a former director in the Monetary Authority of Singapore who was charged and found guilty of breaching the Official Secret's Act in 1992 was fined only S$1,500, an amount that allowed him to contest as a PAP candidate.[44]

Apart from the rules governing candidate eligibility, Singapore's law also requires candidates to place a large monetary deposit to stand for legislative election. In the 1948 Legislative Council election, only a deposit amount of S$500 was required of each candidate. But by the 2011 GE, the deposit amount increased to S$16,000.[45] While the rationale to impose a monetary deposit is to screen out farcical candidates, the large sum ends up privileging resource-rich PAP candidates and deterring the poorer opposition candidates. So far, only independents or opposition candidates have forfeited their deposits as they failed to secure at least 12.5 percent of the valid votes in their constituencies. This precedent discourages others from joining the opposition cause, exacerbating the problem of uncontested seats, which exceeded more than 50 percent in the 1991 and 2001 GEs. The high number of uncontested seats implies that a disproportionate number of PAP MPs have assumed office by "appointment," while more than half of the electorate did not exercise its right to vote.[46]

Most legislatures prohibit MPs with dual mandates.[47] Legally, senior officers from the Singapore Public Service are not allowed to hold public office and be an

---

[42] The three provisions are (1) the Constitution of Singapore (The Legislature – Part VI), (2) the Parliamentary Elections Act (Chapter 218), and (3) the Political Donations Act (Chapter 236) and Subsidiary Legislations.

[43] For the lawsuits against JBJ and his party members, see the WP website at http://www.wp.org.sg/party/history/1981_1986.htm.

[44] See Mauzy and Milne (2002: 134–136) for a summary of the key lawsuits and Worthington (2003: 155–163) for an account of the "accidental prosecution" of T. Shanmugaratnam.

[45] The amount of electoral deposit is calculated based on 8 percent of the total allowance payable to MPs in the preceding year. Press release by the Prime Minister's Office, December 13, 2007.

[46] Tan 2013.

[47] Except in France and Germany, 46 other countries do not allow public servants to serve simultaneously as elective officers at the national levels. See Massicotte, Blais, and Yoshinaka 2004.

MP at the same time.[48] Yet, this prohibition does not prevent the PAP from recruiting from state institutions. In fact, the civil service, statutory boards, and the armed forces are the PAP's prime recruiting grounds. Handpicked candidates from state institutions with no prior party experience are parachuted into constituencies and fast-tracked into ministerial positions. For example, in the 2011 GE, half of the 24 new PAP candidates were from the military, statutory boards, or government-linked companies. As Table 3.3 shows, most elected MPs were former bureaucrats (40.2 percent) and professionals (27 percent). In fact, an average of 49 percent of the PAP MPs – nearly half of the House – were drawn from state institutions.

Likewise, the bulk of the cabinet ministers were also from the elite administrative service or the military. For example, in the cabinet formed in 2011, 46 percent of the 15 ministers were former civil servants, generals, or senior military officers.[49] See Table 3.4. And between 2001 to 2011, only an average of 10 percent of the ministers were from the private sector. Another key feature of Singapore's cabinet is that most of the ministers (73 percent) were all government scholars or received government funding to study in prestigious foreign universities.

To most observers, the politicization of the civil service is a key feature of Singapore's political system that is distinctively un-Westminster style.[50] In fact, it behaves more like what Chan calls an "administrative state" as the division between the party and state is unclear and there is a strong horizontal integration of government elites to the ruling party.[51] Also, incumbency advantage and access to state resources allow the PAP to unload traditional party functions to para-political organizations such as the People's Association, the Community Development Centers, and community centers, bolstering the leaders' policy formulation capacity and penetration into the grassroots level.[52] As Worthington notes:

In Singapore, hegemonic rule is achieved not through democratization but through oligarchic means. The bureaucratic, political and business elites are integrated through a bourgeois party which uses meritocratic assessment based on educational and other achievements to select the public sector and political leadership. Because of the high degree of penetration of the state into the market and society, the party selected elite also penetrates these sectors thus perpetuating oligarchic control.[53]

The following sections examine the institutionalization of the PAP's cadre system and the implications of an elitist leadership selection model that fosters oligarchic control.

---

[48]   The Singapore Public Service employs some 110,000 public officers in 15 ministries, more than 50 statutory boards and 9 organs of state.

[49]   They are Lee Hsien Loong, Lim Hng Kiang, Lim Swee Say, Lui Tuck Yew, Teo Chee Hean, and George Yeo.

[50]   Iwasaki 2003; Worthington 2003; Vennewald 1994.

[51]   Chan 1976.

[52]   Tan and Tan 2003.

[53]   Worthington 2003: 10.

TABLE 3.3. *Occupational Background of MPs (1988–2011)*

Year (%)	2011–	2006–2011	2002–2006	1997–2001	1992–1996	1988–1991
Bureaucrats	16 (18.4)	14 (16.9)	11 (13.1)	13 (15.7)	13 (16)	14 (17.3)
Government-Linked Companies (GLCs)	5 (5.7)	4 (4.8)	4 (4.8)	3 (3.6)	4 (4.9)	4 (4.9)
Military	7 (8.0)	6 (7.2)	6 (7.1)	6 (7.2)	5 (6.2)	3 (3.7)
Government Officials	35 (40.2)	24 (28.9)	21 (25.0)	22 (26.5)	22 (24.7)	21 (25.9)
Professors	5	7	10	14	16	15
Teachers	2	2	1	2	4	6
Academics	7 (8.0)	9 (10.8)	11 (13.0)	16 (19.3)	20 (24.7)	21 (25.9)
Medical Doctors	7	8	9	4	4	4
Lawyers	14	13	10	7	5	5
Others	3	1	5	3	2	1
Professionals	24 (27.6)	22 (26.5)	24 (28.5)	14 (16.9)	11 (13.6)	10 (12.3)
Trade Union Links	8 (9.2)	4 (4.8)	8 (9.5)	3 (3.6)	5 (6.2)	7 (8.6)
Company Managers	17 (19.5)	17 (20.5)	14 (16.7)	18 (21.7)	18 (22.2)	14 (17.3)
Party Staff	0	2 (2.4)	0	1 (1.2)	1 (1.2)	3 (3.7)
Journalists	2 (2.3)	4 (4.8)	5 (6)	6 (7.2)	5 (6.2)	1 (1.2)
Unknowns	1 (1.1)	1 (1.2)	1 (1.2)	3 (3.6)	3 (3.7)	4 (4.9)
Total of MPs	87	83	84	83	81	81

Source: Calculated based on data from Singapore Parliament and Singapore election websites.

TABLE 3.4. *Occupation Profiles of Cabinet Ministers (2001–2011)*

Background (%)	2011	2009	2008	2006	2004	2003	2001
Government Scholars	11 (73.3)	15 (71.4)	13 (65)	12 (66.7)	13 (68.4)	13 (72.2)	14 (82.4)
Administrative Service	3 (20)	5 (23.8)	4 (20)	3 (16.7)	3 (15.8)	3 (16.7)	3 (17.6)
Civil Service /Statutory Board	7 (46.5)	7 (33.1)	10 (50)	10 (55.6)	11 (57.9)	11 (61.1)	10 (58.8)
Government-Linked Companies	0 (0)	3 (14.3)	3 (15)	3 (16.7)	3 (15.8)	2 (11.1)	2 (11.8)
Military	7 (46.6)	6 (28.6)	4 (20)	4 (22.2)	4 (21.1)	4 (22.2)	4 (23.5)
Private Sector	0 (0)	5 (23.8)	3 (15)	1 (5.6)	1 (5.3)	1 (5.6)	1 (5.9)
Total Ministers	15	21	20	18	19	18	17

Note: Ministers have multiple work portfolios and backgrounds; hence, percentages do not add up to 100 percent.
Source: Calculated based on data from official Singapore cabinet website and PAP website.

INSTITUTIONALIZED SUCCESSION

This study focuses on leadership succession, as it is the gravest threat to hegemonic party stability. As Huntington says: "the institutional strength of a party is measured in the first instance by its ability to survive its founder or the charismatic leader who first brings it to power."[54] In hegemonic parties, leadership succession is critical as the rules and procedures governing who can or cannot stand as candidate affects the composition and representativeness of the legislature.[55] Broadly, leadership succession consists of two parts: elite recruitment and candidate selection. Elite recruitment refers to the process through which individuals are inducted into active, high-profile political roles; candidate selection is part of this wider recruitment process. Candidate selection is thus an intraparty mechanism by which parties select their candidates before the general election.[56]

A party with an institutionalized succession system is expected to be more stable, as it has a predictable incentive structure that can attenuate the uncertainties of power struggles. Studies show that in institutionalized parties, leadership selection asserts a centripetal movement – toward the "strong center" in the party – to whoever has the monopoly to nominate and select candidates.[57] Higher centralization is more likely to solidify the authority.

In a party, leadership succession may be considered institutionalized if the selectorate has autonomy over the selection criteria and the process is routinized and governed by formal and informal rules.[58] The selectorate is autonomous if it retains exclusive rights and jurisdiction over candidacy requirements and can exclude any outsiders or nominate or appoint its candidates without external interferences.[59] Conversely, if the selectorate is too large or has little control over the quality of candidates, then its autonomy is low. For example, inclusive parties that hold primaries rather than appoint their senior party officials usually have low autonomy. If there are formal and informal rules, established guidelines governing the selection for top party and national leadership positions, and these rules or procedures are accepted without contest by a large number of party members, then systemness is high. Conversely, if the rules are circumvented to suit the needs of one individual or a particular group or challenged by a majority of party members, then systemness is low. A party may be unevenly institutionalized, display high autonomy and low systemness or vice versa.

[54] Huntington 1968: 409.
[55] Gallagher and Marsh 1988; Hazan and Rahat 2006.
[56] Czudnowski 1975; Barnea and Rahat 2007.
[57] Panebianco 1988: 60.
[58] Party selectorate refers to the body that selects the candidates. It can consist of one person or many people (including the whole nation). Hazan and Rahat 2006: 110.
[59] Lovenduski and Norris 1993: 321.

Uneven institutionalization could bring about unintended consequences, undermining accountability and the linkage between party leaders and members.

THE PAP'S CADRE SYSTEM AND COHESION

The PAP was formed in 1954 by a group of British educated, middle-class men. It originated as a left-wing mass party and had co-opted Chinese-speaking, left-wing unionists to expand its support base. In the early years, three events dramatically altered the PAP's organization: a failed takeover attempt by the left-wing faction in 1957 and two party splits in 1960 and 1961. The near takeover of the Central Executive Committee (CEC) by the left-leaning faction was a critical juncture as the moderate leaders learned how inclusiveness and intraparty democracy could weaken party cohesion.[60]

After the near takeover, founding PAP leader Lee Kuan Yew reorganized the mass-based PAP into a cadre party[61] Thus, 1958 marked the end of PAP's experiment with intraparty democracy whereby members had met annually to elect the CEC.[62] Instead, a bloc voting system was instituted so that only full cadres were allowed to vote in the biannual election of the CEC. PAP's organization change meant that the party now retained high autonomy in deciding who was in and out of the inner circle.[63]

Originally, PAP's early inclusiveness attracted laborers, unionists, and students. However, the party split in 1961 changed the membership composition and included a movement to attract more English-speaking, higher educated, middle-class members.[64] To ensure only approved, selected members could become cadres, measures such as selection board and cadre-training classes were introduced.[65] In 1998, the cadre membership was estimated to be around 1,000, around 7 percent of the total party membership of 15,000. Annually, only about 100 candidates are invited to interview for cadre membership. To be considered as a cadre, the candidate must be recommended by a senior PAP member and undergo three interview panels consisting of cabinet ministers and MPs.[66] This secretive and regular selection process suggests that the PAP retains high systemness in the elite recruitment process.

[60] For more on the PAP's early party splits, see Pang 1971; Fong 1979; Lee 1998.
[61] The organizational overhaul was also inspired after Lee's visit to Rome in 1958, where he was reminded of the resilience of the Catholic Church. As he recounts: "the folly of adopting a democratic constitution had left it open to capture through the penetration of its own party branches. We discussed several possible changes to ensure that it could never happen again" (1998: 271).
[62] The CECs from 1954 to 1957 were elected by all party members. However, this changed after 1957, and the CEC is now elected only by party cadres.
[63] Four categories of membership (probationary, ordinary, probationary cadre, and cadre) and re-registering of membership were introduced to prevent takeovers. See Pang 1971: 35.
[64] Shee 1971: 166.
[65] Lee 1998: 280.
[66] Koh 1998.

The CEC is the pinnacle of the PAP's decision-making body and is dominated by the party secretary who selects the cadres and who, in turn, endorses the proposed candidates for the CEC at a biannual party conference. As Pang has aptly described, the CEC voting process is a "closed system" in which "the cardinals appoint the pope and the pope appoints the cardinals".[67] Consisting of 18 members, the CEC is essentially the party selectorate, and most of the CEC members are also cabinet ministers.

The exclusive and regularized cadre recruitment process fosters PAP's cohesion as it filters like-minded members into the inner circle and excludes those with extreme or alternative views. Even though, technically, being a cadre comes with no extra incentives or privileges,[68] the sense of exclusivity on being the select few serves as a "collective incentive" and fosters a sense of belonging.[69] As the PAP's former assistant secretary general once said: "You know you are among the elite, the trusted few. People are quite happy when told they have become cadres."[70]

KEY FEATURES OF THE PAP'S CANDIDATE SELECTION

Conventionally, a person interested in political office would register with a party, work up the rank and file, cozy up to the leaders, and hope to be nominated as a candidate. But this is not the case for the PAP. The PAP avoids vertical integration of its cadres and does not overtly reward party loyalists.[71] Since 1984, the PAP has adopted the rigorous process that the civil service uses in recruiting bureaucrats, specifically, the officers for the administrative service – the apex of the civil service hierarchy.

Unlike other parties, the PAP "talent spots" within the state structures and integrates prospects horizontally into the party. Long-term incumbency and access to the Public Service Commission that administers prestigious government scholarships help identify and channel highly qualified scholars into its party.[72] As suggested earlier, the scholarship scheme is one of the PAP's talent-spotting mechanisms that nurtures outstanding returning scholars who have to serve their scholarship bonds in government agencies and statutory boards.[73] In the latest session of Parliament constituted by 2011, about 30 MPs were former government scholars who were sponsored for higher foreign education. These scholar MPs are now part of the apex of the power elite, groomed for higher

---

[67] Pang 1971: 36.
[68] The PAP prides itself for its clean governance that does not condone gift giving, nepotism, or corruption. However, critics argue that political corruption can manifests itself in different forms; see Tarling 2005.
[69] Panebianco 1988: 54.
[70] Koh 1998.
[71] Mauzy and Milne 2002: 246–247.
[72] Barr 2006; Neo and Chen 2007.
[73] Scholarships awarded by the Singapore government usually come with a bond period of 3 to 10 years. See PSC website at http://www.psc.gov.sg/content/psc/default.html.

leadership roles. This recruitment process that makes use of the civil service scholarship scheme to cream off the best and brightest is well entrenched as Lee Kuan Yew once disclosed:

> Our problem was not to find loyal cadres who can do the rank and file work and running of the party, even to be MPs … and the only way we could overcome that was by going out recruiting, talent spotting … A person who has done well in Singapore's scholarship system will eventually be "spotted" and "headhunters" from the party will look for him. That is the system that has evolved.[74]

Viewed in this way, the PAP cadre party structure could be seen evolving into a party-state, cartel model in which the "colluding parties become agents of the state and employ the resources of the state to ensure their own collective survival."[75]

WHO BECOMES A PAP CANDIDATE?

There is no primary election for the PAP's selection of legislative candidates. Like its exclusive cadre selection, candidate selection occurs through an elaborate screening, nomination, and appointment process. Generally, the PAP's candidate selection consists of the following stages:

Stage 1: Candidates are talent spotted and recommended by PAP activists, corporate leaders, MPs, and senior civil servants to a PAP recruitment committee. Potential candidates are usually top of their cohort from the civil service or the military or professionals from the legal, banking, and health care sectors.[76]

Stage 2: Groups of six to eight candidates are then invited to meet with ministers in tea discussions, which last around 60 to 150 minutes. Around 100 candidates a year get invited for the tea sessions. As a result of the large number of Singaporeans studying or working abroad, tea sessions are now also conducted overseas.

Stage 3: Short-listed candidates undergo two formal interviews by a high-level panel at the party headquarters. Successful candidates are invited to meet the cabinet ministers. However, the CEC reserves the final authority to endorse the selected candidates. In 1997 GE, 24 PAP candidates were fielded out of 300 interviewed.

Stage 4: Weeks before an election, the selected candidates are sent to different constituencies to shadow senior MPs. Before the election, prospective candidates are sent for courses on public speaking and communications skills to handle the media press and questions during the campaign.

---

[74] People's Action Party 1999: 133.
[75] Katz and Mair 1995: 5.
[76] In the 1984 GE, about 2,000 potential names were drawn from government scholars, professionals, and party ranks. See Ooi 1998: 372.

Stage 5:   Selected candidates deemed to have ministerial quality will go through
an additional stage of psychological tests with more than 1,000 questions that lasts one-and-a-half days. Based on the potential appraisal
system developed by Shell Oil Company, the PAP assesses the candidates' personality and disposition. In each election, five to six candidates identified to have ministerial qualities are groomed for higher
office.[77]

The PAP prides itself for developing a leadership recruitment system based on
meritocracy – the best man or woman for the job. But in reality, the selection
system based on talent spotting is more elitist than meritocratic.[78]

LEADERSHIP SUCCESSION

In the past five decades, the PAP has engineered two party leadership successions. Lee Kuan Yew became the country's first PM when it attained self-
government in 1959. In 1990, he relinquished his PM position and endorsed
Goh Chok Tong in a carefully managed leadership change. While Goh was not
Lee's preferred successor, he had later deferred the choice to the cabinet, which
eventually endorsed Goh as its leader.[79] The first leadership succession was
completed when Lee gave up his secretary general position two years later
after Goh became prime minister. While Goh was widely viewed as a "seat
warmer" for Lee's son, he held on to his position for 12 years and earned respect
for his consensus-based leadership style.[80] Meanwhile, Lee's son, Lee Hsien
Loong, waited and supported Goh as deputy PM.[81]

There is no primary election for the PM position. However, in 2004, Goh
formalized a three-step procedure for PM selection that begins with a meeting of
all cabinet ministers to nominate a leader based on consensus; this is followed by
another meeting by all the PAP MPs to show their support of the PM's nomination in a separate venue. At this stage, the PAP MPs are permitted to nominate
other candidates, if they disagree with the PM's nomination. The MPs' nomination will then be considered by the party's CEC in a separate meeting. The
CEC retains the right to endorse the final decision.

Following this procedure, Lee Hsieng Loong, Singapore's third PM, was
selected in August 2004. The formalization of the selection of the PM is significant, as it provides a mechanism to mediate the possibility of an internal split or
leadership challenge. As Goh says, "The confidence of MPs is important. I want
to put in place a process so that, in future, if there is a contest for the position,

---

[77] Neo and Chen 2007: 334.
[78] Tan 2008.
[79] Mauzy and Milne 2002: 115–116.
[80] Welsh et al. 2009.
[81] Lee's diagnosis of lymphoma in 1992 was another reason why Goh remained as PM longer than
expected.

there's a process to follow."[82] This new process increases systemness as it offers a way for the MPs to nominate an alternative candidate and mitigate any arbitrariness. In the event of disagreement, there is a mechanism to close ranks. In Singapore's short history under the PAP, two PMs have stepped aside for a younger successor. Even though the fourth PM successor has not been identified, the precedent of PMs stepping down for a younger successor is expected to continue. As former PM Goh said: "In the PAP, we have institutionalized a planned and orderly system of political succession. The old generation systematically identifies and prepares the next generation to take over. It steps aside when the successor generation is ready."[83]

IMPLICATIONS AND POTENTIAL PROBLEMS

In most authoritarian regimes, the question of leadership succession is perilous, as it raises expectations and changes that could destabilize the balance of power. For example, when Taiwan was under the Kuomintang's rule in the 1980s, speculation on the potential successor of ailing strongman Chiang Ching-Kuo was banned.[84] Typically, authoritarian leaders want to hold on to power for as long as possible and show little interest in developing a means of providing a successor. However, this is not the case in Singapore. In fact, the PAP obsesses about succession and considers internal renewal a priority.

In Singapore, leaders groom the next generation of leaders and the PMs retire voluntarily — not an easy feat, considering how coups and mass protests are often the mechanisms for leadership change in neighboring states. However, at the higher level, retired PAP leaders do not leave the political scene completely but continue to remain in office to lend expertise as senior ministers or minister mentors. Increasing the number of executive positions and expanding the cabinet work as face-saving strategies that allow the old guard to exit graciously and mitigate power struggles. The creation of more cabinet positions also fosters elite cohesion as it compensates the outgoing leader with a prestigious position and salary, and it also allows the incoming leader to tap his predecessors for knowledge and expertise – a win-win situation for both young and old leaders.

As Mainwaring and Scully remind us, "evaluations of party system institutionalization are not static ... unilinear nor irreversible."[85] Despite the PAP's institutionalized leadership succession system, its survival as a party organization may still be deinstitutionalized for the following reasons. First, while the horizontal integration of elites promotes elite unity, it does not foster vertical ties between leaders and members. This suggests that the PAP's institutionalization is uneven. In fact, its party membership has not increased for the past 35 years. The

[82] PAP 2004.
[83] Petir 2004.
[84] Chang 1984.
[85] Mainwaring and Scully 1995: 20–21.

PAP leadership is acutely aware of its image problem and has launched an aggressive recruitment drive to appeal to younger Singaporeans and to address the gap between leaders and members. For example, the PAP Policy Forum was initiated in 2004 as a feedback mechanism to reach out to youngsters via social media. In addition, the PAP is encouraging intraparty democracy by allowing direct elections for party committees such as the Youth Wing, the Women's Wing, and district branches. It is still too early to assess the effects of these initiatives.

Second, unlike most parties that prize party loyalty and grassroots experience, the PAP recruits widely from outside the party and "parachutes" candidates without strong party ties or grassroots experience to stand in elections. For example, the PAP candidate Dr. Koh Poh Koon had only joined the PAP three weeks before he was declared the candidate for the Punggol East by-election on January 26, 2013.[86] Over time, this parachuting practice may undermine the relevance of the PAP as the primary organization that nurtures and supplies candidates. As Singaporeans learned that they do not need to join the party to be considered as a candidate, they may be less inclined to join the PAP and serve in the grass roots. Also, ambitious cadres may be frustrated by the PAP's recruitment from outside the party. Party careerists who are leapfrogged and excluded from the parachuting scheme may just defect, leading to membership decline.[87]

Third, the PAP is behaving more like a party-state than a party. The party-state fusion is worsened by the overlapping CEC and cabinet membership. In fact, Mauzy and Milne argue that the PAP as a party exercises little influence as the "CEC is only a rubber stamp for government decisions, and that the party has lost is role in giving direction to society."[88] The PAP organization is lean, with fewer than ten salaried administrative staff in a small headquarters located far away from the city center. The party relies more on state resources to develop a sprawling network of para-political organizations to serve the constituencies. Without party-building efforts, the PAP may risk losing its organizational strength, coherence, and mobilization capacity.[89]

Finally, the PAP's nominally meritocratic candidate selection is a "ruthless winnowing process" that promotes elitism and the "politics of envy."[90] It is widely known that Singapore politicians are among the highest paid in the world.[91] As the ruling elites are rewarded more financially, the growing income inequality in the country could evoke a sense of resentment, social disengagement, and envy among those excluded from the system. The elite-selection

---

[86] The Punggol East by-election was triggered by former MP Michael Palmer's resignation after an extramarital affair. Saad 2013.

[87] Hirschman 1970.

[88] Mauzy and Milne 2002: 49.

[89] See Croissant, Bruns, and John 2002: 236 for a contrary view.

[90] Barr 2006; Tan 2008.

[91] The PM earned more than S$3 million before a review committee slashed it to S$2.2 million after 2011. See Politicians' Salaries: Leaders of the Fee World 2011; Chua 2012; Reuters 2012.

process may also lead to inbreeding of ideas as the ruling class renews itself with people of the same mind-set. Indeed, in hegemonic regimes such as Singapore's, the PAP's candidate selection is the "choice before the choice" that decides the composition of the Parliament. As this chapter has tried to show, the Parliament is now filled with technocrats, experts, former military officers, and professionals. With few MPs with party, union, or grassroots experience, members of Parliament may lack empathy for the problems of the ordinary people and become disconnected from the grass roots.

CONCLUSION

Most observers contend that the PAP's cohesion and resilience owed much to Lee Kuan Yew's forceful personality. Yet, this chapter has tried to show that institutions and institutionalization matter more than charisma or ideology in ensuring the survival of the hegemonic party system. Lee and his successors have institutionalized a process by which the PAP as an organization has incorporated the founder's values. The PAP's exclusive, centralized, and autonomous selection method has helped foster elite cohesion and prevent internal splits. By institutionalizing charisma, access to power is now less arbitrary and not tied to any one individual or a particular group. As Lee Kuan Yew once said: "My colleagues and I have institutionalized honesty, integrity and meritocracy into the systems we have created. Each generation of leaders has the duty to recruit the people of integrity, ability and commitment as their successors."[92] With time, the regular tea sessions, interviews, and psychological tests have become acceptable means to produce an elite-based government.

Current literature tends to equate party system institutionalization with democratic consolidation. However, as Tuong Vu's (Chapter 6, this volume) and Meredith Weiss's (Chapter 2, this volume) studies on Vietnam and Malaysia, respectively, have shown, this is not necessarily the case. Likewise, this chapter's focus on Singapore's hegemonic party shows how party institutionalization fosters the "iron law of oligarchy," limits internal dissent, and constrains electoral competition. The proposed two-level analysis is thus an attempt to avoid conflating party and party system institutionalization and to demonstrate how uneven institutionalization could bring about undemocratic outcomes.

In Singapore, the PAP leaders have put in place a series of institutional incentives and constraints at the regime and party organization levels to prevent factionalism and defection. The elite recruitment and candidate selection foster cohesion as the party selectorate retains complete control over the processes. Factionalism, personality, and money politics are mitigated by the supposedly meritocratic, performance-based selection criteria. Aside from the party whip who maintains party discipline, the cadre system and a strong concentration of

[92] Rodan 2009: 192.

power in the PAP's small elite circle also help hold the party together. The PAP's institutionalized candidate selection system suggests that the party is better prepared than most hegemonic parties to withstand the uncertainties of leadership change. Despite the rise in opposition challenges and demands for more political pluralism in the country, Singaporeans may have to contend with a hegemonic party system for some time to come.

REFERENCES

Barnea, Shlomit, and Gideon Rahat. 2007. Reforming Candidate Selection Methods: A Three-Level Approach. *Party Politics* 13(3): 375–394.

Barr, M. D. 2006. The Charade of Meritocracy. *Far Eastern Economic Review* 169: 18–22.

Bunce, Valerie J., and Sharon L. Wolchik. 2010. Defeating Dictators: Electoral Change and Stability in Competitive Authoritarian Regimes. *World Politics* 62(1): 43–86.

Chan, Heng Chee. 1976. *The Dynamics of One Party Dominance: The PAP at the Grassroots*. Singapore: Singapore University Press.

Chang, M. H. 1984. Political Succession in the Republic of China on Taiwan. *Asian Survey* 24(4): 423–446.

Cheong, Yip Seng. 2012. *OB Markers: My Straits Times Story*. Straits Times Press. Available from http://www.stpressbooks.com.sg/OB-Markers-My-Straits-Times-Story.html. Accessed January 11, 2013.

Chua, Lee Hoong. 2012. Pay, Bonuses: What Exactly a Minister Gets. *Straits Times*. Available from http://www.straitstimes.com/The-Big-Story/The-Big-Story-1/Story/STIStory_755542.html. Accessed January 14, 2012.

Croissant, A., Gabriele Bruns, and John Marei. 2002. *Electoral Politics in Southeast and East Asia: A Comparative Perspective*. Singapore: Friedrich Ebert Stiftung.

Czudnowski, M. 1975. Political Recruitment. In Fred I. Greenstein and Nelson W. Polsby (Eds.), *Handbook of Political Science*, pp. 155–242. Reading, MA: Addison-Wesley.

Fetzer, Joel. 2008. Election Strategy and Ethnic Politics in Singapore. *Taiwan Journal of Democracy* 4(1): 135–153.

Fong, Sip-chee. 1979. *The PAP Story: The Pioneering Years*. Singapore: Times Periodicals.

Freedom House. 2011. Freedom in the World 2011 Survey. Available from http://freedomhouse.org/template.cfm?page=594. Accessed December 27, 2011.

Gallagher, M., and M. Marsh. 1988. *The Secret Garden: Candidate Selection in Comparative Perspective*. London: Sage Publications.

Gandhi, J., and A. Przeworski. 2007. Authoritarian Institutions and the Survival of Autocrats. *Comparative Political Studies* 40(11): 1279.

Geddes, B. 2003. *Paradigms and Sand Castles: Theory Building and Research Design in Comparative Politics*. Ann Arbor: University of Michigan Press.

George, Cherian. 2012. *Freedom from the Press: Journalism and State Power in Singapore*. Singapore: NUS Press. Available from http://www.uhpress.hawaii.edu/p-8808-9789971695941.aspx. Accessed August 14, 2012.

Gomez, J. 2006. Restricting Free Speech: The Impact on Opposition Parties in Singapore. *The Copenhagen Journal of Asian Studies* 23(1): 105–131.

Hazan, R., and G. Rahat. 2006. Candidate Selection: Methods and Consequences. In R. S. Katz and W. Crotty (Eds.), *Handbook of Party Politics*, pp. 109–122. London: Sage Publishing.

Hicken, A., and E. M. Kuhonta. 2011. Shadows from the Past: Party System Institutionalization in Asia. *Comparative Political Studies* 44(5): 572–597.

Hirschman, A. O. 1970. *Exit, Voice, and Loyalty: Responses to Decline in Firms, Organizations, and States*. Cambridge: Harvard University Press.

How to Rig an Election: Weighing the Votes. 2012. *The Economist*. Available from http://www.economist.com/node/21548946/print. Accessed January 15, 2013.

Huntington, S. P. 1993. American Democracy in Relation to Asia. In Robert Bartly (Ed.), *Democracy and Capitalism: Asian and American Perspectives*, pp. 27–44. Singapore: Institute of Southeast Asian Pub.

Huntington, S. P. 1965. Political Development and Political Decay. *World Politics* 17(3): 386–430.

Huntington, S. P. 1968. *Political Order in Changing Societies*. New Haven: Yale University Press.

Hussin, M. 2002. Constitutional-Electoral Reforms and Politics in Singapore. *Legislative Studies Quarterly* 27(4): 659–672.

IBA Report. 2008. *Prosperity versus Individual Rights? Human Rights, Democracy and the Rule of Law in Singapore*. London: International Bar Association (IBA).

IPS. 2011. IPS Post-Election Forum 2011. *IPS*. Available from http://www.spp.nus.edu .sg/ips/Post_Election_Forum_080711.aspx. Accessed January 15, 2013.

Iwasaki, I. 2003. State Bureaucrats, Economic Development, and Governance: The Case of Singapore. In Y. Shimomura (Ed.), *The Role of Governance in Asia*, pp. 349–381. Singapore: Institute of Southeast Asian Studies.

Jeyaretnam, Kenneth. 2012. Statement on Michael Palmer's Resignation. Available from http://thereformparty.net/about/press-releases/statement-on-michael-palmers-resig nation/#.UMh_YWLS5qk.twitter. Accessed January 15, 2013.

Katz, R. S., and P. Mair. 1995. Changing Models of Party Organization and Party Democracy: The Emergence of the Cartel Party. *Party Politics* 1(1): 5–28.

Koh, B. S. 1998. Singapore: The PAP Cadre System. *Straits Times*. Available from http:// www.singapore-window.org/80404st1.htm. Accessed April 26, 2014.

Koh, G. 2006. IPS Post-Election Survey Report. *Institute of Policy Studies*. Available from http://www.lkyspp.nus.edu.sg/ips/Survey_Report_postelection.aspx. Accessed July 13, 2012.

Lee, K. Y. 1998. *The Singapore Story: Memoirs of Lee Kuan Yew*. Singapore: Times Pub.

Levitsky, S. 1998. Institutionalization and Peronism: The Concept, the Case and the Case for Unpacking the Concept. *Party Politics* 4(1): 77.

Levitsky, S., and L. Way. 2002. The Rise of Competitive Authoritarianism. *Journal of Democracy* 13(2): 51–65.

Lindberg, Staffan. 2009. *Democratization by Election: A New Mode of Transition*. Baltimore: Johns Hopkins University Press.

Lovenduski, J., and P. Norris. 1993. *Gender and Party Politics*. London: Sage Publications Ltd.

Magaloni, B. 2006. *Voting for Autocracy: Hegemonic Party Survival and Demise in Mexico*. New York: Cambridge University Press.

Mahtani, Shibani. 2012. Debate over Blog Limits Intensifies in Singapore. *Wall Street Journal*. Available from http://blogs.wsj.com/searealtime/2012/03/01/debate-over -blog-limits-intensifies-in-singapore/. Accessed January 12, 2013.

Mainwaring, S., and T. Scully. 1995. *Building Democratic Institutions: Party Systems in Latin America*. Stanford: Stanford University Press.

Massicotte, L., A. Blais, and A. Yoshinaka. 2004. *Establishing the Rules of the Game: Election Laws in Democracies*. Toronto: University of Toronto Press.

Mauzy, D. K. 2002. Electoral Innovation and One-Party-Dominance in Singapore. In J. F. Hsieh and D. Newman (Eds.), *How Asia Votes*, pp. 234–254. New York: Chatham House.

Mauzy, D. K., and R. S. Milne. 2002. *Singapore Politics under the People's Action Party*. Routledge.

Meleshevich, A. 2007. *Party Systems in Post-Soviet Countries: A Comparative Study of Political Institutionalization in the Baltic States, Russia, and Ukraine*. Basingstoke, UK: Palgrave Macmillan.

Neher, Clark D. 2002. *Southeast Asia in the New International Era*. Boulder, CO: Westview Press.

Neo, B. S., and G. Chen. 2007. *Dynamic Governance: Embedding Culture, Capabilities and Change in Singapore*. Singapore: World Scientific Pub Co Inc.

North, D. 1990. *Institutions, Institutional Change and Economic Performance*. Cambridge: Cambridge University Press.

O'Donnell, G., and P. C. Schmitter. 1986. *Transitions from Authoritarian Rule: Tentative Conclusions about Uncertain Democracies*. Baltimore: Johns Hopkins University Press.

Ooi, C. S. 1998. Singapore. In W. Sachsenroder and U. E Fringes (Eds.), *Political Party Systems and Democratic Development in East and Southeast Asia*, Vol. 1, pp. 343–402. Aldershot, VT: Ashgate Pub Co.

Panebianco, A. 1988. *Political Parties: Organization and Power*. New York: Cambridge University Press.

Pang, C. L. 1971. *Singapore's People's Action Party: Its History, Organization, and Leadership*. Singapore: Oxford University Press.

PAP. 2004. Petir. Available from http://www.pap.org.sg/news-and-commentaries/petir -archives#.UPcnregyF1Y. Accessed January 16, 2013.

Pempel, T. J. 1990. *Uncommon Democracies: The One-Party Dominant Regimes*. Ithaca: Cornell University Press.

People's Action Party, 1999. *PAP 45th Anniversary Book: For People, through Action, by Party*. Singapore: People's Action Party Publication.

Petir. 2004. *People's Action Party, 1954–2004: Petir, 50th Anniversary Issue*. Singapore: People's Action Party Publication.

Politicians' Salaries: Leaders of the Fee World. 2011. *Economist*. Available from http:// www.economist.com/node/16525240. Accessed October 4, 2011.

Rajah, Jothie. 2012. *Authoritarian Rule of Law: Legislation, Discourse and Legitimacy in Singapore*. New York: Cambridge University Press.

Randall, V., and L. Svasand. 2002. Party Institutionalization in New Democracies. *Party Politics* 8(1): 5–29.

Reuters. 2012. Singapore PM Faces 36 Pct Pay Cut, Still World's Best Paid. *AJW by the Asahi Shimbun*. Available from http://ajw.asahi.com/article/asia/south_east_asia/ AJ201201040046. Accessed March 19, 2012.

Rodan, Garry. 2004. *Transparency and Authoritarian Rule in Southeast Asia: Singapore and Malaysia*. New York: Routledge.

Rodan, Garry. 2009. Accountability and Authoritarianism: Human Rights in Malaysia and Singapore. *Journal of Contemporary Asia* 39(2): 180–203.

Saad, Imeda. 2013. PAP Fields Koh Poh Koon as Its Candidate for By-Election. Available from http://www.channelnewsasia.com/stories/specialreport/news/1247058_189/1/.html. Accessed January 19, 2013.

Sartori, G. 1976. *Parties and Party Systems*. New York: Cambridge University Press.

Sartori, G. 2005. *Parties and Party Systems: A Framework for Analysis*. Colchester: ECPR Press.

Schedler, Andreas. 2002. The Menu of Manipulation. *Journal of Democracy* 13(2): 36–50.

Shee, P. K. 1971. *The People's Action Party of Singapore 1954–1970: A Study in Survivalism of a Single-Dominant Party*. Bloomington: Indiana University Press.

Tan, K. P. 2008. Meritocracy and Elitism in a Global City: Ideological Shifts in Singapore. *International Political Science Review* 29(1): 7–27.

Tan, Kenneth, and Andrew Tan. 2003. Democracy and the Grassroots Sector in Singapore. *Space and Polity* 7(1): 3–20.

Tan, Netina. 2012. "Winner-Takes-All": A Study of the Effects of Group Representative Constituencies (GRCs) in Singapore. Paper presented at the Effects of District Magnitude Conference, Lisbon. Available at http://www.districtmagnitude.ics.ul.pt/papers/. Accessed April 26, 2014.

Tan, Netina. 2013. Institutional Sources of Hegemonic Party Stability in Singapore. In *Stability and Performance of Political Parties in Southeast Asia*. Singapore: ISEAS.

Tarling, Nicholas. 2005. *Corruption and Good Governance in Asia*. New York: Routledge.

Tey, T. H. 2008. Singapore's Electoral System: Government by the People? *Legal Studies* 28(4): 610–628.

Thio, Li-Ann. 1997. Choosing Representatives: Singapore Does It Her Way. In G. Hassall and C. Saunders (Eds.), *The People's Representatives: Electoral Systems in the Asia Pacific Region*, pp. 38–58. Sydney: Allen and Unwin.

Thio, Li-Ann, and Kevin Tan. 2009. *Evolution of a Revolution: Forty Years of the Singapore Constitution*. New York: Routledge.

Vennewald, W. 1994. *Technocrats in the State Enterprise System of Singapore*. Asia Research Center, Perth, Western Australia: Murdoch University.

Welsh, Bridget, James Chin, Arun Mahizhnan, and Tarn How Tan. 2009. *Impressions of the Goh Chok Tong Years*. Institute of Policy Studies and National University Press. Available from http://www.spp.nus.edu.sg/ips/pub_goh_chok_tong.aspx. Accessed January 16, 2013.

Worthington, R. 2001. Between Hermes and Themis: An Empirical Study of the Contemporary Judiciary in Singapore. *Journal of Law and Society* 28(4): 490–519.

Worthington, R. 2003. *Governance in Singapore*. London: RoutledgeCurzon.

4

Party System Institutionalization in Japan

Kenneth Mori McElwain

INTRODUCTION

The literature on party systems is composed of two related strands. Studies of emerging democracies typically ask whether the party system is *institutionalized*: are parties the primary legislative and electoral actors, with deep social roots and routinized patterns of interaction? Those of established democracies, on the other hand, are more concerned with whether the party system is in *equilibrium*: given status quo socioeconomic and political institutions, are the number of parties and ideological cleavages stable? As this volume's editors propose, these two approaches are based on distinct conceptions about the role of parties in democracy. In a celebrated quote, Schattschneider (1942: 1) writes, "Political parties created modern democracy and modern democracy is unthinkable save in terms of parties." In new democracies, parties are seen as organizations whose existence – before, during, and after democratization – is crucial but fragile. Scholars of established democracies, by contrast, assume that parties are here to stay and focus instead on more granular distinctions in the character of the party system.

My goal in this chapter is to integrate these two literatures through the lens of party system institutionalization in Japan. Japan has had the longest history of party politics in Asia, but its functions and salience have varied over time. Parties emerged during the autocratic Meiji period, and they played a valuable role in political liberalization. Despite being derailed by military governments during World War II, parties quickly became a focal point of legislative politics during and after the U.S. occupation. They took on many of the organizational characteristics of their prewar predecessors, and the primary partisan cleavage in Japan, interregional fiscal redistribution, retained its salience throughout. In this sense, the Japanese party system has been institutionalized for a long period of time: legislative politics – both in the autocratic and democratic periods – was the province of political parties that represented urban versus rural socioeconomic divisions in society.

However, this long history of party system institutionalization belies changes in institutional equilibria. Between 1925 and 1994, Japan (mostly) used the same multimember district, single nontransferable vote (MMD-SNTV) electoral formula, which had two profound effects on the party system. First, it produced multiparty competition, and combined with high degrees of malapportionment, it prioritized rural over urban interests. Second, it incentivized candidates to develop clientelistic linkages with voters through the redistribution of public works. The results were conservative dominance, the result of the bloc's strengths in overrepresented rural regions, and weak party-voter linkages because of the greater salience of candidate qualities over partisan ideologies.

After the electoral system was altered to a mixed member majoritarian (MMM) formula with parallel single-member plurality and proportional representation tiers, parties began to realign into new patterns of interaction. First, the electoral system pressured minor parties to merge with bigger counterparts, gradually producing a two-party system. Second, parties have been marketing themselves more aggressively, with the result that voters now pay more attention to a candidate's party affiliation than his or her individual qualifications or background.

There are three key differences between these two equilibria. The new system better matches traditional notions of party institutionalization: parties compete based on *programmatic* platforms, rather than promises of greater fiscal redistribution to their supporters. However, voters still lack durable partisan identities, resulting in *weaker linkages* to parties than they had to candidates under MMD-SNTV. As a result, the new system is significantly more *volatile*. Weak partisan identification produces more vote turnover across elections, generating fluctuating coalition patterns and unstable governments. The lesson is that while we typically see more institutionalization as an unadulterated good for emerging democracies, we need to be more cognizant of trade-offs under different institutional equilibria.

Japanese political history is a lens through which we can peek at one possible path of party system institutionalization in other Asian nations. Other chapters in this volume, particularly Erik Kuhonta's discussion of Thailand (Chapter 12), note the centrality of elite factionalism and patron-client relations in early democratic governance. These same features were salient in Japan, originating with the regional inequalities and institutional architecture of Meiji Japan. However, postwar industrialization and urbanization steadily tapered popular satisfaction with clientelistic redistribution, and electoral reform in 1994 further incentivized programmatic party competition. These are not theoretically surprising: the political science literature has long argued that richer voters are less amenable to clientelism and that the electoral system shapes the party system. This predictability of Japanese party politics is perhaps the strongest indicator that the party system is deeply institutionalized.

THE INSTITUTIONALIZATION OF POLITICAL PARTIES

The Emergence of Parties in Autocratic Japan

The modern Japanese state began with the Meiji Restoration of 1868. Disgruntled samurai from the Satsuma and Choshu domains in Western Japan overthrew the feudal Tokugawa Shogunate based in Edo (now Tokyo), replacing it with a centralized, autocratic government built around the *de jure* supremacy of the Meiji Emperor. These revolutionary samurai served as *genro*, or elder statesmen, to the government and wielded power through the extra-constitutional Privy Council, the main advisory body to the emperor. The Meiji Constitution of 1889 established a Diet (parliament) with an elected Lower House (House of Representatives) and a peerage-based Upper House (House of Peers). However, actual policy-making power was retained by the oligarchic *genro*, who could issue imperial commands with quasi-statutory and decree powers via the Privy Council (Duus 1998).

The oligarchs jealously guarded their power against the Diet, but internal rivalries quickly cracked their unity. The first breaking point was the proposed invasion of Korea. The foreign incursion was opposed by government leaders but backed enthusiastically by samurai seeking to recapture their social and economic statuses, which had deteriorated under the new regime. Lacking sufficient clout in the Privy Council, pro-invasion oligarchs established political parties in the Lower House and sought the support of wealthy landowners (Ibuki 2005). As Ramseyer and Rosenbluth (1995) write, the original goal of these parties was not to promote democracy per se. Rather, dissatisfied oligarchs sought to strengthen their position within the autocracy through the legitimacy conferred by popular support in the Diet. As such, early legislative politics was defined by conflicts between the majority of oligarchs, who wielded power through the Privy Council and dominated the cabinet, and political parties in the Lower House, which had the backing of voters and a minority of oligarchs.

The early party system was not a threat to the oligarchy. Restrictive voting requirements ensured that the Meiji party system only represented conservative political and economic interests. Under the Electoral Act of 1889, suffrage was limited to men older than age 25 who had resided in their district for more than one year and paid at least ¥15 in taxes. Given the economic dislocation and migration caused by rapid industrialization, this rule restricted the electoral franchise to fewer than 500,000 wealthy landowners and businessmen out of 42 million citizens. The Meiji oligarchs instituted additional safeguards in the form of restrictive campaign regulations. Voters were required to sign their ballots in front of election officers, opening the door for government intimidation, and limits were placed on the solicitation of party members.

The development of durable party-voter linkages was also derailed by the 1900 Electoral Act, which introduced multimember districts with single nontransferable votes (MMD-SNTV).[1] Yamagata Aritomo, an oligarch particularly antagonistic toward parties, recognized that MMD-SNTV would force parties to run multiple candidates within districts, generating intraparty fragmentation and raising hurdles against single-party dominance (Ramseyer and Rosenbluth 1995). As predicted, these early parliaments experienced the repeated formation, merger, and dissolution of political parties.

The oligarchs' strategy of deterrence was motivated by the nontrivial and increasingly antagonistic influence of the Lower House. Legislation required parliamentary approval, and cabinets were subject to parliamentary confidence. Over time, political parties became more explicitly anti-oligarchic in nature. Their primary constituency – landed gentry and industrialists – began to chafe under the disconnect between their rising wealth and minimal political clout. Chaotic parliamentary struggles became commonplace. The Lower House would veto budgets and issue no-confidence motions, while the cabinet – anticipating this action – tried to dissolve the Diet preemptively and call for new elections.

The oligarchs themselves were not of one mind: personal rivalries and conflicts over economic and foreign policy continued even after the invasion of Korea was abandoned (Takenaka 2002). The central disagreement was whether the oligarchy should resist any parliamentary encroachment on its authority or attempt to co-opt the nascent party system. Facing intractable legislative conflicts in the Diet, the oligarchs eventually conceded the utility of electoral participation and established parties of their own. The most prominent was Seiyukai, formed in 1900 under the leadership of Ito Hirobumi, one of the main architects of the Meiji Constitution. Because the right to vote was restricted by tax qualifications, the party was an electoral coalition of large landlords, prosperous farmers, and business leaders. A number of alternative elite parties, such as the Kenseikai and Doshikai (each led by other Meiji oligarchs), challenged the Seiyukai's rule, but the party retained its preeminent status until the 1920s.[2]

As the conflict between oligarchs and political parties shifted to the Diet, the defining issue became political liberalization. Most oligarchs were opposed to expanding the franchise, which would not only dilute their authority but also increase the representation of poorer voters and challenge the conservative status quo regime. Many parties were also ambivalent, as the rise of Socialist parties would challenge their legislative dominance, and the very process of competing for votes nationally would strain their coffers (Ramseyer and Rosenbluth 1995). However, public calls for greater representation had been growing for more than a decade, catalyzed by the Rice Riots of 1918 and labor unrest in the 1920s. In

---

[1] Initially, elections were held in a mixture of single- and dual-membered districts.

[2] One strategy of the Seiyukai was to replace MMD-SNTV with single- and dual-membered districts in 1918. Prime Minister Hara Takashi of the Seiyukai had successfully played on Yamagata Aritomo's fear about rising socialism to urge a disproportionate electoral system, which would stamp out the representation of smaller parties (Ramseyer and Rosenbluth 1995).

1925, the oligarchs acquiesced to popular pressure and finally extended suffrage to all males older than age 25.[3] However, they packaged suffrage expansion with enhanced policy powers such as the notorious Peace Preservation Law, which forbade any actions that challenged the Meiji regime.

Political parties also agreed to switch the electoral system back to MMD-SNTV, with three to five seats per district. As the most popular party, the Seiyukai historically backed single-member plurality rules, which magnify the seat share of larger parties. However, the party's preferences shifted after one faction (the Seiyu Honto) split off in 1924. Under the resulting three-party system – the Seiyukai, the Seiyu Honto, and the Kenseikai – each party feared that the other two would merge under single-member districts with plurality (SMDP) rules. MMD-SNTV (with at least three seats per district) increased the prospect that each party would win at least one seat, thus insuring them against temporal fluctuations in popularity (Ramseyer and Rosenbluth 1995; Woodall 1999).

As the country descended into militarism in the 1930s, the power and independence of political parties began to wane (Yamanouchi et al. 1998). A series of political assassinations by military cliques robbed parties of their leaders, and by the 1930s, both the Minseito – the successor to the Kenseikai – and the Seiyukai began to splinter internally over confronting or accommodating the military.[4] Under Prime Minister Konoe Fumimaro's initiative to establish a single-party totalitarian state, both parties disbanded in 1940 to form the Taisei Yokusankai, or Imperial Rule Assistance Association. For the remainder of the Pacific War, competitive multiparty elections were abolished – candidates ran as sponsored or unsponsored by the Yokusankai – and the cabinet came under the control of the military elite.

Although Japan's prewar party system was neither the cause nor the product of full democratization, its role in the liberalization of politics cannot be ignored. The oligarchs controlled the military and exerted influence through the emperor, but the Meiji Constitution required that they address legislative demands. The oligarchs' attempts to co-opt the Diet by establishing their own parties eventually meant that the Diet became the locus for deliberation *between* oligarchs, with legislative seats determining their relative influence. When popular calls for franchise expansion mounted, political actors took up the mantle of full voting rights to further their own goals.

Importantly, the establishment of universal male suffrage pushed parties to expand their operations outside of their rural bailiwicks. Whereas truly left-wing

---

[3] In 1918, Prime Minister Hara had lowered the tax requirement for voting to ¥3, increasing the vote base to 8 million people, about 5 percent of the population.

[4] In 1927, the Kenseikai merged with the Seiyu Honto to form the second major party of prewar Japan, the Minseito. This marriage of convenience only lasted for a year, until the Seiyu Honto rejoined the Seiyukai. However, the Seiyukai and Minseito continued to alternate in power, ushering in a period of party government that is frequently referred to as "Taisho Democracy" (named after the Taisho Emperor's rule).

parties were proscribed, some establishment parties – particularly the Kenseikai – began to develop labor-oriented policies (Ramseyer and Rosenbluth 1995). By contrast, the Seiyukai, as the dominant party of the prewar period, retained its rural base among the landed gentry. In other words, the rural versus urban cleavage that would dominate postwar politics was already apparent in the Meiji autocracy.

Party System Reorientation in the Postwar Decade

As the chapters in this volume show, parties can exist in autocracies, and their pre-democratic organization and function influence their post-democratic institutionalization. As Hicken and Kuhonta argue in the introductory chapter, there are two sources of party system stability in early democracies. Parties that emerged out of grassroots movements and forged the path toward democracy may enjoy a social legitimacy that fosters their long-term success. Those that were agents of autocratic regimes, on the other hand, may leverage their organizational experience and capacities to induce greater certainty in the political process.[5] To a large extent, postwar Japan lacked either archetype. Parties were accepted as crucial mediums for democracy that linked voters to their representatives (and vice versa), but the wartime military autocracy severed any direct connections between prewar and postwar parties. At the same time, because full democratization was only realized through the outside influence of the U.S. occupation, no prewar group could claim historical legitimacy. The result was a decade of party system chaos, as various parties emerged, split apart, or dissolved altogether.

The end of World War II and the enactment of the 1947 constitution brought about fundamental changes in democratic competition. The Diet, not the emperor or oligarchs, would select the prime minister, and members of both houses of parliament would be directly elected by voters.[6] However, two features of the postwar period rendered seamless continuity from the prewar party system impossible.

First, the establishment of universal suffrage and freedom of assembly gave voice to new socioeconomic actors who represented urban, poorer voters.[7] Amid postwar food shortages and escalating unemployment, labor unions mobilized against the formerly privileged business conglomerates (*zaibatsus*) and major landowners. The elimination of autocratic police powers meant that the government could no longer suppress left-wing groups. Socialists and communists – many of whom were imprisoned during the war – quickly established

---

[5] For a fuller treatment of the autocratic role of political parties, see also Grzymala-Busse 2002 on Eastern Europe and Mainwaring and Scully 1995 on Latin America.

[6] The hereditary House of Peers (Upper House) was replaced with the elected House of Councillors.

[7] More specifically, the 1947 constitution expanded suffrage to women and lowered the voting age from 25 to 20.

political parties with deep organizational ties to public and private sector unions. The aggregate effect was to shift the electoral landscape leftward and weaken the ability of right-wing interests to dominate party politics.

Second, the U.S. occupation expelled politicians who had participated in the wartime legislature from the new Diet. This particularly hurt the conservative Progressive Party (1945–1947), as 260 of its 274 legislators were forbidden from electoral competition. The occupation's purge also created a power vacuum, as most politicians with parliamentary expertise were exorcized from the Diet. In their place, many senior bureaucrats from the powerful government ministries joined political parties. Elite civil servants had been culled from Japan's most prestigious universities, and most ministries had been left intact by the occupation (Johnson 1982). These bureaucrats were prized for their political knowledge and enjoyed public prestige, but they lacked the strong electoral base necessary to establish enduring linkages with voters. The net effect was to leave Japan with elite-driven, top-down political parties that had weak social penetration.

By the late 1940s, there was a three-way split in the Diet among the conservative Liberal Party, the centrist Democratic Party, and the left-leaning Socialist Party. The Liberals and Democrats were natural allies, as both espoused a strong security alliance with the United States – one of the main ideological issues of the day – although there were disagreements about the wisdom of demilitarization. The two parties were also composed of conservative politicians from the prewar Seiyukai and Minseito, many of whom were de-purged after the occupation. The left, too, experienced intraparty disputes over accepting the San Francisco Peace Treaty and the continued presence of U.S. military bases. The Socialist Party temporarily split into the "Left Socialists" and "Right Socialists" – each with its own headquarters and electoral strategy – over aggressive versus accommodationist stances on foreign policy.

A number of factors led to the consolidation of the conservatives into the Liberal Democratic Party (LDP) and the progressives into the unified Japan Socialist Party (JSP). In the 1953 and 1955 elections, the Democrats – the political centrists – won a plurality of the votes and chose to rule as a minority government. This came with legislative consequences: without majority support in the Diet, the Hatoyama cabinet faced significant hurdles to passing the fiscal budget. Labor union leaders, fearing a disorganized progressive camp and seeing the opportunity for greater political influence, urged the two wings of the JSP to reunite (Kohno 1997). On the conservative side, business leaders pressured the Liberals and Democrats to form a joint party in opposition to the reunified JSP (Masumi 1985). Competing campaign donation demands from the two conservative parties had strained the coffers of business associations and produced a number of embarrassing bribery scandals. When the JSP reunited, the Liberals and Democrats agreed to form a joint front against the Socialists, and in November 1955, the Liberals and Democrats merged to form the Liberal Democratic Party.

With the consolidation of the conservative and progressive camps into two distinct parties, the political landscape was poised for the classic left versus right

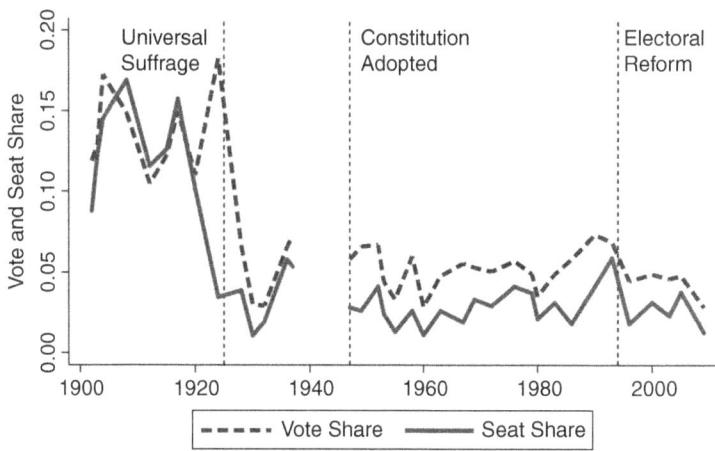

FIGURE 4.1. Representation of Independent Legislators.
Source: *Senkyo Nenkan*, various issues. Published by the Election Department, Local Administration Bureau, Ministry of Internal Affairs and Communications.

partisan divide that is found in many established democracies. While the LDP enjoyed an initial size advantage, the merger could have fallen apart easily had the party failed to win decisive majorities, returning the electoral landscape to three-party competition. Instead of robust competition between the two ideological poles, however, electoral margins continued to widen in favor of the LDP.

Evaluating Party System Institutionalization

At this point, it is useful to evaluate whether we can call the Japanese party system "institutionalized" by the time of mergers of the LDP and the JSP in 1955. The shape of the party system would continue to change with the emergence/dissolution of some smaller parties, in response to the rapid industrialization and urbanization of postwar Japan. However, the fundamental question remains: had the centrality of political parties as the cornerstone of legislative politics taken hold?

We can examine the salience of political parties in two ways. Figure 4.1 plots the proportion of seats and votes held by independent candidates since 1902, when the Seiyukai kicked off the integration of oligarchic politics into the Diet.[8] If political parties have weak salience in the Diet, then we should observe more

---

[8] In 1902, credible government records of election results also started. I have excluded data from the 1942 election, which occurred after the military government halted multiparty competition, and the 1946 election, held immediately after World War II. Candidates were counted as independent if they ran in the election without party affiliation, regardless of whether or not they joined a party afterward.

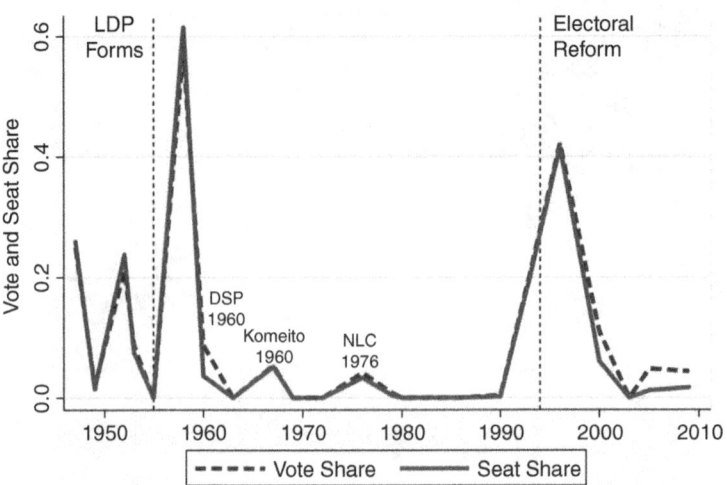

The LDP forms in 1955 and competes in its first election in 1958.

FIGURE 4.2. Representation of New Political Parties.
Source: Senkyo Nenkan, various issues. Published by the Election Department, Local Administration Bureau, Ministry of Internal Affairs and Communications.

candidates competing in elections as independents. The data suggest the opposite. The proportion of independents has been relatively small in Japanese electoral history, and their electoral salience steadily declined throughout the prewar period. Even when universal suffrage was adopted in 1925 – roughly quadrupling the electorate and increasing the representation of poorer voters – voters flocked to established conservative parties or to new centrist groups. The low salience of independent candidates continued in the postwar period, when political parties – particularly progressive groups – drew in any voters disaffected with the preceding regime. Despite ample opportunity for progressive independents to strike out on their own, the postwar ratio of independent candidates hovered around 5 percent, suggesting that legislative politics continued to be seen through the prism of political parties.

Figure 4.2 looks at the continuity of established political parties. Although it is not uncommon to see new parties created – either from scratch or through the merger or dissolution of existing groups – in any democracy, a high frequency suggests voter dissatisfaction with the status quo system. Figure 4.2 shows the proportion of votes and seats held by new parties in the first election after their formation. Parties are counted as "new" if they have never competed in elections in that form. For example, I count the JSP's split in 1952 into left- and right-wing factions as the creation of two new parties, but I do not count the JSP's reconstitution in 1955.

The major event of the postwar period was the creation of the LDP in 1955 (first election in 1958). Since then, minor centrist parties emerged periodically – the Democratic Socialists in 1960, Komeito in 1967, and the New Liberal Club in 1976 – but new parties rarely won more than 5 percent of the votes in their first elections. Given the rapid industrialization and urbanization of Japan after World War II, it is actually quite surprising that they did not play a more prominent role. Indeed, Figure 4.2 suggests that existing parties successfully adapted to changes in the electoral landscape, leaving no space for new actors to enter. The question tackled next is *how* the political establishment co-opted or fended off would-be challengers.

FISCAL CENTRALIZATION SHAPES THE PARTY SYSTEM

Although the postwar system took a decade to stabilize into the multiparty structure of the "1955 System," referring to the LDP's heyday between 1955 and 1993, parties never ceased being the focal point of politics. What, then, was the qualitative nature or content of party competition? As Allen Hicken notes in his chapter on the Philippines (Chapter 13), we can look at the party system on two dimensions: external and internal. The external dimension reflects the relationship between political parties, particularly the number of parties (i.e., its "shape") and their individual policy platforms (i.e., their "issues"). The internal dimension addresses the nature of the linkage between political parties and voters. Do voters develop strong ideological commitments to political parties and their platforms, or are they attached to individual politicians based on quid pro quo exchanges of votes for favors? The former is often called "programmatic" linkages; the latter is referred to as "clientelistic" (Kitschelt and Wilkinson 2007). These distinctions are not purely taxonomical: clientelistic versus programmatic linkages have important implications for the stability of the party system. For example, Erik Kuhonta's chapter on Thailand (Chapter 12) posits that the centrality of patronage and favors in voter-elite ties inhibited the development of durable partisan identification.

The rest of this chapter makes two arguments. First (discussed next), the main cleavage in the Japanese electoral arena has been fiscal redistribution between urban and rural regions. This is a function of the interaction between high degrees of fiscal centralization in the nation's budget and the diverging economic fates of the profitable/industrial and declining/agricultural sectors. Second (discussed in the following section), the clientelistic nature of fiscal redistribution has been shaped by the electoral system. Under MMD-SNTV, clientelistic linkages bound candidates and voters. Candidates promised to bring pork-barrel projects to their districts in exchange for electoral support. This produced a fairly stable party system, as significant swings in legislative representation only occurred when a group of politicians decided to switch party affiliations. After electoral reform in 1994, however, party competition became more programmatic. Vote choice increasingly turned on the party affiliation of candidates, and political campaigns responded by espousing ideological platforms and charismatic leaders. While interregional income disparities have not disappeared, they have been subsumed into broader policy disputes over the future of agriculture in Japan, the merits of infrastructural investment, and the trade-offs between short-term government expenditure and long-term debt accumulation.

Fiscal Centralization

The classic narrative of ideological politics divides parties on the right, which advocate lower taxation in alliance with capital owners, from parties on the left, which prioritize greater income transfers in alliance with labor unions (Lipset and Rokkan 1967; Przeworski and Sprague 1986). Japan differs from this model slightly: fiscal redistribution has divided the electoral landscape based on urban versus rural divisions, not class conflict. Conservatives have catered primarily to rural constituents and urban industrialists; the former provided votes while the latter provided campaign funds. The progressives, on the other hand, only entered the legislative arena after freedoms of speech and assembly were established in the postwar constitution. They forged strong ties to labor unions and established their main locus of support in the rapidly industrializing cities. While other issues have risen to the fore – most prominently, foreign and security policy – interparty differences have largely mapped onto a single spectrum from progressive (*kakushin*) to conservative (*hoshu*). As Kabashima (1999) elaborates, conservatives tend to be pro-business and rural and pro-America, while progressives tend to be pro-worker and urban and anti-America.

Following the formation of the LDP, the Yoshida School of politics, advocating neo-mercantilism and export-driven economic growth, seized the party's reins (Pempel 1998). Much like its prewar counterparts, the Seiyukai and Minseito, the LDP received significant backing from business conglomerates. The party advocated private property, low taxes, weaker unions, and market competition, albeit under the direction and coordination of the government (Johnson 1982). Yukio Noguchi (1997) argues that the LDP's 1955 System, based on the tight network between the LDP, bureaucrats, and big business, actually has its roots in the prewar period. During World War II, the military government funneled all social, political, and industrial forces – civilian and military – into the production of military material in "Total War." Noguchi argues that this commitment to state-led production persisted after the war, albeit attuned to the more pacifist belief that economic growth would enrich human life.

Whereas the pursuit of economic growth is not necessarily ideological, new social cleavages emerged from the unequal distributions of the fruits of growth. The fiscal structure of the Japanese government is highly centralized, as local governments collect only one-third of all taxes but spend close to two-thirds of public revenues. Importantly, elite civil servants in Tokyo direct this spending under the watchful gaze of Diet parliamentarians. Local governments are thus heavily dependent on central government transfers to fund social and infrastructural projects.

Interregional fiscal redistribution, particularly in the form of government construction investment, has historically been at the heart of the Japanese budget. Under the feudal Tokugawa Shogunate, provinces enjoyed autonomy in their economic practices, producing significant cross-regional inequalities based on natural resources and geographical proximity to trade routes. With the advent of the Meiji government, however, the oligarchs took greater control over economic management, especially as tax collection was vital to the establishment of a strong, conscripted military.[9] Modern infrastructure, such as roads, bridges, and tunnels, was crucial to the development of industrial networks, and the redistribution of central taxes as public works became tightly linked to job growth and economic success. The practice became further entrenched after World War II with the 1947 Finance Law, which forbade the government from issuing bonds to balance the budget except to finance public works. Although the government has since overridden the stipulation against general deficit financing, this *carte blanche* effectively institutionalized public works as a sanctuary for pork-barreling (Woodall 1996).

Fiscal centralization impacted party system development in two ways. First, it helped the LDP redistribute income from urban areas, where the party was less popular, to its rural bailiwicks (DeWit and Steinmo 2002). Thies (1998) finds that despite gradual urbanization, agricultural spending increased as the percentage of rural electoral districts increased. The postwar economic boom made this redistributive, pork-barrel–oriented strategy more effective, as urbanization left rural areas impoverished and dependent on LDP largesse to survive. Second, fiscal centralization put pressure on local government officials to affiliate with the LDP, so that they could gain access to the central government budget. Scheiner (2006) argues that this significantly strengthened the LDP's competitiveness in national elections, as ex-local politicians – who affiliated with the LDP to cajole more redistribution – made the best candidates for the Diet.

As a result of the government's redistributive policies, income stratification has been limited in postwar Japan. Figure 4.3 plots the Gini coefficient in Japan between 1960 and 2000 in two ways: using household income directly and using household income adjusted for social insurance benefits and costs. Keeping in mind that high values of the Gini coefficient denote more inequality, Japan has had relatively mild income disparities despite a rapid growth in per capita GDP. This is particularly apparent when examining the adjusted Gini coefficient, which incorporates much of the income redistribution policies of the government. Historically, Japan has had one of the lowest Gini coefficients around the world, on par with Denmark and Sweden and significantly lower than the United States or Great Britain.

---

[9] Even after the advent of party politics, the Seiyukai and Minseito focused on mustering the political support of prefectural governors, who were appointed by the Home Ministry (Masumi 1985). Governors exercised discretion in the promotion of local industries and the enforcement of election laws, and so parties competed to install their preferred candidates.

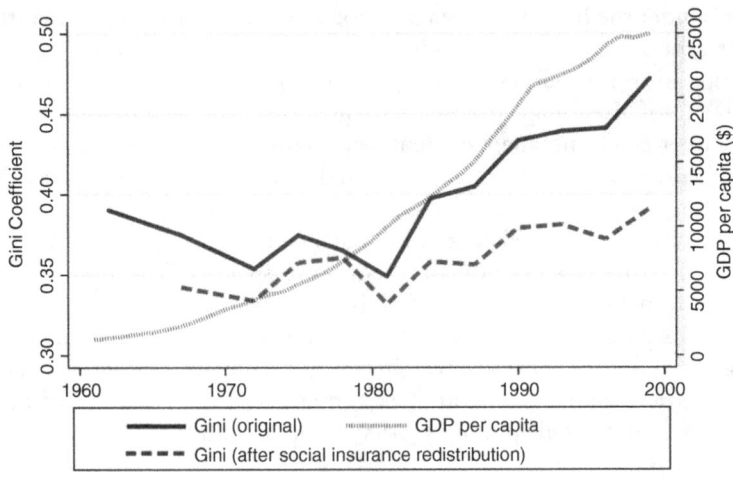

Gini coefficient for household income. Data taken from Ministry of Health, Labor, and Welfare.

FIGURE 4.3. Gini Coefficient in Japan (1960–2000).
Source: Shotoku Saibunpai Chousa Houkokusho, various issues. Published by the Directorate of Policy Planning, Japanese Ministry of Health, Labor, and Welfare.

Weak Secondary Cleavages

The interregional fiscal transfer scheme minimized the formation of durable class conflicts between employers and workers. Although the Japan Socialist Party was the natural ally of labor unions, it could only lock in about 15 to 30 percent of manual workers and salaried employees, in contrast to the LDP's success in corralling 70 to 80 percent of farmers and 55 to 65 percent of small business owners (Richardson 1997, table 2.2). Blue-collar ambivalence to the JSP was the result in part of the economic structure's co-optation of labor interests. In a movement called *shunto*, or "spring wage offensive," unions would annually renegotiate wages with employers. This produced a continuous and incremental adjustment of wages, which redistributed economic growth to workers and contributed to socioeconomic stability (Fukatsu 1995).

In addition to these distributive cleavages based on urbanization, the Japanese party system was also divided by ideational cleavages. The most salient dimension was foreign policy, specifically the U.S.-Japan Security Treaty (which permitted American bases) and Article 9 "Peace Clause" of the Japanese constitution (which forbade war as an element of foreign policy). For most of the postwar period, Yoshida's philosophy of low military spending and a close alliance with the United States dominated LDP politics (Pyle 1996; Samuels 2007). However, as the US military commitment to Asia grew – beginning with the Korean War, and then with disputes in the Taiwan Strait and the Vietnam War – American demands for burden sharing mounted. In response, the LDP warmed to limited remilitarization to fend off U.S. pressures to revoke

Article 9. Progressives, on the other hand, defended the importance of the Peace Clause as a national commitment to peace. Pacifist sentiment in the electorate made increased military spending unpopular, and opinion surveys consistently showed support for preserving Article 9 and against remilitarization (Katzenstein 1996; Samuels 2007).

In terms of votes and seats, however, Japanese remilitarization and Article 9 were low-salience electoral issues. The Socialist and Communist Parties managed to corner some popular support for their firm defense of the status quo, and these positions yielded electoral gains when exogenous shocks such as the Vietnam War provoked popular backlash against the United States. However, Miyake, Nishizawa, and Kohno (2001) show that most voters retained stable, positive sentiments toward the United States, favoring alignment with the American/Liberal coalition over the Soviet/Communist sphere. Although foreign policy attitudes developed into recognizable ideological differences between supporters of the LDP and the JSP, its low salience meant that foreign policy was a losing electoral cause for progressive parties.

MMD-SNTV: STABLE, CLIENTELISTIC PARTY SYSTEM

An analysis of ideological differentiation helps us understand which issues political parties can compete over. However, they do not necessarily explain which issues *will* become electorally salient, and how parties will go about providing those goods or services to voters. This section and the next explore the role of political institutions, particularly the electoral system, in shaping the nature of the party system.

Multiparty Competition

The external dimension of political parties is defined by the number of political parties and their relative balance of power. In the Japanese context, why were there five stable parties through most of the postwar period, with the LDP on the right, the JSP and the JCP on the left, and the DSP and Komeito in the center? There is an extensive political science literature on the relationship between electoral institutions and the party system.[10] The underlying cause is strategic behavior by voters and politicians: rational actors will not invest resources (votes, time, money) on lost causes. Fringe candidates should opt out of elections they cannot win; even if they decide to compete, strategic voters should choose to

---

[10] One of the most cited works in political science is Maurice Duverger's 1954 argument that single-member districts (one seat per district) tend to have two effective or competitive candidates, whereas multimember districts (more than one seat per district) produce multi-candidate competition. Other prominent scholars who have examined the relationship between electoral and party systems include Rae 1967, Sartori 1976, Cox 1997, and Taagepera and Shugart 2002.

support candidates with greater viability. In his seminal study, Steven Reed (1991) posits the "M+1" rule: where the number of seats in a given district equals M, we should expect to see M+1 competitive candidates. The mechanism is straightforward: a candidate needs to win $1/(M+1)$ share of the total votes to guarantee victory. In a one-seat district, 50 percent of the votes will win a seat; in a two-seat district, 33 percent of the votes will do the job. To the extent that strategic behavior or simple market forces will weed out weaker parties, we should see a convergence toward M+1 competitive candidates.

From 1925 to 1942, and again from 1947 to 1994, Japan used a multi-member district, single nontransferable vote system (MMD-SNTV) system, which divided the country into electoral districts with three to five seats each. As discussed in earlier sections, this system was purposefully chosen in 1925 as a compromise between the three principal parties – Seiyuto, Kenseikai, and the Seiyu Honto – to ensure that each would win at least one seat. Because the average district magnitude (M) in postwar Japan under MMD-SNTV was four, it was possible for an average of five candidates or parties (M+1 = 5) to be competitive in each electoral district. Indeed, even during the initial instability between 1945 and 1955, five parties emerged: Liberals, Democrats, the left- and right-wing Socialists, and the Communists.

The mergers that created the LDP and the unified JSP made sense contextually, as business and union interests each sought to maximize their representation in the Diet. However, this quasi–two party system was unsustainable in the long run, because centripetal pressures were insufficient to overcome disagreements within the LDP or the JSP. This institutional perspective allows us to better understand opposition fragmentation from 1955 to 1993.

The first party to emerge after 1955 was the Democratic Socialist Party (DSP), which formed in 1960 as an offshoot of the JSP's right-wing faction. The DSP was backed by Domei, the private sector workers union, and advocated greater political compromise with conservative parties and labor moderation with corporations.[11] The second new party was the Komeito, which formed in 1964. The primary support of the party (which remains in operation today) is a Buddhist organization, the Soka Gakkai, making it an outlier in Japan's otherwise secular political landscape. Komeito's urban orientation and centrist policy platform draw the party some additional support from nonunionized workers and small business owners. The final new actor, the New Liberal Club (NLC), was established in 1976 when an LDP faction split off to protest Prime Minister Tanaka Kakuei's corruption scandals, although it later rejoined the LDP in 1986. The NLC maintained a strong partnership with the LDP even

---

[11] Private sector unions had the legal right to engage in industrial action, including strikes and sit-ins, which gave them more bargaining leverage in the market. By contrast, public sector unions – which backed the JSP – were forbidden from labor disruption tactics. As a result, the latter was more confrontational in the political arena, relying on the JSP to win policy concessions, whereas the former was more willing to work with the conservative LDP.

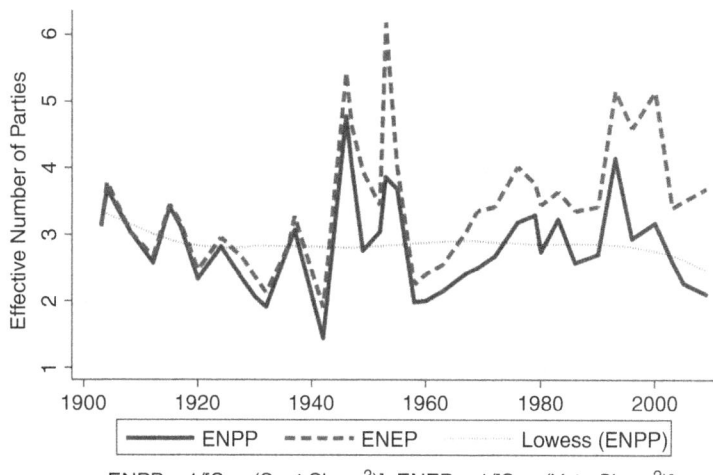

FIGURE 4.4. Effective Number of Parties.
Source: Senkyo Nenkan, various issues. Published by the Election Department, Local Administration Bureau, Ministry of Internal Affairs and Communications.

during their split, even joining forces in the Diet when the latter fell short of a parliamentary majority.

The question here is why these particular parties emerged after 1955, and what effect they had on the shape of the party system and parliamentary competition. Two factors come into play. First, Kohno (1997) argues that the success of new political parties is a function of the MMD-SNTV system. New parties did better in districts where $M=5$, because the vote share needed to win a seat was smaller. Second, socioeconomic and structural transformations influenced the emergence of these particular parties. Whereas a larger district magnitude would support more candidates, it is not clear whether we would see more conservative, centrist, or socialist parties. In Japan, most of the "new" votes up for grabs were in metropolitan areas, where urbanization and industrialization unmoored voters from traditional allegiances in their home districts. Scheiner (1999) demonstrates that new parties tended to run candidates in urban districts where voters had weaker identification with the larger parties. Although these newcomers did not greatly harm the LDP, whose support base was in rural areas, the proliferation of floating voters diluted the JSP's urban strength, leading to the emergence of union-based parties such as the DSP that fragmented the progressive vote.

Even with the rise of new political groups, the Japanese party system remained relatively stable throughout its history. Figure 4.4 plots the effective number of parties from 1900 to 2009. The effective number of parties is an empirical measure that weights political parties by the size of their vote or seat share, so that larger parties are counted more than their smaller counterparts.

The result is a variable used to measure the number of competitive parties.[12] The effective number of elected parties (ENEP) weights parties by their share of votes; the effective number of political parties (ENPP) does the same by the share of legislative seats. I count "minor parties" and "independent candidates" as two parties, when official government records report them as such.

Given the continuous usage of MMD-SNTV, we would expect to see a stable number of parties persist over time. The Lowess curve in Figure 4.4 shows the smoothed average for ENPP over time. While the introduction of universal suffrage, World War II, postwar uncertainty, and the emergence of the LDP all produced short-term shocks in the party system, we can observe a relatively robust average of three parties over a century of legislative competition.

Japan's 1.5 Party System

The MMD-SNTV electoral system fostered multiparty competition. What has not yet been touched on, however, is the imbalance in the party system. Electoral theory simply predicts that we would see M+1 competitive candidates per district, where M is the number of seats per district. It would be reasonable to expect, then, that Japanese elections with M≈4 should produce a balanced system with five, roughly even-sized parties.

In reality, however, the LDP enjoyed single-party majorities between 1955 and 1993. And as Figure 4.4 shows, Japan's legislative history has been characterized by three to four competitive parties. Various observers have described this as Japan's "1.5 party system": one dominant party (LDP) competing against a weaker main opposition (JSP) and a smattering of minor urban parties (DSP, Komei, JCP). Although a fuller treatment of the causes of the LDP's electoral success is beyond the purview of this chapter, it is nevertheless necessary to explain why this imbalance persisted over time.

As Ordeshook and Shvetsova (1994), Cox (1997), and Clark and Golder (2006) note, the relationship between district magnitude (M) and the number of parties is conditional on the number of salient issue dimensions. If M=4, we should observe a maximum of five competitive parties. However, for five parties to actually manifest, there must be five distinct policy issues or positions that voters care about. Moreover, for there to be five equally sized parties, these five policy positions must be important to an equal subset of voters. Japan's 1.5-party system exemplifies this nuanced interaction between political cleavages and the electoral system. For one, the urban versus rural dimension overwhelmed other issues such as class conflict or foreign policy. As a result, there was no clear reason for five equally sized parties to survive, especially as the JSP struggled to forge its identity around the secondary issue of foreign policy.

---

[12] More specifically, ENEP = $1 / \Sigma(V_i^2)$, where V_i is the proportion of votes won by party i. ENPP reproduces this calculation by using the proportion of seats instead. For more detail, see Laakso and Taagepera 1979; and Lijphart 1994.

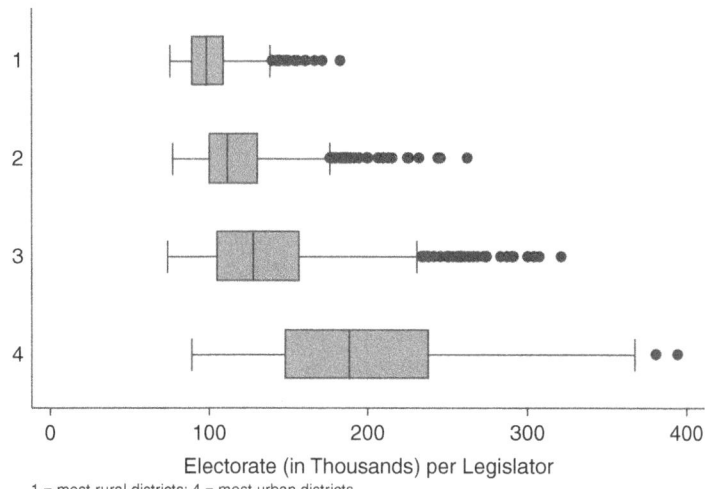

FIGURE 4.5. Malapportionment by Level of Urbanization.
Source: Data shared by Steven Reed, Chuo University; personal communication with author.

The more important factor, however, was the rapid urbanization of the nation, which distorted the representation of urban versus rural districts. If seats were allocated to districts based on population parity (i.e., perfect apportionment), the electorate-to-M ratio would be constant across districts. In Japan, however, industrialization and urbanization led to distorted malapportionment favoring rural districts (Ohmiya 1992). In effect, the LDP could continue to win a majority by catering to a pro-LDP electoral minority in rural areas because each rural vote was more valuable than an urban vote.

An important point here is that the LDP purposely fostered malapportionment. Although Japanese law mandates redistricting every five years, the LDP ignored this stipulation except when the Supreme Court threatened to void election results, typically when the population disparity between the most- and least-represented districts exceeded 3:1 (Ohmiya 1992; McElwain 2008). This produced a sizeable boon to the LDP, as urban regions – where the opposition parties were more competitive – have been serially undervalued in elections. Figure 4.5 depicts this in graphical form. The boxplots represent the number of voters per legislator in Japanese electoral districts between 1950 and 1993. The vertical axis represents the Asahi Newspaper's four-point coding of each electoral district, where 1 = rural and 4 = metropolitan. We can see that rural districts typically have far fewer voters per legislator (median less than 100,000) than do urban districts (median less than 200,000). This system worked in the LDP's favor: it needed to win half the votes to obtain a median rural seat than progressive parties did for urban seats.

Higher levels of political participation in rural regions encouraged the LDP to solidify its support among farmers by equalizing income distribution through budgetary redistribution (1984). The dominance of conservative parties in rural areas dates back to the prewar period, when suffrage restrictions and constraints on political freedoms limited the electoral participation of left-wing parties and urban (poorer) voters. When these hurdles were lifted during the U.S. occupation, the new left-wing parties tried to establish their own support base, but their success was limited to urban areas where conservatives lacked an established foothold.

In effect, the 1955 System was less a 1.5-party system than it was two different party systems in urban versus rural areas. In the less-developed countryside, the LDP's promise of fiscal redistribution generated strong electoral majorities. In the rapidly expanding urban regions, however, voters experienced a net loss from fiscal reallocation, and their concerns increasingly turned to negative externalities from industrialization, such as rising housing costs and environmental degradation. Scheiner (2006) calls this Japan's "parallel party system": LDP dominance in rural areas and two-party competition in urban areas.

MMD-SNTV System Breeds Clientelistic Party-Voter Linkages

The institutionalization of the party system is not just about shape (number of parties) or issues (ideological cleavages). What also matters is the internal organization of individual parties and their relationship with voters. As the editors describe in the introductory chapter, "The stability of interparty competition must necessarily depend on the presence of cohesive and ideological organizations creating a setting for patterned electoral contests" (pp. 3–4). Japanese parties have traditionally eschewed stable policy platforms, before and after the war. Instead of ideological cohesion, legislators and voters were linked by redistribution based on the exchange of private goods – notably pork-barrel projects – for votes at the ballot box. However, the party system has largely been stable, suggesting that there are multiple equilibria to party institutionalization.

Looking within the LDP, Fukui (1970) posits that the structural characteristics of postwar parties emerged before World War II. The two main prewar parties, Seiyukai and Minseito, shared organizational features that the LDP adopted decades later: policy committees that aggregated the preferences of different MPs, overseen by an executive council that cut across policy areas. While many senior political officials were ousted by the U.S. occupation, the party organs of the Seiyukai and Minseito survived intact. The leadership positions were filled instead by retired bureaucrats, whose ministries were strengthened after the purging of wartime politicians and who could provide much-needed policy competence.

Partisan identification hinges on the persistence of demographic or socioeconomic factors, such as income, region, or occupation, which determine (or proxy for) electoral preference. As Richardson (1997) argues, however, the correlation between economic class and party attachment in Japan is weak,

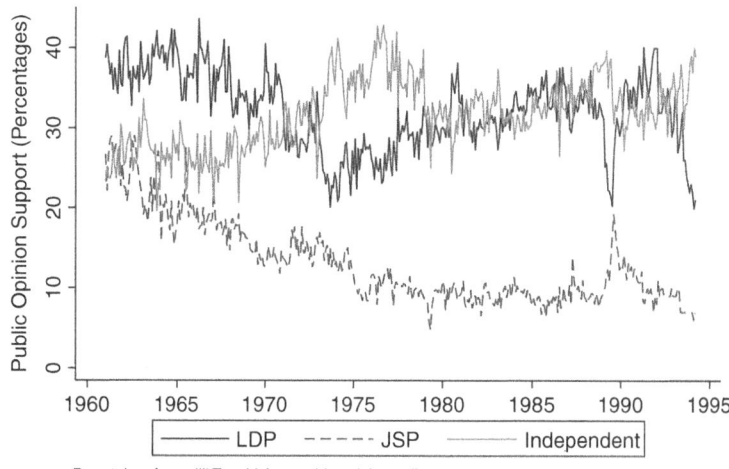

Data taken from *Jiji Tsushin's* monthly opinion polls.

FIGURE 4.6. Public Support of Political Parties (1960–1994).
Source: *Jiji Seron Chousa Tokuho*, various issues. Published by Jji Tushinsha (Tokyo, Japan).

especially among salaried middle-class workers. Regional divisions are some-what stickier, especially in rural areas where the LDP has dominated the vote. However, rapid urbanization inhibited the development of durable party attach-ments, as more and more voters faced different policy appeals or candidate choices as they moved to different parts of the country.

If anything, Japanese voters have become more nonpartisan over time. Figure 4.6 plots data from the *Jiji Tsushin*'s monthly opinion polls on voter affinity to specific parties during the MMD-SNTV period. I focus on three primary groups: the LDP, the JSP, and independents.[13] The JSP's support has been declining since the early 1960s; by the mid-1970s, only 10 percent of voters claimed to like the party. While the LDP has remained stagnant, it has routinely outpaced the JSP by about 20 percent. By contrast, the fastest-growing segment of voters has been political independents.

In some ways, this is a rational response to the fickle policy stances of Japanese political parties. Kobayashi (1997) reviews the preelection policy promises of political parties and finds that campaign platforms lack consistency, giving voters little partisan substance to latch on to. The result is what Miyake, Nishizawa, and Kohno (2001) term overwhelming *relative* support for the LDP: support for the LDP fluctuated over time, but opposition parties suffered even greater drop-offs.

An illustrative turning point came in the 1970s. The LDP had benefited from double-digit GDP growth in the 1960s, when 35 to 40 percent of voters

---

[13] Independent voters are survey respondents who reported that they do not support any party.

expressed strong preference for the party, but domestic and foreign policy crises challenged voter assessments of the LDP (Miyake et al. 2001). The two oil shocks of 1973 and 1979 slowed the rate of economic growth; the Vietnam War and "Nixon shocks"[14] raised anti-American sentiment in the country; and urban voters came face to face with the negative externalities of the growth-at-all-cost policies of the LDP.

These transformations in the social, economic, and international environment should have provided the opposition parties with ample opportunity to bring new voters into their fold. Instead, the greatest growth was in the ranks of independent voters. If the party system is based on competitive, programmatic politics, then voters who are disillusioned by the status quo government should be able to locate alternative policy visions among opposition parties. That a large fraction of the electorate remained dissatisfied with any party, however, implies that the party system lacked a vibrant programmatic component.

Miyake et al. (2001) go so far as to argue that the 1.5 party system, with dueling LDP versus JSP competition, only existed until the late 1960s. Since then, the LDP's main competitor has been independent voters, whose allegiance was up for grabs. This finding is bolstered by Figure 4.6, which showed an inverse relationship between LDP support and independents. In fact, the correlation between the two variables (1960–1994) is −0.74. The correlation is similarly negative at −0.65 between the JSP and independents. By contrast, LDP and JSP support is positively correlated at 0.43, indicating that both parties are primarily losing votes to independents, not to each other.

In contrast to classic notions of internal party institutionalization, however, the lack of entrenched partisanship among the electorate did not engender party system instability. Ballot decisions in Japan have depended on the personal characteristics of individual candidates, not their party affiliation. Scheiner (2006) shows that candidate "quality" – defined by past political or policy experience – better predicts electoral success than party affiliation. Under MMD-SNTV, parties emphasized the personal qualities of their candidates over their policy platforms. Because each district had three to four seats but voters could pick only one candidate, co-partisans from major parties were forced to compete against one another. As same-party candidates could not differentiate themselves ideologically, they highlighted their personal competence at extracting pork-barrel projects or patronage from the central government's coffers instead (Curtis 1971; Ramseyer and Rosenbluth 1993; Kohno 1997).

As legislative clout over redistribution depended on affiliation with the majority party in the Diet, there were relatively few cases of defection by LDP legislators prior to the 1990s. Given strong incumbency advantage, the party system remained stable as long as candidates did not switch parties frequently.

---

[14] Nixon Shock refers to two events in the early 1970s: (1) President Richard Nixon's decision to pull the United States out of the Bretton Woods gold standard system and (2) Nixon's unannounced (to the Japanese) trip to and diplomatic recognition of the People's Republic of China.

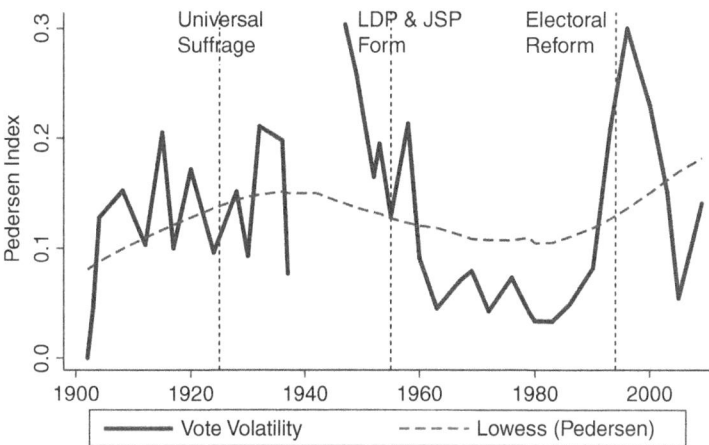

FIGURE 4.7. Vote Fluctuations across Elections.
Source: *Senkyo Nenkan*, various issues. Published by the Election Department, Local Administration Bureau, Ministry of Internal Affairs and Communications.

When progressive parties began to coordinate candidate nominations to avoid costly vote splitting, the magnitude of vote instability fell even further (Baker and Scheiner 2004). In effect, party system alignment changed only when political elites switched teams, not when voters' ideological preferences evolved.

We can demonstrate this point in two ways. Figure 4.7 depicts aggregate shifts in votes between parties, as measured by the Pedersen Index.[15] A value of 0.1 indicates that 10 percent of the total votes changed hands between political parties. Higher values thus denote larger vote swings between parties. In the prewar period, approximately 15 percent of the total votes went to different parties than in the previous election. Despite upheaval in the first postwar decade, the party system quickly stabilized, with less than 10 percent of votes changing hands by 1960. This period of tranquility continued until the 1990s, when anticipation of electoral reform resulted in the creation of new parties (more on this in the next section).

Figure 4.8 looks at vote stability from the perspective of candidate perform-ance. If voters have strong allegiances to individual candidates, then short-term changes in the electoral environment – scandals among co-partisans, fluctuations

---

[15] The Pedersen Index = 0.5 * [Abs($V_{i,t} - V_{i,t-1}$)], or the sum of the absolute change in vote share for every party divided by two (Pedersen 1979). One difficulty with the Pedersen estimation is how to count the vote shares of new parties. I apply the following rules. When a party splits, the new party fragment with the largest vote share counts as the official successor. When multiple parties merge, I use the vote share of the largest predecessor as the basis for the vote swing.

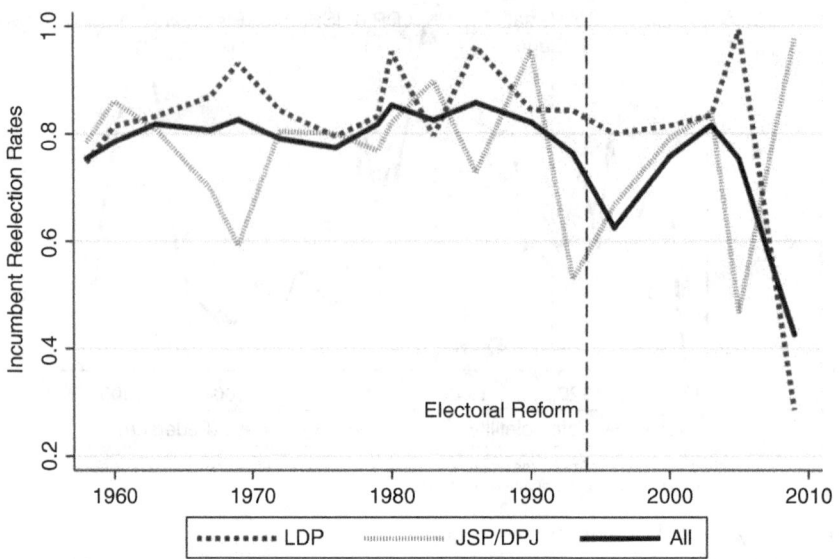

FIGURE 4.8. Stability of Incumbent Reelection Rates until Reforms.
Source: Data shared by Steven Reed, Chuo University; personal communication with author.

in economic growth or unemployment, environmental disasters – should have weak effects on their reelection probabilities. To that extent, I calculate the proportion of incumbent LDP and JSP candidates who were reelected. As a precursor to the next section, I have also listed the performance of the main post-JSP opposition parties after electoral reform, namely the New Frontier Party (NFP; 1996) and the Democratic Party (2000 onward). While the JSP did slightly worse than the LDP, more than 80 percent of incumbents from both parties routinely won. Given minimal levels of party switching by legislators until the 1990s, strong clientelism generated a stable party system, as voters rarely changed their ballot choices regardless of their sentiments about political parties.

MMM: UNSTABLE, PROGRAMMATIC POLITICS

The stabilization of the Japanese party system depended on two institutional factors: the high degree of fiscal centralization, which defined interregional distribution as the primary political cleavage, and the MMD-SNTV electoral system, which promoted multiparty politics and clientelistic party-voter linkages. The traditional party system had its merits. Despite the socioeconomic upheavals of the postwar era, the party system experienced relative stability, as characterized by the LDP's single-party dominance and low level of vote turnover. The theoretical implication, however, is that if either factor changed, we should observe a shift in the shape, issues, and stability of the party system. This does not necessarily mean that the party system should become less institutionalized. Rather, the party system could adapt to a new institutional equilibrium.

The transformative moment in Japan came in 1993, when the LDP was ousted from power. The successor coalition government fulfilled its mandate to replace the MMD-SNTV electoral system with a new system that combined single-member district-plurality (SMDP) with a proportional representation (PR) tier. Thus began a decade of party system realignment toward a less stable two-party system based on programmatic competition.

Electoral Reform

A number of factors contributed to the LDP's falling popularity in the 1980s. Postwar industrialization diminished agriculture's labor market share, shrinking the LDP's electoral base. The gradual reduction of trade barriers, forced by foreign criticism of Japan's huge trade surpluses, also disproportionately harmed the LDP's core constituency. Economic slowdown, exacerbated by the bursting of the asset bubble in the early 1990s and accompanying spikes in unemployment, soured voter perceptions about LDP competence (Miyake et al. 2001). The LDP's reckless spending on pork-barrel politics also came back to haunt the party, as a 3 percent consumption tax to defray ballooning government deficits resulted in the party's defeat in the 1989 Upper House election.

A more immediate problem was the revelation of high-profile scandals, illustrating the cronyism, corruption, and clientelism that underlay the 1955 system (Schlesinger 1997). Although voters and interest groups may have tolerated the inefficiencies of pork-barrel politics as long as the economic pie was growing, their willingness to support LDP clientelism disappeared once the pie began to shrink. More importantly, voter disenchantment exacerbated internal fissures within the LDP. Traditionally, belonging to the LDP conferred control over fiscal redistribution and the reputation of being an effective economic manager. These benefits became polluted, however, with the emergence of bribery scandals and the bursting of the economic bubble.

By the early 1990s, political reform had become synonymous with electoral system change. Many reformists advocated a switch from the traditional MMD-SNTV electoral system to a Westminster-style, SMDP system. Ozawa Ichiro, a top lieutenant in the LDP, also pushed for electoral reform, arguing that an SMDP system would promote two-party competition. This would, in turn, (1) increase government accountability, because small swings in vote share would produce large swings in seat shares and (2) foster ideological competition, because voters would have an easier time differentiating the political views of two parties than of five. However, these reforms were opposed by many LDP legislators, who feared that electoral reform would force them to move to new districts and abandon their established political networks (Christensen 1994; Reed and Thies 2001a; McElwain 2008).

Given the weakening ties binding the LDP, however, this recalcitrance toward reform led to a series of factional defections, notably by Ozawa himself. The 1993 election was a watershed moment, as it ousted the LDP from majority status in the Lower House for the first time. However, no opposition party had enough seats to form a majority government. Instead, all non-LDP parties (except for the Communists) joined an eight-party coalition government to adopt a mixed member majoritarian (MMM) electoral system.[16] This new rule created two electoral tiers: 300 single-member districts and 200 proportional representation seats distributed in eleven regional blocks (since shrunk to 180). Voters would have two ballots: one to pick a candidate for their smaller single-member district, and another to pick a party (closed-list) in the larger regional block. The plurality winner would obtain the SMDP seat, and the PR seats would be divided among parties based on their share of regional block votes.

The eight-party coalition collapsed after the passage of electoral reform and was succeeded by a short-lived minority government. The next stable government was a surprising coalition of the two major parties of postwar Japan: the LDP and the JSP. Between June 1994 and January 1996, these two parties and the smaller Sakigake partnered to form a coalition government under Murayama Tomiichi, the first Socialist prime minister since 1948. The opposition struggled to come up with a viable counterpart to the LDP. For the 1996 election, the centrist groups – Renewal (Shinseito), Democratic Socialists, Japan New Party, and Komeito – coalesced into the New Frontier Party (NFP, or Shinshinto) under Ozawa Ichiro's leadership. Some center-left opposition parties, including JSP and Sakigake dissidents, formed the Democratic Party of Japan (DPJ). The 1996 election, which was the first under the new MMM electoral system, strengthened the LDP's hold on power. By contrast, the remnant of the JSP was decimated, falling from 14 percent to 3 percent of the seats. The NFP and the DPJ fared better, but they were unable to overcome the combined majority of the LDP-JSP-Sakigake partnership.

The 1994 to 1996 period reveals conflicting insights about the social penetration of political parties and, by extension, the institutionalization of the party system. On the one hand, the JSP's decision to join with its bitter rival in exchange for the premiership speaks to the top-down, non-ideological commitment of legislators. On the other hand, the decimation of the JSP – because of legislative defections and voter disgust – reveals that voters were not as ignorant or dismissive of ideological differentiation as politicians expected.

The failure of Ozawa's New Frontier Party to oust the LDP led to a new round of party realignment. Komeito split off in 1998 to compete in that year's Upper House election independently, and many of the remaining progressive parties

---

[16] For more on the partisan debate regarding electoral reform, see Narita 1996; Curtis 1999; Reed and Thies 2001a; McElwain 2008.

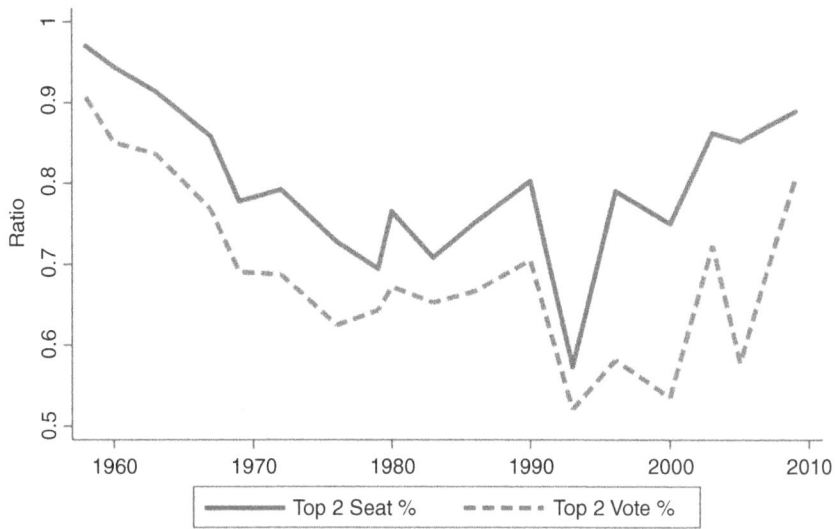

FIGURE 4.9. Multi-Partyism to Bi-Partyism.
Source: *Senkyo Nenkan*, various issues. Published by the Election Department, Local Administration Bureau, Ministry of Internal Affairs and Communications.

decided to join the DPJ. Ozawa himself created a smaller Liberal Party and joined the LDP's coalition with Komeito between 1998 and 2000. The LDP-Komeito-Liberal coalition remained intact until 2003, when Ozawa once against switched affiliations, joining the opposition DPJ.

As a result of party switching (many by Ozawa himself), the party system landscape had realigned significantly over ten years. The JSP – now rebranded as the Social Democratic Party (SDP) – had become a minor opposition party. The NFP, once seen as the main opposition challenger to the LDP, folded after two years. Left standing were the LDP and DPJ – the two major players in Japanese politics as of 2012.

Lurching toward a Two-Party System

The stated purpose of electoral reform was to create a two-party system that would foster ideological competition, party-centric politics, and government accountability. To assess the realization of these objectives, we must distinguish electoral competitiveness at the national and district levels. Figure 4.9 depicts the Lower House seat shares of the two largest parties in the Diet since 1955. The LDP remained the plurality party until 2009, although it did not have a unilateral majority in 1996, 2000, or 2003. The New Frontier Party was the primary opposition in the 1996 election, but the Democratic Party took its place in 1998. The representation of the top parties fell prior to electoral reform, when major factions defected from the LDP. As the MMM system took hold, however, Japan moved toward bi-partyism, as seen by the 90 percent combined seat share held by the LDP and the DPJ in 2009.

The most noticeable change is in an omitted category: the representation of minor parties. The Social Democrats (which succeeded the JSP) are now a fringe player in the Diet. Over the past five elections since 1996, it has only captured an average of 6.1 percent of the votes and 2.2 percent of the seats. The Communist Party is in a similar situation, with 9.3 percent of the votes and 3.0 percent of the seats. The exception is the Komeito, which was in a coalition government with the LDP between 1999 and 2009. Komeito is in a unique position because of stable support from the Soka Gakkai, a religious organization whose membership has actually risen since 1990. The Komeito's vote share has stayed stable at around 13 percent.

By contrast, the two-party seat share of the LDP and the DPJ has increased from less than 80 percent in 2000 to more than 90 percent in 2009. Averaging across the five elections from 1996, the ratio of votes between the largest and second-largest parties in the Lower House has been 1.22. This is a much closer distribution of seats than the 2.16 ratio that divided the LDP and the JSP between 1955 and 1993. However, their individual vote and seat shares have waxed and waned. The DPJ increased its seat share from 1996 to 2000 to 2003, suffered a big loss in the 2005 election, but then won a resounding victory over the LDP in 2009.

Taken together, the decline of minor parties and the increased competitiveness of the major parties reflect the emergence of a two-party system. The stability of this new status quo, however, is conditional on the frequency of party switching and mergers, which were rampant in the mid-1990s. It is difficult for elections to revolve around two ideologically coherent parties if there are recurring changes in the identity and membership of those parties. Since 1993, there have been more than 100 party-switches involving LDP members, whereby a politician leaves, is kicked out, and/or later rejoins the LDP (often *en masse* with his or her faction). The reasons for party switching vary by case and include generational conflicts within the LDP hierarchy (Kato 1998), ideological disagreements about electoral reform (Reed and Scheiner 2003), and the need to tap government funds for pork-barrel projects (Saito 2009). Wholesale party dissolutions and mergers were originally more pronounced within the opposition camp, as the New Frontier Party briefly took up the opposition leader's mantle in 1996, only to give way to the Democratic Party after one election. In fact, none of the new parties that emerged in the 1993 election – Shinseito, Nihon Shinto, or Sakigake – currently exists. Of the pre-1993 parties, Komeito agreed to join the NFP in 1996, only to break off in 1998 and ultimately join a coalition with the LDP. The Democratic Socialists no longer exist, and the JSP has become a rump party.

A common theme of these party switches and mergers is that they involve strategic realignment by parliamentarians, rather than the bottom-up emergence of new grassroots organizations. This top-down pattern of party system change suggests that the impetus for realignment is not clear-cut ideological differentiation between the LDP and the DPJ, but rather elite-level bargaining and positioning. Electoral reform created the strongest impetus for realignment, because the new mixed member system penalizes smaller parties that cannot win a plurality of seats in the SMDPs. Party switching continued for more than a decade, because of uncertainty about voter priorities and ideological cleavages. Given voter dissatisfaction with the LDP and the inability of new opposition parties to capture an electoral majority, office-seeking politicians lacked clarity about which camp to align with. This, in turn, produced lurches toward two-party competition rather than a smooth pattern of realignment.

Current stability does not, however, necessarily preclude party realignment in the future. One of the effects of party switching in the 1990s is that neither the LDP nor the DPJ has internally coherent ideological principles. No one epitomizes this phenomenon as much as Ozawa Ichiro, who was considered hawkish within the LDP when he left in 1993 but became the leader of the progressive DPJ between 2006 and 2009. In certain cases, party leaders have resolved intraparty tensions by taking drastic steps. In 2005, Prime Minister Koizumi kicked out LDP legislators who opposed his signature bill on postal privatization. Many of the ousted politicians chose to form their own minor parties, and their ranks grew after the 2009 election when the LDP was trounced by the DPJ. Ozawa himself was delisted from the DPJ in 2012 (along with close to 40 faction members), because of his repeated criticisms of the leadership's handling of the March 11, 2011 earthquake and its push to increase the consumption tax. Ozawa quickly founded the People's Life First party, but he joined yet another new group – the Tomorrow Party – in December 2012.

To the extent that political expediency has dictated the pattern of party alignments, we may see further splintering. The December 2012 Lower House election suggests that the predominance of floating voters will continue to play havoc with the party system. The LDP returned to power by capturing 61 percent of the seats, compared to a paltry 12 percent for the DPJ. Many independent voters who had supported the DPJ in 2009 stayed home, resulting in a post–World War II low 59 percent turnout.[17] The most notable feature of the contest was the emergence of the Japan Restoration Party (JRP), a new grassroots party based around Hashimoto Toru, the mayor of Osaka, and Ishihara Shintaro, the governor of Tokyo. The JRP's principal priority is to increase fiscal and regulatory decentralization, although it also espouses a conservative social and foreign policy philosophy. In many ways, the JRP is akin to an urban version of the LDP, and it won 11 percent of the legislative seats by appealing to disaffected voters who had backed the DPJ in 2009. The JRP appears to be an exception to the rule that elite-led bargaining dictates party system alignment. However, its 2012 performance can be considered a

---

[17] An illustrative fact is that the LDP more than doubled its seat share despite winning 2 million fewer votes than in 2009. The DPJ, on the other hand, lost 20 million votes.

disappointment. The media had hyped the JRP as a new "Third Force" in national politics, and while the party successfully won over independent voters in metropolitan areas – the very group that had boosted the DPJ in 2009 – it is not clear if it can develop a partisan core outside of the Osaka region. The JRP is still very young, having only formed in September 2012, and so it may continue to grow in the coming years. However, its reliance on independent voters is a double-edged sword: even though the party benefited from voter disaffection with the established parties in 2012, that support can easily evaporate should independents turn against conservative politics, as they did in 2009.

The Nature of Political Party Competition: Party-Voter Linkages

Reformers in the early 1990s pursued two-party politics to emphasize ideological competition over clientelistic quid pro quos. Strategic party switching suggests that legislators are, indeed, more attentive to the electorate's ideological preferences. If candidate quality still mattered most, then there would be no need for politicians to change allegiances. Although programmatism is difficult to operationalize using existing data, some signs indicate that the old artifices of clientelism are crumbling.

First, the *koenkai*, or personal support network, of individual politicians has become less salient in elections. Whereas *koenkai* played a prominent role in the first MMM election in 1996 (Christensen 1998), electoral reform – which involved massive redistricting to transform 130 multimember districts into 300 single-member districts – severed geographical linkages between the pre-reform *koenkai* and post-reform SMDP boundaries. Taniguchi (2004) reports weaker ties between candidates and interest groups – firms, unions, neighborhood associations – in 1996 than in 1993. At the same time, Reed and Thies (2001b) argue that public financing for political parties, introduced in 1996, has enhanced the resources controlled by the party headquarters relative to individual candidates. The decline in *koenkai* appears to be particularly pronounced for new, younger politicians. Krauss and Pekkanen (2011) report that most politicians continue to develop *koenkai* to hedge against sudden drops in party popularity, but they are no longer sufficient to guarantee reelection for incumbents.

Second, factions are no longer the predominant players within the LDP. Prior to electoral reform, each faction boss would give his followers in the Diet campaign funds and election endorsements in exchange for their support in LDP presidential elections. However, single-member districts simplified candidate endorsements, because there is now only one slot per district. The availability of public campaign funds since 1996 also shifted the locus of money from factions to the party boss (Cox et al. 1999). Factions are still important for managing career advancement in the party and allocating cabinet positions, but their organizational cohesion has weakened.

Perhaps the most consequential change in the nature of party competition is the growing salience of party leaders in the media. Traditionally, LDP leaders were selected based on their proficiency at factional bargaining and negotiations. Since the 1980s, however, media coverage of parliamentary leaders has grown rapidly (Krauss and Nyblade 2005). The introduction of electoral primaries to select party leaders has further increased their visibility (McElwain and Umeda 2011). As voters pay greater attention to party leaders, the electoral benefits of leader popularity have also risen. Popular leaders are valuable to their parties, because they can generate electoral coattails: their speeches, campaign visits, and other public actions can convince independent voters to cast a ballot for their parties' candidates, even if they are indifferent to those candidates personally (Kabashima and Imai 2002; McElwain 2009).

The shift in leader salience has produced a growing emphasis on party affiliation and programmatic policies over clientelism. Reed, Scheiner, and Thies (2009) suggest that the linkage between politicians and voters has begun to shift. Even though election results have historically hinged on which parties have more quality candidates (ex-bureaucrats, ex-local politicians, celebrities), since 2005, party affiliation has proven to be a stronger predictor. McElwain (2012) adds further that elections have nationalized: as local factors such as candidate quality or levels of urbanization decline in salience, vote fluctuations are increasingly correlated across districts. Given the other corroborating evidence about the importance of parties – the media focus on party leaders, the control of political funds – this shift toward more programmatic politics in Japan appears to be decisive. Indeed, Noble (2010) examines the composition of government budgets and finds that public works redistribution – the cornerstone of the LDP's fiscal transfer program from urban to rural regions – has given way to greater emphasis on public goods such as education and social security expenditures.

CONCLUSION: VARIETIES OF PARTY SYSTEM INSTITUTIONALIZATION

Since electoral reform in 1994, we have observed numerous changes to Japanese party politics. The postwar multiparty system has seemingly consolidated into two-party competition between the LDP and the DPJ. Media coverage of politics, the institution of party subsidies, and – most importantly – the switch to a mixed member majoritarian electoral system have increased the importance of party leaders in elections, which, in turn, has shifted public debate from candidate-centered clientelism to party-centered debates.

Despite this fundamental shift in the external shape of the party system and the internal nature of the party-voter linkage, it may be misleading to state that the party system is more institutionalized. Rather, we are observing a change in institutional equilibria, which confers both advantages and disadvantages. The traditional system – built on the MMD-SNTV electoral system – prioritized strong ties between candidates and voters and generated low levels of partisan identification. These characteristics are generally seen as evidence of weaker party system institutionalization, but they also produced a very stable 1.5 party system, based on LDP single-party dominance. The new political landscape following electoral reform certainly appears to be more institutionalized, in that voters seem to care more about programmatic differences than pork-barrel redistribution. However, this new system produces extremely unstable election results and more frequent government turnover, the result, in part, of the continuing weakness of partisan identification. To the extent that difficult policy initiatives take time to draft and implement, rapid changes in government are not net positives for Japanese voters.

What has remained consistent over time, however, is the fundamental institutionalization of the party system itself. Since the late Meiji period, legislative politics has been dominated by political party competition. Once the oligarchs became actively involved in the creation and survival of political parties, parties played a crucial role in expanding the electoral franchise and engaging in interregional fiscal redistribution. While the military autocracy limited the role of parties during World War II, they quickly reemerged during the U.S. occupation. To paraphrase Schattschneider (1942) once again, Japanese politics has become unthinkable without political parties, and political parties will continue to play a critical role in the maintenance of Japanese democracy.

REFERENCE LIST

Baker, Andy, and Ethan Scheiner. 2004. "Adaptive Parties: Party Strategic Capacity under Japanese SNTV". *Electoral Studies* 23: 251–278.

Christensen, Ray. 1998. The Effect of Electoral Reforms on Campaign Practices in Japan: Putting New Wine into Old Bottles. *Asian Survey* 38 (October): 986–1004.

Christensen, Raymond. 1994. Electoral Reform in Japan: How It Was Enacted and Changes It May Bring. *Asian Survey* 34(7): 589–605.

Clark, William Roberts, and Matt Golder. 2006. Rehabilitating Duverger's Theory: Testing the Mechanical and Strategic Modifying Effects of Electoral Laws. *Comparative Political Studies* 39(6): 679–708.

Cox, Gary W. 1997. *Making Votes Count: Strategic Coordination in the World's Electoral Systems.* Cambridge: Cambridge University Press.

Cox, Gary W., Frances McCall Rosenbluth, and Michael F. Thies. 1999. Electoral Reform and the Fate of Factions: The Case of Japan's Liberal Democratic Party. *British Journal of Political Science* 29: 33–56.

Curtis, Gerald L. 1971. *Election Campaigning Japanese Style.* Tokyo: Kodansha International Ltd.

Curtis, Gerald L. 1999. *The Logic of Japanese Politics: Leaders, Institutions, and the Limits of Change.* New York: Columbia University Press.

DeWit, Andrew, and Sven Steinmo. 2002. The Political Economy of Taxes and Redistribution in Japan. *Social Science Japan Journal* 5(2): 159–178.

Duus, Peter. 1998. *Modern Japan.* 2nd ed. New York: Houghton Mifflin Company.

Duverger, Maurice. 1954. *Political Parties: Their Organization and Activity in the Modern State.* New York: Wiley.

Fukatsu, Masami. 1995. Whither Goes the 1955 System? *Japan Quarterly* 42(2).

Fukui, Haruhiro. 1970. *Party in Power: The Japanese Liberal Democrats and Policy-Making.* Berkeley: University of California Press.

Grzymala-Busse, Anna. 2002. *Redeeming the Communist Past: The Regeneration of Communist Parties in East Central Europe.* Cambridge: Cambridge University Press.

Ibuki, Ken. 2005. *Nihon Seitou-Shi: 1980–1947.* Tokyo: Shougaku-sha.

Johnson, Chalmers. 1982. *MITI and the Japanese Miracle: The Growth of Industrial Policy, 1925–1975.* Stanford: Stanford University Press.

Kabashima, Ikuo. 1984. Supportive Participation with Economic Growth: The Case of Japan. *World Politics* 36(3): 309–338.

Kabashima, Ikuo. 1999. An Ideological Survey of Japan's National Legislators. *Japan Echo* (August).

Kabashima, Ikuo, and Imai, Ryosuke. 2002. Evaluation of Party Leaders and Voting Behavior: An Analysis of the 2000 General Election. *Social Science Japan Journal* 5(1): 85–96.

Kato, Junko. 1998. When the Party Breaks Up: Exit and Voice among Japanese Legislators. *American Political Science Review* 92(4): 857–870.

Katzenstein, Peter J. 1996. *Cultural Norms and National Security: Police and Military in Postwar Japan.* Katzenstein, Peter, J. (Ed.) Ithaca: Cornell University Press.

Kitschelt, Herbert, and Steven I. Wilkinson (Eds.). 2007. *Patrons, Clients, and Policies: Patterns of Democratic Accountability and Political Competition.* Cambridge: Cambridge University Press.

Kobayashi, Yoshiaki. 1997. *Politics in Japan, 1955–1993.* Tokyo: University of Tokyo Press.

Kohno, Masaru. 1997. *Japan's Postwar Party Politics.* Princeton: Princeton University Press.

Krauss, Ellis S., and Benjamin Nyblade. 2005. "Presidentialization" in Japan? The Prime Minister, Media, and Elections in Japan. *British Journal of Political Science* 35: 357–368.

Krauss, Ellis S., and Robert J. Pekkanen. 2011. *The Rise and Fall of Japan's LDP: Political Party Organizations as Historical Institutions.* Ithaca: Cornell University Press.

Laakso, Markku, and Rein Taagepera. 1979. "Effective" Number of Parties: A Measure with Application to West Europe. *Comparative Political Studies* 12(1): 3–27.

Lijphart, Arend. 1994. *Electoral Systems and Party Systems: A Study of Twenty-Seven Democracies 1945–1990.* Oxford: Oxford University Press.

Lipset, Seymour M., and Stein Rokkan (Eds.). 1967. *Party Systems and Voter Alignments.* New York: Free Press.

Mainwaring, Scott, and Timothy R. Scully. 1996. *Building Democratic Institutions: Party Systems in Latin America.* Stanford: Stanford University Press.

Masumi, Junnosuke. 1985. *Postwar Politics in Japan, 1945–1955.* Translated by L. E. Carlile. Berkeley: Institute of East Asian Studies, UC Berkeley.

McElwain, Kenneth Mori. 2008. Manipulating Electoral Rules to Manufacture Single Party Dominance. *American Journal of Political Science* 52(1): 32–47.

McElwain, Kenneth Mori. 2009. How Long Are Koizumi's Coattails? Party-Leader Visits in the 2005 Election. In S. R. Reed, K. M. McElwain, and K. Shimizu (Eds.), *Political Change in Japan: Electoral Behavior, Party Realignment, and the Koizumi Reforms.* Palo Alto: Walter H. Shorenstein Asia-Pacific Research Center.

McElwain, Kenneth Mori. 2012. "The Nationalization of Japanese Elections." *Journal of East Asian Studies* 12(3): 323–350.

McElwain, Kenneth Mori, and Michio Umeda. 2011. Party Democratization and the Salience of Party Leaders. *Social Science Japan Journal* 62(1): 173–193.

Miyake, Ichiro, Yoshitaka Nishizawa, and Masaru Kohno. 2001. *55-Nen Taisei-ka no Seiji to Keizai: Jiji Yoron-chousa Data no Bunseki.* Tokyo: Bokutaku-sha.

Narita, Norihiko. 1996. Seiji Kaikaku Houan no Seiritsu Katei: Kantei to Yotou no Ugoki wo Chuushin to shite. *Hokudai Rippo-Katei Kenkyukai Shiryou* 46(6).

Noble, Gregory W. 2010. The Decline of Particularism in Japanese Politics. *Journal of East Asian Studies* 10: 239–273.

Noguchi, Yukio. 1997. The Persistence of the 1940 Setup. *Japan Echo* 24 (Special Issue): 81–89.

Ohmiya, Takeo. 1992. *Senkyo-Seido to Giin-Teisuu no Zesei.* 3rd ed. Tokyo: Hokuju Shuppan.

Ordeshook, Peter, and Shvetsova, Olga. 1994. Ethnic Heterogeneity, District Magnitude, and the Number of Parties. *American Journal of Political Science* 38(1): 100–123.

Pedersen, Mogens N. 1979. The Dynamics of European Party Systems: Changing Patterns of Electoral Volatility. *European Journal of Political Research* 7(1): 1–26.

Pempel, T. J. 1998. *Regime Shift: Comparative Dynamics of the Japanese Political Economy.* Edited by P. Katzenstein. Ithaca: Cornell University Press.

Przeworski, Adam, and John Sprague. 1986. *Paper Stones: A History of Electoral Socialism.* Chicago: University of Chicago Press.

Pyle, Kenneth B. 1996. *The Japanese Question: Power and Purpose in a New Era.* 2nd ed. Washington, DC: AEI Press.

Rae, Douglas. 1967. *The Political Consequences of Electoral Laws.* New Haven: Yale University Press.

Ramseyer, J. Mark, and Frances McCall Rosenbluth. 1993. *Japan's Political Marketplace.* Cambridge, MA: Harvard University Press.

Ramseyer, J. Mark, and Frances McCall Rosenbluth. 1995. *The Politics of Oligarchy: Institutional Choice in Imperial Japan.* New York: Cambridge University Press.

Reed, Steven R. 1991. Structure and Behavior: Extending Duverger's Law to the Japanese Case. *British Journal of Political Science* 29(1): 335–356.

Reed, Steven R., and Ethan Scheiner. 2003. Electoral Incentives and Policy Preferences: Mixed Motives Behind Party Defections in Japan. *British Journal of Political Science* 33: 469–490.

Reed, Steven R., Ethan Scheiner, and Michael F. Thies. 2009. Party-Centered, More Volatile: New Ballgame in Politics. *The Oriental Economist* 8–9.

Reed, Steven R., and Michael F. Thies. 2001a. The Causes of Electoral Reform in Japan. In M. S. Shugart and M. P. Wattenberg (Eds.), *Mixed-Member Electoral Systems: The Best of Both Worlds?* New York: Oxford University Press.

Reed, Steven R., and Michael F. Thies. 2001b. The Consequences of Electoral Reform in Japan. In M. S. Shugart and M. P. Wattenberg (Eds.), *Mixed-Member Electoral Systems: The Best of Both Worlds?* New York: Oxford University Press.

Richardson, Bradley M. 1997. *Japanese Democracy: Power, Coordination, and Performance.*, New Haven: Yale University Press.

Saito, Jun. 2009. "Pork Barrel and Partisan Realignment in Japan." In S. R. Reed, K. M. McElwain, and K. Shimizu (Eds.), *Political Change in Japan: Electoral Behavior,*

Party Realignment, and the Koizumi Reforms. Palo Alto: Walter H. Shorenstein Asia-Pacific Research Center.

Samuels, Richard J. 2007. *Securing Japan: Tokyo's Grand Strategy and the Future of East Asia*. Ithaca: Cornell University Press.

Sartori, Giovanni. 1976. *Parties and Party Systems: A Framework for Analysis*. Cambridge: Cambridge University Press.

Schattschneider, E. E. 1942. *Party Government*. New York: Farrar and Rinehart.

Scheiner, Ethan. 1999. Urban Outfitters: City-Based Strategies and Success in Post-war Japanese Politics. *Electoral Studies* 18: 179–198.

Scheiner, Ethan. 2006. *Democracy without Competition in Japan: Opposition Failure in a One-Party Dominant State*. Cambridge: Cambridge University Press.

Schlesinger, Jacob M. 1997. *Shadow Shoguns: The Rise and Fall of Japan's Postwar Political Machine*. New York: Simon and Schuster.

Taagepera, Rein. 2002. Implications of the Effective Number of Parties for Cabinet Formation. *Party Politics* 8(2): 227–236.

Takenaka, Harukata. 2002. *Senzen Nihon ni Okeru Minshuka no Zasetsu: Minshuka Tojo Taisei Houkai no Bunseki*. Tokyo: Bokutakusha.

Taniguchi, Masaki. 2004. *Electoral Reform in Japan*. Tokyo: University of Tokyo Press.

Thies, Michael. 1998. When Will Pork Leave the Farm? Institutional Bias in Japan and the United States. *Legislative Studies Quarterly* 23(4): 467–492.

Woodall, Brian. 1996. *Japan under Construction: Corruption, Politics, and Public Works*. Berkeley: University of California Press.

Woodall, Brian. 1999. The Politics of Reform in Japan's Lower House Electoral System. In B. Grofman, S.-C. Lee, E. A. Winckler, and B. Woodall (Eds.), *Elections in Japan, Korea, and Taiwan under the Single Non-Transferable Vote: The Comparative Study of an Embedded Institution*. Ann Arbor: The University of Michigan Press.

Yamanouchi, Yasushi, J. Victor Koschmann, and Ryuichi Narita (Eds.). 1998. *Total War and "Modernization."* Ithaca: Cornell University Press.

5

Long in the Making: Taiwan's Institutionalized Party System

Tun-jen Cheng and Yung-ming Hsu*

INTRODUCTION

By any criteria, major parties and the party system in newly democratized Taiwan are fairly institutionalized. The two leading parties – the Nationalist Party or Kuomintang (KMT) and the Democratic Progressive Party (DPP) – are enduring, resilient, and well embedded in their support bases. Factions have existed within each party, and factional conflict can be acute, but factionalism has not undermined party coherence or identity. During the extended period of democratic transition, the two leading parties – at times, in accord with their affiliated partners – have competed fiercely but principally at the ballot box rather than in the streets or under the shadow of democracy-inhibiting forces such as the military or insurgents. By and large, the two political camps have accepted electoral competition as the only legitimate avenue to power, the emotional confrontation on the street over the contested result of the presidential election in 2004 being a notable exception. The magnitude of electoral volatility has been small by comparison with other young democracies in the region. Typically, the dominant KMT ebbed and the DPP flowed, both incrementally rather than abruptly. With the deepening of democratization, electoral volatility increased, especially in recent elections, but the spikes were transitional, caused by a major electoral reform that has effectively eliminated all small parties.

This chapter advances two main arguments. First, parties and the party system in Taiwan had already attained a high level of institutionalization even before the onset of the democratic transition. Such institutionalization was primarily attributable to the authoritarian regime's decision in 1950 (a historic critical juncture) to govern postwar Taiwan via empowering the hegemonic party and holding local elections under a peculiar electoral system, instead of relying primarily on coercion.

* Thanks are due to Allen Hicken, Erik Kuhonta, Kimberley Manning, Jim Glassman, and other participants of the Montreal workshop for their comments on earlier versions of this chapter.

At some point, local elections created "trickle-up" pressure, leading the regime to experiment with controlled national elections, permitting electoral competition for newly created legislative seats. In due course, patterned and orderly interaction between the hegemonic party and the democratic opposition began to take shape. By the time that Taiwan embarked on its democratic transition in 1986, the prototype of a stable party system was already in place. The newly democratized Taiwan seems to have had prefabricated building blocks for a party system that was ready to use after quick assembling. Taiwan's electoral system for county council, provincial assembly, as well as legislative elections – one dubbed the SNTV (single, nontransferable vote in multiple-seat districts) system and one that functions like a proportional representation system, detailed later – was also a piece in the puzzle. Initially, the electoral system was adopted to help the authoritarian regime neutralize the challenge from the opposition in local elections, but it turned out to be a device that nurtured both the hegemonic and opposition parties into the two stabilizers of the party system in newly democratized Taiwan.

Second, a stable party system may be a reflection of, but is not caused by, the most salient social and political cleavage based on national identity in democratic Taiwan. Effectively institutionalized, the two leading parties have been able to define and redefine social and political cleavages more adroitly than any other, and typically smaller and newer, parties. This means that the two leading parties were locked in a game of issue framing and electoral mobilization, a game in which no other parties were able to become serious contenders. The organizational capacity that the two leading parties had developed before the advent of Taiwan's democracy turned out to be their comparative advantage over new entrants in the electoral market. The timing and mode of Taiwan's democratic transition further helped the two parties to consolidate their "first-mover" position vis-à-vis the newcomers.

In the following analysis, we first demonstrate how institutionalized the party system is in newly democratized Taiwan. Following Mainwaring and Scully's definition of institutionalization, we examine the magnitude of electoral volatility, the degree of party fragmentation, the scope of party identification, the legitimacy of elections, and the cohesiveness of the two leading parties in Taiwan. We then examine the factors that contributed to the making of Taiwan's institutionalized party system. We dwell on the impacts of social cleavages, the timing and mode of Taiwan's democratic transition, and Japan's and the KMT's authoritarian legacies on Taiwan's party system.

In the concluding section, we briefly address the consequences of the institutionalization of the party system in Taiwan. The highly institutionalized party system seems to have reinforced political polarization, an undesirable consequence in the eyes of many observers. The two leading parties are so deeply entrenched in their support bases and are so far apart on some fundamental issues that political polarization appears to be unbridgeable. The 2007 electoral reform – probably the most consequential one in the history of democratic Taiwan – may force the two parties to cater to the middle-of-the-road voter and to moderate their polar positions in the ideological spectrum. But this institutional effect is yet to be seen.

STABLE, CONSOLIDATED, AND ENTRENCHED

A hegemonic KMT – led by elites from the mainlander community (who accounted for 15 percent of the total population and retreated to Taiwan in the late 1940s, the other 85 percent being largely those Taiwanese whose ancestors came ashore centuries ago) – monopolized political power for four decades in authoritarian Taiwan, permitting only two friendly (viz. satellite) parties to exist and cracking down on any effort to organize a new political party. As soon as the ruler of the KMT regime embarked on democratic reform in 1986, opposition parties began to mushroom. The newly established Democratic Progressive Party, formed by a unified opposition movement called Tangwai (literally, political activists outside the KMT), led the pack to become the principal opposition party until 2000. The emerging political party system, however, seemed to be highly institutionalized right from the beginning.

For more than two decades since the advent of democracy on the island, the two leading parties have largely dominated the newly created electoral space. Only in one legislative election (held in 2001) was one of the two leading parties (the KMT) relegated to the third-party position. The party system certainly was neither static nor evolving neatly in linearity. Its permutations had ranged from a one-party dominant system to a multiparty system,[1] but it quickly settled for a two-plus party system and now is heading for a two-party system, with the KMT and the DPP as the good old protagonists.

In embarking on Taiwan's democratic opening in 1986, the KMT as the hegemonic party had sequenced and paced change in such a way as to provide breathing space to transform itself into the dominant party, as did the Liberal Democratic Party in Japan, thereby continuously staying in control of power. For a short while, this transformation appeared to be proceeding according to the script. The KMT government opened one-third of the legislative seats for electoral competition in 1986, pensioned off the lifetime legislators – predominantly KMT members – in 1990, phased out the functional constituencies (professional associations capable of electing representatives to legislative bodies) – in which the KMT had built-in advantages – in the mid-1990s,[2] and permitted direct presidential elections beginning in 1996. While taking time to liberalize the polity, the KMT lost no time in reinventing itself. Throughout the second half of the 1980s, the KMT assiduously promoted indigenous, local elites to its leadership ranks. Its new leadership outmaneuvered the KMT's conservative wing to endorse various agendas for Taiwan's democratic change, permitting the party to present itself as a reformist, all-inclusive political force rather than as the conservative and exclusive political force, as depicted by the DPP.

---

[1] Clark 2003: 92–99.
[2] The People's Action Party in Singapore has been as masterful as the KMT in Taiwan in recrafting electoral systems to both include and contain political opposition in political processes. See Netina Tan's chapter in this volume (Chapter 3).

However, as the distinction between the DPP's reformist banner and the KMT's conservative banner began to blur, the DPP astutely injected the issue of Taiwan's relationship with the mainland into electoral politics. In 1990, various factions of the DPP reached an agreement to enshrine the cause of Taiwan's self-determination for its own future in the party's constitution, effectively redefining the DPP as being not only a political reformist party but a nation-building one as well. Not only did this issue cement the ties among various DPP factions, but it also sent a strong signal to voters that the DPP identified with Taiwan and Taiwan only, and that it would turn Taiwan into a normal (viz. *de jure* independent) nation that, with the consent of the majority of Taiwan's people, could be permanently separated from the mainland. In due course, as Taiwanese identity deepened and Chinese identity weakened, the DPP benefited electorally from turning the Taiwan independence versus unification with mainland China (TI-UM) issue into a salient political debate in newly democratized Taiwan. For the KMT, this issue quickly triggered an implosion within its ranks, as some KMT elite were staunchly for unification with the mainland, whereas others were for *de facto* separation.[3] Twice, splinter groups bolted from the KMT to form new parties, the New Party in 1993 (a party for pro-unification elite) and the People's First Party (PFP) in 2000 (a party for those elite who were not happy with the KMT's murky stand on the unification issue and with the KMT's flawed nomination system that was said to be grossly tainted by "black and gold" elements – organized crime and corrupt political bosses). Also in 2000, a small number of KMT elite left and formed a small party called the Taiwan First Alliance in 2001 that is ideologically closer to the DPP. In addition, numerous social groups active in labor rights and environmental movements also formed their own small new parties and fielded candidates in a few legislative (but not presidential) elections. Hence, for a short while, there was a semblance of a multiparty system in the landscape of newly democratized Taiwan.

However, of these new parties, only the PFP deserves the title of "significant third party," thanks to its maverick leader, but it held that title only briefly after the 2001 legislative elections. As soon as the KMT began fine-tuning its stand on the TI-UM issue to try to underscore its Taiwan identity (although without rejecting Chinese identity), cleaning up the black and gold elements, improving and codifying its candidate selection system, and drastically expanding intraparty democracy (for direct election for party leadership and for competitive but indirect election of half of the central standing committee members), the defection to the PFP stopped and, indeed, as the 2004 presidential election approached, many PFP rank-and-file members were all too ready to rejoin the KMT.[4] To the extent that the New Party and the PFP were actively contending for legislative seats, they tacitly or explicitly coordinated with the KMT to avoid fratricide. When it came to presidential, county magistrate, and mayoral elections

---

[3] Cheng and Hsu 1996: 137–173.
[4] For an analysis of the KMT's resiliency, see Cheng 2006: 367–394.

(and for that matter, legislative politics), the splinter parties typically were in a united front with the KMT. Similarly, the Taiwan First Alliance effectively functioned as a junior partner of the DPP on nearly all political occasions, hoping to gain legislative seats at the expense of the KMT or its junior partners, avoiding competition with the DPP candidates for legislative election, and throwing its full weight to the DPP nominees for presidential, county magistrate, and mayoral elections. The three splinter parties, essentially vote mobilizers rather than spoilers of the two leading parties, the KMT and the DPP, also shared a tendency to lose steam after they ran through a couple of electoral cycles. Social movements turned small parties, notably the Greens and the Workers' Party, were basically a flash in the pan, never putting any dent in Taiwan's party system. Thus, the moment of Taiwan's multiparty system was brief and transient. What has really emerged is a party system that can be called a two-plus system, the KMT and the DPP being the constants, orbited by a very small set of splinter parties.

The first indication of Taiwan's stable, consolidated, and entrenched party system is low electoral volatility. In Table 5.1a and the accompanying figure, we track electoral volatility through eight legislative elections from 1986 to 2012 in newly democratized Taiwan. The average volatility rate of the seven observations is 8.39 percent, a low score by cross-national comparison, indicating that an overwhelming number of Taiwan voters have remained glued to leading parties, and that democratic transition in Taiwan has featured a soft landing (rather than collapse or evaporation) of the hegemonic KMT and a gradual ascent of the DPP. There are two spikes of volatility, a modest 12.5 percent swing for the 2001 election, and a more significant 22.07 percent swing for the 2008 election. The 12.5 percent swing was caused by the PFP's strong electoral performance – recall that the PFP was formed by a substantial number of former KMT members in 2000. As discussed earlier, the bulk of the PFP elite had rejoined the KMT after one electoral cycle.

The second spike is also an exceptional episode. In the 2008 general election, nearly all small parties lost their electoral fortune, thanks to crucial electoral reform carried out in 2007 that replaced the proportional representation–like SNTV system with a mixed member system (MMM) that primarily uses the single-member, plurality-based system to elect the overwhelming majority of legislators (details on the two electoral systems follow). This electoral reform compressed the living space for small parties, and the result of post-reform elections has led most small-party elites to contemplate the option of merging with either the KMT or the DPP. Electoral volatility for future legislative elections is expected to return to the normal low level. As for presidential elections, Table 5.1b and the accompanying figures show the consistent leveling off trend. Admittedly, there have been only five elections and, hence, four observations of this genre. But the very fact that the number of competing parties has been dropping from four (1996) to three (2000) to two (2004, 2008, and 2012) suggests that volatility has become a simple function of electoral swings between the two leading parties.

TABLE 5.1A. *Volatility of Taiwan's Legislative Elections (1986–2012)*

Years	1986~2012
Number of Elections	9
Volatility: 1st and 2nd elections	6
Volatility: Last election	6.07
Average Volatility	8.39

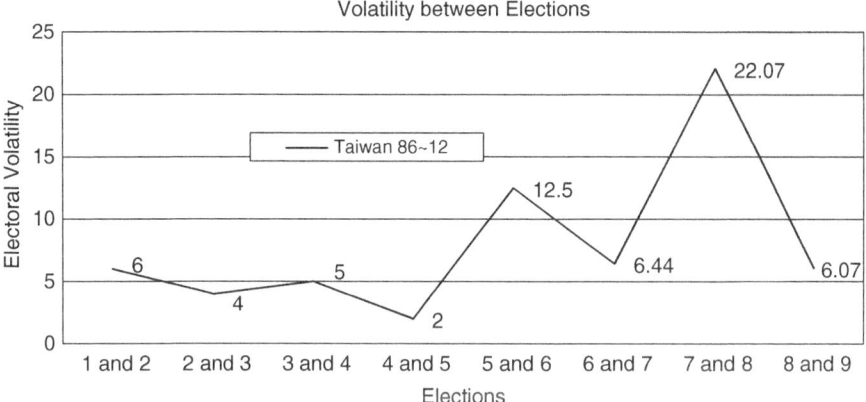

Source: Computed from the data provided by the Central Election Commission.

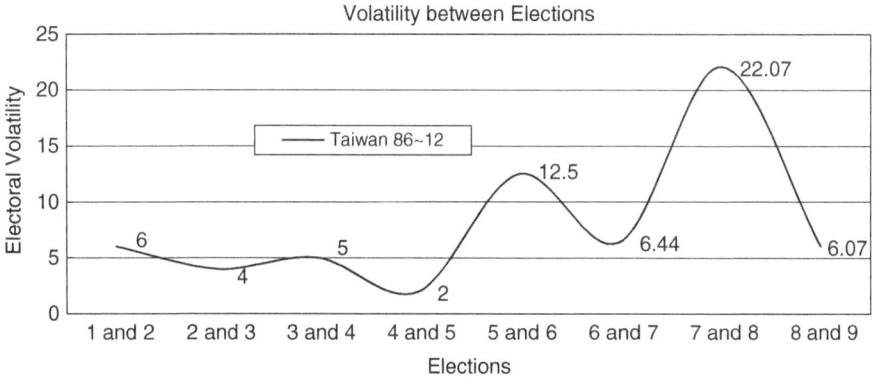

Source: Computed from the data provided by the Central Election Commission.

The low level of party fragmentation is the second indication of Taiwan's highly institutionalized party system. The scores listed in Table 5.2 show how fractionalized the party system has been in Taiwan. Instead of using the Rae index (which ranges from zero to one, zero suggesting the existence of one party only, one suggesting that there are as many parties as there are

TABLE 5.1B. *Volatility of Presidential Elections in Taiwan (1996–2012)*

Years	1996~2012
Number of Elections	5
Volatility: 1st and 2nd elections	24.54
Volatility: Last election	5.33
Average Volatility	12.31

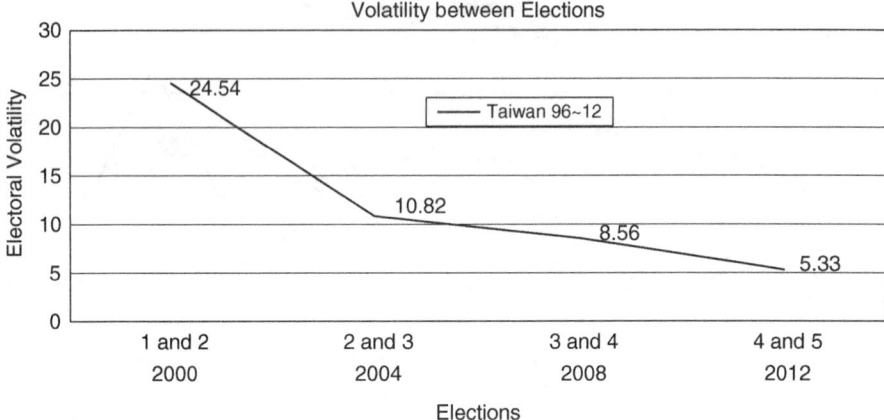

Source: Computed from the data provided by the Central Election Commission.

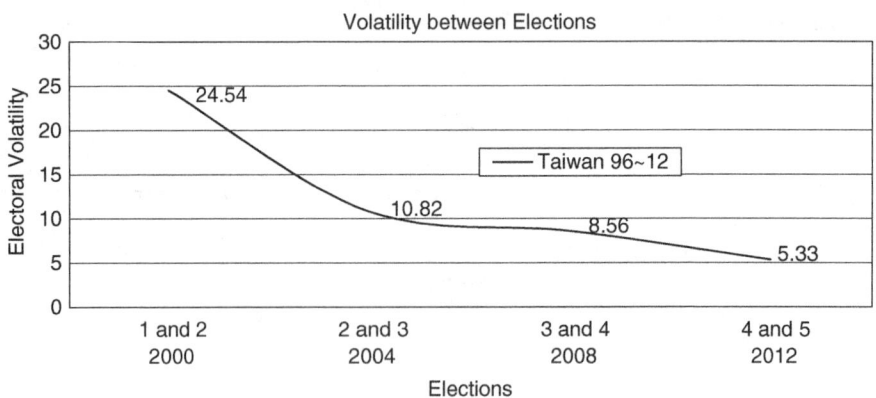

Source: Computed from the data provided by the Central Election Commission.

candidates), we use the Laakso-Taaegepera index that is easily visualized, as the score indicates the number of parties. Table 5.2 identifies an ebb-and-flow pattern and a secular trend. The pattern is that the party system becomes more fragmented during legislative elections and less so during presidential

TABLE 5.2. *Party Fractionalization in Taiwan: The Laakso-Taagepera Index*

	Nv	Ns
1992 Legislative Election	2.49	2.32
1995 Legislative Election	2.91	2.62
1996 Presidential Election	2.71	1.00
1998 Legislative Election	2.97	2.45
2000 Presidential Election	2.91	1.00
2001 Legislative Election-A	4.10	3.47
2001 Legislative Election-B	2.30	2.17
2004 Presidential Election	2.00	1.00
2004 Legislative Election-A	3.79	3.19
2004 Legislative Election-B	2.38	2.19
2008 Legislative Election-A	2.29	1.51
2008 Legislative Election-B	2.25	1.51
2008 Presidential Election	1.94	1.00
2012 Legislative Election-A	2.31	2.04
2012 Legislative Election-B	2.22	1.99
2012 Presidential Election	2.09	1.00

Notes:
1. The presidential election is normally held in March, and the legislative election in December. The timing for the legislative election has been shifted toward January, and the three-year electoral cycle has been expanded to a four-year one to be more synchronized with the presidential election.
2. The Laakso-Taagepera Index N_v is based on the parties' vote shares. The formula is $N_v = 1/\Sigma V_i{}^2$ where V_i is the vote proportion of the ith party. Index N_s is based on the parties' seat shares, using the same formula. The 2001-A and 2004-A indexes are based on a calculation of the vote spread across five parties (DPP, TSU (Taiwan Solidarity Union/Taiwan First Alliance), KMT, PFP, and the New Party), plus a nonpartisan group. The 2001-B and 2004-B indexes calculate the spread across three groups, the Pan Green (DPP and TSU), the Pan Blue, (KMT< PFP, and the New Party) and a nonpartisan group.
3. Using the Laakso-Taagepera index, N = 1 if there is only one party in the system; N = 1.72 if the two parties split the votes 70:30; N = 2 if the two parties split the votes 50:50; N = 2.7 if the three parties split the votes 40:40:20; N = 3 if the three parties split the votes equally by one-third of the total.
Source: Computed by the authors based on data provided by the Central Election Commission.

elections (the two types of election are nonconcurrent).[5] But even during legislative elections, the effective number of parties rarely has exceeded three, the 2001 election being the exception, obviously because of the formation of the PFP by defected KMT elites. This lends support to our assertion that Taiwan's party system has been a two-plus party system. But the declining trend of party fractionalization – irrespective of which type of election we want to focus on – also suggests that a stable two-party (and only two) system is clearly in the making. This leads us to the third indication of party system

---

[5] For ebbs and flows, see Cheng and Hsu 2007: 56–82.

institutionalization in Taiwan, which is that the same two leading parties have remained the anchor of the system.

The two leading parties have remained constant. They have not changed their names, emblems, or fundamental party platforms, and new parties have never replaced them as the main players in the political market (again, the 2001 election being a notable exception). As mentioned, three new parties formed from clusters or splinters of the two leading parties, but the two parties each serve as the center around which these new parties had orbited and into whose nuclei they are now being reabsorbed. The DPP was born as the opposition party and slowly built its strength, while the ruling KMT was never completely routed. Their electoral fortunes may ebb and flow, but they remain the two biggest brands with which the majority of Taiwan voters have been identifying. Table 5.3 provides time series data on party identification in democratic Taiwan. Aside from a brief interregnum from 2000 to 2002 (that can be dubbed the PFP historical moment), the KMT consistently has been identified as the party of one-third of the electorate. The DPP's identifiers have steadily grown in number, inching up from a single-digit level to a high of 20 percent of all voters. Nonidentifiers, or the independents, clearly have shrunk in number; their representation of the voting public has declined rather steadily from 60 percent to a mid-30 percent level. The decrease of independents seems to dovetail with the increase of identifiers with the DPP, hinting that more independents have become comfortable revealing their partisan preference. Put together, more than 55 percent of the electorate are party identifiers, and 40 percent are independents. The two leading parties and their affiliates have also been successful in luring the independents to their camps during elections, leaving other political parties or groupings out in the cold. The high level of party identification with the two leading parties and their affiliates indicates that Taiwan's party system has a certain boundary that a third party or any party based on individual leadership is unable to enter.[6] The high party ID level in Taiwan – close to the level in the United States but far above those in the European polities,[7] probably also suggests that the two parties are well rooted in society and that Taiwan voters – while often disgusted with partisan fighting

---

[6] We are indebted to Eric Yu for this point.

[7] According to Clay Clemens, there is a real debate about the utility of party ID as a concept in Europe. For decades, people such as Helmut Norpoth have argued that party ID is a Michigan invention with relevance solely to politics in the United States, given the evolution of parties not based on social cleavage. Others make the point that European voters identify more with a social subcultural milieu out of which one or more parties spring, and voters within that subculture may feel free to switch parties (e.g., Communist to Socialist, or Liberal to Conservative); moreover, those parties may well change and morph over time or even be supplanted (e.g., Catholic Center to CDU) without losing voters. That being said, surveys have never shown very high party ID in Europe, even when electoral volatility was low and voters tended to more consistently back their own subculture's party(ies) (e.g., in the 1950s to the 1980s). Now, of course, electoral volatility is rising, and there are more shifts, more new parties, and so on. But most political scientists still do not see that – since they never really saw party ID as strong; they see declining party ID as a collapse

TABLE 5.3. *Party Identifiers for the Two Camps (KMT-Centered Blue and DPP-Centered Green)*

Year	KMT	PFP	NP	Blue	DPP	Green	Independent
1992a	34.60			34.60	2.70		62.80
1992b	33.80			33.80	5.40		60.80
1994b	29.00		5.60	34.60	12.10		53.30
1995a	30.50		7.60	42.60	10.50		46.80
1995b	30.00		8.40	38.40	13.00		48.10
1996a	30.90		10.20	41.10	13.90		45.30
1996b	34.80		9.10	43.90	11.20		44.90
1997a	25.90		7.30	37.10	18.30		48.40
1997b	24.20		6.00	30.20	15.80		54.00
1998a	28.10		4.50	32.60	20.70		46.70
1998b	30.30		3.50	33.50	21.20		44.90
1999a	32.80		4.00	36.80	21.20		41.90
1999b	35.30		3.30	38.60	23.20		38.20
2000a	23.10	6.30	2.90	32.30	25.80		41.90
2000b	14.50	17.50	1.00	33.00	26.60		40.30
2001a	14.70	17.00	0.90	32.60	25.60		41.70
2001b	15.00	14.10	0.90	30.00	24.00	25.50	44.40
2002a	14.40	14.80	0.40	29.60	25.90	27.50	43.00
2002b	18.90	13.40	0.70	33.00	24.80	26.50	40.40
2003a	23.50	12.90	0.60	37.00	22.40	24.30	38.70
2003b	21.40	11.20	0.90	33.50	25.10	27.20	39.30
2004a	21.10	8.90	0.50	30.50	28.20	31.00	38.50
2004b	28.00	6.60	0.50	35.10	28.10	29.90	35.00
2005	26.90	3.70	0.50	31.10	20.50	20.50	48.40
2006 (Taipei)	39.60	1.80	2.20	43.60	24.30	25.40	31.00
2006 (Kaohsiun)	29.60	1.60	0.05	31.25	29.50	30.60	38.15
2008a	35.90	0.00	1.20	37.10	23.30	24.10	38.80
2008b	34.30	1.30	1.50	37.10	26.30	27.00	35.90
2010 (Taipei)	47.20	0.60	1.50	49.30	24.60	25.00	25.40
2010 (Kaohsiun)	28.00	0.40	0.20	28.60	31.50	31.70	39.60
2010 (Taichung)	36.10	0.60	0.10	36.80	23.40	23.50	39.60

Note: The KMT, the PFP, and the New Party (NP) combine to form the blue camp; the DPP and Taiwan First Solidarity Alliance are the members of the green camp. Blue and green are the colors of KMT's and DPP's emblems, respectively.

in the parliament – have no qualms entrusting the two leading parties as the articulators and carriers of their interests and ideological preferences.

The fourth indicator – a qualitative one – of party system institutionalization in Taiwan is that the legitimacy of competitive process has been fairly established.

of the old milieu bonds and evermore individualization of voter preference, subject to short- term influences (campaigns, economy, candidates, and the like).

The two leading parties have negotiated nearly all aspects of democratic change, including the steps and timetable for dismantling the authoritarian structure, seven rounds of constitutional amendments, rationalization of electoral districts, and the change of the electoral system itself. Small parties were invited and present, sometimes in disagreement with what the two leading parties had hammered out, but never boycotting the decisions. After each election, the loser's consent typically is given. One notable exception was the 2004 presidential election, in which the outcome, a razor-thin vote differential, was heatedly contested and indeed sparked mass protests and prompt sit-ins.[8] But in the end, the judicial solution prevailed, which makes this incidence more like the United States in 2000 rather than post-Thaksin Thailand. As Christopher Anderson and others expressed it, "How losers respond to their loss ... affects the legitimacy and viability of democratic institutions."[9] Taiwan's competitive party system seems to have passed, at least barely, "the loser's test." A military coup was never accomplished, unlike Thailand, or attempted, unlike the Philippines. Whichever party comes to power has been able to command military, intelligence, and other national security organizations. Ideology-oriented issues – often emotionally charged and blown out of proportion in public discourse – are also dealt with electorally. Whichever party comes to power is able to change history textbooks and rename controversial historical sites (e.g., the Chiang Kai-shek memorial was renamed Democracy Square under the DPP government, but the decision was reversed under the current KMT government).

The cohesion and internal discipline of the two autonomous leading political parties are the final indicators – also qualitative ones – of party system institutionalization in Taiwan. The two parties are neither loosely knitted political groupings, nor front desks for their leaders. Party headquarters for the KMT and the DPP draft platforms, conduct surveys, manage candidate selection for national and local elections and select their own leadership according to codified procedures, and chart strategies for legislative battles. Party switching and the creation of new parties are not common. The two parties have grassroots organizations in society as well as card-carrying rank-and-file members. The KMT has close to 1 million card-carrying members, close to 60 percent of them paying their dues regularly and, hence, eligible to participate in the party primary and party elections for chairperson and party delegates. The DPP's card-carrying members are less than one-tenth of the KMT's, but nearly all of them are extremely active members, participating in the intraparty democratic process. The two leading parties can and do nurture the reputation of their labels and political brand names. A party label is not simply a flag of convenience for candidates. There are factions all right, but party headquarters are typically able to determine party candidates and have been able to discipline the members who deviate from the important party line.

---

[8] For this episode, see Cheng and Liao 2006: 81–102.
[9] Anderson, Blais, Donovan, and Listhaug 2005: 2.

WHAT MOLDED TAIWAN'S PARTY SYSTEM?

The literature on Taiwan's electoral politics is replete with analyses of how ethnic and national identity cleavages have combined to largely determine the structure of partisan competition and shape the party system on the island.[10] Sub-ethnic distinctions have existed in postwar Taiwan between the Taiwanese (85 percent of the population, and early immigrants from the mainland) and the mainlanders (15 percent of the population, coming to the island with a retreating KMT regime in the late 1940s). Most mainlanders have Chinese identity and are the staunchest supporters of the KMT, a party that in its distant past, swore to return to the mainland. It subsequently insisted on preserving the status quo and avoided the hard choice between independence and unification. The KMT currently sees unification with the mainland as an option for Taiwan's future. The DPP by and large is a party for those Taiwanese who adhere primarily to Taiwanese identity and with aspiration for *de jure* Taiwan independence. Ethnic identity (Chinese vs. Taiwanese) and national identity (independence vs. unification) being powerful predictors of Taiwan's electoral choice, it would seem plausible to argue that identity cleavages created a very stable, highly inelastic, and seemingly enduring party system in democratic Taiwan.

However, it is too simplistic and mechanical to attribute the institutionalization of Taiwan's party system to the existence of identity-based political cleavages. Our criticism is based on three observations. First, ethnic and national identity in Taiwan has been changing and may even be in flux; yet, Taiwan's party system has been stable. Ethnic identity is acquired, formed, and mutable. Many of the 15 percent of the population demographically classified as the mainlanders regard themselves as Taiwanese, whereas many of the 85 percent of the population demographically classified as Taiwanese claim some Chinese identity. Fewer and fewer people in Taiwan self-identify as simply Chinese (as of 2014, less than 10 percent of the total population).[11] Szu-yin Ho and I-chou Liu show that more people who previously self-identified as Chinese now hold double identity as both Chinese and Taiwanese, whereas probably as many double-identity people now see themselves as simply Taiwanese (today, close to 40 percent of the total population for each of these two categories). Moreover, ethnic identity and national identity are not coterminous. A person can perceive him- or herself as Chinese but not support unification across the Taiwan Strait. A person self-defined as Taiwanese may support either Taiwan independence or unification with the mainland. A stand on unification versus independence may reveal one's beliefs and values, but it can also be based on a cost-benefit

---

[10] For example, Shyu 2002; Sheng and Chen 2003.

[11] Ho and Liu 2003. It should also be noted that the binary designations, Taiwanese vs. mainlander, have lost their political saliency. The political category of Taiwanese has been long redefined to include all those residing in Taiwan, irrespective of the timing of their immigration into the island. In particular, mainlanders are now defined as "new" Taiwanese.

assessment, which can change according to security and economic conditions across the strait. Thus, if the party system had been primarily a function of identity cleavages, then the changing ethnic identity and a fluid national identity should have destabilized Taiwan's party system.

Second, ethnic and national identities were not the salient political issue at the beginning of Taiwan's democratic transition; they were turned into one at some point, and their saliency may be attenuating now. What initially underlay the partisan cleavage in democratizing Taiwan was the push for and resistance to political reform. The DPP adroitly introduced the TI-UM issue into electoral politics in 1990. Had the DPP highlighted workers' welfare or environmental protection instead of, or even in addition to, the TI-UM issue, the party system would have evolved differently; conceivably, an issue-oriented multiparty system would have developed. Beginning in 2007, with the secular economic slump on the island, the KMT has been able to use cross-strait economic exchanges (avoiding political confrontation with China and, hence, benefiting from China's economic expansion) as the prime issue to override the identity issue. The emerging political cleavage now seems to be between supporters and opponents (or skeptics) of Taiwan's economic integration with China.

Third, while political parties attempt to define the salient issue for electoral competition, voters sort themselves along party lines with respect to the salient issues. The sorting mechanism is an ongoing process.[12] Political parties must fine-tune their positions on the issue dimensions of the day, so as to regroup. The stable and resilient party system in Taiwan hinges on the two leading parties' capacity to manage Taiwan's ethnic and national identity cleavages, or whatever new cleavage that may come into being.[13] The two leading parties have been able to inject issues to shape the political fault line and fine-tune their positions on the issue space to create competitive edges over each other. By highlighting the issue of political reform in the 1980s, the DPP or its predecessor drew a line between the reformists who wanted to dismantle the authoritarian political order as soon as possible and the conservative force that wanted to resist, delay, slow down, or minimize democratic change. The lineup cut across sub-ethnic lines, as many mainlanders were core elements of the *tangwai*, the predecessor of the DPP. The KMT has been able to turn around to follow the DPP to embrace the reformist cause, to cobble together a broad coalition across the sub-ethnic groups to become the bridge and convergence point, and now to present itself as the

---

[12] Communication with Eric Chen-hua Yu, July 29, 2009. See Yu 2008.
[13] Indeed, comparing Taiwan with other democracies in the region, one may suggest that social cleavages do not appear to be a good predictor for party system institutionalization. The party system can be institutionalized in societies without deeply entrenched social cleavages such as in Japan and the United States, while it is very loose and fluid in societies with deeply entrenched social cleavage, such as South Korea (where regional divide is historically embedded) or Thailand (where the urban-rural divide seems unbridgeable). The key factor for party system institutionalization lies more in the development of political parties and less in the pattern and depth of social cleavages.

entrusted party capable of reconciling with Taiwan's formidable adversary, mainland China. The DPP was able to adapt itself as well, from initially being a reformist political force to a party for the cause of Taiwan independence, and this party is now in the midst of redefining itself as a Taiwan-first party that seeks to firmly but gracefully deal with, rather than confront, the mainland. More and more people (including even DPP supporters) have aligned with the KMT's position about cross-strait economic exchanges. Likewise, if the DPP is able to adjust or should the KMT's policy for economic exchanges with the mainland turn sour, the public may switch back to support the DPP.

How did democratic Taiwan get a fairly institutionalized party system? We suggest that the party system in Taiwan had been fairly institutionalized even before the advent of democracy. In a sense, the democratic transition formalized and legalized the two-bloc competition that was already long in the making. The incremental process of institutionalization began when the authoritarian regime began to institute local elections. In addition, the choice of a peculiar electoral system called SNTV (see later discussion) for the authoritarian regime to run local elections and eventually national elections helped institutionalize a *de facto* party system.

The KMT as the ruling party was initially born as a nation-building party in the 1910s, modeled after the Communist Party, with cell-like organization, a guiding ideology, membership, and centralized leadership. As the nation-building party, it awarded itself a sort of political entitlement, assumed a mission of tutoring the polity for constitutional democracy, superimposed itself onto the government, and began its long journey of political hegemony. The party, however, was only barely anchored in a narrow geographical and social base (landlord and bourgeoisie in the lower Yangtze River delta). In 1949, the KMT lost the civil war to the Chinese Communist Party on the mainland and relocated to an island. There, the KMT quickly went through a party reform – essentially bridling factionalism, cleaning up its membership, launching a multi-tiered cadre-training program that would last for decades – and reorganized its party bureaucracy to pair with and, hence, oversee the majority of state and social organizations. The KMT leadership then consigned technocrats to the task of land reform (1951–1953), by which the party extended its arms into the rural sector. Technocrats were then assigned the task of industrial development, turning an agrarian society into an industrial one at a pace with which its party bureaucrats were barely able to keep abreast.

Economic transformation under developmental authoritarianism in South Korea and Taiwan, a contrast with predatory authoritarianism in many other places, is a story told many times.[14] Less dwelt on was how the authoritarian order was ensured in these two newly industrialized nations. Unlike the South Korean military junta that mainly used coercion, often via intelligence apparatus, to neutralize political dissidents, the KMT regime from early on in postwar

---

[14] The literature is huge. For a definitive study, see Evans 1995.

Taiwan had intended to mainly, certainly not exclusively, rely on its own party organization to govern. Coercion was used as well in Taiwan, but more significantly, the party-state interfaced with the politically disgruntled in electoral space at the subnational level. A national-level election under the auspices of the KMT regime was first held in 1946 on the mainland and in Taiwan, a year after World War II ended. After its defeat by the CCP on the mainland and its relocation to Taiwan in 1949–1950, the KMT suspended national elections indefinitely because of a national emergency. Local elections – held in pre–World War II Taiwan on a limited scale under Japanese colonialism – not only were allowed to resume but also to quickly expand to the provincial level.

Why did the KMT regime not suspend local elections altogether?[15] First, local elections were a good way for an émigré regime to govern an unfamiliar society. Elections provided local elites with an arena within which to compete among themselves – indeed, a safety valve to vent whatever grievances they might have harbored after highly redistributive land reform. Local elections were a mechanism for the KMT to divide and rule and to co-opt local elite. The electoral system adopted was the SNTV system, a perfect design for the party organization to serve as coordinator among competing local elites.[16] Second, local elections allowed the KMT party regime to establish a democratic façade, helping keep Taiwan's affiliation with the liberal democratic camp and secure the support of the United States, especially during the first two decades of the Cold War era. Capped at the provincial assembly level, local elections could not possibly dislodge the KMT from the provincial government, not to mention the national government. Still, subnational elections on Taiwan were a showcase when compared to those on the other side of the strait.

Local elections in Taiwan were comprehensive, institutionalized, and quite real. They have been held regularly for both executive and representative elections at the township and county levels since 1950, and for the provincial assembly beginning in 1951. They were real in that they were fairly competitive, and non-KMT candidates could and did win. As Table 5.4a and Table 5.4b show, the candidate-to-seat ratio was consistent at 2:1 for the county councilor election and the provincial assembly elections and at about 3.5:1 for the contested seats for county magistrates and city mayors; the uncontested seats for these executive elections had decreased significantly. Prior to 1986, political

---

[15] The following draws heavily from Cheng and Lin 2007: 164–168.
[16] Under the SNTV system, a voter can cast only one ballot, but a candidate cannot transfer any votes to help elect fellow party candidates. Nomination of an optimal number of candidates and an extremely even allocation of votes among fellow party candidates are utterly essential to a party's fate in this kind of race. See Tien and Cheng 1977. The KMT party leaders with high name recognition and dense local connections were supposed to campaign only for specific party nominees and only in designated subdivisions or responsibility zones within an electoral district. That way, the KMT's votes would be evenly distributed among all viable party candidates rather than unduly concentrated on a few high-profile candidates.

TABLE 5.4A. *Direct Local Elections and KMT's (K) Performance*

	County and City Councillors					County Magistrates and City Mayors				Members of Provincial Assembly				
Year	Seats	Candidates	K Seat %	Seats Contested	Candidates	Seats not contested	K Seat %	K Vote %	Seat Bonus	Seats	Candidates	K Seat %	K Vote %	Seat Bonus
1950	814	1827	63.02	21	90		85.9	N.A.						
1951														
1952	860	1844	60											
1953														
1954	928	1579	70.8	13	38	8	90.5	71.8	18.7	57	110	84.2	68.8	15.4
1957				18	40	2	95.2	65	30.2	66	118	80.3	67.8	12.5
1958	1025	1621	64.1											
1960				13	35	8	90.5	72	18.5	73	126	79.5	65.4	14.1
1961	929	1629	62.32											
1964	907	1563	73.87	15	47	6	81	73.1	7.9	74	137	82.4	63	19.4
1968	847	1262	73.9	15	43	5	85	72.4	12.6	71	129	84.5	75.5	9
1972				11	39	9	100	78.6	21.4	73	121	79.5	68.9	10.6
1973	850	1480	73.53											
1977	857	1271	84	13	36	7	80	70.4	9.6	77	125	72.7	64.1	8.6
1981				17	56	2	78.9	59.4	19.5	77	189	76.6	70.3	6.3
1982	799	1683	80.1											
1985				18	54	3	81	62.6	18.4	77	158	76	69.8	6.2
1986	837	1472	79											
1989				19	69	2	66.6	52.7	13.9	77	157	70.1	62.1	8

(continued)

TABLE 5.4A (*continued*)

	County and City Councillors					County Magistrates and City Mayors				Members of Provincial Assembly				
	Seats	Candidates	K Seat %	Seats Contested	Candidates	Seats not contested	K Seat %	K Vote %	Seat Bonus	Seats	Candidates	K Seat %	K Vote %	Seat Bonus
1990	842	1743	77											
1997				23	80	0	34.8	42.1	-7.3					
1998	891	1952	59											
2001				23	88	0	39.1	35.1	4					
2002	897	2057	44.1											
2005	901	1689	45.4	23	76	0	60.9	50.9	10					
2009	592	935	30.9	17	54	0	70.6	47.9	22.7					

Source: Adapted from Lei (1992: 169–171); Central Election Commission.

TABLE 5.4B. *Direct Elections at National Level and KMT's Performance*

Year	The Legislative Yuan						National Assembly					
	Senior members	Seats up for grab	Candidates	KMT Seats (%)	KMT Votes (%)	Seat Bonus	Senior members	Seats up for grab	Candidates	KMT Seats (%)	KMT Votes (%)	Seat Bonus
1969	468	11	25	72.7	76	-3.3	1,399	15	29	100	79.7	20.3
1972	419	30	55	83.3	70.2	13.1	1,344	53	78	81.13	72	9.13
1975	337	37	61	81.1	78.7	2.4						
1980	309	70	218	80	72.1	7.9	1,152	76	185	80.26	66.4	13.86
1983	270	71	171	87.2	70.7	16.5						
1986	224	73	137	80.8	69.9	10.9	880	84	169	80.95	68.3	12.65
1989	150	101	302	71.3	60.1	11.2						
1991							none	219	627	78.9	69.1	9.8
1992	none	119	403	56.3	53	3.3						
1995	none	122	314	50	45.6	4.4						
1996							none	228	420	53.9	49.2	4.7
1998	none	168	382	53.6	46.1	7.5						
2001	none	168	434	29.2	28	1.2						
2004	none	168	368	33.9	32.7	1.2						
2005							none	300	686	39	38.9	0.1
2008	none	73	283	78.1	53.5	24.6						
2012	none	79	315	60.8	48.1	12.7						

Source: Adapted from Lei (1992: 167–168); Central Election Commission.

opposition quite consistently had grabbed between 30 and 40 percent of the votes in all local elections and between 10 and 30 percent of the seats.[17]

Local elections had steadily and subtly impacted the KMT party organization and the nature of political competition. As mentioned, the KMT was born as a nation-building party, akin to the Institutionalized Revolutionary Party (PRI) in Mexico and the Republican People's Party (RPP) in Turkey, following a nation-alist revolution, but it was initially organized as a quasi-Leninist party.[18] Its defeat by the CCP on the mainland during the civil war convinced its leaders of the necessity for keeping Leninist features, such as cell-like organization, vanguard party membership, and democratic centralism. However, the decision to institu-tionalize local elections compelled it to act as an electoral machine. Local elections entrapped the KMT in a protracted process of organizational change that even-tually led it to institutionalize a controlled, limited electoral competition. First, by institutionalizing local elections, KMT leaders came to rely more and more on voters' voices than on the party's internal disciplinary and auditing units to monitor and assess their cadres.[19] Voters' choices became a useful feedback mechanism for party leaders. Second, local elections nurtured the managerial types of cadres within the party and gave them political clout. These election managers were not necessarily liberal reformers, but their intraparty careers were vested in the KMT's performance of electoral processes, unlike the conservative ideologues who were primarily mindful of maintaining political stability so as to focus on the grandeur of a national mission such as retaking the mainland. The more competitive the KMT candidates, the better election results the party could achieve, and the better off these managerial cadres would be.

Local elections eventually made interparty competition more imaginable and less objectionable to the KMT leaders. The party initially allowed only individual-based, unorganized dissent, and the party indeed used coercion to prevent the formation of a new party at the turn of the 1960s. However, it did not take too much effort for various dissidents to find a way to coalesce, initially by way of dissident journals, and later on through study groups during nonelection times and informal groupings during elections, all without presenting themselves as organized political parties. But clearly they, indeed, were coordinating their actions.

The second effort to smash the opposition took place in 1979, resulting in a famous trial of the leading members of the opposition movement, a trial that not only drew attention from abroad but also unintentionally turned the opposition into an even more adhesive group. The trial publicized the common namesake of the leading wing of the opposition and integrated various generations of opposition movements into a united front called the Tangwai (the predecessor of the DPP). From that point on, the opposition functioned like a party, except in name, taking concerted action. KMT election managers, for their part, also

[17] Lei 1992.
[18] Cheng 2008.
[19] Dickson 1997: 23–35.

treated the opposition as a *de facto* rival political party, fine-tuning nomination and campaign strategies as if functioning under a two-party system. In due course, the election tally also listed the democracy movement people as a separate group right next to the KMT, rather than as part of an unorganized nonpartisan category. Its separate listing on par with the KMT gave the opposition a distinct identity. Thus, before lifting the ban on the formation of a new political party in 1987, the KMT was already facing the reality of organized opposition and *de facto* interparty competition. To paraphrase Dunkwart Rustow, the KMT and the DPP's predecessor had experienced "habituation" in norms, procedures, and expectations of "partisan" competition in an incrementally expanding electoral space that was gradually internalized.[20]

To compete with the political opposition, the KMT made efforts to hone its skills and co-opt local elites. Whereas the party center previously had had the final say about candidate selection, it experimented with various methods of identifying the potential nominees, including opinion surveys of party members, cadres' evaluations, and public opinion polls. Grassroots criticisms typically led the party to alter the candidate selection method. With the expansion of competitive elections, the KMT then set out to further indigenize and pluralize itself, as reflected in the changing composition of party members and leadership ranks. By 1986, the year that the KMT leadership agreed to let Taiwan embark on its democratic transition by lifting the bans on new parties, new press, and full-scale competitive elections, the KMT had long become an essentially Taiwanese party with two-thirds of its rank-and-file members recruited from local society, although its leadership stratum was not yet localized. By 1986, the KMT had had 34 years of experience in running local elections and 11 years of experience in running limited, but increasingly competitive and continually widened central elections.

We certainly would not want to idealize the patterned interaction between the KMT and the DPP or its predecessor in the drawn-out local elections and subsequently newly opened national elections. Prior to democratic transition, jail terms had been quite frequently imposed. In addition, the parameters of competitive elections had been changed unilaterally when the opposition performed all too well at the ballot box. The mayoralty of Taipei city, the national capital, was turned into an appointive office after the opposition had triumphed over the KMT in a few elections. Similarly, the mayoral election for Kaoshiung, the second largest city in Taiwan, was no longer up for grabs when the predecessor of the DPP came close to winning it, prompting the authoritarian KMT regime to elevate Kaoshiung to a national (vs. provincial) municipality. The democratic opposition, for its part, also had been testing the limits of the KMT regime's political tolerance, sometimes triggering suppression and repression, as vividly demonstrated in the 1979 Kaoshiung incident and the subsequent grand trial, mentioned earlier. Street confrontations between the KMT government and the DPP became even more frequent, at least initially.

[20] Rustow 1970.

However, the coercive and confrontational aspect of the interaction between the two leading political forces should not blind us from their incremental organizational adaptation and the mutual learning afforded by competitive elections. As mentioned earlier, the KMT initially allowed only individual-based, unorganized dissent and, indeed, had used coercion to crack down on opposition party organizing efforts. However, it began to tolerate and interact with opposition forces as if functioning under a two-party system. Although initially not permitted to organize, opposition elements astutely joined together by using clubs and political journals as proxies for party organizations. As soon as the political thaw began in 1986, the democratic opposition lost no time in formalizing itself and, in doing so, borrowed from the ruling party all of its organizational components, ranging from membership recruitment and the cadre system to the central committee, central executive, and central advisory systems. The DPP's organizational flowchart mimics that of the KMT, and the DPP also has portrayed itself as a catchall party, proclaiming to represent all those who value democracy and progress, an open-ended pitch that cuts across all social strata (as the nationalist KMT had been positioning itself for some time). As the opposition party began to experiment with various mixed nomination systems, blending primaries, opinion surveys, and other nomination mechanisms (Tables 5.5 and 5.6), the KMT also subsequently appropriated and improved upon what the DPP had adopted. As the DPP aggressively promoted its civil society outreach programs to befriend environmental and women's movement elite and activists, the KMT turned its attention to minorities and urban youth. In short, the two leading parties have been learning from each other about organizational development and management all along.

That the two leading political parties – the KMT and the DPP or its predecessor – had been prepositioning, interacting, and developing their organizational capacities in political society long before the democratic transition certainly suggests a path-dependent explanation of Taiwan's highly institutionalized party system. Age-old partisan competition between the two sides, however asymmetrical it had been in terms of resource distribution, largely laid the foundation for the party system in democratic Taiwan. However, Taiwan's peculiar, permissive electoral system known as SNTV, as well as the timing and mode of its democratic transition also have been conducive to the making of a stable and resilient party system.

It is often argued that Taiwan's SNTV system – a large electoral district system for representative elections (from county councilors and provincial assemblypersons to legislators) – was a party-busting device that nurtured intra-party factionalism, induced members to bolt from the party, and facilitated the formation of new parties.[21] Under the SNTV system, a district has many seats; candidates fill the seats in the order of the number of votes they receive, but a voter can cast only one ballot (rather than as many votes as there are seats), and a candidate cannot transfer any votes to help elect fellow party candidates. The

---

[21] The literature on this is expansive. See Cox 1991; Cox and Niou 1994.

TABLE 5.5. *KMT Candidate Selection for Local Elections*

Time period	Methods	Criticisms Received
1950–1951	Selection by the party center	Method was undemocratic
1954–1957	Primary (however, outcomes not released)	Method fueled factional conflicts
1957–1977	Opinion surveys of grassroots party members; party center then composed the list	KMT leadership had too much say; KMT candidates not as competitive as opposition's
1980–1986	Opinion surveys of grassroots party members; local leaders' evaluations of potential candidates	KMT leadership still had too much say
1989–1992	Closed primary	Many candidates able to mobilize party members for nomination were unable to compete with opposition
1993–1997	Closed primary and opinions survey	
2001	Closed primary and opinions survey (primary results would weigh 50%; opinion polls 50%.)	
2005–present	Closed primary and opinions survey (primary results would weigh 30%; opinion polls 70%.)	

Sources: Huang (1996: 124–125); methods used after 1997 were compiled from KMT's party documents posted on http://www.kmt.org.tw/.

smaller the district, the more an SNTV system is akin to the single-member, plurality system. The larger the district, the more PR-like the SNTV system is. The district magnitude – the number of seats from a district – in Taiwan was typically large, with 7 as the medium, and in some districts, the magnitude was as high as 14. Thus, Taiwan's SNTV system had a strong PR bent. It would allow a candidate to collect votes from a large district to win a seat, an opportunity that this candidate would not have had under the single-member district, plurality-based system. This system encouraged the formation of new parties and defections from existing parties and was probably adopted by the KMT regime to keep the opposition fragmented, as the opposition, unlike the KMT, had neither resources nor coercive mechanisms to deter defection.

However, running elections under an SNTV system poses a critical challenge to all political parties, the KMT included. Nomination of an optimal number of candidates and an extremely even allocation of votes among fellow party candidates are utterly essential to a party's electoral fate.[22] Over-nomination and

---

[22] See Tien and Cheng 1997: 14.

TABLE 5.6. *Legislative Candidate Selection Methods for the DPP (1989–2012)*

Year	Main regulations	Other regulations
1989	Coordination among contenders; if no consensus was reached, closed primary would be held.	If drafted by the party, candidacy would have to be endorsed by 50% of party members.
1992	Coordination among contenders; if no consensus was reached, closed primary would be held in each county.	
1995	Coordination among contenders; if no consensus was reached, party cadres would recommend and a closed primary would be held in each county.	Cadres' recommendation and primary would carry equal weight.
1998	Coordination among contenders; if no consensus was reached, a closed primary would be held in each county, and subsequently public opinion polls would be conducted.	Primary and public opinion polls carry equal weight.
2001	Coordination among contenders; if no consensus was reached, a closed primary would be held in each county, and subsequently public opinion polls would be conducted.	Primary results would weigh 30%; opinion polls 70%.
2004	Coordination among contenders; if no consensus was reached, a closed primary would be held in each county, and subsequently public opinion polls would be conducted.	Primary results would weigh 30%; opinion polls 70%.
2008	Coordination among contenders; if no consensus was reached, a closed primary would be held in each county, and subsequently public opinion polls would be conducted.	Primary results would weigh 30%; opinion polls 70%.
2012	Coordination among contenders; if no consensus was reached, public opinion polls would be conducted.	Opinion polls weigh 100%.

Sources: For the methods used before 2001, see Wang (2001); the methods used after 2001 were compiled from DPP party documents posted on http://www.dpp.org.tw/.

under-nomination would penalize a party as party votes might be spread too thinly, hence, wasted away rather than translated into seats. Vote division is also essential. From the perspective of a candidate, the more votes the better, as that raises one's ranking in the roster and enhances winning probability in a highly uncertain situation. Further, a candidate competes for votes not merely against other party's candidates but also against fellow party candidates. Yet, if a highly popular candidate collects all of the votes that a given party may have, this candidate will be elected with an unnecessarily high number of votes, leaving his or her fellow party candidates unelected. Another party with fewer total party votes but capable of evenly distributing these votes can win many seats, resulting in a seat bonus for this party and seat penalty for the opponent party (seat bonus and seat penalty are measured by the difference between a party's share of total seats and its share of votes). SNTV thus rewards parties that can exercise internal discipline to nominate an optimal number of candidates and can solve the problem of vote division among party candidates, while it penalizes parties that fail on both counts. The threshold for securing election can be low and the fate of candidates is highly uncertain. The coordinating function provided by a party in a condition of high uncertainty is valuable.

By controlling state resources (subsidies to the local governments), the KMT was historically able to broker deals among local faction leaders in rural areas for a time-share arrangement for nominations. If incentives failed, coercion could be used. The KMT was able to sharpen its skills in coordinating local bosses when it came to nominations. If they were not nominated, only a few KMT elite defied or bolted from the party to run as independents, drew away KMT voters, or stirred the muddy water that might have hurt the KMT's electoral fortune. Thanks to its grassroots organizations in rural areas, the state sector (especially the residential compounds of civil and military service), and educational circles, the KMT had effectively allocated its party supporters among various party candidates, a time-proven vote mobilization and division capacity that helped deter defectors. For example, the KMT was able to assign different KMT candidates to be electorally supported by a specific organizations. For example, farmer associations would be told to vote for KMT candidate A, the civilian state sector for KMT candidate B, the military state sector for KMT candidate C, then all three would be elected. If all KMT votes had been cast to support A, then B and C would have lost the race to the opposition party candidates. In addition, the KMT perfected its well-known "responsibility zone" system to prevent its candidates from practicing predatory campaigns and upsetting the party's vote-distributing plan.[23] It took the DPP or its predecessor roughly two decades to learn how to function efficiently under the SNTV system. It experimented with various kinds of nomination systems to avoid over- or under-nomination of its candidates and eventually fine-tuned vote division methods to maximize its seats (e.g., cueing its zealous supporters to coordinate among themselves, using birth dates or geography as a guide).[24] Once the two leading parties had mastered the SNTV system, they

---

[23] For the best study on this, see Liu 1990.
[24] For examples in a constituency with four seats, a party with a very high general level of electoral support, would ask its supporters to vote for this party's four candidates very evenly, those with

TABLE 5.7. DPP's Seat Bonus for Legislative Elections in Taiwan
(1986–2012)

Years	Seats	Votes	Seat bonus
1986	20	25	−5
1989	25	30	−5
1992	33	32	1
1995	35	34	1
1998	32	30	2
2001	42	34	8
2004	40	36	4
2008	18	39	−21
2012	27	44	−17

Source: Computed by the authors based on data provided by the Central Election
Commission.

acquired a competitive edge over small and new parties that would be climbing a
steep learning curve. The SNTV system hence functioned as a barrier to entry for
newcomers and, conversely, as a device that gave the two parties, in tandem, the
first mover's advantage in Taiwan's electoral landscape. The seat bonus tallies for
the KMT and the DPP illustrate this. The seat bonus for the KMT was in double-
digit percentiles before 1972, when the KMT began to open up electoral space
incrementally at the national level and organized opposition began to take shape,
indicating that the KMT was able to organize and mobilize votes to maximize
seats. The seat bonus decreased to a single-digit range afterward, indicating that
the opposition had been able to coordinate to avoid wasting votes (see Tables 5.4a
and 5.4b and Table 5.7).

In 2007, Taiwan revamped its electoral system for the legislature, replacing the
SNTV system with a mixed member district that gives voters two ballots – one for a
candidate, the other for a political party. The legislative election has also been
synchronized with the presidential election. The new electoral system for the
legislature includes a strong component of plurality-based, single-member district
seats (for 73 legislators), a lean component of at-large seats (34 party list legislators),
and a tiny portion of seats (6 legislators for aboriginal communities) using the old
SNTV formula. At-large seats are allocated proportionally to any political parties
that have received more than 5 percent of the total second ballots. This new
electoral system clearly squeezes the living space for smaller parties and favors the
leading party in the election. The single-member, plurality-based electoral formula
can turn a small lead in electoral votes into a big lead in legislative seats, especially
when a strong presidential candidate of the leading party generates coattail effects.
Such bias for the leading party was clearly manifested in the 2008 general elections

birthdates in the spring time supporting A, those in the summer supporting B, those in the autumn
supporting C and those born in the winter time supporting D. This party's votes would be evening
distributed among A, B, C, and D, getting all four candidates elected. Had this party's votes been
all concentrated in a party candidate, say A, then the other three would have lost the election.

when the KMT reemerged as a dominant party. But the new electoral system also permits the second leading party to bounce back, as an improvement of its vote share can significantly correct its share of legislative seats, especially when it has a strong presidential candidate, as shown in the 2012 general elections. Smaller parties, however, have a consistently gloomy fate under the new electoral system, as they have little chance to do well in single-member districts and may not be able to qualify for the distribution of at-large seats. In both the 2008 and 2012 elections, smaller parties were nearly wiped out, barely able to secure a few at-large seats. The new electoral system has been clearly reinforcing rather than undermining a two-party-plus system in Taiwan.

In addition to the electoral system, the timing and mode of the democratic transition also helped stabilize and consolidate Taiwan's party system. In their comparative study of democratization in Latin America and East Asia, Stephan Haggard and Robert Kaufman highlight economic conditions as a key variable determining the processes and consequences of a democratic transition. Under the shadow of economic hardship, many nations experience rupture and disturbance in the process of democratization, but Taiwan embarked on democratic change with the blessing of prosperity and seems to have been able to smoothly and gradually transform its authoritarian structure into that of a democracy. Taiwan's democratization came in the wake of impressive economic development, and its protracted political reform proceeded in economic good times. Did democratic transition under good economic conditions create some period effects and contribute to institutionalization of the party system in Taiwan? Thanks to economic prosperity, the authoritarian regime and the hegemonic party in Taiwan was in a position to take some credit for the economic accomplishments and, hence, had political capital to continue in the electoral market, unlike other parties that would be blamed for economic problems. Electorates for their part probably were more inclined to endorse stable and orderly democratic change than abrupt change and political disturbance that might threaten the prosperity they enjoyed. Thus, in Samuel Huntington's analytical category, the mode of democratic transition in Taiwan is one of transformation, rather than replacement or rupture. The protracted democratic transition in Taiwan was a process of negotiation between two leading parties, rather than an episodic cycle of popular uprising, regime collapse, and the bursting and reshuffling of a new political force. The democratic transition thus consolidated and stabilized, rather than unsettled, Taiwan's political party system. Two-party competition between the KMT and the DPP (with their respective junior and minor partners) gradually became a structural feature, while new parties such as agrarian parties, labor parties, and green parties turned out to be short lived.

CONCLUSION

Taiwan has been endowed with a highly institutionalized party system. In Korea, political parties have gone through numerous rounds of realignment and reinvention, frequently assuming new names and creating party identity crises for both party elites and the public. In the Philippines and Thailand, political parties seem to be functioning more like electoral consortia expediently put together on the eve of each election than as socially embedded organizations. In contrast, the party system in Taiwan is consolidated rather than fluid. Major parties in democratic Taiwan are few, stable, and well rooted in society and able to maintain party discipline. The political market is not chaotic or volatile.[25] The major parties are in a position to make credible commitments to each other and to their supporters.

However, there are also undesirable side effects. First, such a highly institutionalized party system in Taiwan tends to reinforce rather than alleviate political polarization. Partisan divide between the KMT and the DPP (and their respective junior partners) is deeply entrenched and hard to bridge. Under the divided government, political stalemate or gridlock is insurmountable. On power transfer, policy reversal is unavoidable. Second, partisan divide, so built into the system, at times reasserts the social cleavage between two ethnic groups, which as a result of intermarriage and identity change, seem to have become less distinguishable. Many have observed that democratic competition under a highly institutionalized party system indeed may inflame subethnic and identity conflict.[26] Taiwan seems to be no exception, although violence has usually been averted. Ethnic and identity conflicts seem to have been geared toward democratic mobilization only, and perhaps they simply denote overzealous political pluralism.[27] The 2007 electoral change was meant to moderate the polarized party system, inducing the KMT and the DPP to be less obsessed with mobilizing the base and more assiduously catering to the central middle-of-the-road voters. Will this institutional change be able to empower the independents (hitherto overshadowed by party identifiers at both ends) and perhaps loosen or even unpack the party system in Taiwan? The next few elections will provide an answer to this question and perhaps adjudicate between the institutionalist side and the historical side of the path-dependent explanation of party system change.

REFERENCES

Anderson, Christopher J., Andre Blais, Shuan Bowler, Todd Donovan, and Ola Listhaug. 2005. *Losers' Consent: Elections and Democratic Legitimacy.* Oxford: Oxford University Press.
Beissinger, Mark. 2002. *Nationalist Mobilization and the Collapse of the Soviet State.* Cambridge: Cambridge University Press.
Cheng, Tun-jen. 2003. Political Institutions and the Malaise of East Asian New Democracies. *Journal of East Asian Studies* 3(1): 1–41.
Cheng, Tun-jen. 2006. Strategizing Party Adaptation: The Case of the Kuomintang. *Party Politics* 12(3): 367–394.
Cheng, Tun-jen. 2008. Embracing Defeat: the PRI and the KMT after 2000. In Edward Friedman and Joseph Wong (Eds.), *Learning to Lose*, pp. 127–147. London: Routledge.

---

[25] For a comparative study of the four cases, see Cheng 2003.
[26] For this thesis, see Beissinger 2002.
[27] Friedman 2007: 52–53.

Cheng, Tun-jen, and Yung-min Hsu. 1996. Issue Dynamics, Opposition Factionalism, and Party Realignment. In Hung-mao Tien (Ed.), *Taiwan's Elections and Democratic Transition*, pp. 137–173. Armonk, NY: Sharpe.

Cheng, Tun-jen, and Yung-min Hsu. 2007. Party System, Coalition Politics and Cross-Strait Relations. In Peter Chow (Ed.), *Economic Integration, Democratization, and National Security in East Asia*, pp. 56–82. London: Edward Elgar.

Cheng, Tun-jen, and Da-chi Liao. 2006. Testing the Immune System of a Newly Born Democracy. *Taiwan Journal of Democracy* 2(1): 81–102.

Cheng, Tun-jen, and Gang Lin. 2007. Competitive Election. In Bruce Gilley and Larry Diamond (Eds.), *Political Change in China: Comparisons with Taiwan*, pp. 161–183. Boulder, CO: Lynne Rienner.

Clark, Caleb. 2003. Lee Teng-hui and the Emergence of a Competitive Party System in Taiwan. In Wei-chin Lee and T. Y. Wang (Eds.), *Sayonara to the Lee Teng-hui Era*, pp. 91–112. Lanham, MD: University Press of America.

Cox, Gary. 1991. SNTV and d'Hondt are "Equivalent." *Electoral Studies* 10(2): 118–132.

Cox, Gary, and Emerson. 1994. Seat Bonuses under the Single Nontransferable Vote System: Evidence from Japan and Taiwan. *Comparative Politics* 26(2): 221–236.

Dickson, Bruce. 1997. *Democratization in China and Taiwan*. Oxford: Clarendon.

Evans, Peter. 1995. *Embedded Autonomy*. Princeton: Princeton University Press.

Friedman, Edward. 2007. China's Incorporation of Taiwan: The Manipulation of Community Tensions. In Peter Chow (Ed.), *Economic Integration, Democratization, and National Security in East Asia*, pp. 29–55. London: Edward Elgar.

Ho, Szu-yin, and I-chou Liu. 2003. The Taiwanese/Chinese Identity of the Taiwan People in the 1990s. In Weic-chin Lee and T. Y. Wang (Eds.), *Sayonara to the Lee Teng-hui Era*, pp. 149–184. Lanham, MD: University Press of America.

Huang, Teh-fu. 1996. Elections and the Evolution of the Kuomintang. In Hung-mao Tien (Ed.), *Taiwan's Elections and Democratic Transition*, pp. 105–136. Armonk, NY: Sharpe.

Lei, Fei-long. 1992. The Electoral System and Voting Behavior in Taiwan. In Tun-jen Cheng and Stephan Haggard (Eds.), *Political Change in Taiwan*, pp. 149–176. Boulder, CO: Lynne Rienner.

Liu, I-chou. 1990. *The Electoral Effect of Social Context Control on Voters: The Case of Taipei, Taiwan*. Ph.D. dissertation in Political Science. University of Michigan, Ann Arbor.

Rustow, Dankwart. 1970. Transition to Democracy: Toward a Dynamic Model. *Comparative Politics* 2(2): 337–363.

Sheng, Shing-yuan, and Yih-yan Chen. 2003. Political Cleavage and Party Competition: An Analysis of the 2001 Legislative Yuan Election. *Journal of Electoral Studies* 10(1): 7–40 [in Chinese].

Shyu, Huoyan. 2002. Partisan's Territory Lines Redrawn in Taiwan: A Comparison of the Electoral Bases of the DPP, KMT and PFP. *Soochow Journal of Political Science* 14: 83–134 [in Chinese].

Tien, Hungmao, and Tun-jen Cheng. 1997. Crafting Democratic Institutions in Taiwan. *The China Journal* (37): 1–28.

Wang, Yeh-li. 2001. *Comparative Electoral Systems*. Taipei: Wu-nan [in Chinese].

Yu, Eric Chen-hwa. 2008. Dynamics of Partisanship, National Identity, and Issue Cleavages in the DPP Era. Paper presented at the Conference on Democratic Consolidation in Taiwan, Stanford University, May 30–31, 2008.

6

The Making and Unmaking of the Communist Party and Single-Party System of Vietnam

Tuong Vu

INTRODUCTION

Theorists of parties and party systems disagree about how to conceptualize communist parties and communist single-party systems. Some do not accept communist parties' claims to be "parties." Most treat communist single-party systems as a special category separate from other party systems. Not only do communist regimes allow no competitive elections, but critical differences also exist between totalitarian communist systems on the one hand and single-party authoritarian regimes on the other. In this chapter, I argue that there is merit in calling communist systems either single-party systems or single-party dictatorships. Neither concept is perfect; the appropriate use depends on context. It is also useful to separate the communist party from the state dominated by such a party, despite the high degree of overlap between the two in communist countries.

The conceptual discussion clears the ground for an analysis of the Vietnamese case, which has never been accorded in-depth treatment in the literature. Vietnam has one of the longest standing and most stable political regimes in Asia. It also has one of the few remaining communist systems in the world. I use concepts developed by Samuel Huntington to examine separately the historical evolution of the Vietnamese Communist Party (VCP) and the party systems in which it has operated.[1] Essentially the VCP as a *party* has undergone four phases: expansion (1945–1948), institutionalization (1948–1960), deinstitutionalization (1963–1986), and limited reinstitutionalization (1986–present). By contrast, Vietnam's *party system* has experienced three periods: factionalism (1945–1946), institutionalization of the single-party system (1948–1956), and deinstitutionalization (1975–present). During the war from 1959 to 1975,

---

[1] From 1955 to 1975, there were times when multiple parties were allowed in the Republic of Vietnam (South Vietnam). This chapter focuses only on North Vietnam during the civil war.

the single-party system experienced certain problems but remained well institutionalized.

The Vietnamese case illustrates the role of elite politics, violence, war, and rents (external assistance) in the evolution of single-party systems. Huntington's (1968) observation that elite polarization and revolutionary violence are crucial for the institutionalization of communist party systems is borne out in the Vietnamese case.[2] Whereas some analysts have viewed the civil war led by the VCP as catalytic of a durable party system (e.g., Smith 2005: 449), the impact of war is shown here to be ambiguous. War compelled the VCP to either develop an effective military machine or perish. For decades, this machine helped the party not only win the war but also to expand political participation by providing upward mobility to youth. As a tool of violence, the military also protected the VCP's domination over the system. But the protracted civil war caused the party to neglect economic development, to grow dependent on foreign aid, and to ossify. War legacies destabilized single-party rule in the postwar period. Finally, rents have mixed effects similar to war. The unavailability of rents in the first few years was among the factors that compelled the VCP to focus on coalition rather than organization building.[3] Rents (from the Soviet bloc since 1950) offered the VCP crucial resources to secure its domination but gradually corrupted the party and caused the party system to deinstitutionalize. The Vietnamese case suggests that variables such as war and rents are complex, and careful historical analyses rather than snapshots are required.[4]

Theories of party system institutionalization have focused only on competitive party systems and associate institutionalization with democratization. In Vietnam, institutionalization means the establishment of a totalitarian system, while deinstitutionalization is now opening up opportunities for democratization. Despite their liberal biases, these theories are useful for the study of single-party systems, as evidenced in the Vietnamese case. In contrast, theories about the breakdown of communist systems built on the Soviet and Eastern European cases have little leverage in Vietnam (Kalyvas 1999: 336–340). Economic crisis in this case led to the regime's decay but not breakdown. Political reforms in Vietnam have never come close to the (intentional or unintentional) creation of political competition as in the other socialist cases – in part because Vietnamese communists have learned the lesson from their fallen comrades in the Soviet Union and Eastern Europe.

---

[2] By "revolutionary violence," I mean systematic violence guided by ideologies and tactics aimed at restructuring the social order. Huntington's term is "class warfare."

[3] In Smith's (2005: 430) model of single-party formation, the lack of rents forces groups to work hard on both coalition and organization building with the outcome being strong and durable parties.

[4] For example, Smith's (2005: 434–439) analysis of regime formation under Suharto begins in 1965, thus missing the entire dynamic of elite polarization prior to 1965 and the consolidation of the authoritarian regime under Sukarno since 1959. These events were crucial in creating a durable regime under Suharto. For my treatment of the Indonesian case, see Vu 2010: ch. 4.

CONCEPTUAL ISSUES

Parties and Party Systems

As far as communist parties and communist single-party systems are concerned, two major disagreements exist in the literature. Huntington (1968) and Sartori (1976) accept communist parties as parties, but others disagree. Mainwaring and Scully (1995: 2), for example, define "parties" as "any political group that presents at elections, and is capable of placing through elections, candidates for public office." They derive their definition from Sartori but explicitly exclude vanguard revolutionary groups that do not compete in elections yet still call themselves parties.

On single-party systems of which communist regimes represent one variant, Sartori (1976) argues that "single-party systems" is a contradiction in name. Kalyvas (1999) agrees and suggests "one-party dictatorships" as a better concept.[5] Mainwaring and Scully's (1995: 4) definition of "party systems" as "the set of patterned interactions in the competition among parties" similarly excludes single-party systems. All these scholars oppose lumping "mono-partyism" together with "multi-partyism" because the latter operates through competition among political parties while the former does not.

In contrast, other scholars believe in the value of lumping and comparing across democratic and authoritarian systems. First, they note that parties in single-party dictatorships perform many functions that are similar to those parties in democratic systems perform. These parties also recruit and present candidates for public office and more or less aggregate social interests. Second, as Duverger argues, "there is no fundamental difference in structure between single parties and the parties of democratic regimes" (cited in Kalyvas 1999: 326). Essentially, they are modern organizations and bureaucracies.

While acknowledging that both lumpers and splitters have a point, I argue that neither term ("single-party dictatorships" nor "single-party systems") is perfect. Two levels of analysis are involved here: at one level are political regimes, and at the other are political organizations within each regime. As Table 6.1 suggests, "single-party dictatorships" is most useful when these dictatorships are compared to other kinds of dictatorships such as dominant-party, military, personal, or religious dictatorships. The problem with "single-party dictatorships" is the conflation of two levels of analysis. When we juxtapose single-party dictatorships with multiparty systems, the two are not on the same level of analysis.

"Single-party systems" is contradictory by definition because a "system" as a whole must be larger than its constitutive part. In single-party systems, the part is

---

[5] Yet, throughout his article Kalyvas chooses to use the term "one-party systems" anyway, "to avoid further confusion."

TABLE 6.1. *Parties and Party Systems*

Political Regimes	Democratic			Authoritarian/Totalitarian			
Political Organizations	Party Systems[a]			Party-State Systems[a]		Anti-Party[b] or Traditional	
	Multiparty (Indonesia)	Two-party (Philip-pines)	Dominant party (Japan)	Dominant party (Singapore)	Single-party (Vietnam)	Military (Burma)	Personalistic (Brunei)

[a] These terms are from Sartori (1976: 283).
[b] This term is from Huntington (1968: 407).

identical with the whole. Yet "single-party systems" can be useful to identify or compare the character and functions of parties in single-party dictatorships to those of parties in multiparty democracies.[6] The line separating dominant-party systems under democratic and authoritarian regimes is also a fine one, suggesting that elections are not sufficient to distinguish democratic and authoritarian regimes and that Mainwaring and Scully's definition of parties based on elections may be too vague. I thus define "party systems" simply as "the organizational structures of political competition through political parties," and "single-party systems" as "structures in authoritarian or totalitarian regimes in which power is monopolized by a dominant party or a single political party."

In addition to the debates about parties and party systems, another conceptual issue concerns the term "party-state" commonly used for communist political systems. Clearly in these systems, the party is identified with the state, and vice versa. Public office is merely "a byproduct of party office" (Sartori 1976: 44). Analytically, however, the term is not useful. Consider China as an example. As Zheng (1997: 12) argues, the Communist Party and the state are different types of political organization, each with distinctive organizational logic. Zheng shows convincingly that significant conflicts existed between the functions of the state and those of the party under Mao Zedong – the extreme example is the Cultural Revolution during which Mao mobilized the masses to viciously attack the Chinese state. More recently, Saich (2001: 105) has argued, "With the emphasis on economic development and the shift in the party's fundamental legitimacy to its capacity to deliver the economic goods, the objectives of party and state are no longer always synonymous." In this chapter, I separate the Vietnamese Communist Party (VCP) from the state.

Party and Party System Institutionalization

For Huntington (1968: 18–24), party institutionalization involves four aspects, namely, adaptability, complexity, autonomy, and coherence. Adaptability refers to a party's ability to adjust over time as its founders pass away from the scene and as the political environment changes. Complexity refers to the development of subunits and the differentiation of functions within a party. Autonomy means that a party has the capacity to make decisions independent of the pressure and control of social groups, and coherence refers to members' substantial consensus on the party's goals and procedures.

Huntington (1968: 401–403, 412) does not offer a formal definition of party systems but focuses primarily on their ability to structure the

---

[6] Sartori 1976: 283 rejects "single-party systems" and, for comparative purposes, creates terms such as "party-state systems," "party polities," and "mono-partyism" (as opposed to "multi-partyism").

participation of new groups in politics. An institutionalized party system can expand participation through the system and channel the participation of newly mobilized groups so as not to disrupt the system. The institutionalization of a party system is determined jointly by the level of political party institutionalization and by the level of political participation. Specifically, a party system is unstable if the level of participation is high but the parties in the system are only weakly institutionalized. But a low level of participation in the system weakens all political parties vis-à-vis other political institutions and social forces. In short, for a party system to remain stable and politically significant, the level of political party institutionalization must not fall too far behind the level of popular participation, and the higher both levels are the better.

While Mainwaring and Scully (1995: 4–6) accept Huntington's concept of "institutionalization" to mean "the process by which organizations and procedures acquire value and stability," their notion of party system institutionalization includes four factors: the rules and the nature of interparty competition must be stable; major parties must have stable roots in society; electoral processes and parties must be accepted as legitimate; and parties must be autonomous and well organized. Although Mainwaring and Scully discuss only multiparty systems, their concept of party system institutionalization is not too different from Huntington's approach and is, in fact, useful to think about the institutionalization of single-party systems. First, stable rules of interparty competition after all serve to aggregate interests and incorporate new groups into politics – this is political participation for Huntington. In single-party systems, the system is stable as long as new groups are incorporated into it (by means other than competitive elections). Second, stable roots of major parties indicate a high level of political participation in which most citizens identify themselves with a particular party and their political identities are salient to them. Single-party systems are, therefore, institutionalized if most people identify with the ruling party and if they participate in politics in some way to express their loyalty. Third, not only multiparty systems need legitimacy. Single-party systems also need legitimacy for single-party rule – for instance, through some form of meritocratic elitism as in Singapore or communist vanguardism as in Vietnam. Sartori (1976: 42) rightly notes that "the one party [in single-party systems] claims exclusiveness and is therefore acutely confronted with the problem of self-justification and self-assertion." Finally, there is no reason why the ruling party in a single-party system cannot be a socially autonomous and well-organized party.

In addition to conditions for party system institutionalization, another important question concerns the origins of party systems and party system institutionalization. To Huntington (1968: 412–420), the institutionalization of party systems is the final stage of a four-stage historical process in which parties and party systems are born. These four stages are factionalism, polarization, expansion, and institutionalization.[7] During factionalism, individuals and groups compete in a large number of weakly organized alliances. In the polarization stage, groups coalesce into a few relatively stable factions, and a few dominant cleavages emerge that polarize these factions. The next stage involves the emergence and expansion of political parties as they compete for power. Depending on the particular contexts, a single-party, two-party, or multiparty system may emerge in the final stage of institutionalization. Huntington does not elaborate on the institutionalization of party systems, but his theory is useful to understand the evolution of the VCP and Vietnam's single-party system to be discussed next.

THE DEVELOPMENT OF THE VCP AND THE SINGLE-PARTY SYSTEM IN VIETNAM

This section examines the evolution of the VCP and the single-party system in Vietnam. Since assuming power, the VCP has evolved through four phases. It experienced phenomenal growth in its first few years (1945–1948) and became institutionalized from 1948 to 1960. In the next phase (1963–1986), deinstitutionalization occurred as a result of intense factional struggles. Since 1986, leaders have sought to reinstitutionalize the party with limited success. Turning to the single-party system, Vietnam had many political factions in the first year following the declaration of independence in late 1945, but through a process of polarization, a single party (the VCP) came to monopolize power and institutionalized its rule over society from 1948 to 1956. The civil war (1959–1975) had mixed impact on this single-party dictatorship, which began to experience deinstitutionalization after the country was unified in 1975. I argue that this trend has continued until the present time despite the VCP's efforts to halt it.

The Vietnamese Communist Party[8]

The VCP was founded in 1930 in Kowloon under the Comintern's guidance.[9] The first leaders of the party were trained in Moscow and sought to organize it in

---

[7] In a later work, Huntington 1970: 3–48 modifies his argument, proposing three stages instead of four: transformation, consolidation, and adaptation. Whereas the four-stage framework is applicable to all party systems and the final stage (institutionalization) occurs at the birth of a party system, the three-stage framework is particularly tailored to the case of revolutionary parties and the final stage (adaptation) extends much further to the second or third generation of leaders of those parties. I find the three-stage notion not as useful as the original four-stage framework and will not use it here.

[8] For simplicity, I am using the name VCP for the entire existence of this party. The VCP had other names in some periods, such as Indochinese Communist Party (1931–1945), Marxist Study Association (1945–1951), and Vietnamese Workers' Party (1951–1976).

[9] The best account of the party in its early years is Huynh 1982.

the Leninist mold. In their view, the tasks of their revolution involved two interlocking steps: the overthrow of colonial rule and the construction of socialism. The party's strategy was to build an alliance of workers and peasants, but tactically other groups such as intellectuals and landlords were mobilized for short-term collaboration if necessary.

The party operated in secret from both inside and outside Vietnam. It led two failed rebellions (1931–1932 and 1940) and suffered from brutal repression by the colonial regime. Its first five general secretaries died young; they were either executed or died in prison. In 1941, a small group of surviving leaders set up the Viet Minh, a front to unite all Vietnamese, regardless of social classes, to fight for independence. The Viet Minh operated out of the jungle near the border of Vietnam and China. At the time, the party had a small following of a few thousand and little formal structure. In fact, in early 1945 most members were still locked up somewhere in colonial prisons, where many had spent a decade or more.

When the Japanese surrendered to the Allies in August 1945, VCP cadres, groups of Viet Minh sympathizers, and other political groups led demonstrations and took power (Tonnesson 1991; Marr 1995; Vu 2010: ch. 5). Failing to obtain Soviet support, the VCP sought to build as broad a coalition as possible.[10] The new government reflected this effort and was composed of an amalgam of political groups. The VCP had control over the major ministries and its own militia but not the entire state apparatus. Territorially, national government authority was established only in larger towns but not over the entire country. This amalgam was also reflected in party membership. Over the next few years, the VCP attracted many new members. It grew from a few thousand in late 1945 to 20,000 in late 1946. By the end of 1949, membership stood at 430,000 (Vu 2010: ch. 6). The rapid growth in membership indicated party policy during this period, which was not to be strict about the class background or ideological loyalty of new members. Central leaders had little effective control over local party branches. This resulted in fast but unfocused growth as the party sought to broaden membership without emphasizing class background and ideological loyalty. Most new members came from privileged social groups, such as educated urban elites, landlords, and well-to-do farmers. The absolute majority of members came from north and north central Vietnam with few from southern Vietnam, where the French had returned and taken effective control.

In response to this early phenomenal growth in membership, the VCP set up a party organization commission in 1948 to monitor the situation and to make membership policy. By then, VCP leaders were looking forward to the victory of Chinese communists on mainland China and the opportunity to join forces with the Chinese to fight the French. Radical leaders led by General Secretary Truong

---

[10] Stalin did not respond to Ho Chi Minh's repeated requests for Soviet assistance primarily because he was concerned that the French Communist Party would lose popular support if Indochina gained independence. See Goscha 2006.

Chinh feared the "contamination" of the party by the admission of upper-class members and called for tightening the criteria for membership and for other measures to strengthen central control. New party policy since 1948 sought to restrict the growth of membership, to expel members who came from privileged backgrounds, and to intensify ideological indoctrination for all members.

The new policy ended the period of expansion and launched the institution-alization of the party. This coincided with the Viet Minh government's joining the Soviet camp and the arrival of massive Chinese aid and advisers. By about 1960, the VCP had become more or less institutionalized if we use Huntington's four criteria of adaptability, complexity, autonomy, and coherence. First, by then the VCP could show that it had overcome numerous challenges and successfully adapted to great changes in the environment. It began as a revolu-tionary group on the fringe of the colonial society, acquired leadership of the nationalist movement, led the struggle with France for independence until winning control over North Vietnam, and successfully established its rule there. Measured by generational age, however, it is less clear that the party was fully adaptable.[11] On the one hand, by 1960 the party had adapted to leadership changes from Ho Chi Minh (1941–1950) to Truong Chinh (1950–1956) to Le Duan (1958–1986).[12] On the other, Le Duan was of the same generation as Truong Chinh, and both Ho Chi Minh and Truong Chinh remained influential in the Politburo.

Second, through successful adaptation to changing roles, the VCP had become a complex organization by 1960. The VCP now formed the core of the state, and its cadres held most public offices with differentiated roles in administration and in economic and cultural management. The party controlled a powerful military that had earlier defeated the French at Dien Bien Phu. It had nationalized most private property, including land and factories; had taken over the markets of key products; and had brought most social means of communication (newspapers and publishing houses) under state ownership. The party now had branches in most villages and urban neighborhoods in North Vietnam. The land reform (1953–1956), during which about 15,000 landlords or 0.1 percent of the population were executed, had allowed the party to overthrow old power structures in the villages and to promote loyal party cadres to positions of leadership. Party control now

---

[11] As Huntington 1968: 14 explains, "So long as an organization still has its first set of leaders, ... its adaptability is still in doubt."

[12] Ho Chi Minh's role in the party weakened in the late 1940s because he failed to obtain diplomatic recognition not only from the United States but also from the Soviet Union. Ho was criticized by some party leaders for his decision to dissolve the VCP in 1945; even though the party was never really dissolved, this decision led Stalin not to trust the VCP. See Goscha 2006 and Quinn-Judge 2005a. Truong Chinh resigned from the position of general secretary in 1956 after the party rectification campaign and the land reform went awry under his direction Vu 2010: ch. 5. He remained powerful in the Politburo, just as Ho Chi Minh remained influential even after he was gradually removed from the daily management of the state in the early 1950s.

encompassed most aspects of social life in North Vietnam, as one would expect in a communist totalitarian system.

Third, the Marxist-Leninist ideology allowed the party to claim a vanguard position above and autonomous from society. In particular, the VCP claimed to fight against feudalism and imperialism. Even before becoming firmly established in power, communist leaders had challenged powerful social forces such as landlords, first with laws to limit land rent and later with the land reform campaign. Yet the VCP was not beholden to peasants for very long: land reform was only a tactic to mobilize them. As soon as the party felt secure, it took away all land, draught animals, and tools from peasants in the collectivization campaign (1958–1960). Besides ideology, material support from the Soviet bloc since 1950 also enabled the VCP to be autonomous from society. In a society threatened by famine and exhausted after a long war, foreign aid gave the party a crucial leverage against social forces. During its first few years in power (1945–1950), the lack of support from its international allies had forced the VCP to cultivate ties with colonial elites. Material aid from the Soviet bloc enabled the party to purge those elites from the party and the government, creating a more autonomous organization in the process.

Finally, the "organizational rectification" campaign (1952–1956) that was implemented among half of party organizations from provincial level down helped strengthen the coherence of the party, the fourth criterion according to Huntington. During this campaign, which was essentially a brutal purge, most members who came from privileged class backgrounds were expelled and replaced by poor peasants. Previously, party members who came from the upper and middle classes and who made up as much as two-thirds of the party's membership did not wholly support the party's goal of building socialism. They had rallied to the party only because they wanted to fight for national independence. After the purge, the poor peasants who owed the party for their lands, houses, and jobs could be trusted to follow the party to their deaths if necessary. The cohesion of the VCP was also aided by its leaders' tireless efforts at carrying out a cultural revolution, including the systematic propagandization of Marxist-Leninist-Stalinist-Maoist thoughts, values, and methods throughout the ranks of the party and in the broader society (Ninh 2002).

By Huntington's four criteria, the VCP seemed well institutionalized by 1960. Yet within a few years, deinstitutionalization set in as the party under the leadership of Le Duan coped with new challenges in the subsequent period. Duan was from central Vietnam and had spent his career mostly in the Mekong Delta until he replaced Truong Chinh as general secretary in 1958. Duan advocated the use of violence to unify Vietnam early on, but the party adopted his views only after he rose to the top. Under his leadership, the VCP led a protracted war to defeat the government of South Vietnam that was backed by the United States. The war ended in victory for North Vietnam, but the VCP did not become a more institutionalized organization in the aftermath. Evidence is sketchy, but elements of deinstitutionalization can be detected.

First, the VCP under Le Duan (1958–1986) adapted successfully to changing circumstances in the first half of this period but later ossified. Measured by chronological age, not only did the party survive, but it also won the civil war and emerged as the unchallenged ruler over all of Vietnam by 1975. Measured by generational age, the score is mixed. The size of the Central Committee elected in 1976 tripled, allowing new blood into the top leadership.[13] At the very top, however, not until 1986 when Le Duan died was new leadership allowed to succeed the first-generation leaders.[14] From 1960 to 1976, the same 11 Politburo members of the first generation ran the party.[15] All the surviving members of the previous Politburo were retained except one.[16] New faces made up less than half of the new Politburo. Among these new members, all had been of high rank in 1960 – in other words, their elevation was no surprise.[17] First-generation leaders who were in their seventies continued to dominate the Politburo in the 1970s. Several of them died while in office,[18] and the other Politburo members of this cohort retired by the mid-1980s, but the top three still wielded tremendous influence even after they had formally retired.[19]

Measured by functional adaptability, the record is also mixed. On the one hand, the party was able to adapt to new challenges as the war against South Vietnam and the United States escalated in the 1960s. This war required the total mobilization of the North Vietnamese population and the enlistment of full support from the Soviet bloc. The VCP performed these tasks brilliantly over 15 years, leading to its victory. On the other hand, this war was not the first one led by the party, which had accumulated nearly a decade of war making just a few years earlier fighting the French. Peace, not war, was the real litmus test of the party's functional adaptability, and here the VCP failed miserably. There was little new thinking in the policy agenda of socialist construction between the 1950s and the 1970s. Despite the failure of collectivization in North Vietnam prior to unification, the party sought to replicate it in South Vietnam in the late

---

[13] The Central Committee had 44 full members and 31 alternate members in 1960 and 133 full members with no alternate members in 1976. Most full and alternate members in 1960 were retained in 1976, and new members accounted for more than half of the Central Committee in 1976.

[14] At the 5th Party Congress in 1982, several first-generation leaders (but not the most powerful ones) were replaced by younger ones. These were Nguyen Duy Trinh, Le Thanh Nghi, Tran Quoc Hoan, Le Van Luong, and Vo Nguyen Giap. They were replaced by To Huu, Do Muoi, Vo Van Kiet, Nguyen Duc Tam, and Le Duc Anh.

[15] Two died in office: Nguyen Chi Thanh died in 1967 and Ho Chi Minh in 1969.

[16] This was Hoang Van Hoan.

[17] These were Tran Quoc Hoan, Van Tien Dung, Le Van Luong, Nguyen Van Linh, Vo Chi Cong, and Chu Huy Man. Le Van Luong had been an alternate member of the Politburo since 1951 but lost this position in 1956.

[18] These included Le Duan and Pham Hung.

[19] These were Truong Chinh, Le Duc Tho, and Pham Van Dong.

1970s – to the detriment of the economy.[20] The VCP also failed to notice changes in the international environment. Proud of their victory, party leaders expected world powers to bid for their favors.[21] Reckless decisions to occupy Cambodia and ally with the Soviet Union against China (1978–1988) indicated that the party had been addicted to making war and failed to realize the need for peace after three decades of nearly continuous warfare.

Second, on complexity, the VCP had a similarly mixed performance. The party underwent tremendous expansion during the war years. Between 1960 and 1976, party membership tripled from 0.5 to 1.5 million (Dang Cong San Viet Nam, vol. 21: 491 and vol. 37: 705, 764). The number of party cells also tripled, and the number of party committees doubled in the same period. Party organizations also became less differentiated. As the entire society of North Vietnam was mobilized for war, economic, social, and cultural spheres of activity shrank tremendously. Most party and state organizations were geared toward wartime demands. Cadres acquired substantial experiences in military affairs but little else. Tens of thousands of young men and women were thrown into the battlefield every year, including new college graduates.[22] The slogan of the time "All for the front, all for victory" indicated that uniformity but not differentiation was favored as an organizational goal.[23] Uniformity helped the VCP lead the war to a successful outcome but sacrificed its complexity in the process.

After the war, the party expanded its organization to all of Vietnam and made economic development its top priority – so its complexity increased somewhat. Unfortunately, war would resume shortly and last for another decade, meaning that any gains in complexity were limited. By 1986 or eleven years after unification, the VCP still maintained an army of more than 1 million soldiers even though the percentage of military leaders in the Central Committee was lower, and some units were assigned to economic development tasks (Turley 1988: esp. 200). Nearly two-thirds of new party members recruited between 1976 and 1982 came from the army. Seventy-six percent of party members were still from North Vietnam, indicating the party's failure to expand its territorial base to the south after reunification (Thayer 1991: 21).

Regarding the third factor, autonomy, the VCP continued to dominate and be autonomous from society throughout this period. Yet there were many cracks in the edifice after 1975. First, the Marxist-Leninist ideology sounded increasingly hollow in the face of a severe economic crisis that began soon after victory in the civil war. Second, a remarkable trend has occurred since 1976, namely the expansion of the Central Committee to include representatives from state organs

---

[20] For failure of collectivization in North Vietnam, see Kerkvliet 2005. For the failure of socialist construction in North Vietnam in general, see Fforde and Paine 1987.

[21] For an astute analysis of the mind-set of party leaders at this time, see Marr 1991.

[22] Hanoi lost approximately 1 million troops in the war out of a population of about 20 million.

[23] In Vietnamese, "tat ca cho tien tuyen, tat ca de chien thang."

and provincial party branches (Thayer 1988). This expansion reflected the party leadership's desire to adapt to new circumstances, but the change opened up the possibility that the Central Committee could be made to serve the interests of sectoral and local groups rather than those of the central party leadership.[24] As will be seen later, sectoral and provincial interests have become increasingly powerful in recent years after the dominant figures of the first generation passed away from the scene and their successors in the Politburo could not command the same level of prestige and authority.

Fourth, the coherence of the VCP also declined under Le Duan. Duan formed a powerful alliance with Le Duc Tho, who was the head of the Central Organizational Commission with the power to groom and appoint party members to provincial and central leadership positions, including the Central Committee and the Politburo. Although Duan and Tho were never powerful enough to remove the other senior leaders, they monopolized power to an unprecedented extent.[25] Duan and Tho worked closely in the late 1940s in the Mekong Delta. Both were long-term Politburo members but became close after Duan assumed the position of general secretary in 1958. Their ascendancy in the mid-1960s was helped by the split in the Soviet bloc that had tremendous repercussions for all communist parties. The split pit the Soviet Union against China, resulting in intense debates in the VCP about which side it should take in the split (Bui 1995; Grossheim 2005; Quinn-Judge 2005b). Duan and Tho placed their bet with Mao, with the support or acquiescence of most Central Committee members. Based on this support, Duan and Tho carried out arrests of many high-ranking party and military leaders who did not agree with them. The arrests reportedly targeted General Vo Nguyen Giap, the minister of defense, and even though he emerged unharmed, his power was severely curbed. Although factionalism in Vietnam never approached the scale it did in Maoist China, it was significant under Le Duan and made a dent in the coherence of the VCP. As Duan's faction consolidated its grip, fear more than consensus governed intraparty relations.

While factional struggles played out secretly at the top, the base of the party showed signs of decay by the early 1970s. Two trends joined to create this situation. First, party leaders launched two main drives during the civil war to recruit new members – one in the early 1960s and the other in the early 1970s.[26] These two drives primarily accounted for the tripling of membership mentioned earlier, but similar to many campaigns in communist Vietnam, quantity ended

---

[24] The Central Committee in theory is above the Politburo, but in reality this was not the case until recently.

[25] Duan and Tho's faction included key members of the Politburo and Secretariat, including Nguyen Chi Thanh, Van Tien Dung, Pham Hung, Tran Quoc Hoan, and To Huu Nguyen 2012.

[26] Party documents referred to members recruited in the first campaign as "the January 6 Cohort" (the campaign was launched on January 6, 1960, the 30th birthday of the VCP), and those recruited in the early 1970s as "the Ho Chi Minh Cohort" (the campaign was launched in September 1970 to commemorate the first anniversary of Ho's death).

up trumping quality here. An internal report written in 1966 had already raised concerns about the quality of about 300,000 new members who had joined the VCP since 1960. In 1971, an examination of 74 factories discovered that nearly 15 percent of new members admitted since 1970 were "below the standards" set out in the Party Code, and another 19 percent were clearly "of poor quality" (Dang Cong San Viet Nam, vol. 32: 303, 443).[27] Party leaders subsequently launched several measures to improve the situation, but it was reported that expelling low-quality party members was difficult (as it was for any state bureaucrat).

The second trend responsible for the decay was the emergence of a massive informal economy in the late 1960s. As Soviet and Chinese aid streamed into North Vietnam just when living standards sharply deteriorated as a result of the war and poor economic management, an increasing number of party members engaged in corruption by selling rationed imported goods and materials on the thriving black market (Dang Cong San Viet Nam, vol. 34: 265 and vol. 35: 1, 102, 106, 112).[28] The rapid expansion of the party, the poor quality of many new recruits, and the spread of corruption eroded the coherence of the party as war protracted. A significant component of the party by the early 1970s was more interested in war profiteering or in social and political status than in making sacrifices for the revolution championed by the top leadership.

After Duan died in 1986 and Tho retired in the same year, new VCP leaders sought to reinstitutionalize the party. This process has continued for the past three decades and brought many achievements. Yet the deinstitutionalization that began under Le Duan continued on many dimensions. Reinstitutionalization has made the most progress in the criterion of adaptability. The party survived the collapse of the Soviet bloc and has achieved impressive results in economic reform. In the Politburo, the first generation and the transition generation have passed the baton to the second generation.[29] Succession has taken place rather smoothly in now regularly held national party congresses. About one-third of Politburo and Central Committee members have been replaced in each of the last five congresses. A mechanism perhaps designed to smooth out the process of succession is to allow key leaders who have retired to maintain some influence as advisers to the Politburo. Party

---

[27] It is unclear what "below the standards" and "poor quality" meant.

[28] It is ironic to read documents in which Le Duan lectured southern revolutionaries on the methods to organize political struggles in South Vietnam's urban centers, published side by side with reports about the thriving black market in North Vietnam's cities that the communist state under him was desperate to control. For an analysis of state workers involved in the black market in North Vietnam, see Vu 2005.

[29] Transition generation include such leaders as Vo Chi Cong, Chu Huy Man, Nguyen Van Linh, Do Muoi, Vo Van Kiet, and Le Duc Anh. Those of the second generation are Nong Duc Manh, Phan Van Khai, Le Kha Phieu, and Tran Duc Luong. For an account of early years of party reform, see Stern 1993.

leaders have also attended to rejuvenating the party and raising the educational level of members. Members of the Central Committee have become younger and more educated, enabling the party to lead economic development more effectively. Perhaps in response to a more complex society, greater balance of representation among various sectors – gender, age groups, party, military, economic, state, and mass mobilization organizations – has been sought in the composition of the Central Committee (Vasavakul 1997).

Adaptability can also be observed in ideological orientations. Party congresses have dropped Marxist-Leninist principles such as the dictatorship of the proletariat and the alliance of workers and peasants. Since 1991 "Ho Chi Minh thoughts" have appeared beside Marxism-Leninism as part of an official ideology. After two decades promoting a market economy, the party has recently allowed its members to engage in private businesses once deemed exploitative. From organizational to ideological matters, the VCP has veered far away from the rigidity of Le Duan's era. Still, the fundamental disposition of adaptability has been gradualism by which changes were incremental and lacked clear direction.

It is precisely this incremental adaptability that has not (yet) helped create a more complex VCP. Although the party has recovered from a membership decline in the late 1980s, most new recruits still come from the usual pool of state employees and military personnel.[30] Despite many efforts, the party has failed to penetrate new urban areas, remote districts, and private enterprises.[31] Party members can own businesses now, but owners of private businesses who want to join the party are still rarely admitted.[32] Not development but involution seems to be the trend, as the party can grow only by drawing from the state sector and the military already under its control, but not by expanding its roots into a rapidly changing society. Party leaders have launched numerous programs to rationalize the party structure so that the VCP remains relevant and effective. Current initiatives include the formation of huge blocks of party organizations based on similar functions and a pilot project to have party secretaries doubling as government executives at the local level. These institutional reforms are either too recent to evaluate or have brought only limited results.[33]

[30] From 1987 to 1991, the annual number of new recruits fell from about 100,000 to 36,000 Le 1992: 19. By 1998, the number for the first time in a decade rebounded to 100,000 Nguyen 1999: 44. By 2007, the number was about 170,000 Phuc Son 2007: 4. The total number of VCP members in 1986 was 1.8 million or 3 percent of the population Thayer 1991: 21. By 2007, there were 3.2 million members who made up 3.7 percent of the population Quoc Khanh 2007.

[31] In 2007, 0.55 percent of 20,000 private enterprises in Hanoi had a party cell Huy Thinh and Tran Hieu 2007. In Ho Chi Minh City, the rate was much lower, at 0.06 percent Cat Dien and Minh Tuan 2008.

[32] Interview with Nong Duc Manh, general secretary of the VCP. *Tuoi Tre*, April 26, 2006.

[33] See articles in *Tap chi Xay Dung Dang* [Party Building Journal] (1) and (2–3) of 2008.

Incremental adaptability is also insufficient to stem the erosion of the VCP's autonomy as it became increasingly vulnerable to corrupting social influences. We have noted earlier how corruption tied to a thriving black market became widespread among cadres in North Vietnam in the last years of the civil war. Corruption, in fact, exploded when that black market was legalized in the late 1980s. New forms of corruption have emerged since then, and one particularly detrimental form involves the selling of offices. With state agencies generating lucrative rents, party secretaries can now make fortunes by selling state positions to the highest bidders. The party secretary of Ca Mau province was sacked after it was disclosed that he accepted money in return for appointments to top positions in the provincial government. His case was never made fully public, but he turned in 100 million dong ($6,000) that someone tried to bribe him with. He also said that he could have collected 1 billion dong ($60,000) for several appointments if he had wanted.[34] This is not an isolated case. Le Kha Phieu, a former general secretary, revealed that people had tried to bribe him many times with thousands of dollars, presumably to receive favorable appointments.[35] The appointment power has turned party congresses into occasions for patronage networks to compete intensively for positions in the Central Committee, as Martin Gainsborough (2007: 13) describes,

For Vietnamese officials, the key question at a congress is whether someone you are connected to personally or through your workplace moves up or out as a result of the circulation of positions, and what this means for you, your institutions, or your family in terms of the provision or loss of protection and access to patronage. In Vietnam, holding public office gives you access to patronage which can range from access to the state budget and the ability to make decisions about how to spend public money, to the authority to issue licenses or other forms of permissions, to carry out inspections, or to levy fines.[36]

I have mentioned earlier that sectoral and provincial interests have gained greater representation in the Central Committee since 1976. In the past two decades, those interests have gained substantial power at the expense of the Politburo. Provincial leaders now form the largest bloc in the Central Committee (every province is entitled to at least one seat and each of the two largest cities could send at least two). Provincial officials also enjoy many informal channels of influence through dense patronage networks based on places of origin, family relations, or other informal ties. It is not uncommon for local governments to interpret central policies any way they like, ignore central policies with impunity, or comply only when subsidies are provided. After provinces were authorized to approve foreign investment projects up to a certain limit, they have scrambled for those projects on top of the usual competition for a share of the central

---

[34] *Ha Noi Moi* [New Hanoi], April 22, 2008 and *Nguoi Lao Dong* [The Worker], April 28, 2008.

[35] Interview with Le Kha Phieu, *Tuoi Tre* [Youth], May , 2005. He returned the money but tellingly did not authorize any investigation of those who tried to bribe him even though the law allowed the prosecution of bribe givers.

[36] See also Koh 2008.

budget.[37] The central party leadership may be more responsive to local demands than previously, but the autonomy of the party as an organization has declined.

VCP leaders see corruption as a major threat to the regime, but evidence suggests that corruption now involves the highest level, often through family links and crony networks. Patronage and corruption are eroding the party's coherence. The occasional dismissal of a Politburo member (e.g., Nguyen Ha Phan), the premature end to the term of a general secretary (e.g., Le Kha Phieu), the sudden publicizing of numerous corruption charges targeted at certain candidates for the Central Committee before a party congress (e.g., Nguyen Viet Tien) – these cases are clear evidence of patronage rivalries at work (Gainsborough 2007). The advisers (former Politburo members who have retired) have helped smooth out successions but have themselves been involved in many of those factional struggles.

In conclusion, Huntington's concept of party institutionalization has been helpful in understanding the evolution of the VCP since 1945. The party has undergone expansion (1945–1948), institutionalization (1948–1960), and deinstitutionalization (1963–1986). Since 1986, VCP leaders have launched numerous initiatives to reinstitutionalize the party, but the results have been limited. The party displays an extraordinary ability to adapt but has tended to react to challenges when they come. This reactive mentality has not helped the party become more complex and fails to shore up its declining autonomy and coherence. Next, we turn to the single-party system in Vietnam that developed jointly with the VCP.

The Single-Party System

During 1945 and 1946, Vietnam had a system that Huntington calls factionalism, a stage of political development in which political factions rather than well-organized parties compete for power. As mentioned earlier, the VCP was not able to monopolize power when it set up the Viet Minh government in late 1945. This government relied heavily on colonial elites and bureaucrats in its first year (Vu 2010: ch. 5). The colonial elites did not form any party, but they had real personal authority in the ministries they controlled (Justice, Education, Agriculture, and Economy). In the coalition with the VCP were two other groups – the Democratic Party and the Socialist Party, but these were in fact not independent organizations. They had been organized earlier by the VCP to mobilize the support of intellectuals and were controlled by the VCP for the length of their existence.[38]

In opposition to the VCP were the Vietnam Nationalist Party (VNP) and the Vietnam Revolutionary League (VRL), which had operated in southern China

---

[37] At least half of provincial governments have been found to violate national investment laws to attract more foreign investment to their provinces Pham 2007.

[38] The VCP ordered the dissolution of these parties in 1989.

since the early 1940s and were staunchly anti-communist. These parties had some popular following and their own militias. They carried out several attacks on Viet Minh governments in many provinces, but the communists were able to hold on in most places, including Hanoi. Through the mediation of Chinese nationalist generals, the communists agreed to let their rivals join the government in late 1945. The chairman of the VRL was offered the vice-presidency, and VNP leaders received the Foreign Affairs and Economy portfolios. Seventy seats in a newly elected National Assembly were set aside for those two parties. This factionalism could have developed into a multiparty system but it did not. When Ho succeeded in negotiating for French forces to replace Chinese nationalist troops in mid-1946, the VCP purged anti-communists from the government.

The single-party system was institutionalized from 1948 to 1956 while the Viet Minh government was fighting a war with the French. By 1948, Chinese communists were winning in northern China. In preparing to join forces with their Chinese comrades, Vietnamese communists launched a cultural reform campaign to strengthen members' ideological loyalty to the party (Vu 2009). At the same time, the party replaced the colonial elites who had collaborated since 1945 with its members. The process conforms to what Huntington calls "polarization" in his framework. Intense elite polarization split the nationalist movement and those not loyal to communists were eliminated, expelled, or fled to join the emerging French-supported nationalist government under former emperor Bao Dai.[39] A few non-communists served as ministers, but they had no real authority.

The land reform that employed revolutionary violence enabled the party to penetrate every village. In this campaign, the party mobilized peasants to participate in village politics while seeking to eliminate landlords systematically as a class. Fear of persecution was one of the main reasons why nearly 1 million northerners sought refuge in South Vietnam in 1954 (Hansen 2009). This systematic elimination of real and imagined rivals and enemies combined with successful leadership of the war with the French established broad legitimacy or acquiescence to single-party rule.

By 1956, the single-party system had been firmly institutionalized with the VCP's absolute monopoly of power over the North Vietnamese state at all levels of government. Organizations sponsored by the VCP, such as the Women's Association and the Workers' Union, now established branches in most economic, social, and cultural activities. Managers of collective farms doubled as government officials performing local administrative roles. These organizations mobilized people to participate in the system through education, production, services, and national defense. Rival organizations, such as churches, private businesses, independent media, and other private associations, were either suppressed or absorbed into state organizations.

[39] This later became the Republic of Vietnam under Ngo Dinh Diem.

The war against South Vietnam from 1960 to 1975 necessitated the total mobilization of the North Vietnamese population. As the economy stagnated, the war helped the VCP channel popular participation through total mobilization. Millions of young soldiers were sent to fight in South Vietnam or deployed to defend North Vietnam. The participation rate was extremely high: about 70 percent of youth in their early 20s were mobilized to serve in the military until the end of the war (Teerawichitchainan 2009: 74). While schools and universities were closed or moved to rural areas to avoid bombing, opportunities to study in the Soviet bloc were available to children of the elites and some talented youth. Through a police state that maintained tight control and a massive propaganda machine portraying the VCP as the sole savior of the nation from foreign aggression, single-party rule enjoyed a high level of legitimacy.[40]

Yet, war was as harmful to the political system as it was helpful. Using war as an excuse, the Politburo under Duan delayed holding a national party congress for more than 10 years while the top party leadership aged and party organizations above the middle level ossified. As mentioned earlier, the coherence of the VCP was in decline in the early 1970s, which hurt the vitality of the single-party system. Finally, war distracted the VCP and diverted resources away from economic development. As a result, in part, of the war, the North Vietnamese economy was in shambles and came to depend heavily on foreign aid for its needs. In hindsight, this situation did not prepare the VCP for tackling postwar economic challenges.

Indeed, the Soviet bloc sharply reduced aid to Vietnam after the war, and the ensuing economic crisis did not allow much upward mobility for youth. Although the military would soon be involved in wars with Cambodia and China, these conflicts never reached the level of casualties nor required total mobilization as the civil war did. The military remained a major venue of upward mobility, but military careers were far more limited because most mobilized soldiers would be released from service in a few years. War weariness also made military services less enticing to young people and their families.[41] At the same time, harsh punishments given to former South Vietnamese soldiers and officials alienated millions of southerners (Huy Duc 2012, vol. 1: ch. 2). In addition to all these factors were agricultural collectivization and the nationalization of capitalist assets in South Vietnam. By the mid-1980s, 2 million people had fled Vietnam by boat or on foot to neighboring countries. The massive waves of refugees testified to the failure of not only the economy but also the political system. Among the refugees were many southern elites frustrated by the lack of opportunities for political participation and economic survival. The legitimacy of the VCP suffered a deep fall in this period, as evidenced in the

---

[40] For an account of the police state in North Vietnam, see Nguyen 2012.

[41] Troop desertion became a significant problem in the late 1970s Dang Cong San Viet Nam, vol. 41: 106–110.

previously mentioned drop in the annual number of new party recruits by two-thirds from 1987 to 1991.

Since market reforms began in the late 1980s, Vietnam's single-party system has experienced two phases. In the first phase, rising living standards and economic opportunities took pressure away from the political system and restored some legitimacy to single-party rule. Employment opportunities from the new market economy allowed the state to demobilize the military and fire employees in many state-owned enterprises without fearing unrest. As former Soviet republics and Eastern European states slid into chaos in the early phase of democratization, VCP leaders proudly held up single-party rule as indispensable for Vietnam's political stability and economic development. The late 1980s also witnessed the rapid passing away of the first generation of party leaders, which increased upward mobility throughout the political system.

The second phase has begun since a decade ago with the single-party system experiencing serious threats. On the one hand, mass organizations sponsored by the VCP have become irrelevant in a market economy, which takes away their ability to distribute the benefits of the planned economy to their members. These benefits were critical for these organizations to serve the regime effectively as vehicles of symbolic popular participation.[42] On the other hand, the tightly controlled VCP turned off the new middle class (intellectuals, professionals, and students) whose demands for political participation have risen (Thayer 2009).

This deinstitutionalization is, in part, a consequence of the transition away from socialism to a market economy. Before reform, Vietnam had a large state-owned sector and a marginalized, often criminalized, private sector. Because the government controlled most productive assets and commercial activities, jobs in the state sector were highly valued. This is no longer the case. Foreign investment and private companies now account for a larger share of the economy (60 percent) than the state sector (40 percent). Trade and agricultural production have been liberalized. The VCP's political monopoly is no longer supported by the economic monopoly of the state sector, which reduces the value of party membership to those Vietnamese with the ability to compete successfully in the labor market. The VCP's failure to expand its roots is also the result of policies that disadvantaged and exploited peasants to meet the needs of capitalist development. The peasantry used to be the bedrock of support for the VCP, but rural protests now break out frequently.

The VCP's shrinking monopoly of the cultural sphere helps accelerate deinstitutionalization. Rising living standards now allow many families to send their children abroad to study. These children are exposed to ideas different from the indoctrination they receive at home. The recent cases of Le Cong Dinh, who came from a solid "revolutionary family," and Nguyen Tien Trung, whose

---

[42] For the importance of rituals of participation in dictatorships, see Wedeen 1999.

father is a party member and official, attest to the danger of a Western education even for children of the elites.[43] The opening up of Vietnam to foreign trade and other exchanges has fostered the revival of religious activities. Under intense pressure from Western countries, the party has relaxed control over religions. The Internet has provided both access to information normally suppressed by the party and a virtual gathering place for dissidents to organize and publicize their anti-government views.

In the context of rising expectations resulting from economic development, the failure of the VCP to sustain its legitimacy has weakened the legitimacy of single-party rule. Until now, the party has justified single-party rule as inevitable and necessary based on the historical conditions of Vietnam. Official historiography has portrayed other political parties that once competed with the VCP for power as incoherent, misguided, corrupt, and dependent on foreign support in contrast with the VCP being a coherent, progressive, incorruptible, and independent organization. The VCP was a historical necessity if Vietnam was to gain independence and prosperity – so says official propaganda. Since economic reform, the party's refusal to fully disown socialism, the emergence of intensive patronage networks tied to foreign aid and investment,[44] and rampant corruption at all levels of government have made justifications of single-party rule sound hollow, making it difficult for the party to convincingly counter demands by dissidents for political liberalization. Those dissidents have, in fact, formed opposition parties and independent unions seeking to challenge the single-party system.

Finally, the VCP itself has undergone deinstitutionalization since the 1960s. As argued earlier, despite the efforts of second-generation party leaders to revamp the party, its autonomy and coherence have declined under market reform. Political decay is now pervasive at all levels of the organization. As the experience of the post-Stalin Soviet Union suggests, this decay does not mean that the VCP will soon collapse. Still, it contributes to the deinstitutionalization of Vietnam's single-party system.

In sum, the VCP remains more established compared to other parties in Southeast Asia, but it is today only a shadow of its former self. In the long term, the deinstitutionalization of Vietnam's single-party system is opening up possibilities for democratization.

---

[43] Dinh is a lawyer trained in France and the United States, and Trung received his graduate degree in France. Both were tried and sentenced to 7 and 5 years in prison, respectively, for conspiring against the state. For a discussion of their trials, see the Forum in *Journal of Vietnamese Studies* 5(3) 2010: 192–243.

[44] Since the 1990s, Vietnam has become increasingly dependent on Western foreign aid, investment, and markets. Public external debt (mostly official development assistance) is currently estimated to be 25 percent of GDP (31.5 percent if the private sector is included) (World Bank 2008a). Annual remittances from overseas Vietnamese are equal to about 10 percent of GDP. In 2008, for example, remittances, official assistance, and foreign direct investment amounted to nearly 34 percent of GDP (World Bank 2008b).

CONCLUSION

This chapter has argued that it is useful to compare and integrate the insights from theories about single-party systems and other party systems. Despite important differences between the two, concepts developed for competitive party systems are surprisingly applicable to single-party systems. At the same time, Huntington's concepts remain helpful in tracing the evolutionary paths of parties in single-party systems. His conception of party system institutionalization is undeveloped, but nonetheless useful if combined with theories built for competitive party systems. For single-party systems, the key insight from Huntington is to examine them in conjunction with the larger political and economic environment and with the particular trajectory of state development.

The Vietnamese case suggests a distinctive set of causes that explains the institutionalization of single-party systems. This process in Vietnam climaxed in the 1950s under conditions of intense elite polarization and revolutionary violence. From 1945 to 1956, the VCP launched several brutal campaigns to overthrow the basis of any future resistance to its rule in both urban centers and the countryside. These campaigns primarily involved the nationalization of productive assets and private media and the suppression of dissenting intellectuals. These steps secured the long-term domination of the party. Thus, the institutionalization of the Vietnamese system depended crucially on the VCP's ability not just to restrict competition but also to eliminate opposition completely and establish a totalitarian grip on society.

Unlike in some accounts of regime formation, war is found to have had an ambiguous impact on Vietnam's single-party system. War provides justifications for single-party rule and an alternative venue of political participation and upward mobility. At the same time, war incurs economic costs, encourages dependency, corrupts government, and facilitates the personal or factional monopoly of power. Rents have had a similarly complex effect in the Vietnamese case. The lack of rents from 1945 to 1950 forced the VCP to build coalitions, not organization. The fragile Viet Minh regime was consolidated (1951–1958) only when massive rents became available: rents were crucial for the VCP to be more autonomous from social elites, to defeat its foreign enemies and domestic rivals, and overall to secure permanent domination. By the early 1970s, and especially since market reform, rents have eroded the party's coherence and autonomy and hurt the legitimacy of single-party rule. Some party members now believe that a multiparty system is required to cure entrenched corruption.

Interestingly, the Vietnamese case does not follow a unilinear process by experiencing both institutionalization and deinstitutionalization. Whereas the literature has often associated institutionalization with democracy, single-party systems such as that in Vietnam display the opposite relationship. In Vietnam, as in Malaysia and Singapore (see Meredith Weiss [Chapter 2] and Netina Tan [Chapter 3] in this volume), institutionalization created a lasting authoritarian regime and deinstitutionalization is now opening up the possibility for liberalization.

The analysis of deinstitutionalization in the VCP and in Vietnam's single-party system contributes to an understanding of Vietnamese politics at this juncture. Vietnam's ruling party and its single-party system are both falling into decay, even though decay does not mean immediate or eventual breakdown (Kalyvas 1999: 333). To know when and how decay would lead to breakdown, Huntington's formula remains useful. According to this formula, stability is determined by measuring the rate of change in the demands for political participation against the rate of absorption of such demands into the political system.

The separate analysis of party and party system helps us understand more precisely what challenges await VCP leaders. On the one hand, a strong party is essential for a stable single-party regime. A cohesive VCP held the system together for decades prior to the 1970s. The deinstitutionalization of the VCP since then has accelerated the deinstitutionalization of the single-party system. As corruption penetrates the VCP, it delegitimizes not only the party but also single-party rule. In addition, the failure of the party to expand its organization into new socioeconomic spheres means conversely an increasing strength of civil society that will threaten single-party rule one day.

On the other hand, party leaders' efforts to improve the party's autonomy and coherence are important but insufficient. Whereas Vietnamese leaders seem to think that more rapid economic growth will bring greater stability, a slow or moderate rate of growth is in fact in their interest because it is less likely to whip up demands for political participation at a rate that aging party organizations cannot channel effectively. Party leaders' new justification for single-party rule is that only this system can bring political stability needed for economic development, but this justification may not suffice for warding off intense pressures from below for political participation. Nationalism as an alternative basis of legitimacy to socialism may help the party channel those pressures into the system more effectively. Last but not least, policy more favorable to peasants can help the VCP recover its once strong roots in the countryside.

REFERENCES

Bui, Tin. 1995. *Following Ho Chi Minh*. Translated by Judy Stowe and Do Van. Honolulu: University of Hawaii Press.
Cat Dien, and Minh Tuan. 2008. Nang cao chat luong doi ngu can bo trong cac doanh nghiep tu nhan o thanh pho Ho chi Minh [To raise the quality of cadres in private enterprises in Ho Chi Minh City]. *Tap chi Xay Dung Dang* [Party Building Journal] (4): 1–4. Available from http://www.xaydungdang.org.vn/Uploads/Data/2008/4/7.pdf. Accessed 20 January 2013.
Dang Cong San Viet Nam [The Vietnamese Communist Party]. 2002. *Van Kien Dang Toan Tap* [The Complete Collection of Party Documents], Vol. 21. Hanoi: Chinh tri Quoc gia.

Dang Cong San Viet Nam [The Vietnamese Communist Party]. 2004. *Van Kien Dang Toan Tap* [The Complete Collection of Party Documents], Vol. 37. Hanoi: Chinh tri Quoc gia.

Dang Cong San Viet Nam [The Vietnamese Communist Party]. 2004. *Van Kien Dang Toan Tap* [The Complete Collection of Party Documents], Vol. 41. Hanoi: Chinh tri Quoc gia.

Fforde, Adam, and Suzanne Paine. 1987. *The Limits of National Liberation.* London: Croom Helm.

Gainsborough, Martin. 2007. From Patronage to Outcomes: Vietnam's Communist Party Congresses Reconsidered. *Journal of Vietnamese Studies* 2(1): 3–26.

Goscha, Christopher. 2006. Courting Diplomatic Disaster? The Difficult Integration of Vietnam into the Internationalist Communist Movement (1945–1950). *Journal of Vietnamese Studies* 1(1–2): 59–103

Grossheim, Martin. 2005. Revisionism in the Democratic Republic of Vietnam: New Evidence from the East German Archives. *Cold War History* 5(4): 451–477

Hansen, Peter. 2009. Bac Di Cu: Catholic Refugees from the North of Vietnam and Their Role in the Southern Republic, 1954–1959. *Journal of Vietnamese Studies* 4(3): 173–211.

Huntington, Samuel. 1968. *Political Order in Changing Societies.* New Haven: Yale University Press.

Huntington, Samuel. 1970. Social and Institutional Dynamics of One-Party Systems. In Samuel Huntington and Clement Moore (Eds.), *Authoritarian Politics in Modern Society*, pp. 3–48. New York: Basic Books.

Huy Duc. 2012. *Ben Thang Cuoc* [The winning party]. Amazon Digital Services: OsinBook (online book).

Huy Thinh, and Tran Hieu. 2007. Day manh phat trien Dang trong khoi kinh te tu nhan [Pushing party growth in the private economic sector]. *Tien phong*, January 11. Available from http://vietbao.vn/Xa-hoi/Day-manh-phat-trien-Dang-trong-khoi -kinh-te-tu-nhan/70074292/157/. Accessed January 20, 2013.

Huynh, Kim Khanh. 1982. *Vietnamese Communism 1925–1940.* Ithaca: Cornell University Press.

Kalyvas, Stathis. 1999. The Decay and Breakdown of Communist One-Party Systems. *Annual Review of Political Science* 2(1): 323–343.

Kerkvliet, Benedict. 2005. *The Power of Everyday Politics: How Vietnamese Peasants Transformed National Policy.* Ithaca: Cornell University Press.

Koh, David. 2008. Leadership Changes at the 10th Party Congress of the Vietnamese Communist Party. *Asian Survey* 48(4): 650–672.

Le, Phuoc Tho. 1992. Mot so nhiem vu doi moi va chinh don Dang [Tasks to reform and rectify the party]. *Tap chi Xay Dung Dang* [Party Building Journal] (9): 1–33. Available from http://www.xaydungdang.org.vn/Uploads/Data/1992/9/2.pdf. Accessed 20 January 2013.

Mainwaring, Scott, and Timothy Scully. 1995. Introduction. In Scott Mainwaring and Timothy Scully (Eds.), *Building Democratic Institutions: Party Systems in Latin America*, pp. 1–34. Stanford: Stanford University Press.

Marr, David. 1991. Where Is Vietnam Coming From. In Dean Forbes et al. (Eds.), *Doi Moi: Vietnam's Renovation Policy and Performance*, pp. 12–20. Canberra: Department of Political and Social Change, Australian National University.

Marr, David. 1995. *Vietnam 1945: The Quest for Power.* Berkeley: University of California Press.

Nguyen, Duc Ha. 1999. Cong tac phat trien Dang nam 1998 [Work on Party growth in 1998]. *Tap chi Xay Dung Dang* [Party Building Journal] (5): 44–45.

Nguyen, Lien-Hang. 2012. *Hanoi's War: An International History of the War for Peace in Vietnam.* Chapel Hill: University of North Carolina Press.

Ninh, Kim. 2002. *A World Transformed: The Politics of Culture in Revolutionary Vietnam, 1945–1965.* Ann Arbor: University of Michigan Press.

Pham, Duy Nghia. 2007. Luat phap truoc suc ep [The law under pressure]. *Thoi Bao Kinh Te Sai Gon* [Saigon Economic Times], February 12.

Phuc Son. 2007. Kho khan va giai phap trong viec nang cao chat luong to chuc co so Dang va Dang vien [Challenges and solutions in raising the quality of local Party organizations and Party members]. *Tap chi Xay Dung Dang* [Party Building Journal] (11): 1–7. Available from http://www.xaydungdang.org.vn/Uploads/Data/2007/11/12.pdf. Accessed January 20, 2013.

Quinn-Judge, Sophie. 2005a. Rethinking the History of the Vietnamese Communist Party. In Duncan McCargo (Ed.), *Rethinking Vietnam*, pp. 27–39. New York: RoutledgeCurzon.

Quinn-Judge, Sophie. 2005b. The Ideological Debate in the DRV and the Significance of the Anti-Party Affair, 1967–68. *Cold War History* 5(4): 479–500.

Quoc Khanh. 2007. Nang cao nang luc lanh dao, suc chien dau cua to chuc co so Dang [To raise leadership capacity and fighting power of local Party organizations]. *Tap chi Xay Dung Dang* [Party Building Journal] (12): 1–7. Available from http://www.xaydungdang.org.vn/Uploads/Data/2007/12/3.pdf. Accessed January 20, 2013.

Saich, Tony. 2001. *Governance and Politics of China.* New York: Palgrave.

Sartori, Giovanni. 1976. *Parties and Party Systems: A Framework for Analysis.* Cambridge: Cambridge University Press.

Smith, Benjamin. 2005. Life of the Party: The Origins of Regime Breakdown and Persistence under Single-Party Rule. *World Politics* 57(3): 421–451.

Stern, Lewis. 1993. *Renovating the Vietnamese Communist Party: Nguyen Van Linh and the Programme for Organizational Reform, 1987–1991.* Singapore: Institute of Southeast Asian Studies.

Teerawichitchainan, Bussarawan. 2009. Trends in Military Service in Northern Vietnam, 1950–1995: A Sociodemographic Approach. *Journal of Vietnamese Studies* 4(3): 61–97.

Thayer, Carlyle. 1991. Renovation and Vietnamese Society: The Changing Roles of Government and Administration. In Dean Forbes et al. (Eds.), *Doi Moi: Vietnam's Renovation Policy and Performance*, pp. 21–33. Canberra: Dept. of Political and Social Change, Research School of Pacific Studies, Australian National University.

Thayer, Carlyle. 2009. Vietnam and the Challenge of Political Civil Society. *Contemporary Southeast Asia* 31(1): 1–27.

Thayer, Carlyle. The Regularization of Politics: Continuity and Change in the Party's Central Committee, 1951–1986. In David Marr and Christine White (Eds.), *Postwar Vietnam: Dilemmas in Socialist Develop*, pp. 177–193. Ithaca: Southeast Asia Program, Cornell University.

Tonnesson, Stein. 1991. *The Vietnamese Revolution of 1945.* London: SAGE Publications.

Turley, William. 1988. The Military Construction of Socialism: Postwar Roles of the People's Army of Vietnam. In David Marr and Christine White (Eds.), *Postwar*

Vietnam: Dilemmas in Socialist Development, pp. 195–212. Ithaca: Southeast Asia Program, Cornell University.

Vasavakul, Thaveeporn. 1997. Sectoral Politics and Strategies for State and Party Building from the VII to the VIII Congresses of the Vietnamese Communist Party (1991–1996). In Adam Fforde (Ed.), *Doi Moi: Ten Years after the 1986 Party Congress*, pp. 81–135. Canberra: Department of Political and Social Change, Australian National University.

Vu, Tuong. 2005. Workers and the Socialist State: North Vietnam's State-Labor Relations, 1945–1970. *Communist and Post-Communist Studies* 38(3): 329–356.

Vu, Tuong. 2009. "It's Time for the Indochinese Revolution to Show Its True Colours": The Radical Turn of Vietnamese Politics in 1948. *Journal of Southeast Asian Studies* 40(3): 519–542.

Vu, Tuong. 2010. *Paths to Development in Asia: South Korea, Vietnam, China, and Indonesia*. New York: Cambridge University Press.

Wedeen, Lisa. 1999. *Ambiguities of Domination: Politics, Rhetoric, and Symbols in Contemporary Syria*. Chicago: University of Chicago Press.

World Bank. 2008a. *Taking Stock: An Update on Vietnam's Recent Economic Development*. Hanoi. Available from http://web.worldbank.org

World Bank. 2008b. *Vietnam Development Report*. Hanoi.

Zheng, Shiping. 1997. *Party vs. State in Post-1949 China: The Institutional Dilemma*. New York: Cambridge University Press.

7

The Institutionalization of the Communist Party and the Party System in China

Yongnian Zheng

INTRODUCTION

For years, China scholars have been debating the sustainability of the Chinese Communist Party (CCP). Since the crackdown on the pro-democracy movement in 1989, scholars have frequently predicted the fall of the CCP. Immediately after the collapse of the Soviet Union and Eastern European communism, Roderick MacFarquhar (1991) claimed that it was only a matter of time before China would go the same way as these regimes. It seems that more radical reforms and greater openness triggered by the late Chinese leader Deng Xiaoping's southern tour in 1992 did not lead scholars to change such a deeply rooted mind-set. In 1994, Avery Goldstein (1994: 727) stated that "[a]lthough scholars continue to disagree about the probable life-span of the current regime, the disagreement now is usually about when, not whether, fundamental political change will occur and what it will look like."

Surprisingly, although the country has sustained three decades of reforms, more scholars tend to believe in the coming collapse of the communist rule. The issue of the sustainability of the CCP was raised in a recent debate on "Reframing China Policy," organized by the Carnegie Endowment for International Peace, a Washington-based think tank.[1] In the debate, two leading China experts in the United States, MacFarquhar and Andrew Nathan, presented rebuttals of each other's position, with MacFarquhar arguing that the CCP would not be able to sustain itself and Nathan taking the opposite view. According to MacFarquhar,

The [Chinese] political system is fragile ... Despite truly impressive progress in its economy, the PRC's [People's Republic of China] polity is in systemic crisis. VIP visitors to Beijing are exposed to an impressive panoply of power, but this is a fragile

[1] The Carnegie Endowment for International Peace 2007.

regime ... The problems I shall analyze [in the debate] are likely to result in a breakdown in the communist regime in years rather than decades.[2]

Some other scholars seem to share MacFarquhar's pessimistic view. For example, Susan Shirk (2007: 6–7) argued that "China may be an emerging superpower, but it is a fragile one. And it is China's internal fragility, not its economic or military strength, that presents the greatest danger ... Chinese leaders are haunted by fears that their days are numbered."

Despite these suspicions about its fate, the CCP continues to matter in Chinese politics. Today, by any measure, the CCP is the largest political party in the world. At the end of 2009, its membership reached 77.99 million, more than doubling the 37 million in 1978 when the post-Mao reform era began.[3] It rivals the population of a major nation. Were it a nation, the CCP would have ranked as the 17th most populous out of the 196 countries in the world in 2009, ahead of Iran (75.08 million) and closely behind Egypt (78.74 million). The percentage of party members in the population has increased, and it has inched up from less than 0.9 percent in 1949 when the CCP came to power to 5.72 percent in 2008. At the end of 2009, the CCP had 3.792 million grassroots organizations – 183,000 grassroots party committees (the lowest level of party committees), 235,000 general branches, and 3.734 million branches.[4]

On the surface, the CCP has by and large retained the basic features of a Leninist party. It is organized as a giant pyramid, with committees, branches, groups, and other types of party organizations both inside and outside the government. As a general rule, the party (its committees at various levels) makes major policy decisions while the government, namely the State Council, implements those decisions. The party cells embedded in the government bureaucracies ensure that the party's policies are implemented. At the grassroots level, party cells also penetrate virtually all organizations of significant size or importance in society.

So, it seems that the CCP, while facing pressing domestic challenges, is as strong as, if not more so than, when it seized power in 1949. Why has the CCP been able to survive and develop? Scholars point to the CCP's ability to adapt to changing environments. An article in *The Economist* aptly titled "The Party Goes On"[5] describes how the CCP has managed to adapt and is now "vastly more able to govern." Rather than perceiving these adaptations as a "proto-democratization of a Leninist state," the article argues that the CCP is primarily motivated by the desire to remain in power.[6]

---

[2] Ibid.

[3] The Central People's Government of the People's Republic of China 2010.

[4] As a general rule, a party committee should be set up when there are 100 or more party members; a general branch is formed when there are 50 – 100 party members and a branch when there is a minimum of three party members.

[5] The word "Party" as used by *The Economist* carries two meaning. First, it refers to the CCP as the party that has proved its numerous detractors wrong and has continued to carry on. Second, it refers to the celebratory mood (as in a party) that is still continuing.

[6] *The Economist* 2009.

Departing from the previous explanations of the CCP and following the conceptual framework of this volume, this chapter attempts to highlight how the institutionalization of the CCP has helped it survive and develop. The institutionalization of the CCP has been largely ignored or understudied in China studies. Without understanding the CCP's efforts in institutionalization, it would be difficult to make sense of how the party has survived and achieved rapid development in both party membership and organization. Furthermore, I argue that institutionalization involves the introduction and accommodation of democratic elements. In academic circles, the prevalent view is that the CCP, by its nature as a Leninist party, is not compatible with democracy. I argue that the CCP has been actively undertaking efforts to consolidate the one-party system, namely, institutionalizing its relations with other minor political parties and social organizations. During this process, the CCP has accommodated democratic elements to respond to the changing socioeconomic and political demands of the Chinese population. Of course, this does not mean that the CCP will transform itself into a political party as we have seen in the West, or that China will become a Western type of democracy. By contrast, I will point out that the ultimate goal of the CCP's efforts is not to achieve democracy per se but to ensure that it remains in power.

This chapter is divided into two parts. Part One briefly examines the theoretical arguments related to the theses of the demise of the CCP and the CCP's adaptation to changing circumstances; then it establishes an institutionalization thesis in explaining the CCP and its institutional linkages with the state and society. Part Two examines the CCP's efforts to institutionalize itself and its relations with other actors including the state, the so-called democratic parties, and society. Finally, the chapter provides concluding remarks on the CCP and its future.

PART ONE: CONCEPTUAL FRAMEWORK

THE CCP DEMISE AND ADAPTATION THESES

The growing body of literature on the CCP, broadly speaking, encompasses two schools of thought, namely, that the CCP is coming to its demise and that it is adapting for survival. Not surprisingly, a scholar can hold opposite views at different times, depending on the evidence he or she has gathered.

One group of scholars holds the pessimistic view that the CCP is on the decline, doomed to obsolescence or even collapse. These scholars often compare the CCP with other communist parties in Eastern Europe and tend to believe that the CCP will inevitably follow the fate of these communist parties. Writing in the 1980s, X. L. Ding (1994) argued that the 1989 Tiananmen crisis was the result of a legitimacy crisis precipitated by the CCP trying to liberalize the economy while preventing political reforms. This led to an intra-elite conflict between the CCP's ruling elite and the counter-elite, which was made up of politically aware members of the intellectual and professional classes. Ding demonstrates how the counter-elites were able to shake CCP rule by mounting oppositional activities through existing state institutions rather than from without (1994: 1–6).

Andrew Walder (1995) examined the unintended political consequences when the CCP chooses the path of reform and concessions as a response to declining economic performance. As a result of such a reform, Walder argued that a "quiet revolution from within" (minus the role of the citizenry) is unleashed that eventually weakens the centralized party-state structure. By "quiet revolution from within," Walder is referring to "changes in the relationship of higher to lower levels of government, in the relations between superior and subordinate within the CCP and government, and in the interests and orientations of officials within the party-state apparatus, especially in the lower reaches" (1995: 4). Yet Walder is cautious in saying that even though these changes do transform (and indeed undermine) the institutions on which the communist regime is founded, they do not lead ineluctably to any specific political outcome.

In his more recent works, Minxin Pei has argued that China is facing a crisis of governance.[7] According to Pei (2006), the power and strength of the CCP has declined drastically, as evidenced in three areas: (1) the shrinking of its organizational penetration, (2) the erosion of its authority, and (3) the breakdown of its internal discipline. Pei listed rising tension between the party-state and society and mass disenchantment with the CCP as being among the most important manifestations of what he called "decentralized predation" or "predatory autocracy."

Needless to say, Pei is only one in a long row of scholars and analysts who have maintained that the CCP is in serious decline and will wither away. David Shambaugh (2000: 36) argues that one is likely to see a "slow, methodical and continued decay" of the CCP's capacity and legitimacy to rule. Bruce Dickson (2000) maintains that the party's authority and organization are experiencing steady decay and that the reform has weakened its capacity to control the behavior of not only the vast majority of Chinese but also its own officials. Scholarly works like these, plus frequent journalistic descriptions,[8] often lead people to believe in the coming collapse of the CCP. The logic of these works is simple. The CCP will fall because it cannot meet social demands. Political parties, including communist ones, are like plants that need to adapt to changing environments to survive and develop. The CCP, however, is apparently not such an organism. As Shambaugh noted, "Leninist systems are not well equipped to respond to the changing demands and needs of society – precisely because they are intrinsically top-down 'mobilization' regimes rather than posses the feedback mechanisms to hear and respond to aggregated social needs and demands" (Shambaugh 2008: 7).

---

[7] See Pei 2002, 2006.
[8] For example, Chang (2001).

The second group of scholars, who tend to compare the CCP with other political parties in East Asia, argues that the CCP is capable of changing and adapting to the times not only to ensure its survival but also to retain its grip on power. Andre Laliberté and Marc Lanteigne (2008: 3) have opined that the challenges posed by the modernization process have "forced the CCP to seek not only new forms of accommodation, but also adaptation to political realities." They provide case studies of the challenges that the party has been able to successfully manage at the turn of the century. While Shambaugh believes in the progressive decline of the CCP in terms of its control over various aspects of the intellectual, social, economic, and political life of the nation, he also has observed that the CCP has been very active in instituting reforms within itself and within China as a result of the wide-ranging assessments drawn from the 1989 Tiananmen incident and the subsequent collapse of the communist regimes in the Soviet Union and Eastern Europe (2008: 2–3).

Within this overall framework, scholars have focused on the CCP's capability to adapt to new socioeconomic environments. Early on, Bruce Dickson argued that the CCP was in a phase that Samuel Huntington called "adaption." But Dickson also believed that unlike the Kuomintang in Taiwan, the CCP would not follow the path to democratization.[9] In his more recent work, however, Dickson (2005) contends that the initiative of the CCP to recruit private sector entrepreneurs is consistent with the evolution of other East Asian ruling parties. This initiative is an effort to adapt in order to save itself. Dickson believes that this initiative is a pragmatic, adaptive measure. The CCP's strategy of co-optation is working.

Nevertheless, Dickson (2005) continues to doubt whether the CCP is able to accommodate genuine civil society and the organized aggregation of social interests as Leninist parties are by nature intolerant and incapable of ceding such power to autonomous social groups. In her study on China's private entrepreneurs, Kellee Tsai (2007) contends that private entrepreneurs and the emergent middle class are not going to demand regime change. Her study explores a variety of adaptive informal institutions that have permitted the CCP to rebuild and sustain its rule.

It is worth highlighting some key features of this growing body of literature. First, while the CCP is analyzed, it is placed in the broader context of China's socioeconomic transformation. The analyses thus enable us to see how the CCP has responded and adapted to changing environments for survival and further development. Most analyses, however, treat the CCP as a reactive actor, not an active and proactive one. Such a perspective tends to underestimate the role of the CCP in bringing changing environments under its control.

Second, the institutionalization of the CCP has been largely ignored. The CCP has been proactive in bringing itself to a higher level of institutionalization. Without the CCP's great efforts at institutionalization, it is difficult to

---

[9] See Dickson (1997, 2008).

understand how it has been capable of adapting to changing socioeconomic transformation.

Third, the CCP's efforts to accommodate democratic elements have been underestimated. Scholars simply assume that the CCP, by its nature as a Leninist party, is incompatible with democracy and are not prepared to make sense of how the CCP has utilized democratic elements to achieve a greater degree of institutionalization. In this chapter, I contend that whereas accommodating democratic elements does not mean that the CCP will become a full-fledged Western democracy, such efforts do help in its institutionalization. More importantly, the case of the CCP underscores one of the main points of this volume that party institutionalization takes place within nondemocratic systems and can be key to regime stability, adaptability, and longevity.

This chapter aims to perform two specific tasks. First, it explores the efforts of the CCP to institutionalize itself and its relations with other key political actors such as the state and social forces. Second, it demonstrates that there is no contradiction between institutionalization and accommodation of democratic elements. Here, it is necessary to highlight the distinction between the terms "democratic accommodation" and "democracy." Democracy, as is commonly understood in the West, has certain distinctive features such as free and competitive elections on a periodic basis; multiparty systems; checks and balances as well as respect for civil liberties such as freedom of political expression, freedom of speech, and freedom of the press. Democratic accommodation, as used in this chapter, refers to the process of introducing democratic elements or features to an existing political system that is widely regarded as authoritarian. In this case, the CCP may introduce certain democratic elements, but this should not be construed as the CCP committing itself to the ideals of democracy per se. Rather, by accommodating democratic elements, the CCP achieves its continuous domination over other political actors.

THE INSTITUTIONALIZATION THESIS

In the West, scholars simply referred to China's political system as a one-party system. As briefly discussed, many scholars see the inevitable fall of this system, as a system of checks and balances does not exist. The issue is how to explain the fact that the CCP has sustained itself and survived in drastically changing environments. To understand the institutionalization dimension of the CCP, the first task is to make sense of how the party organizes its politics. Elsewhere, I have demonstrated how the CCP is the personification of a modern emperor. It is a highly organized emperor that exercises domination over the state and society, wielding its power in a similar way to what Chinese emperors of the past did.[10] In this sense, the CCP may look like a different animal to political parties we see in most Western countries. However, as other chapters in

---

[10] Zheng 2010.

this volume show, there are strong parallels to dominant parties we observe elsewhere in Asia, particularly Singapore, Malaysia, Vietnam, and Taiwan.

I interpret China's one-party system as a "hegemonic regime," in Robert Dahl's term (1971). A hegemonic regime is a system in which one individual or one organization rules the country. Therefore, to understand the political process of China's one-party system is to understand the process of what I call "hegemonization." Hegemonization is the key feature of the institutionalization of the CCP and its relations with other political actors. It involves two dimensions, namely, domination and legitimation. More concretely, the term "hegemonization" has three connotations in the CCP case. First, the CCP wants to maintain its domination over other political actors. Second, it maintains its domination by accommodating other political actors and soliciting their loyalty. And third, hegemonization is, therefore, an effective tool of legitimation. In this context, I argue that the changing relations between the CCP and other political actors are a dual process of domination and legitimation.

Hegemonization as an effective mode of legitimation places its emphasis on the interaction between the CCP and other political actors. By doing so, I attempt to highlight the following points. First, the interaction between the CCP and other political actors is not always a zero-sum game. Although hegemonization implies the process of the CCP dominating other political actors, this does not mean that these actors are completely powerless. Without these actors, the CCP will not be able to acquire legitimacy from various sectors of society. Second, like the CCP, these actors are active in this process. Politics is relational, and so is power. Legitimation means that the CCP solicits loyalty from other political actors through noncoercive means, and these actors somehow voluntarily accept the domination of the CCP. Both processes of domination and legitimation are struggles between the CCP and other political actors. Third, hegemonization is thus a dynamic process of mutual transformation of the CCP and other political actors. To acquire legitimacy through hegemonization does not mean that the CCP can simply impose its will on other actors; neither does it imply that these actors accept CCP domination without resistance or negotiations with the CCP. It is an interactive process between the two actors, and their continuous interactions lead to mutual transformation.

Figure 7.1 elaborates the dual processes of domination and legitimation, processes that the CCP uses to establish and maintain a hegemonic political order over other political forces in society. The left column represents the dual processes of domination and legitimation of the CCP over other political actors. "A" represents the CCP, and A1, A2, A3... represent other political actors such as the state (including the government, the National People's Congress, the Chinese People's Political Consultant Conference), mass organizations (e.g., the Chinese Communist Youth League, the All China Federation of Trade Unions, and the Women's Federation), and other social organizations (e.g., chambers of commerce and various forms of non-governmental

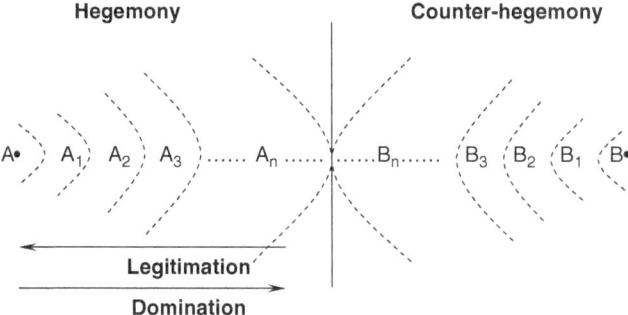

FIGURE 7.1. Hegemonization: Domination and Legitimation

organization). By accommodating other political actors within the boundary of the hegemony, the CCP solicits loyalty from them; by accepting CCP domination, these actors become part of the political process dominated by the CCP.

Within this structure of domination, one can also make sense of hegemonization and legitimation in a Gramscian sense. The CCP is a part of society, a sphere in which it organizes consent and hegemony. According to Antonio Gramsci (in Simon 1991: 48–52), if one organization is to become hegemonic, it has to combine the interests of other organizations and social forces with its own interests so as to create a nationally popular collective will.[11] Similarly, the CCP cannot achieve national leadership and become a hegemonic organization if it confines itself only to its own organizational interests or the interests of other political actors on which it has built its hegemonic position. Instead, to sustain and reproduce its hegemonic position across historical periods, the CCP has to transcend these interests by taking into account the aims and interests of other political forces, linking these with its own interests so as to become their universal representative. By doing so, the CCP realizes the dual processes of domination and legitimation in its relations with social forces.

Society, however, is also the sphere in which subordinate social forces may organize their opposition, struggle for power, and construct an alternative hegemony – a counter-hegemony. The right column of Figure 7.1 points to a possible counter-hegemony. When the CCP is challenged or perceives that it is being challenged by different actors within a possible counter-hegemony (e.g., B, B_1, B_2, B_3...), it tends to use coercive measures against these actors. It is at this juncture that the CCP departs from all political organizations in the liberal-democratic world where political pluralism is norm. The CCP does not allow a counter-hegemony to develop and grow. To achieve that goal through coercive measures is not always effective and, indeed, is often counterproductive as a result of changing socioeconomic environments. Therefore, while not

---

[11]   Simon 1991: 48–52.

surrendering the option to use coercive measures at any point in time, the CCP actively engages and transforms social forces by accommodating them. The political process of CCP politics is thus increasingly becoming open.

Having explained what institutionalization means, the next question is how the CCP has institutionalized its relations with other political actors and social forces. This institutionalization has three layers. First is the institutionalization of the CCP itself. This is important because the CCP is the actor that is realizing its hegemonization. Whether the CCP is strong or weak depends on the degree of institutionalization. Second is the institutionalization of the relationship between the CCP and the state. China has been regarded as a party-state. This, however, does not mean that the party-state is monolithic. Indeed, the CCP and the state are two separable political entities. Third is the institutionalization of the relationship between the CCP and social forces, that is, how the CCP has provided institutional means for social forces to participate in the process of CCP politics.

PART TWO: EMPIRICAL EVIDENCE

THE INSTITUTIONALIZATION OF THE CCP

As the CCP is the sole organizer of political life in China, its institutionalization matters. Once the CCP is weakened, political chaos will follow. The reason is simple. As the CCP does not allow a counter-hegemony to develop, there is no alternative to the CCP. Therefore, the capacity of survival and development heavily relies on the institutionalization of the CCP. A dimension of power relations between individual party leaders and the party as an organization exists within the CCP. Institutionalization in this context means the depersonalization of power within the CCP. The personalization of power strengthens political leaders' personal power but often weakens the capacity of the party in leading political changes and maintaining the domination of the party.

The personalization of the party tends to be associated with a weak party. When strong leaders rule, the party is highly personalized, meaning that its top leaders behave like emperors and build their political parties as an emperorship. This was the case of the CCP under Mao Zedong and to a lesser degree under Deng Xiaoping. The personalization of the political party has not only resulted in highly centralized political power but also rendered it difficult for the party to institutionalize itself. While party leaders are strong, the party itself is weak. To a great degree, the party is often a personal tool for individual leaders to organize and perpetuate personal power. When individual leaders fall, the party is inevitably weakened and may even collapse. As other chapters in this volume show, such a political phenomenon indeed has also existed in other Asian countries in different historical periods, particularly when one party is able to dominate other political parties.

Institutionalizing the CCP thus means depersonalizing it. In this regard, the CCP has built a set of institutions dealing with elite politics. These institutions have greatly increased the level of institutionalization of party politics.

Political exit was established. Political exit is important for elite politics, particularly power succession. Before new leaders can come in, old leaders have to leave. No exit, no entry. For most times in traditional China, the institutionalized rule was that only after the decease of the old emperor could his or her successor formally become the new emperor. An emperor could be removed by factors other than death. Some emperors were forced to give up the throne, at times by various violent means.

For decades after 1949, China did not have a system of functioning political exit. Top leaders were able to hold on to their positions until they died. Mao Zedong died as chairman of the CCP. Even though Deng Xiaoping did not have any formal position in his later years, he was able to exercise great influence through informal channels. The exit problem had troubled both the top leadership and the country because it often had to be solved by a bitter power struggle. To deal with the problem, formal regulations and informal rules have been developed. Among others, term limits and the age limit play an important role in handling elite politics and power succession.

Term limits matter. Now, in general, political leaders including the general secretary of the CCP, the president of state, premier, and holders of other important positions are allowed to serve at most two terms in office, that is, 10 years. This system is not that different from many Western presidential systems.

The retirement system for aged cadres was formally established in the early 1980s. Candidates for ministers, provincial party secretaries, and governors have to be younger than age 65, and those for deputy ministries, deputy provincial party secretaries, and deputy governors younger than age 60. The main problem lies in retiring top senior leaders, namely those in the Political Bureau and especially in the Standing Committee. Although Deng did not specify the retirement age for these positions, he was able to retire aged senior political leaders. During Deng's tenure, the average age of Political Bureau members was reduced from 71 in 1982 to 62.1 in 1992.

Since the era of Jiang Zemin, the age factor has become increasingly important in handling power succession.[12] After the Fourteenth Party Congress in 1992, unwritten rules about retiring top leaders were developed. In 1992, a consensus was reached that no one in the Political Bureau except for Jiang Zemin should be older than 70.[13] This also applies to candidates for the premier and vice-premier positions (or their equivalent levels in the party sector). At the Sixteenth Party Congress in 2002, all leaders in the Political Bureau and its Standing Committee who were older than age 70 retired, and all new leaders now are younger than age 70. Li Ruihuan, the chairman of the Chinese People's

[12] See Zheng (2000, 2003).
[13] Baum 2000: 24.

Political Consultative Conference (CPPCC), retired when he was 68. Jiang Zemin remained an exception, even though he no longer held a position in the Political Bureau. At the Seventeenth Party Congress in 2007, Zeng Qinghong, who was regarded as part of the core leadership, retired at age 68.

Since Jiang Zemin's time, most senior leaders have been able to exit from politics peacefully and gracefully. During the Fifteenth Party Congress in 1997, Qiao Shi retired gracefully from all power positions. Regardless of whether Qiao retired voluntarily or was pushed out, his retirement was widely regarded as a major step for the CCP in resolving its endemic problem of retiring senior leaders. At the same congress, General Liu Huaqing also gracefully exited from the Standing Committee. Since then, no military man has occupied a place in this most powerful decision-making body in China. This exit system has functioned well.

While the term limits and age limits have severed effective institutional constraints on personal dictatorship, the CCP leadership has also developed what it called "intraparty democracy" (or intraparty elections) to deal with factional politics and to choose its successors. Mao was certainly able to stand above all institutions to choose his successor. He chose Liu Shaoqi first, and then Lin Biao. He failed in both cases as a result of intraparty power struggles, but he was still able to choose Hua Guofeng before his death. The way Mao chose his successor was no different from that of the emperor in the premodern era. Under Deng Xiaoping, the situation changed slightly. Deng and his generation of leaders realized the danger of Mao's way of conducting power succession, and, indeed, many of them including Deng himself became victims of Mao's personal dictatorial power. Therefore, Deng put much emphasis on the so-called collective leadership. After the 1989 pro-democracy movement, Deng, together with other elders, appointed Jiang Zemin as the general secretary of the CCP. Then, at the party's Fourteenth Congress in 1992, they also appointed Hu Jintao as member of the Standing Committee of the Political Bureau to succeed Jiang Zemin.

Greater institutionalization took place during the post-Deng era. The fact that Hu Jintao was appointed as Jiang's successor by the late Deng Xiaoping means that Jiang Zemin no longer had power to appoint his own successor when he retired from all formal positions. But this does not mean that there was no other way Jiang could work to ensure the continuity of his legacy and policies. Factional politics came to play an important role then. In 2002, when Jiang was retired from the position of the general secretary, Hu succeeded him. In terms of formal procedures, this meant a successful power succession, indeed the first smooth power succession in the history of the CCP. However, although Hu led the Standing Committee of the Political Bureau, he lacked factional support. There was virtually no one on the Standing Committee whom he could count on for support. In contrast, even though Jiang had relinquished his senior party post, he could count on six supporters among the nine members of the Standing Committee – Wu Bangguo, Jia Qinglin, Zeng Qinghong, Huang Ju, Wu Guanzheng, and Li Changchun. Indeed, the expansion of the Standing Committee from seven to nine was Jiang's way to strengthen his faction.

When Hu took over from Jiang in 2002, the new leadership was defined as the central leadership with Comrade Hu Jintao as the General Party Secretary. Whereas Deng had backed Jiang for the leadership role, Jiang did not do so for Hu. That meant that Hu had to work harder than Jiang to consolidate his power and make himself one among the core of leadership. Like Jiang, Hu has consolidated his power by building up his power base – the Chinese Communist Youth League.

The fact that Hu has consolidated his power does not mean that he is powerful enough to handle power succession. As with Jiang, Hu cannot choose his own successor. As a matter of fact, his personal power is even weaker than Jiang's in planning and arranging future leadership. Therefore, Hu has to resort to other means to handle power succession. The Seventeenth Party Congress in 2007 was regarded as vital for power succession because the lineup of the future leadership had to be made. As it turned out, this party congress brought Xi Jinping and Li Keqiang into the Standing Committee of the Political Bureau as candidates for general secretary and premier, respectively, after Hu Jintao and Wen Jiabao. China observers did not know how this arrangement was made until after the party congress when the Xinhua news agency published a lengthy on-the-spot report on how the new leadership was formed.[14] It is worth citing the story at length:

On June 25, 2007, over 400 people, including members and alternate members of the Sixteenth CPC [Communist Party of China] Central Committee and leading officials of relevant departments participated in picking proposed members of the Political Bureau from a list of almost 200 candidates. Hu Jintao presided over the event and set, on behalf of the CCP Central Committee, the conditions for the selection of new Political Bureau members, with emphasis on political firmness, capacity, and image among Party members and ordinary people. The candidates must be 63 or younger and were at least a minister, according to the rules.

The democratic recommendation of the new Party leadership is of great importance to the CCP, which has more than 70 million members and is managing a country with a population of 1.3 billion, Hu was quoted as saying. On September 27, the Standing Committee of the Political Bureau of the Sixteenth CCP Central Committee met and approved the candidates of the new central leadership of the Party. On October 8, the Political Bureau of the Sixteenth CCP Central Committee discussed and approved the list, before proposing the list of candidates to the First Plenary Session of the Seventeenth CCP Central Committee and the First Plenary Session of the Seventeenth CCP Central Commission for Discipline Inspection.

On October 21, the Seventeenth CCP National Congress elected the Seventeenth CCP Central Committee and the Seventeenth CCP Central Commission for Discipline Inspection. And a day later, the Seventeenth CCP Central Committee elected a new central leadership of the Party.[15]

---

[14] Liu, Sun and Liu 2007.
[15] Ibid.

Although the degree of democracy in the so-called democratic process of electing the new party leadership is still negligible, it is certainly true, as the report stated, that for the first time, participants of the Central Committee's plenary session could recommend candidates to the Political Bureau. The report thus regarded this event as a milestone in the history of the party's efforts to develop internal democracy. As no single leader can dictate power succession, new institutions and methods, including ones with democratic elements, have to be instituted. Indeed, the Bo Xilai affair before the Eighteenth Party Congress in 2012 is an indication of the need to facilitate intraparty democracy.[16] Without formal rules and norms, ambitious politicians like Bo would challenge the legitimacy of the party leadership through all possible means.

INSTITUTIONALIZATION OF PARTY-STATE RELATIONS

To maintain dominance over the government, the CCP has made great efforts to institutionalize its relationship with the government. Over the years, neither the party nor the government has been satisfied with the current structure of their relationship. The parallel system of party and government from the national to local levels has led to political inefficacy and administrative inefficiency. As the boundary between the party and the government blurs, the two are in consistent conflict. What is called *wolidou* (literally, "infighting") could paralyze the governance system, especially during a crisis. This seems inevitable as the blurring of the boundary between the party and the government also makes less clear the responsibility of each. Many reform measures have been carried out to institutionalize the party-state relationship. Meanwhile, these reforms also aim to establish the rule in which the party maintains its domination over the government.

The three-in-one system

The three-in-one system refers to the linking of the offices of the state president and the chairmanship of the CMC (Central Military Commission) with the position of the party general secretary. Today, the party general secretary (the head of the ruling party) is concurrently the head of the state (state president) and the highest commander of the military (chairman of the CMC). This system somewhat resembles the semi-presidential system in other countries.

Before 1992, China's system was the same as the Vietnamese system in which different leaders hold three positions. But at the party's Fourteenth Congress in 1992, in an attempt to institutionalize party-state relations, the

---

[16] Bo Xilai, the former Communist Party chief in Chongqing, was once seen as a high flyer tapped for top office. But he was expelled from the Communist Party because of a scandal over his corruption in 2012 and was given a life sentence in 2013. His wife was given a suspended death sentence for the murder of British businessman Neil Heywood in 2012.

three-in-one system was established. Both the state presidency and vice state presidency have become the most important positions in the Chinese leadership. Hu Jintao was the vice state president for several years before he succeeded Jiang. Similarly, Xi Jinping was the vice state president before he succeeded Hu. Institutionalization has not only brought about some level of division of functions between important public offices, but it also legitimizes the party's command over the military. While the basic principle of "the party commands the gun" remains largely unchanged, this power is now vested in a formal office, which acts on behalf of the party. This is evident in the institutional arrangement of the CMC. Although the CMC is one organization, it goes by two names in public, namely, the party's CMC (*zhonggong zhongyang junwei*) and the state's CMC (*guojia junwei*).

As the state president and chairman of the state's CMC, the party general secretary and his office are given a legitimate base to perform governmental functions. There is an informal division of labor between the state president office and the premier's office in the State Council, namely, the government's executive branch. The state president office is in charge of foreign affairs, national defense, national security, and public security, whereas the State Council is in charge of economic and civil affairs. Several ministries such as National Defense, National Security, Public Security, and Foreign Affairs are under the jurisdictions of the state president office even though they are located in the State Council. Major decisions in these areas are made by the party (general secretary office) in the name of the state president office. Of course, the State Council has to bear the responsibility of policy implementation.

Party secretary as head of people's congress

At the provincial level, the secretary of the provincial party committee concurrently acts as the head of the people's congress. This institutional arrangement is now in place in most of China's provinces and cities. Although this arrangement is often interpreted as the effort by the CCP to strengthen its domination over the people's congress, the underlying rationale behind it can also be explained in terms of the institutionalization of the party-state relationship.

According to China's constitution, the National People's Congress (NPC) is "the highest organ of state power" (article 57); and "the NPC and the local people's congresses at various levels are the organs through which the people exercise state power" (Constitution of the People's Republic of China: article 2). In reality, the NPC and local people's congresses are often rubber stamps of the party, meaning that party organizations make major decisions first and then ask the NPC and local people's congress to approve. In both Mao's and Deng's eras, the NPC and local people's congresses were usually headed by a powerless retired senior party cadre or a government official.

This situation has changed since 1989. During the pro-democracy movement, many NPC leaders showed their ambitions. Hu Jiwei, then editor of *People's*

Daily and a member of the Standing Committee of the NPC, attempted to use the NPC to nullify the State Council's martial law. After the crackdown, the Party leadership began to strengthen the party's control over the NPC and local people's congresses. Since the early 1990s, the NPC Standing Committee has been headed by a member of the Political Bureau Standing Committee, such as Qiao Shi, Li Peng, and Wu Bangguo. At the provincial level, the secretary of the provincial party committee heads the people's congress.[17]

Indeed, according to Zhao Ziyang, the arrangement was initiated in the 1980s when political reform became the important agenda of the party leadership. The arrangement was expected to help in the reconciling of the two contradictory sources of power: the NPC as the highest organ of state power in theory and the CCP as the highest power in reality (Zong 2007: 147). This comment by Zhao can be interpreted in the following way: the party secretary as the head of the people's congress gives the party the legitimate means to influence the government. The CCP as the only ruling party has maintained its domination over the government. During the 1980s debate on political reform, the separation of the party from the government became the theme. If the party and the government became two separate bodies, then the question was how the party could exercise its domination over the government. The party and the NPC (and local people's congresses) have similar functions: according to China's constitution, the NPC and local congresses are to supervise the government at different levels. So, by being actively involved in the activities of the NPC and local people's congresses, the party at different levels establishes a legitimate means to supervise and maintain its domination over the government. Therefore, this new involvement has led the CCP to exercise direct control over provincial people's congresses on the one hand and over provincial party secretaries' face-to-face interaction with local people's representatives on the other. Provincial party secretaries now need to listen to and take the representatives' opinions into consideration before provincial party committees can make important decisions.

More space and greater autonomy for professionalism

To institutionalize party-state relations, ideological reliability has to give way to allow more professionalism in the ranks of government officials. To boost effective governance, the CCP, since the mid-1990s, has begun to loosen its grip on the state to give professionals more autonomy in the day-to-day running of the country. The most visible signs are those within the State Council. Over the years, the council has come under the economic and social management of professionals. The posts of premier, vice-premier, state councillor, ministers, and vice-ministers are now filled by professionals. This is especially so for positions at the ministerial and vice-ministerial levels. The rise of professionalism largely reflects the increasing need for expertise in dealing with the complexities of new

---

[17] Zheng and Li 1998.

social and economic issues. In 2007, China had the first two non-communist cabinet appointments, namely, Minister of Science and Technology Wan Gang and Minister of Health Chen Zhu. Minister Wan, an expert in the automobile industry, has been chairman of the China Zhi Gong Party since December 2007; Minister Chen, a medical doctor, does not have any affiliation to a political party. The political implications of these two appointments should not be exaggerated. However, they do mean that professionals now play an increasingly important role in handling daily state affairs.

Professionalism has also been injected into both the NPC and local people's congresses. The NPC is largely an inefficient platform because of its big size, which hovers around 3,000. It convenes for only a short period annually; its annual conference usually spans about 10 to 14 days. Moreover, the structure of its meeting, which is made up of full-day plenary sessions, is not suited for lengthy deliberations. To overcome these shortcomings, NPC reforms since the early 1990s have focused on expanding the Standing Committee and establishing various special committees.

Over the years, the Standing Committee has been expanded to its present strength of 161 members. The expanded Standing Committee functions as a "miniature-NPC" – its small size allows more frequent and efficient consultations as compared to the NPC as a whole, yet it is large enough to accommodate different social and political bases, particularly those that include non-CCP members. The expansion of this group of "first-among-equals" serves to raise the quality of motions tabled during annual NPC conferences and allows follow-ups on NPC decisions when the need arises.

The NPC has nine special committees in the areas of foreign affairs, finance, education, minorities, and agricultural and rural affairs. The number continues to increase. Special committees usually draw their members from two sources: government officials who have previously served in various state organizations and specialists in particular fields. These special committees provide expertise and public office experience both in the law-making process and in the supervision of the daily functioning of the government (the State Council and its various ministries). Professionalization has altered the role of the NPC from that of a rubber stamp to one that is capable of overseeing governmental operations.[18]

INSTITUTIONALIZATION OF PARTY-SOCIETY RELATIONS

Although the CCP maintains its domination over society, it is a part of the society. Certainly, the CCP cannot sustain its domination by imposing its will onto society. To sustain such domination, the CCP has attempted to institutionalize its relations with society by establishing various institutions that link the CCP and other social groups.

---

[18] For example, see Tanner (1998); Peerenboom 2002.

TABLE 7.1. *Functional Groups of the Eleventh CPPCC (2008)*

	Functional Group	Deputies	Percentage
1	Chinese Communist Party	98	4.38
2	China Revolutionary Committee of the Kuomintang	66	2.95
3	China Democratic League	65	2.91
4	China Democratic National Construction Association	65	2.91
5	China Association for the Promotion of Democracy	45	2.01
6	Chinese Peasants and Workers' Democratic Party	45	2.01
7	China Zhi Gong Dang	30	1.34
8	Jiusan Society	45	2.01
9	Taiwan Democratic Self Government League	20	0.89
10	Non-party Deputies	65	2.91
11	Youth League	12	0.54
12	Trade Unions	63	2.82
13	Women Associations	67	3.00
14	Youth Associations	29	1.30
15	Industry and Commerce Associations	65	2.91
16	Associations of Scientists	44	1.97
17	Taiwan Associations	15	0.67
18	Overseas Chinese Associations	30	1.34
19	Arts and Entertainment	147	6.57
20	Science and Technology	112	5.01
21	Social Sciences	68	3.04
22	Economy	145	6.48
23	Agriculture	65	2.91
24	Education	107	4.78
25	Sports	22	0.98
26	Media and Publishing	46	2.06
27	Medical Care	90	4.02
28	People's Diplomacy	39	1.74
29	Social Welfare	36	1.61
30	Minorities	105	4.69
31	Religions	65	2.91
32	Hong Kong	126	5.63
33	Macao	29	1.30
34	Guest Deputies	166	7.42
	TOTAL	2237	100.00

Source: Compiled by author based on data from Bo and Chen 2008: 12.

Among various institutions, most notable is the Chinese People's Political Consultant Conference (CPPCC), which institutionalizes the CCP's relations with the so-called democratic parties and key functional groups. The CCP has divided the whole society into 32 functional groups, including the democratic parties, and then co-opted them into the regime through various institutions, mainly the CPPCC (see Table 7.1).

The eight other political parties, known as the democratic parties, were formed during China's long struggle to become a new nation. According to China's constitution, multiparty cooperation and political consultation are fundamental to its political system. In this light, the CPPCC is the principal institution through which the non-communist parties and other functional groups supposedly work in tandem with the ruling party. However, as indicated in Table 7.1, this multiparty cooperation actually means the dependency of these democratic parties on the CCP. According to *People's Daily*, "the CCP and the democratic parties are totally equal under the Constitution but politically, the latter is subject to the leadership of the former."[19]

These eight democratic parties have to work within certain constraints. Instead of opposing and out-performing one another as is common with political parties in the West, these democratic parties have to abide by the emphasis on "multi-party cooperation and political consultation under the leadership of the CCP."[20] Under this system, the eight democratic parties can participate in and deliberate on state affairs as long as they recognize the leading and ruling position of the CCP. In turn, the CCP will engage in political consultation with the eight democratic parties on major state guidelines and policies and key state affairs before making and implementing decisions.

In a one-party state such as China, the quasi-government, quasi-civil CPPCC is useful in serving as a vital link between state and society, especially in channeling feedback to the political leaders. The crux is how to better translate feedback into policy that effectively reflects societal needs and sentiments. The answer lies in greater institutionalization and devolution of power to enable the CPPCC to develop "sufficient regularity" and "perceived importance" in Kenneth Lieberthal's words (2004: 206). For example, adopted proposals from delegates can be made legally binding to deepen CPPCC's political influence. Whether this will take place ultimately depends on the state's willingness to carry out political reforms that inevitably require it to share or relinquish some of its power.

In the 1980s, Deng Xiaoping made an important speech at an enlarged meeting of the Political Bureau that sparked debates on political reforms, including for China's legislature. Some, such as Liao Gailong, suggested dividing the NPC into two houses; others such as Song Richang floated the idea of turning the CPPCC into the upper chamber.[21] As the idea had been mooted in the 1980s, however, there has been little, if any, progress toward that end. The focus of reform has since shifted to the CPPCC's functional groups. A 2006 government document on the CPPCC urged "the study and reasonable set up of functional

---

[19] *People's Daily* 2010.
[20] White Paper 2007.
[21] O'Brien 1988: 354.

groups, expand their unity and strengthen their inclusiveness."[22] Today, the CPPCC has 34 functional groups.[23]

The CCP has also actively employed other means to engage in institutionalizing its relations with society to ensure its own sustainability amidst rapid socioeconomic transformation. The institutionalization has taken several forms, including opening its political process to different social forces, establishing grassroots democracy, and accommodating a rising civil society.

Opening the CCP to All Social Groups

The CCP has gradually opened itself to social groups, and it is now becoming a catchall party. This is best reflected in the composition of the CCP membership. Overall, the CCP has been undergoing a transformation from a party composed predominantly of peasants and workers to a more broad-based party.

During Mao's era, the CCP was a revolutionary party dominated by workers and peasants. In 1956, the two groups made up 83 percent of the membership. When Deng Xiaoping came to power, he initiated a technocratic movement that replaced workers and peasants with technocrats. Since then, the representation of workers and peasants has generally experienced a downward trend from 64 percent in 1981 to 48 percent in 1994 to 29 percent in 2005.[24]

In fact, membership in today's CCP is very much a product of the reform era. At the end of 2008, party members who joined the party in the reform era (after October 1976) numbered 54.89 million or 72.29 percent. In comparison, the revolutionary generation (those who joined the party before October 1, 1949, when the People's Republic of China was founded) had shrunk to less than 1 percent (0.97 percent or roughly 733,000) of the party's membership. Those who joined before the Cultural Revolution (1949–1965) made up 10.53 percent (8 million) and those during the Cultural Revolution (1966–1976) claimed the remaining 16.21 percent (10.31 million).

Whether in terms of the CCP total membership or of its newly recruited members, it is clear that the CCP has gone beyond its traditional worker and peasant base to incorporate other social classes such as managers and professionals from businesses and students. Doing so does not mean that the CCP will ignore the interests of the workers and peasants. The CCP's purpose is to ensure that it has as wide a social base as possible so that it can be an inclusive party in line with the changing socioeconomic dynamics of society. Staying relevant is paramount to remaining in power.

---

[22] "Zhonggong zhongyang guanyu jiaqiang renmin zhengxie gongzuo de yijian" ("The Central's opinion on strengthening the work of the CPPCC").

[23] Wang Dejun 2010.

[24] Zheng 2009: 193–194.

Grassroots Democracy

Grassroots democracy refers to a process of democratization from below. Central to this type of democratization is political participation. This means that certain political processes are open to the participation of individuals or social forces that have a say in decisions and policies that directly impact them. Two main aspects include local elections and the greater emphasis on public supervision of the conduct of CCP and government officials. It is worthwhile to bear in mind that grassroots democracy is taking place within limits set by the CCP. It reserves the right to intervene to halt any practice or action that it regards as posing a threat to its hold on power.

Local elections were first introduced at the village level in the late 1980s as part of the CCP's effort to restructure rural governance after the collapse of the commune system established in Mao's time. In the late 1970s, China initiated rural reform that was characterized by radical decentralization and was based on the household responsibility system, which decentralized property rights to individual families in rural areas. The rapid introduction of this system led to the collapse of the old system of governance, that is, the production brigade system of collective agricultural activities and eventually the collapse of the commune system. Hence, the party-state leadership decided to restructure the governance system at the basic level. In 1987, China's Parliament or the NPC passed the Village Committee Organic Law of the PRC (for Trial Implementation). According to the law, village committees would be established with a view to ensuring self-government by the villagers in the countryside, who will administer their own affairs in accordance with the law, and promoting socialist democracy at the grassroots level.[25]

Since the mid-1990s, the election system has developed rather impressively. According to the Ministry of Civil Affairs, which has been in charge of implementing the election system, by early 1997, more than 80 percent of China's 930,000 villages had conducted at least one round of relatively democratic elections. By 2001, this system had spread to the whole country.

This top-down reform does not mean that the CCP wants to give up its control in the countryside; instead, it is aiming at strengthening the rule of the party in rural areas by accommodating democratic elements (Li and O'Brien, 2000). So, while the village committee was elected by villagers, the CCP committee continued to exist. The rapid spread of rural democracy, however, soon created contradictions between the elected committee and the party branch in the same village. Whereas the elected village committee draws its legitimacy from villagers, the party committee members, who are nominated, often faces challenges in dealing with the former, despite the fact that the party committee is a rung higher than the village committee. To solve

---

[25] See the Organic Law of the Villagers Committee of the People's Republic of China (for Trial Implementation) 1987.

this contradiction, more and more provinces have developed a system of having two ballots, whereby the party secretary in a village is subject to a popular vote, meaning that in these places both committees are elected.[26] In this way, the parallel structure of the party and the village branch has continued to coexist although the basis of their legitimacy has been transformed.

Going beyond the village level, the CCP has also implemented direct elections at the township level – the basic level of administration in China – on an experimental basis. In the mid-1990s, China experienced its first township elections for key township officials. Since then, the new election practices have been extended to many townships in several counties in a number of provinces.[27] The positions open to elections have been extended from township vice-mayors to township mayors, and sometimes even township party secretaries. The number of cases increased from a dozen in the mid-1990s, to several hundreds in the late 1990s, and to several thousands by the early 2000s. Compared to village elections, township elections are more constrained by various factors such as size, diverse needs of different villages, and tight political control, leading to the coining of the term "semi-competitive elections" by the scholarly community.[28]

Unlike the village committee election, which is legally backed, the holding of township elections is a policy decision. They have not been legalized. Hence, they remain controversial even though they are now widespread.[29] The political support from the leadership at both the central and local levels is the key factor that has facilitated the implementation of this system.[30] Besides village and township elections, China is experimenting with other kinds of democratic elements such as the election of urban community committees, allowing independent candidates to run for local people's congresses, the emergence of what China called "rights-democracy," and social movements.[31]

---

[26] For example, Li 1999. The two-ballot system originated from Hequ County in Shanxi Province.

[27] The end of 1998 saw the first breakthrough in upgrading the direct election to the township level with the experiment of Suining County in Sichuan Province. However, the immediate official reaction of the central leaders was negative. They regarded the Buyun township direct election as a violation of the Constitution, which stipulates the election of township government leaders by the Township People's Congress. Despite this reaction, less competitive elections than Buyun Township were organized in several provinces including Sichuan, Guangdong, Shanxi, Hubei, Jiangsu, and Yunnan. See Dong 2008: 158.

[28] For example, Lai 2008.

[29] Dong 2008.

[30] Li 2002.

[31] The "rights-democracy" refers to citizens from marginalized or disadvantaged social groups asserting or defending their rights by a variety of means, including through formal institutions such as competing in local elections and asserting the right to recall a delegate to the local people's congress whom they deemed incompetent, corrupt, or unwilling to represent voters' interests.

Accommodating a Rising Civil Society

On the surface, the rise of civil society does not favor the CCP's domination over society. Elsewhere in the world, civil society has played a key role in overthrowing authoritarian regimes. However, the CCP has actively engaged in civil society by accommodating it. The relationship between the party-state on the one hand and civil society on the other hand has undergone a dramatic change after more than three decades of reform and opening up. The CCP used to be completely averse to any social organizations or groupings that it did not sanction, perceiving them as harboring ulterior motives including mounting a direct challenge to its hold on power. Yet, over the course of reform and opening up, the CCP's aversion to bottom-up initiatives has been ameliorated somewhat.

This shift in attitude can be attributed to three main factors. The first is that the reform and opening up have led to a more diversified socioeconomic environment characterized by rising expectations and more varied demands on the part of the population. Not all of these expectations and demands can be met by the CCP. There is, therefore, more room for civil society to fill the void. This process is largely beyond the CCP's control. The second is that the CCP has recognized that civil society can play a positive role in providing certain services as long as it does not challenge the authority of the CCP. By allowing civil society room to maneuver, the CCP will be able to harness its resources and networks to better meet the needs of a more diversified population. In this way, the CCP can better govern society. The third and most important factor is that the CCP will be able to accommodate social forces by allowing them to organize themselves. The reason is simple: it is easier for the CCP to deal with organized social forces than unorganized individuals. Therefore, to allow the rise of organized social forces is a major endeavor of the CCP to institutionalize its relations with society.

The development of non-governmental organizations (NGOs) in China has demonstrated how the CCP can institutionalize its relations with social forces. NGOs in China can be broadly divided into three categories, namely, social organizations, civil non-enterprise institutions, and foundations. Their numbers have increased steadily over the years. Social organizations comprise the largest group of NGOs in China, followed by civil non-enterprise institutions and foundations. According to the Ministry of Civil Affairs, at the end of 2008, there were a total of 414,000 NGOs in China. Of this figure, 230,000 were social organizations (an increase of 8.5 percent from 2007), 182,000 were civil non-enterprise institutions (an increase of 4.6 percent from 2007), and 1,597 were foundations (an increase of 19.2 percent from 2007). These NGOs are involved in diverse areas such as education, culture, science and technology, health, labor, civil affairs, sports, environmental protection, legal services, intermediary services, religion, and agriculture.

Despite their apparent strength in numbers, these NGOs, while not strictly government agencies, are subject to the CCP and government control through various regulations and oversight mechanisms. For instance, according to existing regulations, an NGO must first find a relevant ministry in China that is willing to sponsor its registration. This can be hard to come by because ministries are careful not to be associated with a potentially controversial organization. Even after this is secured, the sponsoring department can unilaterally terminate the relationship at will and the NGO must then resume the arduous search for a new sponsor.[32]

The significance of NGOs in China thus varies, depending on their nature and functions. In the economic sphere, the government has strived to reduce its direct management role by establishing intermediary organizations such as trade associations and chambers of commerce to perform coordination and regulatory functions. In the social welfare sphere, the government also wants to foster the growth of NGOs so as to offload some of the burden of welfare service provision. In the social development sphere, the government wants NGOs to mobilize societal resources to supplement its own spending.[33] These NGOs are expected to perform their role according to the official line, that is, as a helping hand, and play a limited independent role.

In general, in areas such as poverty reduction, health, the environment, social welfare, and charity provision, NGOs are encouraged and allowed to play a greater role. However, in more sensitive areas such as religion, ethnicity, political reforms, and human rights, the influence of NGOs is much weaker. Also, some NGOs are more powerful than others. Most commercial-related organizations such as business associations at different levels and in different regions are extremely powerful in influencing the government's policy-making process: it is not difficult to find business professionals sitting in the people's congresses and the People's Political Consultative Conferences at different levels of government, whereas workers and farmers are not allowed to organize themselves and thus lack effective mechanisms to articulate and aggregate their interests.

The influence of particular NGOs in China may also depend on the timing. Today, the government-dominated All-China Federation of Trade Unions (ACFTU), an important government-sponsored social organization, has recognized the need to play a role by taking a more proactive approach to articulate workers' rights in order to claim its legitimacy in an age of a market economy. Given current economic difficulties that have resulted in increasing layoffs and labor disputes, there is an impetus for the ACFTU to play a more active role. In doing so, it can become an effective conduit to channel and allay workers' grievances. During the Sichuan earthquake that struck China in May 2008,

---

[32] Some people have described the search for a sponsoring department as "finding a mother-in-law," and the legal requirements for these "mothers-in-law" are very high. There is also the regulation that if there is already a social organization active in the same or similar area of work, there is no necessity for a new organization. Financial requirements for registration also pose another obstacle for social organizations. National level social organizations must have a minimum of *RMB* 100,000 (US$14,600) at hand, while local social organizations must have at least *RMB* 30,000 (US$4,380). See Liang 2003.

[33] Howell 1997.

the CCP and government officials also realized that NGOs could play a role in disaster relief and assistance. They could not only mobilize resources but also render assistance on the spot, particularly those with relevant expertise. However, the effectiveness of these NGOs on the ground often depends on a number of factors, including their credibility, their ability to coordinate their work with that of local officials, and the mind-set and attitude of local officials toward them.[34]

CONCLUSION

The CCP is determined to stay relevant to the needs of a more complex and diversified society. To do so, the CCP has engaged in extensive institutionalization that accommodates democratic elements. As discussed in this chapter, the CCP has consolidated its status as the core of China's political system. The movement toward internal institutionalization deemphasizes the role of individual leaders but places an emphasis on institutions. The intraparty democracy, be it factional competition or internal elections, now plays a key role in achieving the goal of collective leadership. Meanwhile, the CCP has also rationalized its relations with the state. While the state continues to depend on the CCP, it is now gaining more autonomous space in managing social and economic affairs in the country.

The CCP has also endeavored to institutionalize its relations with social forces. It has expanded its social base to incorporate new social groups beyond the traditional support base of workers and peasants. It is committed to strengthening consultation with and taking on board the views of members in the other eight democratic parties that represent specific constituents despite their small size. While the CCP is not prepared to withdraw from society, it is actively engaged in developing grassroots democracy, recognizing that civil society has a role to play within China's one-party system.

It is too early to tell whether the CCP will become a political party like those in the West, but all these instances show that the CCP is not averse to democratic elements or democratization. In developing the so-called democracy with Chinese characteristics and in line with its ideological bearings, the CCP appears prepared to accept or experiment with whatever works. However, what is adopted, the form it will take, and the pace of these changes are likely to be gradual and may not necessarily proceed in a linear direction. At the end of the day, the CCP, as the ruling party, will want to ensure that it remains in power through such democratic adaptations. It is determined to chart its own political path forward. Therefore, the nature of the political system that emerges at the end of the day is likely to be different from Western-style democracy.

[34] "Zhenqu NGOs, yaobai zai jintui zhijian" 2009.

REFERENCES

Baum, Richard. 2000. "Jiang Takes Command: the Fifteenth National Party Congress and Beyond." In Hung-mao Tien and Yun-han Chu (Eds.), *China under Jiang Zemin*, pp. 15–32. Boulder: Rienner Publishers. 2000.

Bo, Zhiyue, and Chen Gang. 2008. China's 11th National People's Congress: What's New?" *EAI Background Brief* No. 374. East Asian Institute, National University of Singapore, March 19.

The Carnegie Endowment for International Peace Reframing China Policy: The Carnegie Debates, Carnegie Endowment for International Peace, October 5, 2006. Available from http://www.carnegieendowment.org/events/index.cfm?fa=eventDetail&id=916&&prog=zch. Accessed February 19, 2007.

The Central People's Government of the People's Republic of China, The Statistics on the Membership of the Communist Party of China. Available at http://www.gov.cn/jrzg/2010-06/28/content_1639416.htm. Accessed August 29, 2010.

Chang, Gordon, 2001. *The Coming Collapse of China*. New York: Random House.

The Constitution of the People's Republic of China. 1994. Beijing: Foreign Languages Press.

Dahl, Robert A. 1971. *Polyarchy: Participation and Opposition*. New Haven and London: Yale University Press.

Dickson, Bruce. 1997. *Democratization in China and Taiwan: The Adaptability of Leninist Parties*. Oxford: Clarendon.

Dickson, Bruce. 2000. Political Instability at the Middle and Lower Levels: Signs of Decaying CCP, Corruption, and Political Dissent. In David Shambaugh (Ed.), *Is China Unstable? Assessing the Factors*, pp. 41–56. Armonk, NY: M.E. Sharpe.

Dickson, Bruce. 2005. Populist Authoritarianism: China's Domestic Political Scene. Paper presented at the Third American-European Dialogue on China, Washington, DC, May 23.

Dickson, Bruce. 2008. *Wealth into Power: The Communist Party's Embrace of China's Private Sector*. New York: Cambridge University Press.

Ding, X. L. 1994. *The Decline of Communism in China: Legitimacy Crisis, 1977–1989*. New York: Cambridge University Press.

Dong, Lisheng. 2008. "Grassroots Governance and Democracy in China's Countryside," In Zhengxu Wang, Zhengxu, and Colin Durkop (Eds.), *East Asian Democracy and Political Changes in China: A New Goose Flying?* pp. 155–168. Singapore: The Konrad Adenauer Stiftung.

The Economist. 2009. "The Party Goes On", *The Economist*, May 28, 2009, http://www.economist.com/world/asia/displaystory.cfm?story_id=13741467. Accessed July 24, 2009.

Goldstein, Avery. 1994. "Trends in the Study of Political Elites and Institutions in the PRC." *The China Quarterly* 139 (September): 714–30.

Howell, Jude. 1997. "NGO-State Relations in Post-Mao China." In David Hulme and Michael Edwards (Eds.), *NGOs, States and Donors: Too Close for Comfort?* pp. 202–221. London: Macmillan Press Ltd.

Lai, Hairong. 2008. *The Causes and Effects of the Development of Semi-Competitive Elections at the Township Level in China since the 1990s*, Ph.D. thesis, Department of Political Science, Central European University, Budapest.

Laliberté, Andre, and Marc Lanteigne (Eds.). 2008. *The Chinese Party-State in the 21st Century: Adaptation and the Reinvention of Legitimacy*. Park Square, Milton Park: Routledge.

Li, Lianjiang. 1999. The Two-Ballot System in Shanxi Province: Subjecting Village Party Secretaries to a Popular Vote. *The China Journal* 42 (July): 103–118.

Li, Lianjiang. 2002. The Politics of Introducing Direct Township Elections in China. *The China Quarterly* 171 (September): 704–723.

Li, Lianjiang, and Kevin O'Brien. 2000. Accommodating "Democracy" in a One-Party State: Introducing Village Elections in China. *The China Quarterly* 162 (June): 465–489.

Liang, Sharon. 2003. Walking the tight rope: civil society organizations in China, *China Rights Forum*, no. 3. available at http://www.hrichina.org/public/PDFs/CRF.3.2003/Sharon_Liang.pdf. Accessed August 8, 2009.

Lieberthal, Kenneth. 2004. *Governing China: From Revolution through Reform*. New York and London: W. W. Norton.

Liu, Siyang, Sun Chengbin, and Liu Gang. 2007. Weile dang he guojia xingwang fada changzhi jiuan – dang de xin yijie zhongyang lingdao jigou chansheng jishi ("For the Prosperity and Stability of the Party and State: on the spot record of the birth the new party leadership"). The Xinhua News Agency, October 23.

MacFarquhar, Roderick. 1991. The Anatomy of Collapse. *New York Review of Books*, September 26: 5–9.

"Multi-party Cooperation and the Political Consultative System," available at http://english.people.com.cn/92824/92845/92869/6441455.html. Accessed April 12, 2010.

O'Brien. Kevin J. 1988. China's National People's Congress: Reform and its Limits. *Legislative Studies Quarterly*, 13(3): 343–374.

Organic Law of the Villagers Committee of the People's Republic of China (for Trial Implementation). 1987. Asian Legal Information Institute. Available at http://www.asianlii.org/cn/legis/cen/laws/olotvcti575/. Accessed August 6, 2009.

Peerenboom, Randall. 2002. *China's Long March toward Rule of Law*. New York: Cambridge University Press.

Pei, Minxin. 2002. China's Governance Crisis. *China Review* (Autumn–Winter): 7–10.

Pei, Minxin. 2006. *China's Trapped Transition: The Limits of Developmental Autocracy*. Cambridge, MA: Harvard University Press.

Shambaugh, David. 2000. The Chinese Leadership: Cracks in the Façade? In David Shambaugh (Ed.), *The Modern Chinese State*, pp. 26–39. New York: Cambridge University Press.

Shambaugh, David. 2008. *China's Communist Party: Atrophy and Adaptation*. Washington, DC and Berkeley: Woodrow Wilson Center Press and University of California Press.

Shirk, Susan. 2007. *China: Fragile Superpower, How China's Internal Politics Could Derail Its Peaceful Rise*. Oxford, England: Oxford University Press.

Simon, Roger. 1991. *Gramsci's Political Thought: An Introduction*. London: Lawrence and Wishart.

Tanner, Murray Scot. 1998. *The Politics of Lawmaking in Post-Mao China: Institutions, Processes, and Democratic Prospects*. Oxford, England: Oxford University Press.

Tsai, Kellee. 2007. *Capitalism without Democracy: The Private Sector in Contemporary China*. Ithaca: Cornell University Press.

Walder, Andrew (Ed.). 1995. *The Waning of the Communist State: Economic Origins of Political Decline in China and Hungary*. Berleley: University of California Press.

Wang Dejun, Zhengxie jiebie shezhi gaige zanhuan (Slowing down the reform of the CPPCC's functional groups), *Dagongbao (Takungpao)*, available at http://www .takungpao.com/news/08/02/21/ZM-866526.htm. Accessed February 12, 2010.

Wang, Gungwu, and Zheng Yongnian (Eds.). 2000. *Reform, Legitimacy and Dilemmas: China's Politics and Society.* London and Singapore: World Scientific and Singapore University Press.

White Paper on China's Political Party System dated November 15, 2007, available at http://www.china.org.cn/english/news/231852.htm. Accessed July 30, 2009.

Wong, John, Zheng Yongnian, and Li Jinshan. 1998. *China after Ninth National People's Congress: Meeting Cross-Century Challenges.* Singapore and London: World Scientific and Singapore University Press.

Zheng, Shiping. 2003. The Age Factor in Chinese Politics. In Gungwu Wang and Zheng Yongnian (Eds.), *Damage Control: The Chinese Communist Party in the Jiang Zemin Era,* pp. 173–189. Singapore and London: Eastern Universities Press.

Zheng, Yongnian. 2000. The Politics of Power Succession. In Gungwu Wang and Zheng Yongnian (Eds.), *Damage Control: The Chinese Communist Party in the Jiang Zemin Era,* pp. 23–50. Singapore and London: Eastern Universities Press.

Zheng, Yongnian. 2009. Can the Communist Party Sustain Its Rule in China. In Keun Lee, Joon-Han Kim, and Wing Thye Woo (Eds.), *Power and Sustainability of the Chinese State,* pp. 186–209. Park Square, Milton Park: Routledge.

Zheng, Yongnian. 2010. *The Chinese Communist Party as Organizational Emperor: Culture, Reproduction and Transformation.* London and New York: Routledge.

Zheng, Yongnian, and Li Jinshan. 1998. "China's Politics after the Ninth National People's Congress: Power Realignment" In John Wong, Zheng Yongnian, and Li Jinshan (Eds.), *China after Ninth National People's Congress: Meeting Cross-Century Challenges,* pp. 51–92. Singapore and London: World Scientific and Singapore University Press.

Zhenqu NGOs, yaobai zai jintui zhijian (Earthquake zone NGOs, oscillating between progress and retreat), *Nanfengchuang* (a publication under *Guangzhou Ribao* conglomerate), May 12, 2009, available at http://www.nfcmag.com/articles/1505. Accessed August 8, 2009.

Zong, Fengming. 2007. *Zhao Ziyang ruanjin zhong de tanhua (Zhao Ziyang: Captive Conversations).* Hong Kong: The Open Press.

8

Party System Institutionalization in India

Csaba Nikolenyi*

INTRODUCTION

Evidence from the history of electoral and party competition in post-independence India leads us to nuance some of the arguments that Hicken and Kuhonta (2009) advance about the determinants of the institutionalization of Asian party systems. Among others, they claim that the Asian experience teaches us that (1) "to get highly institutionalized party systems it may be necessary to have some form of authoritarian party in power at an earlier point in time";[1] (2) that "more elections [do not] necessarily lead to greater institutionalization"[2]; and (3) that there is "no relationship between electoral institutions and government type with institutionalization."[3] The Indian case study helps us understand some of the limitations of these claims. First, drawing on conventional wisdom in the literature of the Indian party system, we point out that authoritarianism, marked by Indira Gandhi's ascent to political leadership, actually led to a deinstitutionalization of the dominant party, the Congress, as well as the party system.[4] As such, the Indian case shows that the type of authoritarianism and specifically the type of authoritarian party that is in power make an important difference for the future institutionalization of the party system. Similarly to what we find in the Philippines under the Marcos regime, the Indira Gandhi episode highlights that authoritarian interruption may not promote future party system institutionalization unless it is defined by the incumbency of an institutionally strong authoritarian party. Conversely, an authoritarian leader, such as Marcos and Indira Gandhi, who is bent on undermining the institutional

* This research was supported by a Standard Research Grant awarded by the Social Sciences and Humanities Research Council of Canada.

[1] Hicken and Kuhonta 2009: 23.
[2] Ibid.: 20.
[3] Ibid.
[4] Kochanek 1976; Morris-Jones 1978; Manor 1988.

foundations of political institutions that might become alternative loci of opposition will be equally capable of undermining the future institutionalization of the party system.

Second, we show that the passage of time has had mixed effects on party system institutionalization. Overall, the rates of electoral volatility have declined and the party system continues to be dominated by old parties with a long organizational history. Yet, we also note that there have been periodic fluctuations in volatility and that political parties have been losing the confidence of the population, which points to a decline in the legitimacy of their central role in the electoral process. Finally, our third main point concerns the institutional foundations of the dramatic and rapid decline in electoral volatility that has taken place since the 1989 general elections. Challenging recent arguments in the literature that point to a positive correlation between the number of parties and electoral volatility,[5] we claim that the decline in volatility post-1989 has been the direct result of the emergence of a fragmented multiparty system under the first-past-the-post electoral rule. Hicken and Kuhonta expect that with more parties, there will also be greater correspondence between voters and parties' ideal policy positions, which will have positive effects on party system institutionalization.[6] However, they expect party proliferation to be promoted by permissive electoral rules, that is, proportional representation. What is puzzling about India is that a fragmented multiparty system has evolved under the highly restrictive first-past-the-post electoral system. The solution of this puzzle lies in the simultaneous effects of the constitutional change of 1985, which imposed harsh penalties for party switching and defection. The anti-defection law both encouraged the splintering of large catchall parties[7] and led to reductions in volatility by providing "incentives for politicians to invest in the party label."[8]

The chapter consists of two main parts. The next section provides a detailed empirical overview of party system institutionalization in India using the four dimensions proposed by Mainwaring and Scully (1995). In the following section, we assess each of the five hypotheses that Hicken and Kuhonta (2009) put forward in the context of the Indian case material. We stress that (1) the period of authoritarian tendencies, marked by Indira Gandhi's rise to and consolidation of power, weakened party and party system institutionalization; (2) the passage of time seems to have had mixed effects on the institutionalization of the party system; and (3) institutional change, via the anti-defection law, has resulted in the simultaneous fractionalization and stabilization of the Indian party system.

[5] Yadav 2000, 2004; Heath 2005; Nooruddin and Chhibber 2008.
[6] Hicken and Kuhonta 2009: 10.
[7] Nikolenyi 2005, 2009, 2010; Subramanian 2008.
[8] Hicken and Kuhonta 2009: 11.

PARTY SYSTEM INSTITUTIONALIZATION IN INDIA, 1952 TO 2004

In their seminal work, Mainwaring and Scully (1995) identify four criteria to measure the institutionalization of a party system: "stability in the rules and the nature of inter-party competition," the stability of the major parties' roots in society, legitimacy accorded to the electoral process and to the role that political parties play therein, and clearly established and functioning party organizational structures.[9] This section provides an overview of the level of institutionalization of the Indian party system on each of these dimensions.

Stability of interparty competition

Mainwaring and Scully propose to measure the stability of party competition with the Pedersen index of electoral volatility, which takes half of the sum of the absolute values of the difference between parties' vote shares in two consecutive elections.[10] Figure 8.1 calculates the Pedersen scores for Indian elections at two levels of aggregation: the national and the state. In calculating the Pedersen score for every election pair, we treat new political parties as distinct formations whether or not they were formed as a result of the organizational amalgamation of preexisting parties in the previous election. This approach is justifiable given our interest in institutionalization. The alternative strategy would be to treat new parties that are born out of mergers as the continuation of their pre-merger constituents.[11] We believe that the latter approach is more suitable for studies on the stability of the electoral bases of party support, whereas the former is better suited to capture changes in the organizational development of political parties.

Figure 8.1 highlights two significant points. First, the Indian electorate is more stable at the national level than at the state level for almost all elections. Second, Figure 8.1 identifies three distinct stages in the development of the party system in terms of electoral volatility. The first period, from 1952 to 1971, was characterized by moderate levels of volatility with the average national Pedersen score at 26.34 percent over four elections. The second period was marked by a rapid although brief escalation in the volatility of the electorate: between 1971 and 1980, the average Pedersen score was 44.97 percent. Finally, relatively low levels of instability and an average volatility score of 19.89 percent characterize the third period that started with the 1984 general election. Declining volatility in India's national party system has

---

[9] Mainwarring and Scully 1995: 4–5.
[10] Pedersen 1983; Mainwaring and Scully 1995: 6.
[11] Bartolini and Mair 1990.

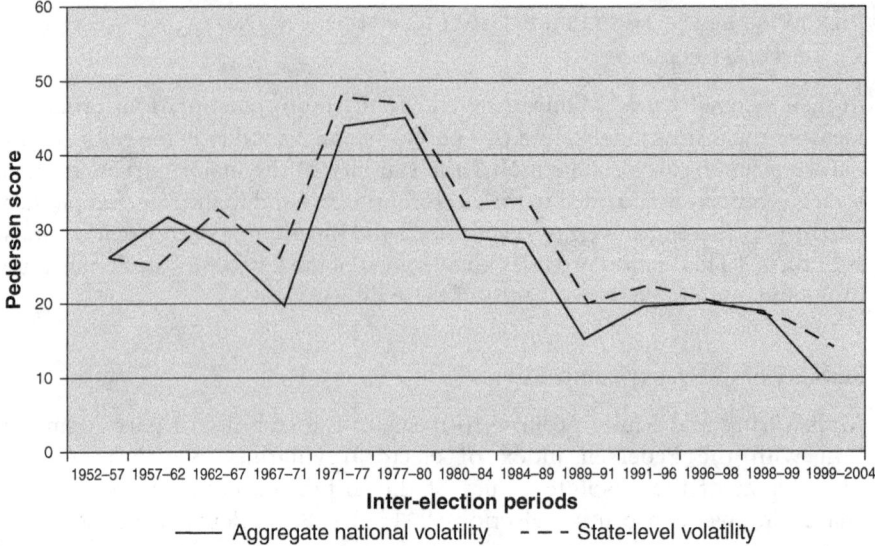

FIGURE 8.1. Electoral Volatility in India (1952–2004).
Source: Author's calculation based on data from Statistical Reports of Lok Sabha Elections (http://eci.nic.in/eci_main1/ElectionStatistics.aspx).

also been reported elsewhere;[12] in fact, Nooruddin and Chhibber actually note that "if anything, volatility is decreasing rather than increasing in the Indian states over time and ... claims that the 1990s were a period of greater party instability are not correct."[13] Indeed, since 1991 the volatility score has never exceeded the 20 percent mark between any two consecutive elections.

The national volatility scores hide considerable variation across the Indian states. Between 1952 and 2004, general elections in 7 of the 18 largest states (Andhra Pradesh, Assam, Kerala, Madhya Pradesh, Maharashtra, Tamil Nadu, and West Bengal) were less volatile than the aggregate national party system (25.74 percent). Kerala is a particularly important outlier as it is the only state with an average Pedersen score that has stayed below 20 percent. Furthermore, electoral instability in the Hindi-speaking states of the North[14] has been considerably more pronounced in comparison with non-Hindi-speaking states. The average Pedersen score in the former is 33.07 percent compared with 25.62 percent in the latter.

---

[12] Linden 2004; Nooruddin and Chhibber 2008.
[13] Nooruddin and Chhibber 2008: 1075.
[14] The Hindi speaking states are the following: Bihar, Delhi, Himachal Pradesh, Haryana, Madhya Pradesh, Rajasthan, and Uttar Pradesh. The non-Hindi states considered for this calculation are as follows: Andhra Pradesh, Assam, Gujarat, Jammu and Kashmir, Kerala, Karnataka, Maharashtra, Orissa, Punjab, Tamil Nadu, and West Bengal.

Parties' roots in society

Mainwaring and Scully propose a number of indicators to measure parties' roots in society.[15] Here, we consider two of these: (1) the seat share of old parties in the most recent election and (2) the average age of parties that have secured at least 10 percent of the legislative seats in recent elections. For our purpose, we define an "old" party in India as one that was formed prior to the first post-independence election held in 1952. Of the 39 political parties that won seats in the Lok Sabha elected in 2004, only 8 were old according to this definition. The following three were officially recognized as national parties by the Election Commission (with the year of their foundation indicated in parentheses):[16] the Indian National Congress (1885), the Bharatiya Janata Party (BJP, which continues the Bharatiya Jana Sangh [BJS] founded in 1951), and the Communist Party of India (CPI, 1928). The remaining five were recognized as state parties: the All-India Forward Bloc (1939), the Dravida Munnetra Kazagham (1949), the Akali Dal (1920), the Revolutionary Socialist Party (1940), and the Jammu and Kashmir National Conference (1932). In spite of their small number, these eight old parties controlled almost two-thirds, 64.2 percent, of the seats in Lok Sabha in 2004. In other words, old parties dominate the Indian party system, which is an important indicator of an advanced degree of institutionalization. The second measure also supports this finding. The average age of the two parties that won at least 10 percent of the Lok Sabha seats in 2004, the Congress (38.3 percent) and the BJP (21.4 percent), was 92 years.

It is worth noting that among the eight old parties, the three national formations are considerably older than the five state parties. The average age of the three old national parties in 2004 was 83 years while that of the five state parties was only 68. Moreover, while these three parties are in a clearly dominant position vis-à-vis the more recent national parties, the five old state parties are not as strong relative to the younger state parties. In the 2004 election, the three old national parties grabbed 80.5 percent of the 364 seats that were won by all national parties, while the remaining 20 percent went to three other national parties with a combined average age of only 22 years. In contrast, of the state parties, which won a total of 159 seats in 2004, the five old formations accounted for only 20 percent of the seats. This finding points to a more advanced level of institutionalization, at least on this dimension, among national rather than among state parties.

Legitimacy

To assess the degree of legitimacy that is accorded to political parties, we have consulted the World Values Survey results for India. The survey asks

---

[15] Mainwaring and Scully 1995: 12–13.
[16] For a discussion on the rules of party recognition in India, see Nikolenyi 2008.

TABLE 8.1. *Confidence in Political Parties (in percentages)*

	1990	1995	2001
A great deal	13.00	11.00	8.5
Quite a lot	40	28.40	19.6
Not very much	26.6	28.2	32.30
None at all	16.3	16.2	23.40

Source: World Values Survey (http://www.wvsevsdb.com/wvs/WVSAnalize.jsp).

respondents one particularly relevant question about their confidence in political parties at three points in time: in 1990, 1995, and 2001. Table 8.1 shows the breakdown of respondents' answers to this question.

The numbers point to a rapid decline in the level of confidence in political parties throughout the 1990s. At the beginning of the decade, more than half of the respondents had either "a great deal" or "quite a lot" of confidence in them. By the middle of the decade, that number dropped to 39 percent, and by 2001 it declined even further to 28.1 percent. The percentage of respondents who indicated having the most confidence in political parties ("a great deal") did not change much; however, the share of those who indicated having "quite a lot" of confidence declined by 20.4 percent during this period. Simultaneously, the number of respondents who expressed either "none at all" or "not very much" confidence in political parties has been steadily increasing from 42.9 percent in 1990, to 44.4 percent in 1995, and eventually 56.7 percent in 2001. The fact that more than half of the respondents expressed weak or no confidence at all in political parties by 2001 may be taken as an indication of weak party institutionalization in India, at least on the dimension of legitimacy.

It is important to reiterate that the Indian party system experienced a fundamental transformation in the 1990s as it moved from one-party dominance by the Congress Party to a coalitional pattern of a competitive multiparty system.[17] The new party system has presented political parties with considerable challenges for adjustment, especially with regard to the formation and maintenance of coalition governments, which some parties met with more success than others.[18] For instance, the Congress Party has been able to form stable governments, either alone as from 1991 to 1996 or in coalition since 2004, but the other parties have had a much more varied record. Therefore, it is possible that respondents have expressed their frustration with political parties as the latter were trying to adjust to the challenges of power sharing and coalition governance at the national level.

---

[17] Singh 1990; Saxena 1996; Yadav 1996; Chhibber 1999; Sridharan and Varshney 2001; Chakrabarty 2006.
[18] Sridharan 2003, 2005.

TABLE 8.2. *Confidence in Parliament (in percentages)*

	1990	1995	2001
A great deal	19.6	11.5	13.7
Quite a lot	45.5	41.9	27.9
Not very much	22.6	18.9	21.5
None at all	10	9.4	12.2

Source: World Values Survey (http://www.wvsevsdb.com/wvs/WVSAnalize.jsp).

Respondents' declining confidence in political parties seems to be affecting their confidence in the national parliament also. This is hardly surprising given that the efficacy of the legislature in a parliamentary democracy critically hinges on the successful operation of political parties. Table 8.2 reports this result. Clearly, confidence in parliament has been declining although not as steeply as for political parties: a majority of respondents consistently expresses "a great deal" or "quite a lot" of confidence in the national legislature. However, this percentage has been getting smaller over time, as it has dropped from 65.1 percent in 1990 to only 41.6 percent in 2001.

Party organization

The regulatory framework established by the Election Commission of India makes it mandatory for all registered political parties to have basic organizational structures in place. As a prerequisite for registration, parties have to file their written constitution with the commission; they have to submit documents pertaining to their internal organizational elections; and they have to provide detailed accounting of their revenues and expenditures. In spite of the apparent convergence toward institutionalization of party organizations, Indian political parties have had different experiences with, and followed different models of, party organization over time. We assess these differences by comparing the three old national parties that have had the longest institutional continuity: the Congress, the BJP and the CPI. The three parties were founded on two organizational principles: whereas the Congress Party was built as a mass party, the BJP and the CPI were formed as cadre-based organizations.[19] The Congress and the BJP have maintained their respective organizational principles; the CPI modified its cadre structure at its 1958 Congress in Amritsar at which the party resolved to become a mass party capable of winning national elections.[20]

The organizational framework of the Congress was designed to prepare the party for the task of governing after the end of British rule. Therefore, the party's organizational units reflected the administrative structure of the Indian state

[19] Malik and Singh 1994:140.
[20] Rodriguez 2006: 228.

rather than the allocation of electoral boundaries.[21] Every state (*pradesh*) of India was divided into a number of administrative districts (*zila*), which were different from and much larger than the individual electoral districts, and it would be along these *zila* and *pradesh* lines that the Congress Party would be fundamentally organized. The state (*pradesh*) Congress committee, as opposed to the constituency associations, was in charge of implementing the strategic directives of the party high command at the local level as well as making recommendations for the nomination of candidates in the electoral districts. According to Singh, "in the Indian National Congress Party ... while the national and state party organizations seem to reflect a fair degree of branch-type structural formalization and articulation, the district and subdistrict local party organizations fall closer to the 'machine-type' party organizations."[22] It is further indicative of the high level of institutional development that characterized the organization of the Congress Party in the first post-independence decades that no Congress prime minister occupied the post of party president simultaneously between 1954 and 1978.[23] As a result, institutionalization prevailed over the personalization of political leadership and power within the party.

This high level of institutionalization, however, was methodically undermined by the new political process created by Indira Gandhi, who adopted a more personal and plebiscitary style of leadership.[24] Under Indira Gandhi's leadership (1966 to 1984), the Congress Party suffered severe internal deinstitutionalization: organizational elections were abandoned and decision making in both the party and the government was centralized in the office of the prime minister.[25] Breaking with the past norm, Indira Gandhi assumed the posts of both prime minister and Congress president between 1978 and 1984. In fact, this practice was continued by successive Congress Prime Ministers Rajiv Gandhi (1985 to 1991) and Narasimha Rao (1992 to 1996) and came to an end only in 2004 when Congress President Sonia Gandhi ceded the prime ministership to Manmohan Singh following intense pressure and criticism from the opposition over her Italian nationality.

After the assassination of Indira Gandhi, her son Rajiv tried to reform the Congress Party on assuming leadership of both party and government. He sought to reintroduce organizational elections, pass internal reforms that would keep the Congress government subordinate to the Congress Party, and strengthen the ideological foundation of the party by systematically training and educating party workers.[26] In an effort to weaken the position of the established

---

[21] Weiner 1967: 40–41; Kochanek 1968: xxi–xxii.
[22] Singh 1981: 28–29.
[23] For a discussion of the division and separation of internal functions as part of institutionalization, see Panebianco 1988.
[24] Heginbotham 1971; Kochanek 1976; Manor 1988.
[25] Manor 1988: 70; Kohli 1990: 339–346.
[26] Kohli 1990: 345.

Congress elite that was strongly opposed to these plans, Rajiv Gandhi ensured that a large number of incumbent Congress legislators in both the national and the state legislatures would not be renominated in the 1984 Lok Sabha and the 1985 State Assembly elections.[27] If carried out, the planned reforms might have contributed significantly to the reinstitutionalization of the Congress Party in the long run. However, severe electoral reversals in state elections and staunch internal opposition eventually led to the abandonment of these reforms. Therefore, the beginning of the new party system in the 1990s found the Congress Party in a condition of organizational decay and deinstitutionalization.

Changes in membership figures reflect the ups and downs of the Congress Party's organizational health. Kochanek documents that between 1945 and 1950, the number of primary members increased from 5.5 to 17 million.[28] Although it declined to 4.5 million in 1957, it shot back to almost 11 million the following year. In 1965 and 1967, the number of primary party members stood at 17 and 11 million respectively. Kochanek attributes these extremely large swings in primary membership to the expectation of internal organizational elections, which provide "the opportunities of competing faction to gain advantage by seeing that the electoral rolls are as full as possible even to the extent of padding the rolls with bogus members."[29] Interestingly, the same pattern was repeated some 20 years later when Rajiv Gandhi announced that after a hiatus of two decades, the party would hold organizational elections once again. As on previous occasions, the expectation of organizational elections triggered the enrollment of new members; however, "over 60 percent of the enrolled members were either non-existent or were not eligible for membership."[30]

The active membership base of the Congress Party also fluctuated but at far lower levels. It reached its peak in 1949 with 400,000 active members but dropped to its lowest point at 40,000 in 1954. By 1967, the Congress Party regained some of its active members, but it could still count only 200,000 in its ranks. In a report commissioned by the 81st All-India Congress Session, held in 2001 in Bangalore, the Congress Party's Committee on Party Finances indicated that there were "at present an estimated 11 lakh [1,100 000] Active Members in the Congress."[31]

In contrast to the Congress Party, the BJP and the CPI have not suffered from institutional decline and have been able to maintain quite strong party organizations. At the time of its (re)formation, the BJP made changes to both its formal structure and its key policy documents to distance itself from its predecessor, the

---

[27] Ibid.: 341.
[28] Kochanek 1968: 343.
[29] Ibid.: 344.
[30] Kohli 1990: 349.
[31] Congress Party.

BJS.[32] However, the fundamental character of the party's cadre-based organization and the party's advocacy of Hindu nationalism have remained unaltered. The key leaders of the new party, such as A. B. Vajpayee, L. K. Advani, R. Vijaya Raje Scindia, and M. M. Joshi were high-ranking officers of the BJS, and they all had close associations with the two most important organizational supporters of the BJS: Rashtriya Swayamsewak Sangh (RSS, National Volunteer Organization), an avowedly cultural organization with a trained cadre of followers dedicated to the observance and propagation of Hindu values, and the Vishwa Hindu Parishad (World Hindu Council). The RSS has played a particularly important role in the development of both the BJS and the BJP. Instead of becoming a political party itself, the RSS has consistently lent the support of its organizational machinery and an ideologically motivated and educated cadre to help the electoral prospects of the Hindu nationalist parties.[33]

In contrast to the Congress, the BJP never allowed dual leadership of both party and government. Although the relations between the party's organizational and legislative wings have been often conflictual, the separation of leadership roles has allowed the party organization to maintain its superiority over the party in parliament. In further contrast to the Congress, the BJP has held regular organizational elections.[34] Although there are no reliable data on changes in party membership over time, in the early 1990s the party claimed to have about 10 million members.[35]

Party organization was a central political and ideological concern to the CPI. The party followed the "democratic centralist" model of party organization that was proposed by the Communist International from its inception to 1958.[36] The organizational reforms that were passed by the party's Amritsar Congress that year aimed at relaxing the strict ideological nature of the party institutions. For example, the Politburo became the Central Executive Committee and the basic organizational units, the communist cells, were transformed into branches. Interestingly, after the split of 1964, the Communist Party of India (Marxist, CPM) and later the Communist Party of India (Marxist-Leninist) readopted some of these ideologically motivated organizational features while the CPI continued to evolve along the mass party model.[37] At the time of their split, the CPI had a membership of 1.7 million versus the CPM's 83,000. Twenty years later, the CPI claimed only 480,000 members against the CPM's 370,000.[38] At the end of 1997, the CPI claimed 560,723 members against the CPM's 717,525.[39]

---

[32] Graham 2006: 159.
[33] Malik and Singh 1994: 158–166; Jaffrelot 1998; Manor 2005: 59.
[34] Malik and Singh 1994: 155.
[35] Ibid.: 140.
[36] Rodriguez 2006: 228.
[37] Ibid.
[38] Ibid.
[39] Hardgrave and Kochanek 2000: 314–315.

Of the three old national parties, the Congress has suffered the most organizational stress in terms of factionalism, splits, and fission. The first major schism took place in 1969 soon after Indira Gandhi became prime minister,[40] followed by three further splits during her leadership in 1978, 1979, and 1981. These splits resulted in the formation of the Indian National Congress (Indira), which remained the official Congress standard bearer; the Indian National Congress (Urs); and the Indian Congress Socialist respectively.[41] In the 1990s, yet another wave of splits shook the party, leading to the creation of seven more Congress parties. In 1996, four new parties were formed (the Karnataka Congress Party, the Madhya Pradesh Vikas Congress, the Congress (Tiwari), and the Tamil Manila Congress), followed by the Trinamool Congress in 1998, and the Nationalist Congress in 1999. It is indicative of the organizational flux characterizing Indian political parties that five of these seven splinter parties have since rejoined the parent party with only the Trinamool and the Nationalist Congress parties continuing their separate existence.

Of the three old national parties, the BJP is the only one that has not suffered any major splits and schisms, which can be attributed to the dense and tightly knit network of its cadre.[42] The third old national party, the CPI, suffered two major schisms since its foundation in 1928. The first open split took place in 1964 and led to the formation of the CPM by the ideologically more conservative leftist elements of the parent party. The CPM quickly became the larger and politically more successful of the two parties. It established its strongholds in the states of West Bengal and Kerala; in the former, the CPM has actually formed every state government since 1977; in the latter, it has alternated in power with the Congress Party.[43] Five years after its creation, the CPM itself suffered a split when its own extremist members advocating direct revolutionary agitation and action over the moderate reformist approach taken by the CPM seceded to form the Communist Party of India (Marxist-Leninist).[44]

In sum, the organizational strength of India's most established political parties varies considerably. The once dominant Congress Party has suffered the most from internal deinstitutionalization as well as overt splits and defections, whereas the BJS/BJP has been disciplined and stable. The Communist Party, and its main successor the CPM, stands somewhere in-between.

A TEST OF FIVE HYPOTHESES

This section assesses Hicken and Kuhonta's (2009) five rival hypotheses on party system institutionalization in the light of the Indian experience.

---

[40] Hardgrave 1970; Singh 1981.
[41] Mendelsohn 1978.
[42] Manor 2005: 58.
[43] Nossiter 1988.
[44] Rodriguez 2006: 217–220.

1. The Passage of Time

According to the first hypothesis, the Indian party system should become more institutionalized over time. Clearly, there is mixed evidence in support of this expectation. In terms of electoral volatility, Figure 8.1 showed that the evolution of the Indian party system has not followed a strict linear path. Although volatility in the 1990s has declined noticeably compared to its earlier levels in the 1950s and 1960s, a significant increase in the level of electoral instability occurred between the 1977 and 1984 elections. Our discussion on the history of the organizational development of India's main political parties sheds light on the reason for this increase. The 1977 election was marked by the entry and the eventual victory of a new political party, the Janata, which consisted of the amalgamation of the principal non-communist parties that were previously in opposition to the Congress. As we treat every new party as a separate and distinct entity, whether or not it is born out of the merger of existing political parties or if it is a genuine new formation, and as the Janata was so successful at the 1977 polls, the Pedersen score jumped sharply to almost double its previous level.

Electoral volatility remained at a high level in the next election, in 1980, because splits in both the Janata and the Congress Parties resulted in the entry of two additional new parties in the electoral fray: the Janata Party (Secular) and the Congress (Urs). Four years later, in 1984, the organizational unrest continued with two new formations: the Congress (Socialist) and the Lok Dal and the reformed BJS, under its newly adopted BJP label, joining the electoral race. However, given that the Congress swept the polls, the new parties had a much more moderate effect on changes in the overall volatility score. In short, the increase in the Pedersen scores between 1977 and 1984 clearly points to the organizational and institutional instability that beset and characterized the Indian party system at this time.

In addition to the decline in electoral volatility since 1989, party system institutionalization is also promoted by the continued electoral and parliamentary domination of old parties. Although there are many new parties entering India's national elections, they tend to remain on the margins. At the same time, the continuing organizational weakness of one of these large established parties, the Congress, and parties' declining ability to command the confidence of the population suggest that party system institutionalization may be on weaker foundations.

2. Timing or Period Effects

This hypothesis also has mixed support. On the one hand, Hicken and Kuhonta (2009) show that based on the Pedersen values from the first two postwar elections, India appeared to have the most institutionalized party system in all of Asia. This suggests that if the Second Wave of global democratization had a general reductive effect on volatility rates in Asia compared to the Third Wave, then it certainly worked very well in India. On the other hand, Indian volatility scores increased considerably over time compared to those in the other Second Wave democratizers, with the exception of Malaysia. This suggests that the effects of the Second Wave did not last long.

3. The effect of authoritarianism

The Indian evidence qualifies the hypothesis about the supposed positive relationship between authoritarian intervention, especially shorter ones such as those in Thailand and Malaysia,[45] and party system institutionalization. As we have seen, authoritarian intervention in India did not lead to an increase in party system institutionalization. This suggests that the kind of authoritarianism that is in place will make an important difference for the subsequent institutionalization of the party system: much like Marcos' *autogolpe* in the Philippines, Indira Gandhi's Emergency explicitly sought to undermine and weaken Indian political parties to prevent the rise of rival opposition to her rule. In the process, she fundamentally destabilized the party system, which would not return to pre-Emergency levels of electoral volatility until the mid-1980s.

4. Political institutions: the number of parties and the anti-defection law

Of the three sets of institutional variables (parliamentary vs. presidential or mixed forms of government, the electoral system, and the number of parties) identified by Hicken and Kuhonta (2009), only the last one can be conceivably linked to changes in electoral volatility in India given that neither the type of government (parliamentarism) nor the electoral system (first-past-the-post) has changed over time while the party system has been much less stable.[46] Similarly to Hicken and Kuhonta (2009), a number of studies on India have also suggested that the relationship between party system fragmentation and electoral volatility is positive.[47] However, we find evidence to the contrary. Figure 8.2 plots the volatility and the effective number of parties scores in India over time. It clearly shows that the era of high levels of party system fragmentation since 1989 have been associated with an increasing level of electoral stabilization. Mathematically speaking, this negative correlation is possible only if the increase in the effective number of parties is caused by the proliferation of small parties whose entry into the electoral process does not have much of an impact on the overall Pedersen volatility score of the system.[48] In fact, as we see later, this is precisely what has been happening in India.

---

[45] Hicken and Kuhonta 2009: 18.
[46] Note, however, that in the first two elections there were a number of two- and three-member districts in the country.
[47] Yadav 2000, 1996; Heath 2005; Nooruddin and Chhibber 2008.
[48] I owe this point to Allen Hicken.

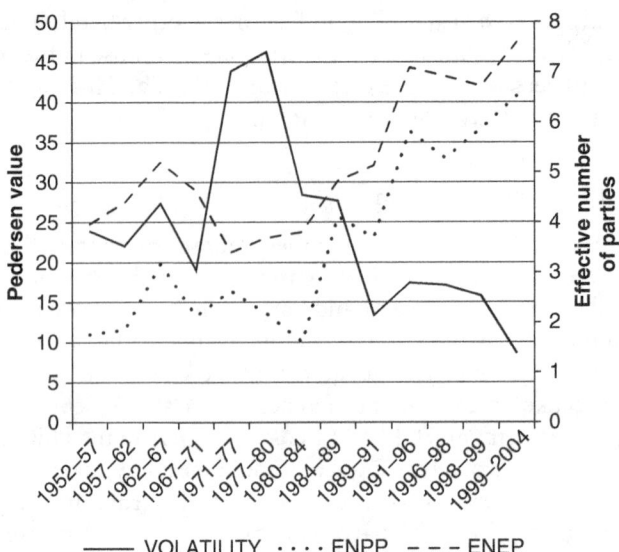

FIGURE 8.2. Volatility and Fragmentation in the Indian Party System.
Source: Author's calculation based on data from Statistical Reports of Lok Sabha Elections (http://eci.nic.in/eci_main1/ElectionStatistics.aspx).

The negative relationship between fragmentation and volatility is a puzzle that makes India a major deviant case compared against much of the available comparative evidence.[49] Of course, it is possible that the relationship between the two variables might be spurious rather than real and causal. In other words, we might imagine that the Indian party system responds with increased levels of fragmentation but reduced levels of volatility to changes that take place in the values of some other un-modeled variable that is the actual cause of both of them. Indeed, studies have suggested that the consequences of one specific institutional change, the passage of the 52nd Amendment to the Indian constitution, popularly known as the anti-defection law, and its subsequent further amendment in 2002, may precisely be this underlying cause accounting for the negative correlation between the number of parties and electoral volatility.[50] This argument also lends support to the point made by Hicken and Kuhonta (2009) that "restrictions on party switching can increase the incentives for politicians to invest in the party label,"[51] which in turn leads to lower rates of volatility.

The introduction of the anti-defection law constituted an integral part of Rajiv Gandhi's package of broader reforms aimed at both the reinstitutionalization of the Congress Party and cleaning up a decaying and increasingly more corrupt

---

[49] I owe this point to Scott Mainwaring.
[50] Nikolenyi 2005, 2008, 2009; Subramanian 2008.
[51] Hicken and Kuhonta 2009: 11.

political system.[52] The timing seemed opportune given that the Congress had just won its largest parliamentary majority ever in the 1984 elections, which were held in the immediate aftermath of Indira Gandhi's assassination. The law, officially passed as the 52nd Amendment to the Indian constitution, was passed at the record speed of only seven days in both houses of parliament. On behalf of his government, Rajiv Gandhi claimed that an anti-defection law was long overdue.[53] Indeed, seven year earlier, in 1978, an anti-defection bill was introduced by the Janata government, as the 48th Constitutional Amendment Bill; however, it was quickly withdrawn amid intense opposition from both the opposition and the government benches.[54] In 1985, the opposition argued during the parliamentary debates that the prime minister was in a hurry to pass the law to ensure discipline and cohesion in his extraordinarily large caucus.[55]

Defections had plagued the Indian party system since its inception. Hardgrave and Kochanek note that there had been "more than 2,700 recorded cases since 1967, most within the state assemblies."[56] According to the report prepared by the Chavan Committee in 1969, a total of 542 instances of defection were recorded between 1952 and 1968, with 80 percent taking place between March 1967 and February 1968. Independents accounted for a large portion of the switches. Defections in the State Assemblies were particularly linked to the pursuit of office benefits: of the 210 defecting state legislators, 116 were given positing in the state government that they helped form.[57]

The 1985 Constitutional Amendment Bill explicitly restricted and punished party switching and indiscipline. It stated that a member of either the state or the national legislature would be disqualified for membership if he or she were to leave the parliamentary unit of the party that elected him or her or if he or she were to vote against the party in violation of the whip. The only loophole provided by the law was that it allowed group defections as long as the defecting group was no smaller than one-third of the parent party that it sought to split away from. Such instances were considered officially recognized splits, and they did not incur the expulsion of the defectors from parliament. Arguably, this loophole may have considerably limited the force of the law.[58] Following recommendations by the Committee on Electoral Reforms in 1990, the Law Commission of India in 1999, and the National Commission to Review the Working of the Constitution in 2002, each echoing that this loophole be closed, parliament passed the 91st Constitutional Amendment, which no longer

---

[52] Kohli 1990: 340–346.
[53] Lok Sabha debates, January 30, 1985: 183.
[54] Malhotra 2005: 8–9.
[55] Rajya Sabha debates, January 31, 1985: 99–102.
[56] Hardgrave and Kochanek 2000: 273.
[57] Malhotra 2005: 5.
[58] Kashyap 2003.

permitted splits as defined in the previous law.[59] Simultaneously, the new law also forbade defectors from being appointed to political office and limited the total number of ministers in both the national and state governments to no more than 15 percent of the total number of legislative seats. Clearly, these provisions sought to ensure that party switching would no longer be used to destabilize governments at either the state or the national level.

As argued elsewhere,[60] the anti-defection law not only discouraged party defections in the legislature, but it also led to an increase in the number of new parties. By increasing deputies' costs of defecting from their party after the election, the anti-defection law actually encouraged would-be deputies to form both smaller and ideologically more compact parties before an electoral race. The incentive to form ideologically more tightly knit parties made sense because such parties, by definition, reduce the scope for conflict between individual deputies and the party leadership relative to ideologically diverse catchall parties. At the same time, the incentive to form small parties with fewer deputies in parliament also made numerical sense, at least until 2003 because of the one-third rule: the smaller the caucus, the easier to organize a collective defection that would avoid the penalty of a by-election for those involved. With the elimination of the one-third rule by the 91st Amendment to the constitution, politicians have even stronger incentives to form small tightly knit parties where the scope for policy compromise is narrower.

The anti-defection law has been effective at keeping defections and party indiscipline at bay. Between 1985 and 2004, only 16 petitions were submitted to the speaker of the Lok Sabha to have individual members disqualified. Of these 16 petitions, only 2 were allowed by the speaker; the remaining 14 cases were either dismissed or "rendered infractuous" because of the dissolution of the House. Overall, only 13 deputies were disqualified for having violated the anti-defection law.[61] In the Rajya Sabha, only two disqualification cases occurred during the entire period 19-year period, both of them allowed. With regard to group defections, that is, allowed splits, the law has been less successful: between 1985 and 2004, there were 22 cases of group defections filed in the Lok Sabha and all but two of them were allowed.[62] However, these defections involved only the smaller political parties, which is not surprising given that the one-third rule was in effect in this period. Indeed, no split was recorded from either the Congress or the BJP, the two largest old national parties. Similarly, the Communist parties also did not suffer splits at this time. Overall, defections and splits have clearly declined in magnitude compared to the numbers that were reported earlier.

[59] Jaitley 2003.
[60] Nikolenyi 2005, 2008, 2009; Subramanian 2008.
[61] Malhotra 2005: 665–670.
[62] Ibid.: 671–679.

At the state level, the number of disqualification requests issued and allowed between 1985 and 2004 have varied greatly; 97 petitions were submitted against 164 members of the different State Assemblies (Vidhan Sabha). Unlike at the national level, the majority of the individual deputies (N=113) who were charged with defection were actually removed from their respective assemblies. Most of the cases (50 out of 97) were launched in only four states, which shows a remarkable degree of concentration of the problem of defection. These states are Uttar Pradesh, the largest state of the India Union; Haryana; and the tiny states of Goa and Manipur. The outcome of the disqualification cases has been highly uneven: most of the deputies who were charged ended up being disqualified in Goa and Manipur, whereas the majority of them had their cases dismissed in Haryana. In Uttar Pradesh, not a single deputy was disqualified on the grounds of defection during this period.

In addition to its effect on party cohesion, the anti-defection law produced an unprecedented increase in the number of parties contesting the election and entering parliament. In the 1989 election, the first one that was held after the anti-defection law had been passed, the number of parties running increased more than threefold, from 33 to 113, compared to the last election held before the passage of the law in 1984. This growth in the number of new parties was particularly concentrated in the category of the small officially unrecognized parties, where their number increased from 9 in 1984 to 85 in 1989! The trend of the proliferation of such tiny unrecognized parties has continued unabated and reached its peak at 321 in the national election of 2009. Furthermore, the number of parties winning at least one parliamentary seat has also increased considerably. The average number of parties entering the Lok Sabha between 1952 and 1984 was 25.8, whereas the average number of parties in the Lok Sabha since 1989 has been 35.2, an increase of 10 parties per parliament on average.

In sum, the effects of the anti-defection law have resulted simultaneously in increasing the number of parties and containing the level of electoral volatility. By increasing the cost of dissenting and exiting from the party, the law has encouraged marginal factions that would otherwise join a broadly based party for electoral purposes to contest the elections on their own as separate entities. The net result has been an increase in the level of party system fragmentation. At the same time, because these splinter parties are small, they do not have a noticeable impact on the overall level of electoral volatility. Moreover, by discouraging large-scale defections from and splits in the large parties, the anti-defection law has had a further stabilizing effect on Indian parties keeping volatility rates under control.

In a number of important publications, Chhibber and Kollmann have offered an alternative view about the sudden increase in the number of parties in India since the late 1980s.[63] They have argued that the fragmentation of the Indian

[63] Chhiber and Kollman 1998, 2004.

party system is the result of the economic decentralization that has taken place in Indian federalism The gist of their account is that as the central government has abdicated economic policy control to the state governments with the onset of economic liberalization, political actors are increasingly more motivated to invest in the formation of state-based parties that focus on capturing and controlling these subnational governments. In other words, the Chhibber-Kollman argument explains the fragmentation of the Indian party system as a matter of increased party inflation in the national party system that is induced by the political incentives generated by economic decentralization. This thesis offers a compelling alternative to the explanation for party system fragmentation that we have provided. However, we suggest that it may be less adequate because, in contrast to the argument based on the consequences of the anti-defection law, it is not consistent with either the fact that national parties do persist and continue to play a pivotal role in the Indian party system or the proliferation of the extremely small unrecognized parties whose origin has nothing to do with the consequences of decentralization.

Strictly speaking, Chhibber and Kollman advance the decentralization argument to account for variation in the level of party inflation over time, which is the difference between the effective number of national parties and the average effective number of state parties. Clearly, party inflation and fragmentation are closely related concepts; however, they are not identical. Party inflation may be high or low regardless of the number of parties at either the national or the state level of aggregation. What matters for inflation is how many more national parties there are relative to the number of state parties. For example, party inflation will be zero if the number of parties at both the state and the national levels is identical, high or low, but party inflation increases as the nationally aggregated number of parties exceeds that at the state level. According to the decentralization thesis, it is party inflation that has been on the rise in India since the late 1980s: the increase in the effective number of national parties has far outstripped the increase in the effective number of state parties as the proliferation of single state-based parties has made the pattern of party competition uniquely state specific in a growing number of states.

We agree that the rise and proliferation of state parties started during Rajiv Gandhi's Congress government (1984–1989) when the shift toward greater subnational control over economic policy took place. However, it is equally true that the main national competitors to the Congress Party, the BJP on the right and the Janata Dal on the center-left of the ideological spectrum, also emerged precisely at that time as viable contenders that could wrest away from Congress its dominant position and hold on the national party system. Similarly to the national level, the principal axis of party competition in a number of major states has come to be defined by the state units of these national parties, many of which would further splinter as a result of the incentives of the anti-defection law. In short, although the decentralization thesis suggests that party system fragmentation should manifest itself in the rise of state-based parties, the evidence actually shows a much more varied picture in terms of the types of parties that have formed and persisted since the late 1980s: there are more parties of all kinds, national, state based, and most importantly unrecognized tiny formations than ever before. Although the rise in state parties may be attributed to the consequences of decentralization, the overall rise in the number of all sorts of other parties is not consistent with this thesis: there is no theoretical reason why decentralization should have resulted in the rise of national parties and the extraordinary increase in tiny political parties documented earlier. At the same time, our argument that locates the central cause of party system fragmentation in the consequences of the anti-defection law is consistent with the fact that there would be an increase in the number of all sorts of political parties: state based, national, and unrecognized.

5. Crosscutting cleavages

Cleavages have a mixed effect on party system institutionalization in India. On the one hand, India occupies the median position on electoral volatility in the sample of Asian democracies in spite of having the highest fractionalization score.[64] In so far as greater fractionalization indicates more clearly defined cleavages, which should lead to lower rates of volatility, this is surprising. At the same time, the relative level of cleavage crosscutting is consistent with Hicken and Kuhonta's expectation: in terms of both crosscutting and volatility, India is the median among the Asian democracies.

It is important to mention that two major lines of cleavage have emerged in the party system since the late 1980s: Hindu nationalism and the rise of the Other Backward Castes (OBCs), championed by the BJP and the Janata Dal respectively.[65] Although the two parties formed a successful electoral alliance in 1989 against the Congress Party, they parted ways soon after and have not cooperated ever since. During its brief term in office (1989–1991), the Janata Dal government introduced the reservation policy recommended by the Mandal Commission, according to which members of OBCs are entitled to reserved employment quotas in the public sector. While this policy resulted in the massive electoral mobilization of the OBCs behind the Janata Dal, it also posed a direct challenge to the BJP's agenda of creating a national electoral base built on a Hindu national and religious identity that cuts across the country's linguistic, regional, and caste cleavages. Since then, the inability of the Janata Dal to build a successful party organization has led to the fragmentation of OBC support behind the multiple competing splinter groups that have split off from the party.[66] Nonetheless, the nature and structure of political cleavages in the Indian party system has been fundamentally redefined by the simultaneous rise

---

[64] See table 5 in Hicken and Kuhonta 2009: 31.
[65] Gould and Ganguly 1993; Jaffrelot 1998; Chandra 1999, 2004; Roy 1999; Yadav 2006.
[66] Fickett 1993.

of Mandal and Mandir,[67] which, as shown in Figure 8.1, corresponds with a reduction in electoral volatility. In sum, even though the BJP remains the only one among the major national parties with a clear cleavage alignment, there still appears to be an overall correlation between the rise of cleavage politics and the concomitant increase in party system institutionalization from the 1990s onward.

CONCLUSION

A number of important points emerge from this discussion on the institutionalization of India's party system. The first is that Mainwaring and Scully's four analytical dimensions of party system institutionalization do not provide a consistent picture of the value and stability of parties and party competition in India. On the positive side, the party system continues to be dominated by long-standing and well-established parties, which keeps electoral instability at bay. On the negative side, the internal organizational strength of India's established parties varies considerably, with the BJP displaying a high level of organizational articulation in contrast to the disarray that characterizes the Janata Dal. Furthermore, survey results reveal that Indian parties' legitimacy appears to be on the decline. Therefore, the evidence about the level of party system institutionalization is mixed.

The second main point pertains to the effects of India's anti-defection law. In contrast to some of the other Asian cases where institutional effects on party system institutionalization are exerted by electoral rules and the system of government, the law appears to be the main institutional source of electoral volatility. The law has led to a simultaneous reduction in electoral volatility and heightened fragmentation in the party system by encouraging the formation of smaller political parties. Considering that this is precisely the opposite of what we find elsewhere, for example, in the Philippines where party system fragmentation and electoral volatility correlate positively, the effects of the anti-defection law in India are both intriguing and puzzling. The subsequent tightening of its provisions in 2003 suggests continued positive impact on electoral stability in the future.

Finally, a third important point to emerge from the Indian case study is that personalized authoritarian rule may very well undermine rather than promote the development of an institutionalized party system. Although India suffered only a short breakdown in its democratic rule (1975–1977), the brief authoritarian interlude under Indira Gandhi only further weakened the political institutions of the country, including political parties, which laid the foundation for future electoral instability in the world's largest democracy. This is very different from some of the other Asian cases in this volume where a strong authoritarian party played a pivotal role in creating the preconditions for an institutionalized post-authoritarian party system.

---

[67] The Hindi word *mandir* means temple; it refers to the rise of the BJP's Hindutva program in contemporary India.

REFERENCES

Bartoloni, Stefano, and Peter Mair. 1990. *Identity, Competition, and Electoral Volatility: The Stabilization of European Electorates 1885–1985.* Cambridge: Cambridge University Press.

Chakrabarty, Bidyut. 2006. *Forging Power: Coalition Politics in India.* New Delhi: Oxford University Press.

Chandra, Kanchan. 1999. Post-Congress Politics in Uttar Pradesh: The Ethnification of the Party System and Its Consequences. In Paul Wallace and Prannoy Roy (Eds.), *Indian Politics and the 1998 Elections: Regionalism, Hindutva, and State Politics,* pp. 55–105. New Delhi: Sage Publications.

Chandra, Kanchan. 2004. *Why Ethnic Parties Succeed: Patronage and Ethnic Head Counts in India.* Cambridge: Cambridge University Press.

Chhibber, Pradeep. 1999. *Democracy without Associations: Transformation of the Party System and Social Cleavages in India.* Ann Arbor: The University of Michigan Press.

Chhibber, Pradeep, and Ken Kollman. 1998. Party Aggregation and the Number of Parties in India and the United States. *American Political Science Review* 92 (June): 329–342.

Chhibber, Pardeep and Ken Kollman. 2004. *The Formation of National Party Systems: Federalism and Party Competition in Canada, Great Britain, India and the United States.* Princeton: Princeton University Press.

Chhibber, Pradeep, and Irfan Nooruddin. 2000. Party Competition and Fragmentation in Indian National Elections: 1957–1998. In Paul Wallace and Prannoy Roy (Eds.), *Indian Politics and the 1998 Elections: Regionalism, Hindutva, and State Politics,* pp. 36–54. New Delhi: Sage Publications.

Fickett, Lewis P. 1993. The Rise and Fall of the Janata Dal. *Asian Survey* 33(12): 1151–1162.

Gould, Harold A. and Sumit Ganguly (Eds.). 1993. *India Votes: Alliance Politics and Minority Governments in the Ninth and Tenth General Elections.* Boulder: Westview Press.

Graham, Bruce D. 2006. The Challenge of Hindu Nationalism: The Bharatiya Janata Party in Contemporary Indian Politics. In Peter Ronald de Souza and E. Sridharan (Eds.), *India's Political Parties,* pp. 155–172. New Delhi: Sage Publications.

Hardgrave, Robert. 1970. The Congress in India: Crisis and Split. *Asian Survey,* 10(3): 256–262.

Hardgrave, Robert and Stanley, Kochanek. 2000. *India; Government and Politics in a Developing Nation.* Fort Worth: Harcourt Brace Jovanovich.

Heath, Oliver. 2005. Party Systems, Political Cleavages, and Electoral Volatility in India: A State-Wise Analysis, 1998–99. *Electoral Studies* 24(2): 177–199.

Heginbotham, Stanley. 1971. The 1971 Revolution in Indian Voting Behavior. *Asian Survey,* 11(12): 1133–1152.

Hicken, Alan, and E. Kuhonta. 2009. Reexamining Party System Institutionalization through Asian Lenses. Typescript.

Indian National Congress Party. Report of the Committee on Party Finances. Available at http://180.179.212.175/en2/index.php/2013-01-02-08-23-8/dr-manmohan-singh -committee-s-report-on-party-finances, access date May 19, 2014.

Jaffrelot, Christophe. 1998. *The Hindu Nationalist Movement in India.* New York: Columbia University Press.

Jaitley, Arun. 2003. *Statement of Object and Reasons, The Constitution (Ninety-First Amendment) Act, 2003.* New Delhi: Lok Sabha.

Kashyap, Subhash C. 2003. *Anti-Defection Law and Parliamentary Privileges.* New Delhi: Universal Law Publishing.

Kochanek, Stanley. 1968. *The Congress Party of India: The Dynamics of One-Party Democracy.* Princeton: Princeton University Press.

Kochanek, Stanley. 1976. Mrs. Gandhi's Pyramid: The New Congress. In Henry C. Hart (Ed.), *Indira Gandhi's India,* pp. 93–124. Boulder: Westview Press.

Kohli, Atul. 1990. *Democracy and Discontent: India's Growing Crisis of Governability.* Cambridge: Cambridge University Press.

Linden, Leigh. 2004. *Are Incumbents Really Advantaged? The Preference for Non-Incumbents in Indian National Elections.* Columbia University Manuscript.

Lok, Sabha. 1985. Lok Sabha Debates, January 30, 1985: 183. New Delhi: Lok Sabha Secretariat.

Mainwaring, Scott, and Timothy Scully (Eds.). 1995. *Building Democratic Institutions: Party Systems in Latin America.* Stanford: Stanford University Press.

Malhotra, G. C. 2005. *Anti-Defection Law in Indian and the Commonwealth.* New Delhi: Metropolitan Book.

Malik, Yogendra K., and V. B. Singh. 1994. *Hindu Nationalists in India: The Rise of the Bharatiya Janata Party.* New Delhi: Vistaar Publications.

Manor, James. 1988. Parties and the Party System. In Atul Kohli (Ed.), *India's Democracy: An Analysis of Changing State-Society Relations,* pp. 62–98. Princeton: Princeton University Press.

Manor, James. 2005. In Part, a Myth: The BJP's Organizational Strength. In Katherine Adeney and Lawrence Saez (Eds.), *Coalition Politics and Hindu Nationalism,* pp. 55–73. New York: Routledge.

Mendelsohn, Oliver. 1978. "The Collapse of the Indian National Congress". *Pacific Affairs,* 51: 41–65.

Morris-Jones, Wyndraeth H. 1978. From Monopoly to Competition in India's Polity. In Wyndraeth H. Morris-Jones (Ed.), *Politics Mainly Indian,* pp. 144–159. Madras: Orient Longman.

Nikolenyi, Csaba. 2005. Institutional Change and Its Consequences: The Rational Foundations of Party System Change in India. In André Lecours (Ed.), *New Institutionalism: Canadian Contributions,* pp. 202–221. Toronto: The University of Toronto Press.

Nikolenyi, Csaba. 2008. Recognition Rules, Party Labels and the Number of Parties in India: A Research Note. *Party Politics* 14(2): 211–222.

Nikolenyi, Csaba. 2009. Party Inflation in India: Why Has a Multi-Party Format Prevailed in the National Party System? In Bernard Grofman, Shaun Bowler, and André Blais (Eds.), *Duverger's Law of Plurality Voting: The Logic of Party Competition in Canada, India, the United Kingdom, and the United States,* pp. 97–114. New York: Springer.

Nikolenyi, Csaba. 2010. *Minority Governments in India: The Puzzle of Elusive Majorities.* London: Routledge.

Nooruddin, Irfan, and Pradeep Chhibber. 2008. Unstable Politics: Fiscal Space and Electoral Volatility in the Indian States. *Comparative Political Studies* 41(8): 1069–1091.

Nossiter, Thomas J. 1988. *Marxist State Governments in India: Politics, Economics and Society*. London and New York: Pinter Publications.

Panebianco, Angelo. 1988. *Political Parties: Organization and Power*. New York: Cambridge University Press.

Pedersen, Mogens. 1983. Changing Patterns of Electoral Volatility in European Party Systems, 1948–1977: Explorations in Explanation. In Hans Daalder and Peter Mair (Eds.), *Western European Party Systems: Continuity and Change*, pp. 29–66. Beverly Hills: Sage Publications.

Rajya Sabha. 1985. Rajya Sabha Debates, January 31, 1985: 99–102. New Delhi: Rajya Sabha Secretariat.

Rodriguez, Valerian. 2006. The Communist Parties of India. In Peter Ronald de Souza and E. Sridharan (Eds.), *India's Political Parties*, pp. 199–252. New Delhi: Sage Publications.

Saxena, Rekha. 1996. Party System in Transition. In Mahendra Prasad Singh and Rekha Saxena (Eds.), *India's Political Agenda: Perspectives on the Party System*, pp. 49–81. Delhi: Kalinga Publications.

Singh, Mahendra Prasad. 1990. From Predominance to Polarized Pluralism: The Indian Party System. *Think India* 2:70–78.

Singh, Mahendra Prasad. 1981. *Split in a Predominant Party: The Indian National Congress in 1969*. New Delhi: Abhinav Publications.

Shridharan, E. 2003. Coalitions and Party Strategies in India's Parliamentary Federation. *Publius* 33(4): 135–152.

Shridharan, E. 2005. Coalition Strategies and the BJP's Expansion. *Journal of Commonwealth and Comparative Politics* 43(2): 194–221.

Shridharan, E., and Ashutosh Varshney. 2001. Towards Moderate Pluralism: Democracy and India's Political Parties. In Larry Diamond and Richard Gunther (Eds.), *Political Parties and Democracy*, pp. 206–237. Baltimore: The Johns Hopkins University Press.

Subramanian, R. S. 2008. *Developing and Testing a Theory of Legislative Party Fragmentation*. Ph.D. dissertation. University of Wisconsin–Madison.

Weiner, Myron. 1967. *Party Building in a New Nation: the Indian National Congress*. Chicago: University of Chicago Press.

Yadav, Yogendra. 1996. Reconfiguration in Indian Politics: State Assembly Elections, 1993–95. *Economic and Political Weekly* 31(2–3): 94–105.

Yadav, Yogendra. 2000. Understanding the Second Democratic Upsurge: Trends of Bahujan Participation in Electoral Politics in the 1990s. In Francine Frankel et al. (Eds.), *Transforming India: Social and Political Dynamics of Democracy*, pp. 120–145. New Delhi: Oxford University Press.

Yadav, Yogendra, and Suhas Palshikar. 2006. Party System and Electoral Politics in the Indian States, 1952–2002: From Hegemony to Convergence. In Peter R. de Souza and E. Sridharan (Eds.), *India's Political Parties*, pp. 73–116. New Delhi: Sage Publications.

9

Party and Party System Institutionalization in Cambodia

Sorpong Peou

This chapter analyses party and party system institutionalization in Cambodia. The country provides an excellent case study that sheds some new light on the theoretical observations made in this volume. Since the country made a historic triple transition in the early 1990s (from war to peace, from command to market economics, and from political authoritarianism to electoral democracy) when four Cambodian armed factions and 18 other foreign states formally signed the Paris Peace Agreements on October 23, 1991, the country's multiparty system and political parties have had more than 20 years to become institutionalized.

The concept of party system and party institutionalization is subject to debate,[1] but this chapter works within the analytical framework developed in this volume. Party and party system institutionalization, as the key dependent variable, is a process not necessarily associated with democratization based on formal or impersonal rules, norms, and decision-making procedures. Institutionalization is defined more or less as a process of stabilization or regularization: party systems become more and more stable over time, and electoral competition becomes less and less volatile because of their growing political legitimacy as measured in terms of growing public support and deepening social roots. Moreover, political parties become less factionalized or more and more organizationally cohesive.

The question to be dealt with here is whether both the political parties and party system in Cambodia have become increasingly institutionalized over time and whether historical legacies explain the levels of party system and party institutionalization. Both Allen Hicken and Erik Martinez Kuhonta make some insightful observations, one of which is that institutionalization can proceed in semi-democratic or semi-authoritarian states (such as Malaysia and Singapore), as dominant parties undermine opposition parties' ability to compete in electoral processes and become institutionalized over time. Party systems that are

Note: I would like to thank the participants in this book's workshop, especially Dr. Manuel Litalien, Ambassador Gordon Longmuir, and the two reviewers for their useful comments. I alone am responsible for what this chapter contains.
[1] In my work, for instance, I develop the concept of democratic institutionalization. See Peou 2007.

increasingly institutionalized are also those that become increasingly stable – because hegemonic parties not only become institutionalized over time but can also push surviving opposition parties to become institutionalized as well. Existing parties that were institutionalized at an earlier point in time, for instance, tend to develop a higher level of institutionalization relative to those that emerged after or more recently.

These insightful observations fit nicely with the theoretical tradition of historical institutionalism, but the key question is whether they enjoy strong empirical support. This chapter advances four main arguments. First, the multiparty system in Cambodia has become more institutionalized in an authoritarian way. The electoral process as a whole has also become less volatile and has gained more legitimacy when assessed in terms of acceptance of the electoral laws; regularity of elections; the National Election Committee (NEC)'s role in managing elections; and a relative decline in the numbers of complaints, protests, and violent incidents before, during, and after polling day. The Election Administration has become institutionally more efficient in technical and organizational terms than in legal and political terms. The NEC in particular tends to prefer informal reconciliation to formal dispute settlement when dealing with election-related complaints and continues to be perceived as politically biased in favor of the ruling party (Cambodian People's Party or CPP). The party system's institutionalization increasingly depends on CPP domination. The system now looks more like a hegemonic one, "in which a relatively institutionalized ruling party monopolizes the political arena, using coercion, patronage, media control, and other means to deny formally legal opposition parties any real chance of competing for power."[2] Sartori adds, "Other parties are permitted to exist, but as second class, licensed parties."[3]

Second, the political parties in the country have become thinly, autocratically, and unevenly institutionalized. The CPP has now emerged as the most institutionalized party in comparative terms, whereas the political opposition seems to remain relatively far less institutionalized or, in some cases, even deinstitutionalized. The country held its first national election in May 1993, after which a coalition government was formed and a fairly liberal constitution was adopted, but the regime led by Prime Minister Hun Sen of the CPP has become increasingly and institutionally authoritarian.

Third, the Cambodia case study validates the hypothesis that the growth of institutionalization is primarily a function of time. The current party system and political parties have had since 1991 to develop. The CPP first emerged as the communist party early in the 1980s, before the opposition parties, which emerged only in the 1990s. The CPP was institutionalized earlier than the opposition and thus developed a higher level of institutionalization relative to those that emerged later. However, time alone does not explain why some parties have become more institutionalized than others or why, for instance,

---

[2] Diamond 2002: 25.
[3] Sartori 1976: 230.

the winner of the 1993 election – the National United Front for an Independent, Neutral, Peaceful, and Cooperative Cambodia (FUNCINPEC) – has become more factionalized and disintegrated (instead of more institutionalized as the CPP became increasingly dominant); nor why the Buddhist Liberal Democracy Party (BLDP) – whose faction was a major signatory of the 1991 peace agreements – ceased to function as a party. Political cleavages did give rise to party and party system institutionalization in this country, but they alone do not explain the low and uneven levels of that institutionalization. If historical legacies matter, cultural and ideological legacies also need to be taken into account. Complex historical legacies help explain why the CPP has become more institutionalized than other parties but has remained far from institutionalized. Historical institutionalism, however, has its explanatory limits: evidence throughout this chapter shows that time functions and historical legacies alone did not necessitate the process of authoritarian institutionalization.

Fourth, party system and party institutionalization in Cambodia was also a product of recent domestic and international policy and politics. At the domestic level, the institutional process was part not only of past legacies but, more importantly, of political performance, regime legitimacy, and domestic power distribution. The CPP leadership has been far more effective than other political parties in terms of both gaining legitimacy through economic performance and consolidating power. At the international level, members of the international community, especially donors, were also partly responsible for the authoritarian and uneven institutionalization of parties and the party system in that they have helped provide the Hun Sen regime with international legitimacy, despite the fact that the CPP has succeeded in consolidating power at the expense of the opposition.

THE AUTHORITARIAN INSTITUTIONALIZATION OF CAMBODIA'S MULTIPARTY SYSTEM

This section assesses the process of institutionalization within the political party system overall and within individual political parties. It covers a period of 22 years: from October 1991, when four Cambodian armed factions signed a peace agreement establishing a multiparty system, to mid-2013. Various indicators show that the multiparty system has now given way to a nascent hegemonic party system, which has become more institutionalized but remains weakly or thinly and increasingly unevenly so.

It may be worth briefly reviewing what this volume means by party system institutionalization. In this volume, both Hicken and Kuhonta make the following arguments based on the work of Samuel Huntington and Scott Mainwaring and Timothy Scully. First, Huntington focuses on the level of institutionalization ("the process by which organizations and procedures acquire value and stability"), which can be assessed in terms of adaptability, coherence, complexity, and autonomy. Mainwaring and Scully, however, focus on party system institutionalization. Second, the concept of institutionalization advanced by Mainwaring and Scully subsumes that of Huntington: institutionalization is thus defined by four factors: (1) stability in the rules and nature of interparty competition; (2) parties having stable roots in society; (3) legitimacy in the electoral process and within parties themselves; and (4) parties becoming cohesive, disciplined, and autonomous. Third, highly institutionalized party systems need not be democratic and may have their roots in authoritarian institutionalized parties.

The Cambodian case study shows that the multiparty system has become more institutionalized over time when assessed in terms of stabilization. The electoral rules governing interparty competition have not been subject to constant substantial revision. New rules for electoral competition were first introduced in the Paris Peace Agreements. The rules, based on an electoral law and a code of conduct regulating participation in the election, included free and fair elections, fair access to the media, and respect for election outcomes. The new constitution (adopted in 1993) reaffirmed these rules. The government also adopted the Law on Political Parties and the Election of Members of the National Assembly (LEMNA) in December 1997 and the Law on the Election of Commune Councils in March 2001 and made some amendments after that (such as one to the electoral law adopted by the National Assembly and enacted on September 17, 2002 aimed at streamlining the electoral process and reducing costs).

The competitive electoral process as a whole also appeared to become more stable. The National Assembly elections of 1993, 1998, 2003, and 2008, the senate elections of 2006 and 2012 and the commune (third-level administrative division below district level) elections of 2002, 2007, and 2012 further reveal a growing degree of stability and electoral regularity within the multiparty system. The electoral process's stabilization can also be assessed in terms of a general decline in the overall numbers of parties, complaints, protests, and violent incidents before, during, and after polling day. The number of political parties registered to compete in the electoral process has declined, indicating that fewer parties mean less polarization, but remained stable overall. At the national level, 20 parties were registered to compete in the 1993 national election; however, the number increased to 39 parties in the 1998 national election and then declined to 23 in the 2003 national election, to only 11 in the 2008 national election and to only 8 in the July 2013 election, and 10 in the 2012 commune election.

The number of violent incidents, complaints, and protests related to the electoral process has also declined in recent years. Major reports by the UN special representative for human rights in Cambodia, regarding the national elections in 1998, 2008, and 2013 and the commune elections in 2002, 2007, and 2012 documented less and less political intimidation and violence, political killings, other instances of violent deaths, as well as the limits of the opposition's access to the media, especially during election time. During the 1998 election, widespread political intimidation and abuses were documented.[4] The 2003 election also witnessed intimidation of voters and political activists across the country but was marked by less violence and political intimidation.[5] In the period preceding the commune polls on February 3, 2002 and after, violence and intimidation remained serious (of the 19 people who were murdered, 17 were political activists affiliated to FUNCINPEC and the Sam Rainsy Party (SRP)).[6] During the period leading to the second commune election in 2007 and the National Assembly election in 2008, cases of political intimidation against political activists were reported to have increased.[7] Overall, however, the level of violence during the 2007 commune election was lower than that of the 2003 election. The 2008 National Assembly election also witnessed a decline in the level of armed violence against members of the opposition. The 2012 commune election was even more peaceful than the previous ones. Only a few activists working for opposition parties were killed in the run-up to the election, but it remains unclear whether the killings were politically motivated. Based on reports by human rights groups confirming "only rare cases of politically moti- vated violence or physical intimidation," the UN Special Rapporteur character- izes the preelection situation in 2013 as "very calm."[8]

The number of complaints and protests has also declined over time. In the 2003 election, for instance, the number of complaints relating to voting, ballot verification, and counting and consolidation of results was 396.[9] The number of complaints in the 2008 election was lower than in the previous elections. The commune elections of 2002 and 2007 also witnessed a decline in the number of complaints: from 800 in the weeks following the 1998 election and 745 in 2003 to 326 in 2007.[10] The number of protests against election outcomes also declined. After the 1993 election, the CPP protested the election results by threatening to divide the country. The subsequent elections resulted in the party's victory and protests by the opposition, but the latter staged fewer and fewer protests against the election results. After the 1998 election, opposition parties staged demonstrations, accusing Hun Sen of fraud and demanding his ouster, which led to violent clashes with the police. The 2008 election saw some initial protests by opposition parties against alleged election fraud, but the protests soon died down as they found themselves in disarray. The post-2013 election situation was more volatile, however, in that opposition members took to the streets in protest against the results.

---

[4] See, for instance, Hammarberg 1998.
[5] Commission on Human Rights (2003: 7–9); Special Representative of the Secretary-General for Human Rights in Cambodia (2003: 8–16).
[6] UN General Assembly 2002: 6.
[7] ADHOC 2008: 14.
[8] Special Rapporteur 2013: 11.
[9] UNDP 2003: 21.
[10] UNDP 2007: 26.

The Election Administration (which included the NEC) has also become more institutionalized over time, especially after the 1998 election, when assessed in terms of technical and organizational development. A report by the International Republican Institute states that *"the NEC's accomplishments appear to have been largely technical in nature."*[11] During the election of 2003, according to the United Nations Development Program, the NEC also "operated a more transparent and participatory process" by scheduling "regular meetings with political parties, NGOs and media representatives" and becoming more "responsive to the preoccupations of Cambodian society as a whole."[12]

Fewer political parties, less election-related violence and intimidation, fewer complaints about election irregularities, less frequent public protests against election results and more technically and organizationally efficient election administration mean more political stability based on coercion and co-option, but not more democratic institutionalization based on higher degrees of political legitimacy. First, the Election Administration remains far from democratically institutionalized, when assessed in terms of formal legal enforcement. The NEC ineffectively enforced the electoral laws or its own directives. The investigation of criminal acts, including politically motivated killings by local police and CPP elements, stalled. The NEC issued directives – often based on appeals from its own chairman – but rarely imposed sanctions on violators. Electoral authorities showed limited accountability for their actions, particularly those related to intimidation and violence during election times. Moreover, policy decisions and subsequent policy actions taken by electoral authorities did not show adequate transparency and accountability. During election times, for instance, the rule of transparency was often challenged when electoral officials refused to implement complicated regulations and procedures or investigate complaints and were reluctant to issue sanctions, preferring instead to rely on conciliation. According to a report by the UN special representative, "While the 2003 elections saw the first application of sanctions by the National Election Committee and its provincial commissions, the electoral authorities were largely ineffective in dealing with serious breaches of the 'Electoral Law.'"[13] During the cooling-off period – the voting and counting days of the 2012 commune election – some 3,000 irregularities (such as intimidation, vote buying, and the destruction of opposition parties' leaflets and logos) were reported.[14] Moreover, the NEC still lacked transparency and its dispute settlement mechanisms remained unchanged: it still relied on reconciliation as an informal means to deal with election complaints.[15]

---

[11] International Republican Institute (n.d.): 7 (italics in original).
[12] UNDP 2003: 6, 7.
[13] Special Representative of the UN Secretary-General for Human Rights in Cambodia (n.d.): 4–5.
[14] COMFREL 2012a.
[15] Ibid

Second, the electoral process has been regarded as still not genuinely free or fair. The NEC has been perceived as being dominated by the CPP. The CPP-dominated Ministry of the Interior controlled the NEC's budget, and the NEC headquarters remains located within the ministry's compound. The ministry also showed more willingness to ban peaceful demonstrations, strikes, and any form of protest against the regime. Before the 2003 election, National Police Chief General Hok Lundy had even made it clear to the public in general and the electorate in particular that post-election protests and violence would not be tolerated. One report, for example, states: "*Many NEC actions – and just as frequently its inaction – reinforced concerns regarding the NEC's political neutrality and contributed significantly to the climate of impunity that allowed for widespread political violence, election law violations, and intimidation of voters.*"[16] Prior to the 2008 election, observers had remained skeptical about the institutional independence of the more technically competent NEC, because its members were still appointed by a few political parties, especially the CPP: the NEC headquarters were still located within the CPP-controlled Ministry of the Interior, and the NEC had no subnational structure and still relied on commune councils, which were dominated by the CPP and took orders from the Ministry of the Interior. There still exists a political atmosphere of insecurity in the country, as people have become increasingly hesitant to raise voices critical of government policies. Before the 2012 commune election, the CPP was still accused of having used state resources, civil servants, and even armed personnel to help it conduct the election campaign. Moreover, the party continued to control state and private media to ensure its electoral victory.[17] The UN Special Rapporteur questioned whether the 2013 elections were free and fair, expressing concerns over the independence of the NEC, freedom of expression, and access to media for all political parties.[18]

Third, popular interest in elections has also declined. According to a survey conducted in August 2007, most Cambodian voters (74 percent) were either somewhat or very dissatisfied with the way democracy worked.[19] The levels of voter turnout also declined. The National Assembly elections saw steady drops in the voter turnout after 1998: 86.78 percent of the eligible voters (1993); 93.74 percent (1998), 83.22 percent (2003), 75.21 percent (2008), and 68.49 percent (2013).[20] The last three commune elections also witnessed steady drops in the voter turnout: from 87 percent of the eligible voters (2002) to 67 percent (2007) and 60 percent (2012).[21]

---

[16] International Republican Institute (n.d.): 7 (italics in original).
[17] COMFREL 2012b.
[18] Special Rapporteur on the Situation of Human Rights in Cambodia (2013: 11).
[19] Ray and Naurath 2008.
[20] International Institute for Democracy and Electoral Assistance, n.d.
[21] Voice of America 2012.

THE LIMITS AND UNEVEN (HEGEMONIC) INSTITUTIONALIZATION OF POLITICAL PARTIES

The extent to which the political parties have become autocratically institutionalized is difficult to assess, but the CPP has definitely become far more institutionalized than any other opposition party. However, party institutionalization remains unevenly authoritarian.

The political opposition has not grown institutionally stronger. Founded in 1978, the royalist party (FUNCINPEC) depended on the personal charisma of its top leader, Prince Norodom Ranariddh, whose party won the 1993 election largely because of his royal status as a son of King/Prince Norodom Sihanouk. Prince Ranariddh would remain president for life. But he soon found himself in the position of being unable to maintain political stability within the party because of personal scandals involving corruption and extramarital affairs, as well as his fallout with Hun Sen. After 1997, FUNCINPEC lost almost all of its political and military muscle and badly disintegrated. Ranariddh was ousted from his party in 2006 and formed a new party, the Norodom Ranariddh Party.

Badly spit, FUNCINPEC won only two seats in the 2008 national election and weakened further after that. The new party leader Keo Puth Rasmey (and its secretary general, Nhek Bun Chhay) has enjoyed less political legitimacy within the party. He remains a political lightweight, and after the poor performance in the 2008 election, a faction within FUNCINPEC sought to oust him.[22] Meanwhile, senior party officials were under pressure to support or defect to the CPP. A series of defections by leading royalists to CPP continued unabated. As of 2008, about 20 high-ranking FUNCINPEC officials had reportedly decided to leave their party for the CPP. In December 2008, for instance, General Serei Kosal of FUNCINPEC (who commanded royalist troops in the fight against Hun Sen's forces after the coup in 1997) finally decided to defect to the CPP. He was reported to have said that he "now recognize[d] the achievement of the national and international policies of the CPP... a party with good discipline."[23] In early 2009, Sun Chanthol (a former minister) also defected to the CPP, followed by the defection of another former minister and former ambassador to Japan, Pou Sothirak. The number of its seats within the National Assembly declined drastically from 58 (1993) to 43 (1998) and to only 2 (2008). Social support for FUNCINPEC weakened over the years, when assessed in terms of the decreased number of voters supporting the party between 1993 and 2013: 1,824,188 (1993), 1,554,790 (1998), 958,426 (2002), 1,072,313 (2003), 277,545 (2007), 303,764 (2008), and only 242,413 (2013).[24]

---

[22] *Phnom Penh Post*, December 15, 2008.
[23] *Phnom Penh Post*, December 10, 2008.
[24] Trustbuilding's Blog 2013.

As recently as 2012 when the last commune election was held, both FUNCINPEC and the Norodom Ranarridh Party received only 396,000 votes. FUNCINPEC won only one seat of commune chief in the election. The Norodom Ranariddh Party did not become more institutionalized either. It performed badly in the 2008 national election: it received only 337,943 votes and two seats (one seat fewer than the new Human Rights Party [HRP]).[25] In December 2008, having finally decided to leave politics, Prince Ranariddh was appointed chief adviser to King Norodom Sihamoni. The party did not even win a commune chief seat in 2012. In August of that year, the party was given a new name (the Nationalist Party) and was subsequently merged with FUNCINPEC. It remains to be seen whether this party reunification will result in further institutionalization.

The Sam Rainsy Party (SRP) has become more institutionalized than FUNCINPEC, but it remains far from stable. The SRP has a history of personalism and intraparty factionalism, which have prevented the party from achieving strong internal unity. When it was first formed in November 1995, it was known as the Khmer Nation Party (KNP), but Sam Rainsy renamed it the Sam Rainsy Party for various reasons, including that the Ministry of the Interior refused to register the KNP because someone else had already done so and the party under that name did not enjoy international support; however, the SRP name was also adopted because no one else within or outside the party could take it away from him. The party is still known for its heavy dependence on the personal charisma of Sam Rainsy. Maintaining loyalty with the party remains a challenge. Defections to the CPP took place. As of November 2009, for instance, more than 100 SRP members, including Sam Rainsy's personal bodyguards, had reportedly defected to the CPP.[26] Those who defected from the party maintained that party committees had no real power, because the president – Sam Rainsy – still controlled the decision-making process. For instance, in 2007 a member of its Steering Committee, Ken Virak, left to form his own party, the People's Power Party, because he had become disillusioned with the SRP. According to Ou Virak, president of the Cambodian Center for Human Rights, "there are some good people in the party that I know that cannot move up in the ranks. There are some very good people who were left out."[27] The party's Steering Committee was nominally in charge of party decision making but apparently no longer had any real power. Sam Rainsy has even proved unable to form an alliance with any other opposition parties such as the HRP, whose institutionalization will be discussed later.

The SRP, however, has gained more popular support than any other opposition party, but the number of voters supporting it declined in the last commune election. Having gained 15 seats in the 1998 election, 24 in the 2003 election,

---

[25] Ibid.
[26] *Khmerization* 2009.
[27] Cited in the *Phnom Penh Post*, December 4, 2009.

and 26 in the 2008 election, the SRP has now emerged as the main opposition party in the National Assembly. The number of voters supporting the SRP steadily increased, as evident in the following election results: 699,665 (1998), 731,150 (2002), 1,130,423 (2003), and 1,316,714 (2008).[28] In 2012, however, the party received fewer votes (about 1,220,000), representing a decrease in its share of the votes from 21.9 percent to 20.8 percent or in the number of commune chief seats from 28 in 2007 to 22 in 2012. The party, however, remains popular in major urban areas but still seems unable to build strong social support far beyond that. The party was regarded as being "like a scared child – the more things happen to them, the more they start to pull back. They refrain from meeting people and they refrain from opening up because of bad experiences."[29]

The only opposition party that appears to have become more institutionalized in recent years is the HRP. Founded on July 22, 2007 and led by the former senator Kem Sokha, the HRP adopted a system of checks and balances based on the idea that its top leaders must be elected and kept in check. Unlike the other parties that operate on the strict basis of one-person rule, top HRP leaders are elected at its convention. During the 2008 election, the party participated in elections for the first time and succeeded in taking third place, having won three seats in the National Assembly. The 2012 commune chief election resulted in the party winning 18 commune chief positions. Still, it is too early to say how institutionalized the party became because it agreed in July 2012 with the SRP leadership to form a new party called the Cambodia National Rescue Party (CNRP).

Inaugurated on September 12, 2012, the CNRP may become more institutionalized, but it still faced the challenge of competing for power against the CPP in the National Assembly 2013 election, in which it received far more votes than expected: 2,946,176. However, it is far from clear that the new party will be able to maintain and enhance its political unity. Only time will tell, as the party remains nascent and resource-poor. The CNRP has now launched the Cambodian Democratic Movement for National Restoration to raise funds and promote its values, but it is likely to face suppression if and when it becomes a growing threat to the CPP.

There is no doubt that the CPP has now developed the best party organization in the country. Following the UN intervention in the early 1990s, the CPP expanded its party structure at provincial, district, commune, and village levels. It has important party committees: Standing, Permanent, and Central. The Central Committee has 263 members (compared to only 64 in the early 1990s). Party members at the local and provincial levels, however, still do not have an effective communication system with their national party leaders. CPP members of parliament' provincial offices hardly function; their staff members

---

[28] Trustbuilding's Blog 2013.
[29] Ibid.

remain too few in numbers, cannot provide information asked for, and had no or little contact with their MPs, 90 percent of whom lived in Phnom Penh on a permanent basis. Moreover, the local party structure remains rudimentary. There was no financial transparency: sources of funds and expenditures were said to have been disclosed only to the Finance Committee and the Central Committee. Party members received no financial information. The CPP has now developed the ability to sustain itself better than other parties and has been able to maintain its members' loyalties. Party disunity appears to have become less of a problem. Defection to other parties has been nearly nonexistent: only a few CPP officials have defected to other parties – such as CPP Economic Police Department Deputy Director Nhim Kim Nhol (CPP police colonel), who joined the SRP (Sam Rainsy Party) in October 2002.

The party has become less factionalized in recent years. Some top party leaders did not support Hun Sen's coup in 1997 after a period of escalating political tension between the CPP and FUNCINPEC, for instance. According to Gordon Longmuir, a former Canadian ambassador to Cambodia, "The most perilous period for Hun Sen came immediately after the 1997 coup de force, which had been opposed by Sar Kheng, the co-Minister of the Interior, General Ke Kim Yan, the Armed Forces Commander, and, most importantly, Chea Sim, the President of the Party."[30] Sar Kheng sought to protect Ho Sok (FUNCINPEC secretary of state for the Ministry of the Interior) but failed: General Hok Lundy (police chief), Hun Sen's main ally, succeeded in extra-judicially executing Ho Sok. Longmuir adds: "Hun Sen's loyal military and police forces stood behind him and this persuaded 'moderate' CPP forces to stifle their reservations."[31] Hun Sen also came under criticism in 1998 for having failed to win majorities in areas previously considered CPP strongholds. Before the 2003 election, the question of party leadership had surfaced and the internal struggle for power continued unabated, as two dominant CPP factions sought to overcome each other. In 2005, Hun Sen publicly attacked General Ke Kim Yan, saying that the general would be fired if he disobeyed orders because the prime minister controlled the armed forces. Even after the 2008 election, the struggle for power within the party continued, finally leading to the dismissal of Ke Kim Yan early in 2009. Meanwhile, Hun Sen continued to consolidate his power by appointing his political loyalists as top military and police commanders and working against any CPP members seen as threatening to him. The anti–Hun Sen CPP faction has been subdued but not defeated. Hun Sen has cautioned against party members regarded as still capable of challenging his political position. In May 2012, for instance, he warned against any attempts to reshuffle the government administration that would diminish his grip on power, targeting two top CPP leaders: Chea Sim (CPP and senate president) who could not prevent the removal of his protégé (Ke Kim Yan) and Heng Samrin (National Assembly president). Hun

---

[30] Gordon Longmuir (n.d.): 6.
[31] Ibid.

Sen made it clear that he was his own master in 1977 when he led the revolt against Pol Pot and remains so today. In his words, "Nobody could represent as the master of Hun Sen, not even ... Heng Samrin and ... Chea Sim; they could not be my masters."[32]

The CPP has also become more institutionalized than any opposition parties in terms of its ability to mobilize, sustain, and expand social support. The party membership was small in the 1980s –between only 12,500 and 30,000 or about 0.36 percent of the population.[33] In more recent decades, its social support has grown, as its impressive victories during the 1998, 2003, and 2008 national elections and the 2002, 2007, and 2012 commune elections as well as its continued countrywide domination over communes and villages has shown. The number of people who voted for the party in national elections increased steadily from 1,533,471 in 1993, to 2,030,790 in 1998, to 2,447,259 in 2003, to 3,492,374 in 2008, but dropped slightly to 3,235,969 in 2013 (although the opposition maintained that the number was much lower).[34]

In short, the party system and political parties have become somewhat more institutionalized over the past two decades, but the general level of institutionalization remains low and uneven, when assessed both quantitatively and qualitatively in terms of electoral volatility and legitimacy (parties' social roots, their organizational effectiveness, and intraparty political unity). If there is any evidence of growing stability, it seems to have less to do with a higher degree of institutionalization than with consolidation and personalization of political power. The party system's institutional development remains rooted in personal politics that are more hegemonic than democratic. The CPP has kept winning more seats at the expense of opposition parties and has emerged as the most institutionalized party; however, its institutional stability lies in the growing concentration of power in the hands of a few elite members, most notably Hun Sen. The process of party and party system institutionalization can thus be considered to go hand-in-hand with hegemonic party politics.

THE MERITS AND LIMITS OF HISTORICAL INSTITUTIONALISM

This section tests the proposition that time functions and historical legacies matter when we seek to explain the process of party system and party institutionalization. As will be shown, the proposition has both some empirical support and limited explanatory power.

The hypothesis that party system and party institutionalization is a matter of time has some empirical support. Cambodia's current party system is still young. Until the end of World War II, the country had never developed a party system. Between World War II and 1953, when Cambodia gained independence, the

---

[32] Hul 2012: 18.
[33] United Nations 1990: 84–85
[34] Trustbuilding's Blog 2013.

French allowed parties to be established and elections to be held. But the parties and the party system were soon subject to repression by then-King Norodom Sihanouk, who sought to strengthen his own political party (Sangkom Reastniyum, based on Buddhist socialism) as the hegemonic one. Left without any hopes for political victory, members of the opposition, led by leftist elements, either sought to cooperate with Sihanouk or carried their activities underground. In 1970, Sihanouk was overthrown and the Khmer Republic was established. The new regime under the leadership of President Lon Nol (1970–1975) had little time for the building of a party system and political party institutions. A civil war began, and a new wave of electoral politics emerged and a new multiparty system was briefly established. Cambodia was once again subject to the ravages of war, which left political parties, and the party system, weakly institutionalized. The Pol Pot regime lasted no more than four years. It came to power after five years of war and sought to build a communist party. The regime brought down all the pre-1975 political institutions. The Khmer Rouge did seek to build new institutions; however, its leaders found themselves immersed in violent struggles and self-destructed; the war with Vietnam also consumed them and led to their downfall in early 1979. The new socialist regime (known as the People's Republic of Kampuchea, PRK later renamed the State of Cambodia, SOC) had to start building new institutions from scratch. The party system was quickly established but remained rudimentary, with the ruling Communist Party the sole party allowed by law.

Since the early 1990s, the political party system has become more institutionalized. The current system has developed over a period of 20 years. As noted earlier, Cambodia clearly shows a degree of party system institutionalization with some continuity in this process. From the early 1990s to 2012, the country enjoyed a more stable period in which it institutionalized a party system. The five National Assembly elections (1993, 1998, 2003, 2008, and 2013), the two senate elections (2006 and 2012), and the three commune elections (2002, 2007, and 2012) show that time matters.

The holding of regular elections has allowed political parties to develop. The hypothesis that party institutionalization is more likely over time with an authoritarian regime thus has some empirical support. If the CPP has become more institutionalized than other parties in the country, it is because it also has the oldest party structures and has had more time to build them. Throughout the 1980s, the Communist Party remained the only political party and the most dominant political institution. The party adopted "a line and policy based on the creative application of a genuine Marxism-Leninism."[35] It was organized into four levels: central, provincial, district, and commune. The Party Central Committee (which had five party commissions, some of which may have been quite elaborate) had 64 members who elected the 13 members of the Politburo

---

[35] United Nations 1990: 86, citing a report by the Fourth National Congress of the United Front for the Construction and Defense of the Kampuchean Motherland Front.

(comprising the secretariat of the committee). By the time Cambodia held its first election in 1993, the CPP had enjoyed more than 10 years to prepare itself as a party. By 2012, the CPP had had more than 30 years to institutionalize itself.

Opposition parties, by comparison, have not become as institutionalized as the CPP. They emerged as armed resistance forces. Both the FUNCINPEC and the Khmer People's National Liberation Front/Buddhist Liberal Democratic Party (KPNLF/BLDP) were founded after the Vietnamese invasion of Cambodia in 1978 and were preoccupied with the war against the PRK/SOC. Their armed forces and supporting populations were scattered along the Thai-Cambodian border and were subjected to military attacks from both the PRK/SOC and Vietnamese forces. The armed resistance factions turned themselves into political parties only when they began to prepare for the 1993 election. The two armed factions turned political parties were 10 years younger than the CPP.

The passage of time alone, however, does not necessarily or automatically lead to higher levels of party system and party institutionalization. Even the monarchy – the oldest and most institutionalized system of government, which has endured for centuries – has weakened to the breaking point. Time did not help FUNCINPEC and the BLDP become more institutionalized: as noted earlier, both in fact became less and less institutionalized, as intraparty factional politics grew intense. The BLDP split and ceased to function, and FUNCINPEC splintered and barely survived. The CPP is far from becoming institutionalized, despite the fact that it has been the oldest party in Cambodia. The basic questions regarding time functions as an independent variable for explaining institutionalization are how long it takes for political systems and parties to become institutionalized and at what point can we consider them institutionalized and why.

What other variables help shed light on the limits and uneven levels of party and party system institutionalization in Cambodia? In general, historical institutionalism also places emphasis on past trajectories or path-dependent development. Policy choices being made today are constrained by choices made early in the development of a particular institution. This perspective can help explain particularities and specificities, or the diversity of party systems in different countries.[36] As is shown next, historical institutionalism has explanatory power: historical legacies also matter but only if they include cultural and ideological legacies, which help explain authoritarian institutionalization.

The hypothesis that historical cleavages give rise to party institutionalization also has some empirical support. Although economic class-based, religious, and ethnic cleavages have not been a key factor for party institutionalization, political cleavages have been. The Paris Peace Agreements, which led to the 1993 election, had much to do with the fact that competing political factions were waging war in Cambodia. The 1991 agreements turned the armed factions

---

[36] Hopkin 2002: 263.

into political parties, each of which competed in the election. Political cleavages thus have given rise to party system and party institutionalization.

However, these pronounced political cleavages have also prevented greater institutionalization. One could, in fact, argue that they have contributed to the crisis of legitimacy within the party system and political parties. The party system has not enjoyed as much legitimacy as it could have. The opposition, as noted earlier, tended to claim that the NEC favored the CPP and thus challenged election results, although its criticism has now become less severe. Political cleavages within political parties, especially those in the opposition, kept them factionalized, internally unstable, and prone to defection.

Earlier party policy decisions also matter. Some anti-CPP observers blamed FUNCINPEC's leadership in particular for having made several strategic errors early on, particularly by agreeing to share power with the CPP after it won the 1993 national election. According to critics, this decision was fateful: it allowed the CPP to remain part of the state structure and to gain political strength to the point where it subsequently weakened the royalists. Another error of judgment was that the royalists never attempted to transform themselves into a modern party, moving away from elitism and toward building a strong social basis. The decision to keep FUNCINPEC as a royalist party did not allow it to maintain a strong social basis (despite the popularity of Sihanouk and Ranariddh, who relied on his traditional legitimacy at the expense of enhancing legitimacy through good policy performance and technical rationality). As a result, the party became fragmented when Ranariddh was implicated in various scandals, and his downfall led to its splintering into small factions. The inability of FUNCINPEC to transform its leader-dependent structures into a democratic party helps explain why the royalist party did not develop institutionally but in fact became deinstitutionalized.

Historical institutionalism can help explain authoritarian institutionalization if traditional "values, norms, interests, identities and beliefs" are taken into account.[37] Many Cambodia scholars regard traditional norms in this country as authoritarian. Authoritarianism existed for centuries and remains resilient.[38] Cambodian culture does not promote compromise – a norm generally regarded as "alien" to Cambodia.[39] Cambodian culture may help explain why the CPP in particular emerged as the most institutionalized party. The monarchy remained highly centralized; Cambodians viewed their kings as divine, and many Cambodians still regard their government as a father figure rather than a servant. Many of the human rights NGOs are run by leaders who remain institutionally authoritarian, resist efforts to promote decentralization, and tend to score low for institutional accountability and transparency. Their staff appear less active and feel estranged from their leaders.[40] Cultural norms are

---

[37] March and Olsen 1989: 17.
[38] For cultural explanations, see Heder 1995: 425–429.
[39] Peang-Meth 2001: 333.
[40] Vijghen 2001: 21.

thus consistent with authoritarian institutions in general and authoritarian institutionalization within the party system and parties in particular.

If election administration has not become more institutionalized as determined earlier, it is also because the previous socialist regime had established few elaborate electoral procedures and authorities – the highest of which were the Electoral Council (made up of representatives of the Central Committee of People's Revolutionary Party of Kampuchea (PRPK) and the United Front for the Construction and Defense of the Kampuchean Motherland, whose role was to provide "solid supports of the state" and to follow the party as the United Front's "leading core" – or various mass organizations, which came under the auspices of the United Front.[41] The regime also held National Assembly elections on May 1, 1981, providing some 8,000 polling stations. After that, no new national elections were held. Only partial elections were held in 1986, with the limited purpose of filling vacancies, and the five-year mandate of the existing National Assembly was renewed in 1986 for an additional five-year term (due to expire in 1991). Elections at the village level were held sporadically, depending on whether a community was considered "organized." Thus, throughout the 1980s, little party system institutionalization took place: Cambodia held only one national election. The socialist regime maintained a one-party system. Building strong armed forces and providing public employees, the masses, and the armed forces with political and ideological education seemed to be the main tasks. With such institutional legacies, one could thus make the case that the process of party system institutionalization should not be expected to mature any more quickly than it has.

The fact that the CPP has become more institutionalized than other parties also has something to do with its past disciplinarian socialism. Critics attribute the authoritarian institutionalization of the CPP to the fact that "the CPP is tightly disciplined along classic Stalinist lines – a structure that it has used to its advantage."[42] Socialist policy legacies helped the CPP become institutionally more cohesive, disciplinarian, and disciplined than anti-communist opposition parties in the country. When compared with other political parties, the CPP has developed the best system of disciplining its party members and has built the strongest party network in the country. Because of its tight control over its party members, the CPP has developed the capacity to prevent the defections experienced by other parties (most notably FUNCINPEC and the SRP), largely because it has succeeded in consolidating its power at their expense (thus having more power to deter potential defectors).

Overall, however, the explanatory power of historical legacies still remains indeterminate. Although post-communist states did come from similar starting points in terms of ideology – that is, single-party systems – they have moved in diverse and radically different directions, "ranging from prosperous social

---

[41] United Nations 1990: 222–230.
[42] Jeldres 2001: 350.

democracies to sultanistic or even dynastic regimes."[43] Cultural legacies help explain why authoritarian politics may persist and why authoritarian parties still persist in Cambodia, but it cannot explain why they fall or disintegrate and give way to multiparty electoral politics in other countries. Cultural and ideological explanations tend to exaggerate the stability of authoritarianism. Traditional culture resists the introduction of modern cultural values, but it does not explain party and party system institutionalization in some societies where traditional values used to persist.[44] Culture always seems more dynamic than static.[45] When manipulated by elites to serve their ends, traditional values may be discredited.[46] Past choices and decisions are no doubt important, but some questions continue to nag at us, such as which choices and decisions, who makes them, and under what circumstances?

MAKING MORE SENSE OF UNEVEN AUTHORITARIAN INSTITUTIONALIZATION IN THE PARTY SYSTEM AND PARTIES

The fact that Cambodia's multiparty system and the CPP have now become more institutionalized than in the past but remain weakly institutionalized requires further explanation. Time functions and historical legacies often depend on other variables such as performance, power relations, and international legitimacy.

The CPP has succeeded in institutionalizing itself because its government has performed well economically. The overall trend in economic growth has been positive over recent decades with high GDP growth rates: 6.2 percent (2002), 8.6 percent (2003), 10.0 percent (2004), 13.4 percent (2005), 10.7 percent (2006), 10.1 percent (2007), 7.5 percent (2008), 7.8 percent (2011), 6.2 percent (2012). The economy was expected to grow by 7.2 percent in 2013 and to pick up to 7.5 percent in 2014.[47] The economy has benefited from growth in several sectors such as the construction, garment, and tourism industries; fiscal stability (although inflation has risen in recent years); and fairly balanced budgets. The CPP government's good economic performance has no doubt contributed to its recent electoral successes, as well as the fact that many Cambodian voters have seen no effective political alternatives. Other country cases such as Singapore, Malaysia, and even China also show that performance legitimacy based on economic development helps institutionalize party systems dominated by ruling

---

[43] King 2000: 168.

[44] For critiques of cultural determinism and relativism, see Chaibong 2004: 93–107.

[45] Culture does not always determine political behavior; it can also be seen as constructed by elites to justify their authoritarian rule. The debate over Asian values, for instance, resulted from the strategy of Asian elites to maintain their authoritarian regimes. See, e.g., Kausikan 1993: 24–51; Zakaria 1994: 109–126; Mahbubani 1995: 100–111; Kausikan 1997: 24–34.

[46] Some Asian elites do not accept the primacy of Asian values seen as antidemocratic; see Kim 1994: 189–194.

[47] Asian Development Bank 2013: 219.

parties. Time will not be on their side if ruling parties fail to perform well economically.

The CPP has also proved itself more effective than the other parties at using bribery to buy votes and co-opt opponents. Its Central and Provincial Offices own businesses, such as transportation rentals and real estate;[48] it has become the richest party in the country and can thus afford to build up its party structures and consolidate its base of social support – unlike the opposition parties, which tend to experience financial difficulties. In addition, the Hun Sen government has had more resources to reward those who jumped on its band-wagon. However, opposition parties have had far fewer resources than the CPP and thus have been less able to develop their institutions and prepare for elections. During the 2012 election, for instance, FUNCINPEC spent less than $200 on each contested commune, the Norodom Ranarridh Party about $200, the HRP about $300, the Sam Rainsy Party about $1,500, whereas the CPP was the biggest spender – about $9,000.[49]

The extent to which some political parties have performed more effectively than others also depends on the changing dynamics of power distribution and relations. The 1991 Paris Peace Agreements reflect on power relations among the political contenders who could not destroy one another by force and thus chose to compete for power through the ballot box. The fact that FUNCINPEC agreed to share power with the CPP after the 1993 election was not simply a strategic error: the decision also had to do with the reality of asymmetrical power relations – essentially, the fact that the CPP was a far more powerful contender that could not be pushed out of the political arena. As a political and military force, FUNCINPEC was no match for the CPP, which controlled state institutions, including the communes across the country, and had built a superior military force. The 1997 coup against Ranariddh and the subsequent quick decimation of the royalist forces further reveal that FUNCINPEC could never have afforded to govern the country on its own after its electoral victory in 1993. The SRP has also been effectively subject to political repression. The CPP has thus become more institutionalized than the opposition because its leadership has proved itself more effective than the opposition in consolidating power.

The CPP's successes also had much to do with the growing support it has received from members of the international community, especially donors – both bilateral and multilateral. Donors have also allowed the CPP's institutionalization to develop more effectively than that of any of the opposition parties. The acts and omissions of external agencies have also affected the domestic balance of power (after the signing of the 1991 agreements), which has shifted in favor of the CPP. The Paris Peace Agreements turned three resistance factions into separate parties competing for power in the electoral process, but left the

[48] Interview with Chantha Muth of the National Democratic Institute, Phnom Penh, Cambodia. January 24, 2006.
[49] COMFREL 2012a.

SOC/CPP intact. The agreements included the Khmer Rouge, but the United Nation Transitional Authority in Cambodia (UNTACT) did not do enough to disarm the rival factions and thus left the CPP in the best military position to weaken its opponents.[50] UNTAC also played a role in allowing the CPP to force the royalists to share power after the party had lost the 1993 election.

The CPP has benefited from the support of the international community because of the latter's concern about the return of the Khmer Rouge, which had committed mass atrocities during its reign of terror. Although the 1991 agreements made no mention of the need to put Khmer Rouge leaders on trial for their crimes, there was an implicit commitment to doing so. It is important to remember that the United Nations and its member states, especially those in the West, were supportive of the idea of putting Khmer Rouge leaders on trial. The Extraordinary Chambers in the Court of Cambodia (ECCC) was finally established in 2007 with the aim of imprisoning surviving Khmer Rouge leaders, but the ECCC made no commitment to trying any of the top CPP leaders who were also former Khmer Rouge officials (including Hun Sen, Chea Sim, and Heng Samrin).

While historical legacies help explain why the international community adopted the anti–Khmer Rouge policy, it would be incorrect to conclude that donors make decisions on this basis alone. The UN decision was based more on *realpolitik* than democratic politics: the CPP's political and military power meant that it had the ability to derail the electoral process UNTAC had initiated. Even though insisting on regular elections, few donors have funded political party building because of political sensitivities and fears of the CPP's negative reactions should external efforts be made to help build the opposition. The lack of external support for political party building has contributed to the general weakness of the opposition and allowed the CPP to grow stronger.[51] The international donors have been supportive of the CPP government, despite their public expressions of displeasure with its human rights record. Between 1993 and 2008, Cambodia received more than $7 billion in foreign aid. After the 1997 coup, Japan and other donors suspended their aid to Cambodia but resumed it soon after. The donor community has even increased its aid in recent years, despite the evidence of Hun Sen's authoritarian behavior. Cambodia received about $600 million per year. In 2006, donors pledged to give Cambodia $601 million for development in 2007. The country received $550 million in 2004. In 2012, however, the amount of aid increased to $1.38 billion.[52] All this has conferred further international political legitimacy on the Hun Sen regime.

---

[50] For more on this, see Peou 1997.

[51] Peou 2007: 175.

[52] Voice of America 2014. *As Foreign Aid Increases, Questions about Conditions.* (June 2). Available at http://www.voacambodia.com/content/as-foreign-aid-increases-questions-about-conditions/1664821.html. Accessed June 20, 2014.

While it has enjoyed international legitimacy evidenced by large amounts of foreign assistance for Cambodia's development, the CPP regime has also bene-fited from post–Cold War geostrategic interests other major states have pursued. Rivalries between China and both Japan and the United States are discussed elsewhere in my work,[53] but it is worth stressing that both Japan and the United States worry about the rise of China and seem reluctant to push the CPP into the Chinese camp. Meanwhile, China has been making efforts to keep Cambodia away from Western influence and has now become one of its biggest donors. By 2012, China's aid to Cambodia in the form of grants and loans had reached $2.7 billion, making China the second-largest donor after Japan. China has become the biggest source of military aid to Cambodia, with no real strings attached.[54]

For its part, the United States has sought to improve bilateral relations with Cambodia. Washington has considered the Asian country to be most coopera-tive in the war against terrorism. Before General Hok Lundy's death in 2008, the U.S. government had invited him to Washington and even awarded him a medal. This was an about-face, as Washington had previously rejected his visa appli-cations on the grounds that he was alleged to have been involved in criminal activities. In 2008, Washington provided 31 trucks to Cambodia's Ministry of Defense, along with $7 million in military aid. Then, in January 2009, Washington signed an agreement with Cambodia to establish a military attaché between the two countries. A confidential source to me also indicated that Washington wanted to build a military base in Cambodia, although this is unlikely to materialize. In spite of Hun Sen's authoritarian behavior, Washington has sought closer ties with Cambodia, apparently in an attempt to counter growing Chinese influence over Southeast Asia.

Cambodia's Election Administration would not have become institutional-ized to the extent that it did had members of the international donor community not funded the elections. Following the end of the Cold War, donors agreed on the need for electoral democracy in Cambodia. The UN, with the collective support of the Security Council, acted as Cambodia's transitional authority, preparing and supervising the 1993 multiparty election. The remit of UNTAC had an electoral component, perhaps the most successful one, that laid the foundation for the development of the Election Administration, particularly the NEC. International donors have provided various forms of support to the subsequent elections, including financing. Almost $2 billion was spent on the UNTAC operation; donors then provided $26 million for the 1998 election, $15 million for the 2002 election, $4.5 million for the 2003 election, and $6.50 million for the 2007 election.[55] Without financial and technical support from external actors, the party system may not have become institutionalized to the extent that it has. The CPP regime has benefited from such international support,

[53] Peou 2007, 2009.
[54] Heng 2013; Thayer 2013.
[55] For more on this, see Peou 2007.

knowing that its legitimacy would be sustained if Cambodia held elections on a regular basis, even if they were not as free and fair as demanded by members of the donor community.

CONCLUSION

Cambodia's democratic institutionalization, beginning in 1993, has now given way to authoritarian institutionalization. The country's political parties, and the party system overall, seem to have become more institutionalized than at any time in the pre-1993 period, when assessed in terms of both electoral regularity and growing stability in interparty electoral competition. The electoral process has also witnessed a relative decline in the overall level of political violence and the overall number of election-related complaints and protests against election results. The party system appears to have become increasingly institutionalized, but the levels of its institutionalization are uneven: the Election Administration has become more efficient in technical and organizational terms than in legal and political terms. The growth of stability within the party system is also still based more on coercion than consent as the system has become more hegemonic than competitive. None of the political parties has enjoyed unconditional legitimacy if assessed in terms of reliance on consent rather than coercion, and, more importantly, their institutionalization is limited by varying degrees of disunity among party members and social support (though the CPP has been more effective than the opposition in achieving party unity and gaining social support).

The Cambodian case study validates the proposition that party systems and parties can become more institutionalized over time, but it calls into question any proposition that such institutionalization is a fixed process and that hegemonic party systems are bound to push opposition parties to become more and more institutionalized. Cambodia's experiences of authoritarian rule – from the time when Prince Sihanouk remained dominant to when the Hun Sen regime began to run the country – did not help institutionalize the party system based more on consent than coercion, nor did they help institutionalize opposition parties to the point where they become stable or effectively functional. Thailand's party system institutionalization under Prime Minister Thaksin (2001–2006), to take another example, "was blocked by a de facto one-party rule."[56] Time functions often depend on changing circumstances and time is always on the side of those who succeed in imposing their will and visions on others. The fact that the Cambodian party system and political parties have become more institutionalized also has to do with the end of the Cold War, good economic performance, and the support Cambodia has received from the international community. The CPP has been effective in gaining domestic and international legitimacy.

---

[56] Ufen 2008: 343.

Time functions also depend on historical legacies, which help shed additional light on the limited and uneven degrees of party system and party institutionalization in Cambodia. Past political cleavages and policy decisions and previous cultural and ideological orientations form complex historical legacies that help explain authoritarian institutionalization within the party system and political parties in the country; however, they do not determine institutional trajectories, as institutional change is possible. Past legacies only facilitate or constrain institutionalization. Other variables also matter, including the specifics of recent policy decisions, party and personal strategies, and leadership effectiveness. The CPP has become more institutionalized than any other party because of support from other states, which, competing over their interests, have supported the Hun Sen regime with the hope that it would not move against them.

In short, historical institutionalism enjoys some explanatory power, as both time functions and legacies matter to the extent that they help shed light on authoritarian institutionalization or incremental change in the process of party system and party institutionalization. These variables, however, do not necessarily determine institutional trajectories in a path-dependent fashion; otherwise, we cannot explain institutional fluctuations as well as democratic changes in countries such as Japan and Germany after World War II and in some former communist Eastern European states and Indonesia in the post–Cold War world. Degrees of institutional development thus depend on other variables such as new ideas and decisions, effective party leadership and strategy, domestic power distribution and relations, and international politics and circumstances.

REFERENCES

ADHOC (Cambodian Human Rights and Development Association). 2008. *Human Rights Situation 2007*. Phnom Penh: February.

Asian Development Bank. 2013. *Asian Development Outlook: Asia's Energy Challenge*. Available at http://www.adb.org/publications/asian-development-outlook-2013-asias-energy-challenge. Accessed July 20, 2013.

Chaibong, Hahm. 2004. The Ironies of Confucianism. *Journal of Democracy* 15(3): 93–107.

COMFREL (Committee for Free and Fair Elections in Cambodia). 2012a. *Press Statement on Final Assessment and Findings of 2012 Commune Council Elections*. Phnom Penh: COMFREL, June 20.

COMFREL (Committee for Free and Fair Elections in Cambodia). 2012b. *Report on Misuse of State Resources for Political Party Purposes*. Phnom Penh: COMFREL, May.

Commission on Human Rights. 2003. *Situation of Human Rights of Cambodia*. UN Doc. E/CN.4/2004/105, December 19. Available at http://www.refworld.org/docid/4090ffeb0.html.

Diamond, Larry. 2002. Thinking about Hybrid Regimes. *Journal of Democracy* 13(2): 21–35.

Hammarberg, Thomas. 1998. Monitoring of Political Intimidation and Violence. Unpublished report, July 18–25.

Heder, Steve. 1995. Cambodia's Democratic Transition to Neoauthoritarianism. *Current History* 94: 425–429.

Heng, Pheakdey. 2013. *Chinese Investment and Aid in Cambodia a Controversial Affair.* EASTASIAFORUM. Available at http://www.eastasiaforum.org/2013/07/16/chinese -investment-and-aid-in-cambodia-a-controversial-affair/. Accessed December 20, 2013.

Hopkin, Jonathan. 2002. Comparative Methods. In David Marsh and Gerry Stoker (Eds.), *Theory and Methods in Political Science.* New York: Palgrave Macmillan.

Hul, Reaksmey. 2012. In Speech, Hun Sen Warns against Contesting His Position. *The Cambodia Daily* May 17: 18.

International Institute for Democracy and Electoral Assistance. *Voter Turnout Data for Cambodia.* Undated. Available at http://www.idea.int/vt/countryview.cfm? CountryCode=KH#_topdoc_.

International Republican Institute. N.d. Cambodia 2003: National Assembly Elections. Washington, DC: IRI. Available at http://www.iri.org/sites/default/files/ Cambodia's%202003%20National%20Assembly%20Elections.pdf. Accessed May 13, 2005.

Jeldres, Julio A. 2001. Cambodia's Fading Hopes. In Sorpong Peou (Ed.), *Cambodia: Change and Continuity in Contemporary Politics*, pp. 349–358. Burlington, VT: Ashgate.

Kausikan, Bilahari. 1993. Asia's Different Standard. *Foreign Policy* 42 (Fall): 24–51.

Kausikan, Bilahari. 1997. Governance That Works. *Journal of Democracy* 8 (April): 24–34.

Khmerization. 2009. Sam Rainsy's bodyguards defected to the CPP. November 28. Available at http://khmerization.blogspot.com/2009/11/sam-rainsys-bodyguards -defected-to-cpp.html. Accessed December 6, 2009.

Kim, Dae Jung. 1994. Is Culture Destiny? The Myth of Asia's Anti-Democratic Value. *Foreign Affairs* 73 (November–December): 189–194.

King, Charles. 2000. Post-Postcommunism: Transition, Comparison, and the End of Eastern Europe. *World Politics* 53(1): 143–172.

Longmuir, Gordon. N.d. Cambodia 2003: Political/Economic Assessment and Risk Analysis. Unpublished confidential report.

Mahbubani, Kishore. 1995. The Pacific Way. *Foreign Affairs* 74 (January–February): 100–111.

March, J., and J. Olsen. 1989. *Rediscovering Institutions.* New York: Free Press.

Peang-Meth, Abdulgaffar. 2001. Understanding Cambodia's Political Development. In Sorpong Peou (Ed.), *Cambodia: Change and Continuity in Contemporary Politics*, pp. 67–80. Burlington, VT: Ashgate.

Peou, Sorpong. 1997. *Conflict Neutralization in the Cambodia War: From Battlefield to Ballot-Box.* Kuala Lumpur, New York, and Singapore: Oxford University Press.

Peou, Sorpong. 2007. *International Democracy Assistance for Peacebuilding: Cambodia and Beyond.* Basingstoke, UK: Palgrave Macmillan.

Peou, Sorpong. 2009. Re-Examining Liberal Peacebuilding in Light of Realism and Pragmatism. In Edward Newman, Roland Paris, and Oliver Richmond (Eds.), *New Perspectives on Liberal Peacebuilding.* Tokyo and Paris: United Nations University Press.

Ray, Julie, and Nicole Naurath. 2008. Cambodians to Vote, but Dissatisfied with Their Democracy. Available at http://www.gallup.com/poll/109114/Cambodians-vote -dissatisfied-their-democracy.aspx? Accessed October 31, 2009.

Sartori, Giovanni. 1976. Parties and Party System: A Framework for Analysis. New York: Cambridge University Press.

Special Rapporteur on the Situation of Human Rights in Cambodia. 2013. UN Doc. A/HRC/24/36. August 5. Available at http://cambodia.ohchr.org/WebDOCs/ DocReports/3-SG-RA-Reports/A-HRC-24-36_en_SR_report_2013_ENG.pdf. Accessed January 29, 2014.

Special Representative of the Secretary-General for Human Rights in Cambodia. 2003. *Situation of Human Rights in Cambodia.* UN Doc.E/CN.4/2004/105. December 19, 2003. Available at http://cambodia.ohchr.org/WebDOCs/DocReports/1-SR-SRSG -Reports/SRSG_HR_CMB19122003E.pdf

Special Representative of the Secretary-General for Human Rights in Cambodia. Undated. The 2003 National Assembly Elections. Unpublished report.

Thayer, Karlyle. 2013. The Tug of War over Cambodia. USNI News. February 19. Available at http://news.usni.org/2013/02/19/the-tug-of-war-over-cambodia. Accessed December 19, 2013.

Trustbuilding's Blog. 2013. Cambodian National Elections Results since 1993. Available at https://trustbuilding.wordpress.com/2013/06/18/cambodian-national-elec tions-results-since-1993/. Accessed December 20, 2013.

Ufen, Andreas. 2008. Political Party and Party System Institutionalization in Southeast Asia: Lessons for Democratic Consolidation in Indonesia, the Philippines and Thailand. *The Pacific Review* 21(3): 327–350.

UNDP (United Nations Development Program). 2003. *National Assembly Election in Cambodia, 27 July 2003.* Phnom Penh: UNDP, September.

UNDP (United Nations Development Program). 2007. *Report on the 2007 Commune Council Elections in Cambodia.* Phnom Penh: UNDP, April 1.

UN General Assembly. 2002. *Situation of Human Rights in Cambodia.* UN Doc. A/57/230, September 27.

United Nations. 1990. *Report of the United Nations Fact-Finding Mission on Present Structures and Practices of Administration in Cambodia.* New York: United Nations, June.

Vijghen, John L. 2001. *Cambodian Human Rights and Democracy Organizations* (Phnom Penh: Experts for Community Research), April.

Voice of America. 2012. *Analysts: Low Cambodian Vote Turnout Blow to Opposition.* June 8. Available at http://www.voanews.com/content/analysts-low-cambodian -voter-turnoutblowopposition/1204944.html. Accessed October 20, 2012.

Zakaria, Fareed. 1994. Culture Is Destiny: A Conversation with Lee Kuan Yew. *Foreign Affairs* 73 (March–April): 109–126.

Explaining Party System Institutionalization in Indonesia

Paige Johnson Tan*

INTRODUCTION

In 2009, Susilo Bambang Yudhoyono's Partai Demokrat (PD) came seemingly out of nowhere to capture 150 seats in Indonesia's parliament, almost tripling its previous tally. In recent years, nationalist parties have acquiesced to the passage of Islamic-inspired legislation at the center and at the regions, seemingly violating their own ideological bases. In addition, parties are widely excoriated in the media as self-seeking, corrupt, and devoid of ideology. Finally, many parties' organizational structures slumber between elections. These phenomena reflect Indonesia's relatively uninstitutionalized contemporary party system. Why does a party system become institutionalized or fail to do so? Why does it become institutionalized in the ways that it does and in the strength that it does?

This chapter uses the ideas from Hicken and Kuhonta's Introduction for this volume to examine independent Indonesia's four distinct party systems. The chapter then analyzes the factors that explain the observed levels of party system institutionalization (PSI), with particular reference to the hypotheses Hicken and Kuhonta test for Asia as a whole in their introductory chapter.

Based on Hicken and Kuhonta, the Indonesia cases do not point to the significance of the passage of time as a factor in institutionalization. Indonesia has gone through several upheavals in its party systems; even within the authoritarian New Order, volatility was high, then low, then rose again. Also, as a Third Wave democracy, Indonesia's parties are relatively uninstitutionalized, as the period effect would predict, but the parties began life early, some as early as the 1920s, and were major actors in the country's national liberation struggle. Despite this, they failed to institutionalize. Hicken and Kuhonta arrive at the

* Thanks to Erik Kuhonta, Allen Hicken, Suranjan Weeraratne, Tuong Vu, and others at the Montreal Conference on Party System Institutionalization for their many fine comments. Responsibilities for continued faults are, of course, mine alone.

"troubling conclusion" that an authoritarian regime may be positive for PSI. For Indonesia, the country paid the authoritarian price but did not get the prize of a stable party system. Sukarno, Suharto, and the military set out to destroy Indonesia's political parties. In large part, they succeeded, with long-lasting impacts.

Political institutions are vital in determining PSI, though the electoral system in Indonesia did not push in the direction first expected by Hicken and Kuhonta. More importantly, laws on the nature of parties, their breadth, necessary size, and a threshold law for entering parliament have all significantly impacted the number and shape of political parties. Moreover, Indonesia's parties have separated themselves from their exclusive roots in the country's social cleavages and have become more catchall in nature. This may have negative effects for party-voter connection and thus PSI, but it can have positive effects in reducing the heat in interparty competition and improving the scope for interparty cooperation. In addition to the factors explored by Hicken and Kuhonta, the Indonesian case suggests the importance of economic performance, international intervention, zeitgeist, and elite choice in determining PSI.

EXAMINING PARTY SYSTEM INSTITUTIONALIZATION

In *Building Democratic Institutions*, Mainwaring and Scully discuss four features that are key to examining institutionalization of parties and the party system.[1] The first criterion deals with stability in interparty competition within the party system. This element is important in evaluating institutionalization because it suggests stability over time in the number of parties in the system, their relative strengths, and their relationships with the electorate. Hicken and Kuhonta focus on stability in interparty competition in understanding PSI across Asia. In particular, they highlight volatility as their key measure of stability in interparty competition. In the case of Indonesia, I explore stability in interparty competition and volatility as a measure; however, to understand the Indonesian parties and party systems in more depth, I also explore Mainwaring and Scully's other criteria of PSI – parties with stable roots in society, party legitimacy, and party organization.[2]

---

[1] Mainwaring and Scully 1995.

[2] Stable roots refer to institutionalized systems that have parties with strong connections to the population. If parties have strong roots in society, swings in support from election to election will be kept to a minimum. This can help moderate competition and offer predictability. Legitimacy of parties and elections: if party competition through elections is viewed as the only legitimate means of forming a government, behavior will be structured on that basis. This can have the effects of moderating competition among the parties and preventing the rise of anti-system politicians. Party organizations: to provide structure to the system, the parties must develop some solidity as organizations. Personalistic, charismatic parties rarely meet this threshold as parties fail to develop their organizations and struggle to survive their founders.

PARTY SYSTEM INSTITUTIONALIZATION IN INDONESIA[3]

Party System 1, Parliamentary Democracy: 1945–1958

The first Indonesian party system existed from the independence era through the late 1950s. Major parties were at first appointed to a legislative assembly; these parties collaborated to form the government as preparations for elections were made. After the 1955 parliamentary elections, 28 parties were represented in parliament. The effective number of parties,[4] a measure that accounts for parties' weight as well as number, was just 6.3, as the vote was strongly consolidated among the top four parties, which took 78 percent of the vote.

The main parties during the period were the (1) Partai Nasional Indonesia (PNI, 22.3 percent in the 1955 parliamentary elections), a party emphasizing secular-nationalism and the unitary state and centered on president and founding father Sukarno; (2) Masyumi (20.9 percent), emphasizing federalism for Indonesia's diverse population and modernist Islam; (3) Partai Nahdlatul Ulama[5] (PNU, 18.4 percent), associated with the Nahdlatul Ulama (NU) traditionalist Muslim organization of Java's rural areas, which tempered its assertion of Islam with nationalism; and (4) Indonesian Communist Party (Partai Komunis Indonesia [PKI], 16.3 percent), which was Marxist and strongly secular. The key point of tension in the system was between Islam and Marxism. As time wore on, this contributed to a party system that was highly polarized and combative.

We have only two national votes by which to determine volatility in the first party system. The vote results in the September 1955 parliamentary elections and December 1955 Constituent Assembly elections are striking. The vote volatility was just 2.56 between the two (admittedly proximate) elections.[6] This suggests that in 1955 at least, voters were not splitting their tickets. This is positive for PSI. The vote was not done and settled at this 1955 level, however. Provincial elections in Java in 1957 showed strong gains by the PKI. Fears that the communists were imminently going to come to power contributed to ratcheting up the feeling of polarization.

Though vote shares were changing, the parties did have strong regional bases, indicative of possibilities for stable interparty competition and stable roots. The PNI, PNU, and PKI were Java-based parties.[7] The PNI won 24.6 percent of the

---

[3] I have written on institutionalization of Indonesia's party systems from 1945 to 2002 in my Ph.D. dissertation. Many of the observations here on the earlier party systems are based on this work. For more, see Johnson 2002.

[4] The effective number of parties is calculated by squaring each party's share of the vote, summing the squares and dividing one by the result.

[5] The Partai Nahdlatul Ulama split from Masyumi in 1952.

[6] Volatility is calculated by squaring the absolute value of the change in vote for each party and dividing the result by two. From September's to December's vote, PNI's vote moved up just 1.65 percent, Masyumi's down 0.33 percent, NU's up 0.06 percent, and PKI's up 0.11 percent.

[7] The population of Java makes up roughly half the Indonesian total.

vote in Java provinces and just 13 percent in Java itself. The PNU did best in East Java, unsurprisingly, as it was the home base of the NU. The PKI also drew votes from Java and from ethnic Javanese elsewhere in Indonesia, particularly in plantation areas. Masyumi, on the other hand, was strongest off the island of Java. It scored 32.5 percent off Java and 18.5 percent on.

The parties also appeared to have bases in the country's *aliran*, or population streams. The PNI was a nationalist party based solidly among the country's secular, nominal Muslims.[8] The PKI also drew from the nominal Muslim community. Modernist Muslims, generally urban, pious, and oriented to a purified Islam, were the natural constituency for Masyumi. Finally, traditionalist Muslims were the base of the PNU.[9]

Despite the parties appearing to have streams in the population receptive to their messages, the parties' legitimacy drained quickly over the period. Though participation in the 1955 elections was high (91.5 percent), popular attitudes toward parties were often negative. The parties were seen to be narrow, self-interested, and corrupt. They argued over small matters while the country appeared to be falling apart as a result of regional rebellions and economic distress. Governments rose and fell in rapid succession. No matter how the communists scored in elections, they were locked out of government at the national level. The parties in the Constituent Assembly were unable to agree on even the most basic outlines of the state.

Other people and organizations competed with the parties for popular loyalty, too. In particular, President Sukarno and the military participated in delegitimizing the parties. Sukarno had long taken an integrationist line, trying to harmonize nationalism, religion, and communism (denying cleavage, in effect). In the late 1950s, Sukarno began to rail against the "disease of parties," this in a 1956 speech called "Let Us Bury the Parties."[10] The military, too, never accepted the civilian parties' supposed supremacy.

Party organizations were generally weak, and Indonesia's parties in the early period could be seen as parties of notables. They existed in the capital Jakarta but had little organization outside. Parties experienced frequent splits as groups within competed for power. Parties generally followed the least costly means to achieve their ends, developing support by colonizing the bureaucracy, co-opting local leaders, appearing to be big organizations to attract further support, and using communal buzzwords and charisma to mobilize support from the electorate. The PNI drew support from Sukarno's charisma. The PNU completely lacked autonomy from its sponsoring organization NU and was tied to the charisma of the various *kyai*, religious experts, making up the NU. Masyumi

---

[8] Following Clifford Geertz, these are referred to as *abangan* Muslims. Their Islam is syncretic, at home with pre-Islamic religious beliefs and practices.

[9] Traditionalist Muslims were pious but more syncretic than their modernist coreligionists. They owed allegiance to rural religious teachers known as *kyai*.

[10] Sukarno quoted in Feith and Castles 1970: 81–83.

was factionalized, particularly prior to the NU split in 1952. The PKI was a notable exception to this rule on organization. Hindley observes that because of the party's failed rebellion at Madiun in 1948 and its virtual elimination thereafter, the PKI had to rebuild its organization to come back.[11] The party was also the wealthiest, with well-established and stable channels of funding. Its subsidiary organizations (such as unions and women's wings) were disciplined under party control.

This first party system showed some promising signs, such as parties that, despite their youth, appeared to have roots in regions of the country and streams of the population. The majority of the signs, though, were negative for institutionalization: party competition was ideological and highly polarized. Vote shares were still fluctuating. Parties were young and weak as organizations, with the PKI as an exception. The parties' legitimacy fast dissipated to the point that even those with an interest in defending democracy barely uttered a whimper as Sukarno dismantled the system.

Party System 2, Guided Democracy: 1958–1965

The second party system was brief, from the late 1950s to mid-1960s and coincided with Sukarno's assumption of power in his Guided Democracy. Sukarno used this term to suggest that this system would allow representation but without the cacophony of the parliamentary democracy period. The key poles in the system were Sukarno himself, the military, and the PKI, with Sukarno often acting as balancer[12] of the other two groups.

The system of electoral competition among parties was disbanded; so we are unable to measure volatility under Guided Democracy. The number of parties was reduced, with Masyumi and the Socialist Party banned in 1960. Just ten parties were permitted in 1961. The parties continued to struggle with one another in ways that were highly polarized ideologically. The PKI grew stronger and had Sukarno's ear. It carried out unilateral actions, *aksi sepihak*, in the rural areas, ranging from demonstrations to land seizures. It sought to arm a "fifth force," potentially supplied by China. The military, dominated by anti-communist elements, harassed communists, shutting down party branches as well as harassing left-wing media. The entire country teetered on the edge as Sukarno aged.

Despite the absence of elections, parties continued to exist and demonstrated their roots in the population. In fact, Sukarno was never able to ban them entirely; his position was more precarious than it appeared, and he occasionally needed the parties as allies. Prominent parties participating in the Guided Democracy regime included the PNI, PNU, and PKI; these represented the

---

[11] Hindley 1966. The party had 100,000 members in 1952 and upward of 20 million by 1965 in the party and its affiliated subsidiary organizations.

[12] Balancer or puppet master, *dalang*, as the Indonesian allusion goes.

nationalist, Muslim, and communist facets in the nation's population, respectively. By the time of Guided Democracy, many of the parties were several decades old, demonstrating some rootedness.

The parties were demagogued as a source of the nation's problems. In 1960, Sukarno filled the parliament with appointed representatives of the military as well as functional groups such as labor, youth, and women's organizations; thus, parties were no longer the unique inhabitants of legislative institutions and controlled only about 46 percent of the seats. Moreover, the parliament's role was limited by the creation of rival, nonparty power centers. Cabinet members, regional government leaders, and even civil servants had to abandon party affiliations. That Sukarno was able to diminish the parties in these ways with little push back is evidence of the depths to which the parties had sunk in popular perceptions of their legitimacy.

Further, parties were limited to assenting to policies determined elsewhere and encouraged to use their networks to mobilize support for government policy; even Sukarno's PNI became just a "follower from behind."[13] Parties were forced to adhere to the president's ideological utterances, such as supporting socialism in Indonesia, for example. These changes in function had implications for party organizations that generally weakened during the period of Guided Democracy. Moreover, the military consciously attacked all party organizations, not just those of the communists, by stripping away subsidiary organizations.

The tensions between the communists and the military eventually led to the Guided Democracy's violent dissolution. A murky coup and counter-coup on September 30, 1965 led to the military's assumption of power and the bloody elimination of the PKI as a force in Indonesia.

Party System 3, The New Order: 1965–1998

The New Order regime of General Suharto was authoritarian, and elections were neither free nor fair. Golkar, the government's electoral vehicle, used government time, funds, and facilities to support its campaigns. All candidates had to be vetted by the regime. Media were controlled. Large numbers of political prisoners were held, and violence and intimidation were used to keep the population in line.

With the strength of economic growth as a carrot and a quiver full of coercive sticks, the regime was durable, lasting for more than 32 years. According to Ed Aspinall, elections in Indonesia were "designed to parade the New Order's invincibility," not as meaningful contests of choice.[14] Golkar achieved between

---

[13] Sjamsuddin 1984: 20. Sukarno had hammered the party loyal to him with the decree banning civil servants from party membership. PNI had long been based in the bureaucracy.

[14] Aspinall 1997.

60 percent and 75 percent of the vote in elections held regularly from 1971 to 1997. Volatility was low, though not uniform, ranging from 2.1 to 11.8.

The party system was simplified as the PKI was quickly banned and suppressed. Golkar, the government party, was a pro-army collection of social groups formed in 1964 and dominated by the bureaucracy, the military, and party patron Suharto.[15] In 1973, Islamic parties were forced to coalesce into the Partai Persatuan Pembangunan (PPP, United Development Party). Nationalist and Christian parties were forced to gather together in the Partai Demokrasi Indonesia (PDI, the Indonesian Democracy Party). According to the new president, General Suharto, "with one and only one road already mapped out, why should we then have nine different cars (parties)?"[16]

Ideological polarization was basically disallowed as the PPP and the PDI were compelled to support the government's program as a condition of participation. After 1984, parties were not allowed to have a basis different from the government-approved *Pancasila* (five principles) ideology; thus, the Islamic party was not allowed to have Islam as its basis and was called the United Development Party, rather than a name more evocative of Islam. The PPP and PDI had ambiguous status as opposition parties – participation, such as holding legislative seats, was dependent on the goodwill of the regime.

Parties did have roots in different parts of Indonesia. Opposition to Suharto was more Java-based and urban (though Aceh regularly and heavily supported the PPP); support for the government was strongest on the Outer Islands such as Sulawesi. Bureaucrats were compelled to support the ruling party and to make sure that their families and underlings did the same. The military was a further prop for the regime, with military officials positioned throughout the government structure and occupying key roles in the Golkar Party.

The existence of the PPP and PDI in the system reflected the streams of Islam and secular-nationalism dating back decades. Golkar was originally secular-nationalist in orientation but greened, became more Islamic, over the years to incorporate some Islamic aspirations as well. These facts suggest some party rootedness. However, the regime consciously depoliticized the population, cutting into roots that had been planted in the past. Election windows were narrow, campaigns were short, and parties were prohibited from organizing below the regency (sub-province) level. The population was supposed to be a floating mass, *massa mengambang*, asked every five years for its assent but basically depoliticized.

As under Sukarno's regime, parties were excoriated during the New Order as sources of division, corruption, and self-seeking in government speeches, slogans ("politics no, development yes!"), television news, and ideological indoctrination, among other channels. The regime as a whole had some

---

[15] Under New Order law, Golkar technically did not have the status of a party. Party/election laws provided for two parties and one Golkar after 1973. However, the party fulfilled the functions of a party according to customary usage of the term in political science.

[16] Suharto quoted in Schwarz 1999: 32.

legitimacy, particularly as a result of the decades of economic growth it delivered. Golkar achieved its highest-ever vote in 1997 (74.5 percent), the year before Suharto was toppled.

Unsurprisingly, Golkar grew as an organization over the course of the New Order. It was a rare institution, like the military and state bodies, to have national breadth. It eventually brought together hundreds of organizations and millions of bureaucrats, in addition to elites in the regions, particularly the Outer Islands. It had access to large sums of money, but it was not autonomous. Suharto, the chair of the party's Board of Patrons, played different pieces of the organization, such as the military, bureaucrats, and later pious Muslims, against one another. Further, the Golkar organization was shadowed at the province level and below by military bodies that were strongly influential. All parties had strong control of their national parliamentary delegations through legislative work rules that allowed them to recall wayward parliamentarians. Laws on parties and elections permitted the parties to determine party lists in the proportional representation elections. Both of these features compelled parliamentarians who wished to continue to serve in politics to tow the party line.

As mentioned, the PPP and PDI were not allowed to organize below the regency level, as part of the regime's drive to depoliticize the population. Also, subsidiary organizations such as unions were removed from party control. The parties were divided and ruled as the regime often intervened in leadership disputes. The most famous incident occurred in 1996 when Megawati Sukarnoputri, daughter of Indonesia's founding father Sukarno, was ousted from the PDI leadership, making her an icon of the fledgling Indonesian democracy movement. Party funding for the opposition came in large part from the government, thus keeping the notional opposition docile, dependent, and without strong networks.

Observers of the mature New Order would have characterized the system as institutionalized. However, looking at the parties, the situation was far less institutionalized than it appeared. Volatility in interparty competition was low in the global perspective, and competition was generally modest. Only Golkar established roots during the period, setting up a strong base in the bureaucracy and among the elites in the regions. The party was factionalized, however, with civilians, military, and other groups competing for influence. Much of Golkar's seeming strength relied on Suharto the man and the authoritarian regime he had built for support. Opposition party organizations were deliberately kept weak and factionalized and were not allowed to organize at the grass roots.

The legitimacy of the party system and elections is difficult to measure, as opinion polling from the period is either nonexistent or unreliable. Certainly there was coercion involved in the 1997 elections, but not all of Golkar's astounding 75 percent of the vote can be attributed to force. For at least some Indonesians, the regime was doing a good job. It was delivering growth, domestic peace, and increased standing for the country in the world – until the Asian financial crisis hit.

Suharto's opponents spun the crisis as the result of the regime's many failings: unequal growth, the wealth gap, crony capitalism, and the first family's kleptocracy. Some within the military wanted to use force against student protesters, while others did not. Violent riots and interethnic violence brought the crisis to a crescendo. Protesters occupied parliament, and elites defected from Suharto. Even Golkar head and Speaker of the House Harmoko called publicly for Suharto's resignation on May 18, 1998. An isolated Suharto stepped down May 21.

Party System 4, The Reformasi Era: 1998–Present

With the downfall of Suharto, Indonesians began to set up the infrastructure of a new democracy; this process was called *reformasi*, reform. Parties formed in the hundreds, so many that activists grew concerned at the apparent over-proliferation of parties. In 1999, a total of 48 parties were approved to compete in the elections, with 21 securing representation in the lower house of parliament (DPR). In 2009, a total of 38 parties qualified to compete.[17] The revised election law for the 2009 elections mandated a 2.5 percent threshold requirement for parliamentary representation (parties scoring below 2.5 percent of the vote would not score any seats in the national parliament); this reduced the number of parties seated in parliament to 9 (the threshold would rise again to 3.5 percent for 2014). The effective number of parties has fluctuated from 5.1 in 1999 (showing strong concentration of the vote among the top parties) to 6.2 in 2009. Volatility from 1999 to 2004 was 28.55, and from 2004 to 2009, 29.81. These figures are higher than those given by Hicken and Kuhonta for Asia as a whole as well as for Latin America, but lower than figures for post-Soviet states. Table 10.1 shows vote results for parliamentary elections from 1999 to 2009.

In the contemporary Indonesian party system, ideological polarization is minimal. At first, there were fears of an Islamist-secularist divide or an authoritarian versus democracy divide[18] and competition seemed heated; however, these divisions were quickly made murky as all the significant parties ran for the center, attempting to reach out to many segments of voters. Partai Keadilan[19] emphasized political Islam in 1999 and Islamic law thereafter,[20] but by the 2004 elections it had switched its emphasis to clean governance and public service, topics that could win wider support: "Islamists who were unwilling to broaden

---

[17] The peace agreement drawing the Aceh separatist conflict to a close (2005) allowed Aceh special prerogatives such as the right to be the only region to have single-province political parties. Six parties from Aceh were allowed to compete solely in that region in 2009.

[18] Referred to as status quo vs. reform.

[19] For the 2004 elections, renamed Partai Keadilan Sejahtera.

[20] The Jakarta Charter would have required the state to enforce Islamic law on all Muslims. Some Islamists claim that this requirement was removed from the country's first constitution in contravention of an understanding achieved with Muslims.

TABLE 10.1. *Share of Votes and Seats, Indonesian Parliamentary Elections under Reform*

Party	Results 1999 (Share of the Vote)	Seats	Results 2004 (Share of the Vote)	Seats[b]	Results 2009 (Share of the Vote)	Seats
Demokrat	–	–	7.5	55	20.9	150
Golkar	22.4	120	21.6	128	14.5	107
PDI-P	33.7	153	18.5	109	14.0	95
PK/S	1.4	7	7.3	45	7.9	57
PAN	7.1	34	6.4	53	6.0	43
PPP	10.7	58	8.2	58	5.3	37
Gerindra	–	–	–	–	4.5	26
PKB	12.6	51	10.6	52	4.9	27
Hanura	–	–	–	–	3.8	18
Other	12.1	39	19.9	50	18.3	0
Total	100.0	462[a]	100.0	550	100.0	560

[a] In 1999, 38 seats were reserved for the military.
[b] Some seat allocations in 2004 decided in Constitutional Court.
Sources: Johnson (2002); Tan 2006; KPU Media Center 2009.

their message have seen their electoral support dwindle much faster … or have forsaken the electoral process altogether in favor of non-electoral political mobilization."[21] Susilo Bambang Yudhoyono's *Partai Demokrat* (PD), coming seemingly out of the nationalist stream, represents itself as "nationalist-religious," formally bridging the country's streams.[22] The party has also silently acquiesced to Islamizing measures at the center, such as the anti-pornography law, and in the regions, such as the stoning of adulterers in Aceh, in a desire not to alienate Muslim voters.

There is little left-right polarization because of the decimation of the Indonesian Communist Party in 1965–1966 and the effectiveness of the machinery of repression and propaganda thereafter.[23] Megawati's *Partai Demokrasi Indonesia Perjuangan* (PDI-P) sets itself as the voice of Indonesia's poor. Megawati's statements also tend to take a more autarchic/nationalist position in regard to international financial institutions and international investment

[21] Pepinsky, Liddle, and Mujani 2010: 8.
[22] "Nasionalis-Religius" was listed under the party name at the top center of the Partai Demokrat official website (Partai Demokrat 2010).
[23] There is one far left party, the small Partai Rakyat Demokratik, that was unable even to qualify for the 2009 elections.

issues. Despite these differing emphases, the lack of polarization in the system appears to make competition among the parties smoother (Mietzner highlights the "centripetal" nature of competition[24]) and allows cooperation in the legislature. Presidents in the reform era have generally ruled with large cross-party coalitions and multiparty unity cabinets. Some scholars and commentators have expressed concern that this party-to-party cooperation has taken on collusive tones, with large coalitions sharing the spoils of governance.[25]

One area in which Indonesia appeared high on institutionalization at the beginning of the reform era was parties with stable roots among the voters. Parties appeared in 1999 that looked similar to those of 1955, when the last democratic elections were held. Parties used the name Masyumi or borrowed old Masyumi symbols (also Islamic symbols), such as the crescent and the star. Dwight King found in his study of the 1999 elections that the same geographic areas supported the same types of parties in both 1955 and 1999, suggesting strong rootedness.[26] Table 10.2 elucidates the parties and their social bases of support, along with the 1999 election results.

TABLE 10.2. *Top-Scoring Political Parties from the 1999 Elections and Their Social Base of Support*

Party	Share of the Vote	Social Base of Support
Partai Demokrasi Indonesia Perjuangan	33.7	Secular-nationalist, poor
Partai Golongan Karya	22.4	Secular-nationalist, bureaucrats, military, provincial elites
Partai Kebangkitan Bangsa	12.6	Nahdlatul Ulama (NU), traditionalist Muslim organization
Partai Persatuan Pembangunan	10.7	Traditionalist NU, modernist Muhammadiyah and other Islamic groups
Partai Amanat Nasional	7.1	Muhammadiyah, modernist Muslim organization
Partai Bulan Bintang	1.9	Dewan Dakwah Islam Indonesia, modernist Muslim organization
Partai Keadilan (Sejahtera)	1.4	Network of college campus mosques, Muslim Brotherhood inspired
Partai Keadilan dan Persatuan Indonesia	1.0	Secular-nationalist, military-linked
Other	9.1	Various
Total	100	

Source: Johnson (2002).

[24] Mietzner 2008.
[25] For example, Slater 2004.
[26] King 2003.

PDI-P and Partai Kebangkitan Bangsa (PKB, the National Awakening Party) are centered on Java and Bali, with Golkar more an off-Java party. Partai Keadilan Sejahtera (PKS), the Prosperous Justice Party, appears to do best among pious Muslims in urban areas, with a real stronghold in Jakarta. Partai Amanat Nasional (PAN), the National Mandate Party, has strength in Yogyakarta, home base of former leader Amien Rais, as well as on the island of Sumatra. Partai Demokrat, the big winner in 2009, appears to be the only party among the top finishers without a clearly defined regional constituency.[27] PD did well across the nation. It won five of the six Java provinces and did well on the Outer Islands, challenging Golkar in many areas.

In addition to geographic rootedness, parties are longer lived than they might at first appear. One measure Mainwaring and Scully suggest for examining rootedness is the age of the parties winning more than 10 percent of the vote – the older the average age, the more rooted the parties. In Indonesia, in 2009, the average age of parties winning more than 10 percent of the vote was 37 years.[28] This suggests parties with some roots and staying power. But this figure must be used cautiously, as only three of Indonesia's many parties crossed the 10 percent threshold.

Despite the geographic rootedness we see in the parties and the big parties' long life spans, voters are moving from party to party from one election to the next. Going into the 2009 parliamentary elections, almost 30 percent of the vote was still undecided according to respected pollster Lembaga Survei Indonesia (LSI).[29] LSI polls from 2004 to 2009 showed PD support fluctuating from 7 to 24 percent, rising to 50 percent after Susilo Bambang Yudhoyono's (SBY) strong victory in the July 2009 presidential polls;[30] indeed, proof that nothing succeeds like success. Respondents expressing a feeling of closeness with a particular party were at 58 percent around the presidential elections in 2004.[31] This tapered off by the end of 2004 and has hovered in the 20s or even teens since January 2006. This is a low level of party identification and suggests low levels of party rootedness.

The parties are widely loathed. In the 2006 East Asia Barometer poll, 55.8 percent expressed not very much trust or none at all in the political parties.[32] From 2004, the rise of Susilo Bambang Yudhoyono, seen as a nonpartisan problem solver, has been an important indicator of dissatisfaction with the political parties.

---

[27] Partai Persatuan Pembangunan is in a state of flux. In 1999, the party did well in strongly Muslim areas such as Aceh. However, its vote has collapsed nationally, and it is presently unclear if any regional strongholds continue to exist or whether the party is on the verge of being eclipsed.

[28] In 2004, the average age of parties winning 10 percent of the vote was 48. It was 39 in 1999.

[29] Lembaga Survei Indonesia, Undated-a, polling from October to November 2008.

[30] Lembaga Survei Indonesia, Undated-b, polling from April 2004 to September 2009.

[31] Lembaga Survei Indonesia, Undated-c, polling from November 2003 to July 2009.

[32] East Asia Barometer 2006: Q 009.

In addition to being widely disliked, parties are seen as weak organizations. Splits have touched most of the major top parties. In fact, all but two of the nine parties taking seats in 2009 had experienced splits or were themselves splits. Factions typically appear around competing leadership personalities, as in Partai Persatuan Pembangunan, for example, and also in regard to alternative political strategies; Golkar and PDI-P have faced repeated leadership tussles over whether to go into opposition or be part of the government.[33]

Representatives of the parties are generally loyal, helped by laws and parliamentary work rules that enable parties to remove disobedient parliamentarians. But this is a rare bright spot for the parties' organizations. A landmark court decision in 2008 moved Indonesia firmly to an open-list proportional representation system, thus weakening the parties' ability to decide who gets elected. Moreover, party poverty has led to the nomination of "affluent, powerful and popular figures for key positions in local government," leading to a cohort of elected officials with little connection to the party notionally represented.[34] Many party functions have been outsourced to independent pollsters and consultants, further hollowing out the parties.

The many personalistic and patrimonial parties are another indicator of weak institutionalization. Megawati Sukarnoputri (known as Mother Mega) is the PDI-P, just as PD is known as "SBY's fan club." Can the parties survive without their leaders? There is talk of Megawati passing the reins of the PDI-P to her daughter Puan Maharani. That would indeed confirm PDI-P as a "monarchy-based party," according to Lili Romli.[35] There has been talk of dynasty in PD as well, with SBY's son, Edhie Baskoro, or wife, Kristiani Herrawati, taking the helm before the next elections.[36]

Surveying Indonesians, Liddle and Mujani find that they "turn to individual leaders rather than to political parties to achieve [their] goals, and they set standards for those leaders – personal integrity, social empathy, professional competence."[37] Like PDI-P, Partai Amanat Nasional (PAN), and PD, Gerindra and Hanura are also strongly based around their leaders. What is Gerindra without Prabowo? Hanura without Wiranto? Further demonstrating the trend to nominate celebrity candidates PAN is known jokingly as Partai Artis Nasional, the national artists' party for being composed of musicians, actors, and other celebrities. Liddle and Mujani directly link Indonesia's personalistic parties with the high volatility in interparty competition.[38]

---

[33] In Golkar, those favoring participation in government have won out. In the PDI-P, Megawati has in recent years favored staying in opposition.

[34] Kleden 2009: 22.

[35] *Jakarta Post*, April 30, 2009.

[36] In both the PD and PDI-P, there appear to be internal struggles between groups that might be called party "institutionalists" and others, "monarchists," seeking to perpetuate the family line. Both groups operate from a variety of motives.

[37] Mujani and Liddle 2010: 45.

[38] Ibid: 46–47.

The parties are weak financially. State funding was offered at the outset of the reform era and then drastically curtailed, leaving the parties without stable access to funds.[39] Parties in the regions appear to have sold their nominations to wealthy outsiders to generate funds.[40] Corruption scandals as with PD treasurer Muhammad Nazaruddin (convicted in 2012) suggest pilferage occurs for party purposes as well personal enrichment.[41] Party funds are poorly reported and poorly audited, so the true state of party finances is little understood.

The institutional parties, Golkar and PKS, best show professionalization. Both parties have extensive organizations that exist regardless of election cycles. They engage in extensive internal cadre development programs and have a strong presence on the web (websites, YouTube channels). This is an important reminder that strong (individual) parties and strong party systems are not always one and the same. PDI-P does not appear to believe that it needs much of an organization, trading on Megawati's charisma. The party's Internet presence was until recently quite minimal: the official website was usually "being improved" or "experiencing problems."[42]

To sum up PSI in the reform era, the parties are relatively uninstitutionalized. Volatility is in the high 20s. Parties have scrambled for the center and all pitch some combination of Islam, nationalism, justice, security, and jobs. There is some geographic rootedness, but vote shares appear still to be in flux. The legitimacy of the parties is low, and turnout at elections has declined at each national election of the reform era (from 93 percent in 1999 to about 70 percent in 2009). Turnout in regional elections is often lower, reaching as low as about 40 percent. Party organizations are in general factionalized, episodic, and personalistic, though there are exceptions in individual parties. On a positive note, the tone of interparty competition has grown more moderate over the decade.

THE REASONS BEHIND THE OBSERVED LEVELS OF PARTY SYSTEM INSTITUTIONALIZATION

With an understanding of the institutionalization of Indonesia's various party systems, we can now begin an analysis of reasons for change. In the Introduction, Hicken and Kuhonta propose a number of hypotheses to explain changes in PSI in Asia. I now discuss their hypotheses with reference to Indonesia.

---

[39] Mietzner 2007.
[40] Buehler and Tan 2007.
[41] In his trial, Nazaruddin implicated other high-level PD officials including Angelina Sondakh, Andi Mallarangeng, and Anas Urbaningrum and explained how the schemes benefited the PD as a party. See Mietzner 2012: 122.
[42] Checked http://www.pdi-perjuangan.or.id/ on April 9, 2009 and July 28, 2009.

Passage of Time

Hicken and Kuhonta hypothesize that the number of parties and volatility will decrease with the passage of time; in the end, however, they are not able to show that this holds. The number of parties in Indonesia has fluctuated widely with the banishments, simplifications, and a reopening of the system in 1998. A look at the effective number of parties in 1955 and 2009 shows a striking but perhaps accidental similarity: 6.3 in 1955 and 6.2 in 2009. Examining just the reform era, the number of parties seated in parliament has declined, from 21 after the elections of 1999 to just 9 after the 2009 contest. The effective number of parties, though, has risen slightly over the reform era from 5.1 in 1999 to 6.2 in 2009. Even with a decline in the number of parties in parliament, it is unclear that the passage of time is the factor most responsible for bringing that about. More influential, I argue later, are institutional changes.

Volatility is difficult if not impossible to measure across the totality of Indonesia's party systems because of the ruptures caused by the imposition of systems without electoral competition (Guided Democracy) or with extremely unfair competition (the New Order). We can see that vote by population stream has changed from the 1950s to the contemporary system. As an illustration, Islamic parties received 44 percent of the vote in 1955. In 2009, they received just less than 30 percent. In 1955, Islamic parties took two of the top three spots in the elections. In 2009, they took none of the top three spots. This reflects a change in the party system and change within the parties themselves as they have moved in a catchall direction.

Hicken and Kuhonta raise the issue of data and passage of time as factors in change in PSI. The authors point out that most data come from democracies, so acquiring data on passage of time in a country like Indonesia, with long periods of authoritarian rule, should be instructive. I found that the hypothesis of increased institutionalization of the party system over time does not hold for Indonesia's authoritarian New Order period, at least as measured by volatility. Volatility actually rose during the New Order from 3.4 from the first to second elections to 11.8 from the fifth to sixth elections. If we look inside the parties, institutionalization is a mixed bag. Golkar institutionalized in many ways, but it was kept dependent on Suharto and factionalized. The PPP and PDI were deliberately kept in organizational tatters by the regime, with shifting, dependent leadership groups and no roots to the ground. The parties as a whole were demonized, as was the entire concept of fair competition of parties for power.

Hicken and Kuhonta observed a drop in volatility from second to third elections. Looking just at Indonesia's reform era, this pattern was not observed. Volatility rose slightly from 28.55 from the first to second elections to 29.81 from the second to third elections. This rise was largely the result of the sudden rise of PD, the collapse of PDI-P, and the slow leak of support away from Golkar.

Timing/Period Effect

Hicken and Kuhonta posit that First and Second Wave countries will have more institutionalized party systems than Third Wave countries, as popular attachments to parties will grow during the vital process of pushing for the expansion of suffrage. Testing their hypothesis across Asia, the authors find that party systems formed earlier are more institutionalized, as in Malaysia and Singapore. Indonesia is an ambiguous case, however, as parties formed early, were interrupted during long years of authoritarian rule, and formed again later for democracy in the Third Wave.

The parties in the first party system of parliamentary democracy had long lineages, some going back as far as the 1920s. Parties were active participants in the struggle for independence and would have been expected to establish linkages with the population, as they were embedded in the country's social cleavages. But the first party system failed to become institutionalized. The parties' own weaknesses and the ideological crafting of Sukarno and the military contributed to sweeping the parties and the system of parliamentary democracy aside.

If we examine Indonesia as a Third Wave country and just look at its democratization since 1998, the country is indeed weakly institutionalized as the hypothesis would hold. Volatility remains in the high 20s. There are large numbers of swing voters from one election to the next. Party rootedness has declined from earlier periods as catchall parties have de-aligned from their streams. Anti-party views prevail. Party organizations have failed to develop, with a few notable exceptions.

NATURE OF PRIOR REGIME

Hicken and Kuhonta's strongest finding is that the nature of the prior regime is vital in explaining institutionalization of the party system. They arrive at the "troubling conclusion" that getting an institutionalized party system may require enduring a period of authoritarianism (is the benefit worth the cost?). In this volume, the cases of Malaysia, Singapore, and Taiwan demonstrate the degree to which a regime with authoritarian features can contribute to institutionalization. Indonesia, though, paid the price, enduring decades of authoritarianism, but did not get the prize of an institutionalized party system. Authoritarian regimes can obviously contribute to institutionalization, but they can also decidedly contribute to deinstitutionalization. In Indonesia, Suharto, as with Sukarno before him, propagandized, legislated, arrested, and divided and ruled all in the interest of destroying the political parties. This has had long-term effects on the status of parties today. The chapter on Taiwan (Chapter 5) highlights the KMT's democratic local elections that set the stage for democratic elections at higher levels. No such process occurred in New Order Indonesia.

In fact, Indonesia appears to fit well with Geddes and Frantz's finding for Latin America as cited by Hicken and Kuhonta that the old party system does not just reappear after authoritarian leaders, who have repressed old parties and created new ones, are replaced. The parties of the authoritarian period initially dominate the free elections. This was the case in Indonesia. The three New Order legacy parties – Golkar, PPP, and PDI-P – took 68 percent of the vote in the 1999 elections. Golkar, the party of the authoritarian regime during the New Order, came in second in the 1999 and 2009 elections and won the elections of 2004 outright. Golkar has been one of the strongest parties organizationally in Indonesia's new democratic environment, although it too has had its problems such as splits. Over the years of the dictatorship, Golkar established networks, built loyalty, and fostered relationships with voters that have lasted into the reform period. One interesting outcome of the nature of the prior regime may be the greening, Islamizing, of Golkar under the New Order. This may have set the stage for the catchall parties of the reformasi period by establishing a hybrid party, at once a home for secular-nationalists and, later, also pious Muslims.

Despite the initially strong performances, however, the vote commanded by the New Order legacy parties has been declining. In 2009, these parties took just 33.8 percent of the vote, down from 68 percent in 1999. This, too, fits with Geddes and Frantz's work, as they found in Latin America that the party system eventually fragments as the parties crafted during the authoritarian period weaken and new parties rise. Golkar continues to hang on, but its vote share has declined. The party survived numerous splits,[43] but splits before the 2009 elections appear to have taken a toll: Gerindra and Hanura took 8.2 percent of the national vote, Golkar 14.5 percent last time around. Together, Golkar and the splits took 22.7 percent in 2009, a hair above Golkar's 21.6 percent from 2004. PDI-P's vote has crashed from 33.7 percent (1999) to 14 percent (2009). The PPP appears to be weakening, perhaps fatally, declining from 11 percent in 1999 to just 5.3 percent in 2009. The party appears to suffer from the general weakness of Islamic-only parties (PPP – an absence of charismatic leadership and questioning of its raison d'être – and has not moved significantly in a catchall direction).

The PDI-P has weakened dramatically, but its strong vote in 1999 might have been the outlier rather than the weak vote in 2009. In 1999, the party received a strong boost from reformist votes, votes the party would not capture again. I question, too, whether the party's survival into the reformasi period is a result of the institutional legacy of the New Order PDI or other factors such as Megawati's charisma, her victimhood by the New Order regime, her descent from founding father Sukarno, and the party's secular-

---

[43] Significant splits include Edi Sudrajat's Partai Keadilan dan Persatuan, Tutut's Partai Karya Peduli Bangsa, as well as Wiranto's Hanura, and Prabowo's Gerindra. In 2010, Surya Paloh, another thwarted leadership contestant, launched the National Democratic movement, potentially the kernel of another party.

nationalist, pro-poor orientation. I would argue that any party Megawati had created in 1998 would have been the PDI-P with or without the connection to the old New Order PDI.

Other historical factors beyond the nature of the prior regime appear to matter for PSI. The Communist Party, destroyed in 1965 and 1966, has not reemerged. The entire hard left has remained suppressed after the violence of the 1960s and 30 years of authoritarian rule and anti-communist propaganda. For this reason, there is little left-right polarization in the current party system. Further, the military's role in the national liberation movement and its reluctance to play second fiddle to civilian politicians contributed to the willingness and the ability of the military to expel the parties from power: first partially with Guided Democracy and then more completely with the New Order.

Political Institutions

Hicken and Kuhonta hypothesize that as far as the electoral system is concerned, a proportional representation (PR) system may contribute to greater institutionalization of the party system as voters may be able to choose parties closest to their ideal preference points; thus, their links to their preferred parties may be stronger. For Asia as a whole in contrast, as the authors found, a PR electoral system was associated with higher volatility and, thus, greater instability in interparty competition. Under conditions of authoritarianism and unfair competition, Indonesia used a PR system and achieved low levels of volatility (ranging from 2 to 12). However, in an environment of free competition during the reformasi period, PR has been associated with volatility in the high 20s. The sheer number of parties in the country's large-magnitude PR electoral system has also contributed to delegitimizing the party system in the minds of citizens, a negative for institutionalization.

Hicken and Kuhonta consider other political institutions that might impact PSI, such as electoral rules that emphasize parties (positive for institutionalization) and presidentialism (negative for institutionalization). In the beginning of the reformasi period, Indonesia's electoral rules strongly emphasized parties: voters chose party symbols rather than individuals in 1999 and 2004,[44] parties made lists of candidates who were then elected based on party performance and party-determined rankings. Parties had strong control over their delegations because of their ability to decide who could run for office and the candidates' position on the list. Even after elections, parties frequently used resignation letters obtained in advance to manipulate the composition of their parliamentary delegations. In addition, only parties or coalitions of parties commanding more than 20 percent of the parliamentary

---

[44] The rules were changed to allow voters to choose individuals in 2004, but few took advantage of this new, poorly socialized feature of the voting system. Only 2 of 560 seats in the parliament were filled in this way.

vote (or 25 percent of the parliamentary seats) were allowed to nominate candidates for president.[45]

The balance between the individual and the party has been changing across the reform era, tilting more toward the individual over time. Independent candidates can now run for office at the local level; previously, only parties could sponsor candidates. Voting for parliament has morphed into an open-list PR system (begun in 2004, made mandatory by a court decision in 2008), which puts much greater emphasis on the individual winning the highest vote total in the constituency. From the perspective of PSI, these newly empowered individual legislators can lead to deleterious effects for the party as a whole because the party is unable to act as a unit. Further, parties are much less visible on candidate election materials, if we contrast materials from 2009 with those from earlier elections. This all plays a role in cutting the link between voter and party and building a link between voter and individual candidate.

As for presidentialism, whereas Hicken and Kuhonta could not find Asia-wide support for a connection between presidentialism and institutionalization or a lack thereof, Indonesia appears to offer support for an association between presidents and weak parties. But Indonesia had poorly institutionalized parties even when it followed a parliamentary system with a weaker presidency in the 1950s. In the reform era, parties have certainly formed around individuals and their presidential aspirations, as evidenced with Susilo Bambang Yudhoyono and PD, Wiranto's Hanura, and Prabowo's Gerindra. This has had deleterious implications for PSI, as the focus on individuals means the potential for short-lived, organization-poor parties.

In addition to the institutions highlighted by Hicken and Kuhonta, an array of particular institutional features can significantly foster or inhibit PSI. Threshold laws have determined which parties can be represented in parliament (only those with more than 2.5 percent of the vote for 2009). This has effectively reduced the number of parties in parliament to nine. The threshold rose to 3.5 percent in 2014, putting further pressure on small parties. It will be harder to be recognized as a party and compete in the general elections with stricter requirements for membership spreading across the nation. Reducing the number of parties is in line with popular aspirations and should improve the legitimacy of the party system and thus increase institutionalization.

Another type of threshold requirement determines which parties can compete in subsequent elections automatically, without going through cumbersome processes of re-naming, re-registering, and re-qualifying. The threshold is the reason that beginning in 1999 the Partai Keadilan (the Justice Party) morphed into the Partai Keadilan Sejahtera (the Prosperous Justice Party) in

---

[45] This has been raised from 3 percent of the vote/5 percent of the seats in 2004. In 1999, the president was elected indirectly through the Majelis Permusyawaratan Rakyat, the upper house of parliament.

2004. The qualification requirement contributes to a feeling of tumult in the political system. Only a few parties seem the same from one election to the next.

Political Cleavages

Reviewing the literature, Hicken and Kuhonta propose that cleavages in the population are good for PSI. If parties tap into cleavages, they should be able to count on dependable support from one election to the next, thus lowering volatility. The situation in societies with crosscutting cleavages is seen to be less promising. Catchall parties form, and attachment to party is weaker. But in Hicken and Kuhonta's findings, ethnic fractionalization on its own does not appear to be associated with any particular outcome as far as volatility is concerned.

Indonesia has high levels of ethnic fractionalization (EF), with an EF score of .77. The measure of crosscutting was also high, at .73. Indonesia has had parties based on cleavages during the period of parliamentary democracy in the 1950s and parties that are moving toward catchall status during the present *reformasi* period. In both periods, levels of volatility were high, and PSI was low. Further, some areas of cleavage in Indonesia have been deliberately ignored as far as the party system is concerned. Ethnic or island-based identities[46] have been removed from the party system by the laws that allow only parties of sufficient national breadth.[47] We may assume that this single rule has strongly impacted the institutionalization of the party system as the parties have removed one significant pole of identity from exploitation. In an alternative political universe, in which ethnic parties had competed during the last decade-plus, Indonesia might be a profoundly different country today.

If we look at other measures besides volatility for PSI, though, we may come to different conclusions regarding fractionalization. If we consider the party system as a system of interactions, high levels of embeddedness of parties in social schisms can contribute to competition that takes on an end-times quality, as did competition during the Guided Democracy. This contributed to destabilization, a coup d'état, the assumption of power by a military regime, and the complete restructuring of the party system.

Parties in Indonesia have moved in a catchall direction in the present period, which makes sense for the party leaderships given Indonesia's high score on the

---

[46] Only Aceh is allowed to have local parties, a result of the 2005 peace agreement that gives that territory special status within Indonesia. The Aceh parties compete only for local offices in Aceh, not as Acehnese representation to the center. For that, the Acehnese must still rely on the existing cross-island political parties.

[47] Requirements for 2014 specify that parties must have 1,000 members nationwide, offices in all 33 provinces (and at least 30 members per province), as well as offices in 75 percent of the cities in the provinces and 50 percent of cities/regencies within those provinces. These requirements have grown progressively tighter across the reform period.

crosscutting dimension of cleavages. With a military man as its focus, PD would seem to come out of the traditionally secular-nationalist stream. However, PD portrays itself as "nationalist-religious" and has supported Islam-focused measures at the center and in the regions. The religious PKS has stressed good governance and moderated some of its Islamic demands. Indonesia offers support for the notion that party identification is weaker in systems with catchall parties. In a 2006 East Asia Barometer poll, 64 percent of respondents expressed lack of closeness with any political party.[48] In two surveys in 2009, Liddle and Mujani found voters' expression of closeness with a political party averaged a low 22 percent.[49]

Additional Factors

Hicken and Kuhonta limit their consideration to a testable number of hypotheses about PSI across Asia. However, the Indonesia case brings up a number of ideas that might be further considered. First, the economy seems to have been a key feature in legitimizing or delegitimizing the parties and party systems in both democratic and authoritarian periods, thus determining the degree to which they had a chance to institutionalize. Under parliamentary democracy, the fruits of liberation were slow to appear. The quibbling politicians and parties were in large part blamed. Later, Suharto lived and died by this sword. The "Father of Development" rested much of his regime's legitimacy on its ability to deliver growth. In the tumult of the Asian financial crisis, the 13.8 percent economic contraction in 1998 contributed to the regime's complete delegitimation. In fact, Indonesia's democratic experiment since 1998 appeared to be tottering until brisk growth returned in the mid-2000s. Poll after poll has demonstrated that Indonesians' number one concern was the economy, with jobs and prices of primary importance.

Moreover, scholars of parties tend to overlook international factors in examining the institutionalization of party systems. In Indonesia during the Cold War, communist versus non-communist global competition was reflected in communist versus non-communist polarization domestically. Other countries directly abetted this polarization, as China supported Indonesia's Communist PKI, and the United States intervened to support non-communists, such as regional rebels in Sumatra and Sulawesi in the late 1950s and the military's eventual assumption of power in the mid-1960s. Suharto fell in 1998 partially because the Cold War was over and the international zeitgeist had changed, and his authoritarian regime appeared to be swimming against history's tide internationally.

In the reformasi period, other international actors have played a role in the establishment of the new party system and democracy. The United Nations

---

[48] East Asia Barometer 2006: Q 062.
[49] Mujani and Liddle 2010: 41.

Development Program (UNDP) invested millions in support of vote-monitoring organizations and voter education. The International Foundation for Election Systems has supported polling, the drafting of laws related to parties and elections, and the conduct of elections by the election commission. The International Republican Institute and National Democratic Institute, two U.S.-centered NGOs affiliated with the major U.S. parties, have supported party training, the development of female parliamentarians, party communication, and professionalization in general. International political consultants have advised Indonesia's parties and candidates. The ways in which these international interventions have impacted PSI merit further study.

Within the confines of institutions and historical circumstances, as well as international influences, individual members of the elite have made choices that affected Indonesia's party system in important ways. When the new party system was germinating in 1998–1999, party leaders often took the path of least resistance and engaged in communal mobilization. This had effects on the high levels of polarization in the early part of the transition.

Across both authoritarian and democratic periods, elites also chose to cultivate an environment in which parties were viewed as illegitimate. Sukarno, president in the 1950s and 1960s, railed against the parties and replaced them partially in parliament with functional group representatives. Suharto, too, propagandized against the parties, saying that they were too divisive in a heterogeneous country. Indonesians were taught that only the moderate *Pancasila* ideology could preserve the nation. This seems to be an important contributor to the decline of narrow political Islam as manifested in the parties (even as Indonesians as a whole have gotten more pious) and the rise of catchall parties. The party system in the reform period works within the confines of this crafted anti-party legacy. The rise of SBY can in part be explained by his emphasis on non-partisan, non-ideological solutions to the problems Indonesia faces.

Suharto also took important steps to transform the parties organizationally. He cut the roots between parties and individuals, preventing the parties from organizing at the local level. He kept his own Golkar party dependent on himself. Suharto's personal foundations channeled millions for electoral purposes. The president also kept factions within Golkar divided to prevent any group from challenging his top spot.[50] Suharto made conscious choices to structure the party system, and these choices have had long-term effects in the weakness of the New Order legacy parties, the personalistic nature of political parties, the factionalization of Golkar, and Golkar's status as the first catchall party.

---

[50] For these reasons, I disagree with Hicken and Kuhonta's assertion that Golkar had autonomy and coherence.

CONCLUSION

An examination of the degree of institutionalization in Indonesia's four party systems and the reasons behind the levels of institutionalization observed allows us to evaluate the hypotheses on PSI that Hicken and Kuhonta test for Asia as a whole. Passage of time was not significant in the Indonesian case. The period effect, too, is ambiguous. Indonesia's parties formed early but failed to institutionalize. As a Third Wave democracy, Indonesia is relatively under-institutionalized as would be expected. History certainly matters, but a prior authoritarian regime has not been an unmitigated positive factor for PSI in Indonesia. Sukarno and Suharto tore down parties conceptually and institutionally. The rise of Golkar as a catchall party may be one of the most interesting and infrequently observed legacies of the authoritarian regime.

In addition, political institutions have been shown to matter. Indonesia's proportional representation system has produced a multiparty system and high volatility. Laws on threshold and qualification for contestation have served to limit the numbers of parties and the types of parties that may contest. The Indonesian cases show, too, that it is possible to get beyond cleavages. This has both positive and negative impacts for PSI. On the negative side, parties are less rooted in defined groups that can offer support from one election to the next. However, on the positive side, politics can be turned down a notch, reducing the polarization and combative competition. Beyond the factors that Hicken and Kuhonta test, the economy, international factors, and elite choice all seem to play significant roles in shaping PSI in Indonesia.

REFERENCES

Aspinall, Ed. 1997. What Price Victory? The 1997 Elections. *Inside Indonesia* 51 (July–September). Available at http://www.insideindonesia.org/feature-editions/what-price-victory-the-1997-elections.
East Asia Barometer. 2006. Indonesia. Available at http://www.jdsurvey.net/eab/AnalizeQuestion.jsp. Accessed July 24, 2012.
Buehler, Michael, and Paige Tan. 2007. Party-Candidate Relationships in Indonesian Local Politics: A Case Study of the 2005 Regional Elections in Gowa, South Sulawesi Province. *Indonesia* 84 (October): 41–70.
Hindley, Donald. 1966. *The Communist Party of Indonesia: 1951–1963*. Berkeley: University of California Press.
Johnson, Elaine Paige. 2002. *Streams of Least Resistance: the Institutionalization of Political Parties and Democracy in Indonesia*. Ph.D dissertation. University of Virginia.
King, Dwight. 2003. *Half-Hearted Reform: Electoral Institutions and the Struggle for Democracy in Indonesia*. Westport: Praeger.
Kleden, Ignas (Ed.). 2009. *Indonesian Political Parties: From Party Machinery to Political Volunteerism*. Jakarta: Indonesian Community for Democracy.

Lembaga Survei Indonesia. Undated-a. Available at http://www.lsi.or.id.

Lembaga Survei Indonesia. Undated-b. Trend Pilihan pada Partai Politik. Available at http://www.lsi.or.id.

Lembaga Survei Indonesia. Undated-c. PartyID: Merasa Dekat dengan Partai Politik Tertentu (%). Available at http://www.lsi.or.id.

Mainwaring, Scott, and Timothy R. Scully (Eds.). 1995. *Building Democratic Institutions: Party Systems in Latin America.* Stanford: Stanford University Press.

Mietzner, Marcus. 2007. Party Financing in Post-Soeharto Indonesia: Between State Subsidies and Political Corruption. *Contemporary Southeast Asia* 28(2).

Mietzner, Marcus. 2008. Comparing Indonesia's Party Systems of the 1950s and the Post-Suharto Era: From Centrifugal to Centripetal Interparty Competition. *Journal of Southeast Asian Studies* 39(3): 431–453.

Mietzner, Marcus. 2012. Indonesia: Yudhoyono's Legacy, between Stability and Stagnation. *Southeast Asian Affairs 2012.* Singapore: ISEAS.

Mujani, Saiful, and R. William Liddle. 2010. Personalities, Parties, and Voters. *Journal of Democracy* 21(2).

Partai Demokrat website. Available at http://www.demokrat.or.id/. Accessed June 4, 2010.

Pepinsky, Thomas, R. William Liddle, and Saiful Mujani. 2010. Indonesian Democracy and the Transformation of Political Islam. Paper presented to the Association for Asian Studies, Philadelphia, Pennsylvania, March 2010.

Sjamsuddin, Nazaruddin. 1984. *PNI dan Kepolitikannaya 1963–1969.* Jakarta: CV Rajawali.

Schwarz, Adam. 1999. *A Nation in Waiting.* St. Leonards, NSW: Allen & Unwin.

Slater, Dan. 2004. Indonesia's Accountability Trap: Party Cartels and Presidential Power after Democratic Transition. *Indonesia* 78 (October): 61–92.

Soekarno. 1970. Let Us Bury the Parties. In Herbert Feith and Lance Castles (Eds.), *Indonesian Political Thinking: 1945–1965,* pp. 81–83. Ithaca: Cornell University Press.

Tan, Paige Johnson. 2006. Indonesia Seven Years after Suharto: Party System Institutionalization in a New Democracy, Contemporary Southeast Asia 28(1).

11

South Korea's Weakly Institutionalized Party System

Joseph Wong

South Korea is hailed a model of political and economic modernization.[1] A desperately poor country in the immediate post–World War II period, and one that suffered under Japanese colonialism and followed by a war that cemented the split on the peninsula between the North and South, South Korea has emerged to become one of the world's richest economies. It boasts a diversified industrial economy, having achieved decades of rapid economic growth. And in the late 1980s, Korea began its transformation into a robust democracy, for which a democratic rollback is now virtually inconceivable. Its democracy was won when Korean society mobilized during the mid-1980s in waves of large-scale protests; the military regime responded by capitulating to demands for political change and by introducing real democratic reform almost immediately. Undoing the institutions of the prior military regime has taken time, to be sure, but Korea's young democracy is deepening: former generals have been prosecuted, industrial barons have been constrained, electoral rules have been institutionalized, civil society remains invigorated and attitudes toward democracy have become more favorable over time. Alternations in power have also occurred regularly, such that the former dominant party, once backed by the military, has experienced and accepted electoral defeat, and opposition candidates and parties have taken power in both the executive and legislative branches of government. The transfer of power between incumbent and challenging parties has by and large been smooth.

These successes notwithstanding, the process of democratic transformation in Korea has not come about without significant challenges that remain today. Chief among these challenges is democratic Korea's political party system, which by most measures is considered to be weakly institutionalized. For instance, in their article on independent voters in Korea and Taiwan,

---

[1] Amsden 1989; Wong 2012.

Alexander Tan and his colleagues calculate that "independents" accounted for 48 percent of eligible Korean voters during the late 1990s, a decade after Korea's democratic transition was initiated. What is more, the data used in that study were collected during the 1997 presidential election, at the time when perennial opposition candidate Kim Dae-Jung won the presidency, and when most observers noted a deepening partisan divide, at least rhetorically, among "conservative" and "progressive" parties and voters. Even so, despite the supposed ideological polarization of Korean electoral politics, which seemed to portend a more institutionalized party system, nearly half of those surveyed indicated that they do "not lean toward any parties."[2]

Party identification in Korea was weak and unstable during the 1990s and continues so today. Voters are described as volatile. Party politics and by extension the party system remain unstable and inconsistent. Partisan affiliations among voters and the parties' rank and file are capricious and ephemeral, changing often from one electoral contest to the next. Political parties in Korea are viewed as transitory, rather than institutionally entrenched or relatively fixed points on programmatic or ideological partisan spectrums. Indeed, according to longtime Korea scholar David Steinberg, political parties in Korea are "the weakest link in the democratic process."[3]

This chapter looks to explain why the party system remains so uninstitutionalized in Korea, despite decades of democratic practice. In contrast to Taiwan,[4] the comparative case often evoked as most similar to that of the Korean experience, I argue that (1) political parties were, historically, weakly institutionalized prior to the democratic transition because of the military's entrenchment within the political elite, and its efforts to govern not through professional parties and electoral institutions, as we saw in nondemocratic Taiwan, but rather through the use and threat of military coercion; and (2) the particular politics of democratization in Korea have failed to construct enduring and consistent partisan cleavages that programmatically define parties and institutionalize their positions within the party system.

KOREA'S WEAK PARTY SYSTEM

Even the most attentive Korea watchers find it frustrating to keep straight the continual transformation of parties and the political party system. The former authoritarian party, the Democratic Justice Party (DJP), entered into a grand coalition during the early 1990s to form the Democratic Liberal Party (DLP), which was headed by one of the former opposition leaders Kim Young-Sam, who himself was repressed by the predecessors of the DJP. The DLP was then transformed into the New Korea Party (NKP) during Kim's presidency in 1996,

[2] Tan et al. 2000: 68, 73.
[3] Steinberg 1998.
[4] See Cheng and Hsu, this volume (Chapter 5).

and then again into the Grand National Party (GNP). Korea's main democratic opposition party (or parties, as it were) initially led by Kim Dae-Jung, originated as the Party for Peace and Democracy (PPD) in the late 1980s and then evolved through two iterations during the Kim Dae-Jung presidency of the late 1990s, first the New Congress for National Politics (NCNP) and then the Millennium Democratic Party (MDP). The MDP was later dissolved to form the Uri Party under President Roh Moo-Hyun, which was re-named yet again during the late 2000s to become the United Democratic Party. Meanwhile, dozens of smaller political parties have come and gone throughout Korea's democratic period.

Volatility in parties and the party system – in name and substance – have contributed to voter volatility (i.e., changed votes from one election to the next). Hicken and Kuhonta confirm in this volume that electoral volatility in Korea ranks among the highest when compared to other Asian cases. And Hans Stockton reports that levels of voter volatility in Korean electoral politics measure the highest compared with other late democratizers in Latin America and East Asia.[5] The Korean case stands out.

The uninstitutionalized nature of the political party system in Korea is also reflected in popular (and frankly accurate) perceptions of parties and their inefficacy with respect to governing. Parties are not viewed as the institutional vehicles for consistent policy platforms. They do not present ideological cues for voters. They change names and are reconstituted with the selection of every new party leader. Parties represent the personal means for the attainment of political power, "standing for nothing" as Steinberg argues "aside from the ex cathedra pronouncements of their leaders."[6] Regionalism, and specifically the regional background of party leaders, is still the best predictor of voting behavior in democratic Korea. That until recently subnational levels of government did not exist – and at present are weak in terms of administrative authority – has meant the regional distribution of pork is basically centralized, exacerbating the regionalist-personalist nature of parties and the party system. The holdover of patronage politics and the inability of the state to de-link from industry's commanding heights have also resulted in the continuation of political corruption. Contemporary analysis confirms that voters perceive parties and the formal political system more generally to be an ineffective means to good governance.[7] To be sure, the rise of civic groups and their tremendous influence in Korea's politics are a reflection of people's dissatisfaction with political parties and their ties to privileged interest groups. As Seong puts it, Korea's civic groups have "come to acquire moral, social and political hegemony."[8]

The non-programmatic nature of parties and the party system is reflective of the absence of enduringly stable and predictable political, economic, and social

[5] Stockton 2001.
[6] Steinberg 1998: 80; see also Steinberg and Shin 2006.
[7] Shin 2003.
[8] Seong 2000: 92.

cleavages in Korea's partisan politics, both a cause and effect of weak party institutionalization. The notion of the left has been historically politically taboo, for instance. The idea of the market and the neoliberal enterprise, typically associated with the right, are contested.[9] The conceptualization of the Korean nation is dynamic, reflective of the nation's turbulent past and its uncertain future with communist North Korea, Japan, and even the United States. Yet, some suggest that politics in contemporary Korea may nonetheless be moving toward a more traditional left-right cleavage. The fact that the terms "conservatives" and "progressives" resonate at all in Korea's political vernacular intimates that such party labels and identities are, at least on the surface, meaningful.[10] However, programmatic cues, as well as issue- and policy-based campaigning, still remain second (or third) to other, more prevalent, perceptions of parties and what they stand for. The evidence suggests that parties continue to be personalist, reflective of the prestige and standing of their party bosses and their elite allies. Parties' economic, social, and foreign policy platforms by and large remain inconsistent, undermining notions of a programmatic coherence among parties and the party system more generally.

Gabor Toka writes that party system institutionalization "entails the stabilization and social embeddedness of the major party alternatives and their relative party positions, hence *a regularity* in the patterns of interparty competition."[11] The development of the party system and political parties in Korea fall well short of this benchmark. As I have briefly described, Korean parties have tended to be short lived; voter identification to parties is weak and electoral support is volatile and unstable; party identities continue to be shaped by individual leaders and personalities, and as such, party legitimacy has waned. Parties in Korea's democracy have failed to articulate consistent programmatic agendas, thus weakening the party system more generally. This is puzzling. Why, after two decades of political reform, with the routinization of democratic competition and after repeated iterations of the electoral game, do parties and the party system in Korea remain weakly institutionalized?

EXPLAINING WEAKNESS

The literature suggests several reasons for South Korea's weak party system, some that are complementary, and others that are more narrowly deterministic. With respect to the latter, for instance, Doh-Chull Shin draws on extensive survey data to assert a culturally based explanation for the persistence of personalism in political parties.[12] According to Shin, Korean society remains deeply shaped by Confucian norms. In particular, Shin and his colleague Chong-Min

---

[9] Kim 2008.
[10] Steinberg and Shin 2006; Moon 2009.
[11] Toka 1997: 96, emphasis added.
[12] Shin 1999.

Park contend that Koreans are culturally hardwired with expectations of, and thus the propensity to legitimate, political hierarchy. Moreover, his data strongly suggest that people in Korea are not uncomfortable with individual leaders exercising preponderant authority, a view that parties qua organizations ought to be headed by strong leaders with quasi-moralistic (i.e., beyond political) claims over the exercise of power. Personalist parties are the norm, not the exception in Korea. Shin and Park thus conclude that "contemporary Korean political culture still manifests the Confucian legacy of hierarchical collectivism and benevolent paternalism."[13]

A more agency-based perspective – one that is less involuntary than intimated by more culturally deterministic explanations – rests on the functional exit of political actors from the formal political arena and, by extension, their disengagement from the party system. Political corruption stemming from within political parties and their leaderships has, for example, delegitimated parties and the party system. Holdovers from Korea's authoritarian past, be it patronage politics inside parties or regionalist appeals through the promise of pork, have similarly cast parties and the party system as ineffectual, and even illegitimate, institutions of governance. Political actors – activists, voters, civic leaders – have, therefore, voluntarily exited the formal political party arena in Korea. The number of civic groups in Korea is on the rise; meanwhile, voter turnout in national elections is declining. Borrowing from Albert Hirschman's conceptualization of politics, one might say that political actors in Korea have decided "voice" is less effective than "exit" when it comes to party politics.[14]

The increasing prevalence of civic groups, as one key example of exit, is indeed related to the declining perceived legitimacy of parties and their leaders more generally. The rise of civil society, the politics of mass mobilization, and the growing democratic capacity of the netizen nation have come to append Korea's formal party politics. In 2000, the Citizens' Alliance for the 2000 General Election (CAGE) was formed to check the suitability of legislative candidates and, if need be, publicly blacklist those politicians deemed corrupt by the civic group coalition. According to most accounts, the CAGE had an enormous impact on the election outcome, whistle-blowing on candidates from both the conservative and progressive camps.[15] Its lasting legacy has been to further delegitimate Korean parties and thus reinforce Korea's weak political parties and party system.

Part of the explanation for Korea's weakly institutionalized and unstable party system rests on the internal organization of parties themselves. As many social movement scholars point out, for instance, no institutional channels link formal parties to activist groups within civil society; they exist and operate in disconnected and separate political spheres, not at all socially embedded within

---

[13] Park and Shin 2006: 360.
[14] Hirschman 1970.
[15] See, e.g., Shin 2003.

broader social forces as prescribed by Toka.[16] Parties' continual name changes reflect the ways in which Korean parties, as Steinberg notes, are merely a vehicle for the attainment of personal power, exacerbating the problem of weak partisan identity among voters. The party leader, often referred to as the party "boss," enjoys tremendous power over the party's rank and file, most notably in his or her allocation of party resources for legislative candidates. But parties are not simply organized in institutionally hierarchical ways; it is not the institutionally defined position of party leader that is powerful. Rather, political parties *serve* the party leader. It is the individual party boss who is powerful. Few leadership succession mechanisms exist inside Korean parties, aside from personalized political power plays among party elites, to ensure the transfer of leadership power from one leader to the next, and even then, incoming party leaders reconstitute the party to separate themselves from their predecessor. Leadership succession inside parties remains uninstitutionalized,[17] and thus parties are short lived and party loyalties among the rank and file are idiosyncratic and dependent on patronage ties to particular leaders. In short, party identities are shallow, even within parties themselves.

Korea's political institutions have also shaped the development (or underdevelopment) of political parties. Tun-Jen Cheng articulates a more institutionalist argument to explain weak party institutionalization in Korea. Cheng finds that party system stability actually has less to do with presidential versus parliamentary institutions. Rather, he argues that variations in party system institutionalization have more to do with specific electoral rules. In his comparative study of electoral institutions in Asia, Cheng argues that Korea's electoral system – including single-term limits on the presidency, nonconcurrent legislative and presidential elections, no runoff elections for the presidency, and a single-ballot system for legislative elections – undermines party coherence, rank-and-file identification, and party discipline. These institutional rules of the electoral game, he argues, "weaken the party system and aggravate the divided-government problem" in Korea. Cheng contends that party identification and party loyalties are, therefore, ephemeral.[18]

The arguments developed in the remainder of this chapter to explain Korea's weakly institutionalized parties and party system are intended to complement those outlined earlier. The arguments unfold in two parts. First, I contend that notwithstanding the presence of political parties during Korean authoritarianism in the postwar period, the authoritarian regime was a military regime. The ruling party was one institutional vehicle through which the president governed, though political power was always firmly entrenched in, and backed by, the military and Korea's domestic security apparatus; power was exercised through the use and threat of coercion. Unlike in Taiwan, there existed in Korea a very

---

[16] Toka 1997; see also Chu 1998; Wong 2004a; Lee 2006.
[17] See Dix 1992.
[18] Cheng 2003: 25–27.

weak historical foundation on which to build a democratic political party system. Second, the processes of democratic consolidation in Korea have not resulted in the institutionalization of predictable partisan cleavages along programmatic lines. As Stockton points out, in general, party system institutionalization and "improved democracies are perpetuated by the routinization of a political process based on political parties that are *consistent* to a large degree in their ideological and policy positions, parliamentary and extra-parliamentary discipline, and organization."[19] I argue that in the case of Korea, parties have failed to cement programmatic positions within the party system, thus constraining the development of stronger parties and party system over time. The historical and contemporary bases of these constraints contrast with Taiwan's pre-democratic and democratic experiences; indeed, the comparison with Taiwan, and specifically the arguments presented by Cheng and Hsu in this volume (Chapter 5), is instructive, and thus references to the Taiwan case will be invoked to inform the analysis of the Korean experience.

KOREA'S MILITARY REGIME

Prior to the democratic transition during the late 1980s, the story of Korea's postwar political development was punctuated by moments of democratic flurry that ended with a military coup, which was then followed by the installation of a military regime. This happened in May 1961, when General Park Chung-Hee staged a coup, ending Korea's flawed democratic experiment at the time; the military regime was re-affirmed with the imposition of the highly repressive Yushin Constitution in 1972 by the Park dictatorship, when opposition forces, led by Kim Dae-Jung, began to mobilize. This pattern continued in 1980, when General Chun Doo-Hwan maneuvered during what Mark Clifford calls the "Night of the Generals" to fill the power vacuum left after Park's 1979 assassination and then as president, quickly re-imposed martial law to end abruptly yet another fleeting moment of high democratic expectations.[20] Matters of statecraft, domestic development, and nation building in Korea were managed almost exclusively by military men prior to the democratic transition. This was unlike the case of postwar Taiwan, where the Kuomintang (KMT) set out as early as 1950 to fundamentally reorganize the party to become a highly penetrative, though largely civilian, Leninist party. The ruling party in Korea – the Democratic Republic Party (DRP) under Park and the Democratic Justice Party (DJP) under Chun – remained subordinate to the personal dictates of military generals-turned-presidents.

The imperatives for military coups and military dictatorships were justified in terms of both foreign security concerns and domestic development. Buoyed by a deep sense of postcolonial anxiety, nationalism, and the shame of having been

---

[19] Stockton 2001: 96, emphasis added.
[20] Clifford 1998.

brutally victimized by Japanese imperialist ambitions earlier in the century, Koreans were concerned with maintaining their national security in the postwar period. The continual threat of a North Korean invasion and the loose alliance between the communists to the north with those in the People's Republic of China created the need for strong, disciplined, martial leadership in the South.[21]

The political justification for Korea's postwar military authoritarian regime extended beyond readiness for external threats, however; the military dictatorship was to be the institutional foundation to propel Korea's modernization program, especially the country's economic modernization. As Clifford notes, when "Park and his associates took power the military and its logistical experience was the most modern part of Korean society."[22] The core of Korea's developmental state apparatus, in its earliest formulation during the 1960s, was the military elite. Immediately after the 1961 coup, for instance, the junta, which was then called the Military Revolutionary Committee, was transformed into the Supreme Council for National Reconstruction (SCNR). The SCNR was "composed of the thirty highest-ranking military personnel, including the chiefs of all the branches of the armed forces."[23] And although the Planning Council for National Reconstruction was staffed by civilian technocrats, the members of the council were appointed by the SCNR. Furthermore, a military officer headed each branch of the Planning Council.[24] Paranoid about possible resistance among his allies, President Park depended on the internal security apparatus of the state, notably the Korean CIA (KCIA), to eliminate dissenters within his own political party and the state more generally. Park established a shadow cabinet of his closest political-military allies to check the civilian bureaucracy. As Byung-Kook Kim recounts, Park relied "on the praetorian guards and the military rather than on political parties" to maintain political rule.[25] Though the military largely remained in the barracks, it was clear the security apparatus was loyal to Park, his party, and his personal dictatorship.

The 1970s saw the military strengthen its position within the Korean state, rather than retreat. Whereas in Taiwan during this period, the ruling KMT was increasingly professionalized and broadly more inclusive in its organization, and the political system there underwent a slow but steady process of political liberalization,[26] the Korean regime became more dictatorial. Opposition to the Park regime began to mobilize during the late 1960s, and the ruling party's electoral support slowly waned. Rather than loosening the state's grip on society in response, as we saw with the KMT in Taiwan, Park unilaterally imposed the 1972 Yushin Constitution, which, among other things, turned the National

---

[21] Moon and Jun 2011.
[22] Clifford 1998: 64.
[23] Moon and Jun 2011.
[24] Kim 2011: 88.
[25] Ibid.: 142.
[26] See Cheng and Hsu, this volume (Chapter 5); see also Dickson 1996.

Assembly into a rubber stamp legislature, redirected the top-down Korean economic development toward heavy industries, and effectively guaranteed Park's lifetime presidency. To politically insulate the regime – what Hyug Baeg Im characterizes as Park's "imperial rule" – President Park came to rely even more heavily on "his time-tested centers of coercive power," composed of all branches of Korea's security apparatus, including the army and the KCIA. As Im concludes, during the 1970s "Park was determined to turn South Korea into a garrison state."[27]

Park Chung-Hee was assassinated in 1979. Without a successor, or even a succession plan in place, Korea's political leadership was in disarray. Democratic activists began to stir, and for a moment it looked as though the pattern of military dictatorship in Korea might give way to meaningful political reform; in the end, this was not to be, however. Despite what appeared to be a brief window for a potential democratic turn after Park's assassination, General Chun Doo-Hwan claimed the South Korean presidency via an internal military coup. After suppressing the Kwangju Uprising in 1980, a moment of intense social movement mobilization, Chun re-imposed the might of the military and his autocratic party regime continued to rule coercively under martial law.

One explanation for weak parties and party system in democratic Korea, therefore, must include the history of political party development during the period of authoritarian military rule, a history quite unlike the gradual institutionalization of the KMT in Taiwan and the party's professionalization prior to the democratic transition. Divergent historical paths in political party institutionalization had a significant impact on the dynamics of the democratic transition in both places. In Taiwan, the historical evolution of the KMT as a Leninist and later a competitive political party, along with the gradual development of a viable opposition party throughout the 1980s, meant that "[b]y the time that Taiwan embarked on democratic transition in 1986, the prototype of a stable party system already was in place";[28] this structural precondition was absent in the case in Korea. As Cheng and Hsu argue, along with many other observers of Taiwan's democratic politics,[29] the democratic transition was prompted by repeated electoral challenges posed by a nascent opposition party, then called the *tangwai*. In addition, the ruling and opposition parties engaged in continual dialogue right up to the moment the *tangwai* announced the formation of an official opposition party, the Democratic Progressive Party (DPP), in September 1986.[30] In Taiwan, parties were the main instigators of democratic reform, and the ruling and opposition parties conspired to bring about Taiwan's democratic transition.

---

[27] Im 2011: 233–234.
[28] Cheng and Hsu, this volume (Chapter 5).
[29] For example, Chao and Myers 1998; Rigger 1999.
[30] Rigger 1999.

In Korea, however, the democratic breakthrough was prompted not by the opposition parties and electoral challenges to the ruling party but rather by massive civil society uprisings during the spring and summer of 1987. A groundswell of students, workers, the church, and middle-class activists took to the streets and demanded political reform. Roh Tae-Woo, the presumptive successor to Chun, decided to not repress the opposition social movement. Rather, in June 1987, Roh announced presidential elections later that year and open legislative elections in the spring of 1988. Whereas Taiwan's President Chiang Ching-Kuo was ultimately forced to contend with an electoral challenge mounted by a well-organized opposition party in an increasingly liberalizing political environment, Roh's decision to embark on democratic reform in Korea was pushed, in terms of a more proximate cause, by Korea's *minjung* movement that had developed from within society's grass roots. Put another way, while the KMT's Chiang Ching-Kuo gave in to an opposition *political party*, Roh Tae-Woo capitulated to a well-mobilized oppositional *civil society*. In the drama of Korea's democratic transition that played out in the summer 1987, political parties were minor actors with bit parts.

NON-PROGRAMMATIC PARTIES

One would reasonably expect that the introduction of democratic institutions and democratic contestation would strengthen the role of parties in the formal political arena and hence stabilize and institutionalize the party system in more predictable and consistent ways. Parties, after all, are important organizations with which to win votes; as organizations, parties are integral actors in competing for electoral support. To that end, political parties simplify otherwise complex real-world politics; aggregate political interests; articulate important heuristic cues and ideological stakes in public policy debates; and, therefore create and over time deepen partisan identification among voters. Parties operating in institutionalized party systems are intended to provide clear and consistent alternatives for voters. In short, we should expect the imperatives of democratic competition to encourage, over time, the formation of stable and programmatic political parties and party systems. But this has not been the case in Korea. Why?

One explanation, as I have argued, is that the nature of the authoritarian military regime in postwar Korea stunted the development of a stable party system prior to the democratic transition. To reiterate: in Taiwan, the professionalization of the KMT Party, the gradual formation of a *de facto* opposition party, and the early institutionalization of limited elections were key drivers of the democratic transition. In Korea, on the other hand, party pressures, either from within the ruling party or from the opposition, were not the proximate causes of the democratic breakthrough. Parties, on the eve of Korea's democratic transition, were weak and ineffectual.

Another explanation is institutional. Efforts to institutionally strengthen parties and thus bring stability to the party system were made during the 1980s with the implementation of electoral reform. One significant change made prior to the 1988 National Assembly election was the introduction of a proportional representation (PR) component to the voting system (one-fourth reserved for PR-list candidates), whereby voters cast a ballot for individual candidates in single member district (SMD) contests, but for which that single candidate vote also counted as the PR vote for a political party. Through the use of a party list, this modified PR reform was intended to strengthen party identities, to engender loyalty among the party rank and file, and in turn stabilize Korea's political party system. However, the reform failed to achieve these objectives, Tun-Jen Cheng explains, because the single vote (double counted for the candidate and the party) did not create enough of an incentive for a political party "to nurture its reputation and polish its label."[31] Instead, the institutional incentives of the single ballot, though mixed SMD-PR electoral system, only reinforced what Steinberg and Shin describe as the "traditional entourage system" operating within political parties, by which personal patronage mattered much more than programmatic commitment among party members, and where electoral voting was largely determined by regional affiliation with party leaders.[32]

Herein lies the bigger problem: parties and the party system in Korea remain unstable and weakly institutionalized because of the absence of programmatic lines of partisan competition and partisan affiliation among voters. Given the nature of the military regime, we have some sense as to why programmatic cleavages failed to be institutionalized among parties prior to the democratic transition in Korea. We also have institutional explanations for why partisan differentiation remained weak even after electoral reforms were introduced just prior to the founding legislative elections in 1988. However, it remains puzzling as to why, over time and with the deepening of democratic competition, we have not seen the development of a more programmatic and enduring cleavage-based political party system in Korea. The explanation, I contend, is political and intrinsic to the particular politics of the democratic transition and consolidation in Korea.

Transitioning in Good Times

To get at the answer, we need to revisit the politics of the democratic breakthrough during the 1980s. Elections were an important driver for the democratic transition in Korea insofar as they provided an important signal to the ruling party that its popular support had begun to wane. The ruling DJP led by Chun Doo-Hwan, for instance, polled a little more than one-third of the popular vote

[31] Cheng 2003: 27.
[32] Steinberg and Shin 2006.

in the 1981 and 1985 National Assembly elections. And even with the skewed rules in seat distribution that overwhelmingly favored the ruling party, the DJP maintained just slightly more than half of the assembly seats, down from around a more dominant take of two-thirds a decade earlier. Still, even though elections signaled to the ruling party its declining popularity, the military-backed regime could have chosen to maintain its rule through coercion, as it had done so effectively in the past. In other words, the ruling party's diminishing electoral fortunes alone were not sufficient to compel General Roh Tae-Woo to choose reform over repression. Rather, as I have argued, the more proximate cause and impetus for Roh to initiate democratic reforms during the summer of 1987 was the emergence of societal mobilization under the banner of the *minjung* movement.[33]

Yet, it needs to be emphasized that Korea's was not a democratic transition sparked by a deep-seated revulsion with the state or an unequivocal international condemnation of the nondemocratic regime, such as we saw with the National Party in South Africa or more recently in the various uprisings against autocratic regimes in north Africa and the Middle East. Nor was Korea's democratic breakthrough at all similar to the complete collapse of the former Soviet Union and the Communist Party there. Nor was it the result of a mass-based revolution, as we saw in parts of Latin America and sub-Saharan Africa. The DJP regime was not amid an irreversible crisis of legitimacy.[34] Rather, the Korean economy during the mid to late 1980s was in relatively good shape. Korea, at the time, was soon to join the ranks of the Organisation for Economic Cooperation and Development (OECD) club of advanced industrial nations. Giant firms such as Samsung and Hyundai were poised to win significant global market share in high-revenue, high-employment industrial sectors. Korean workers had received wage increases and continued to expect better employment prospects (even though levels of inequality were widening). Students, always at the vanguard of patriotic reform movements, saw themselves as enlightened and nationalist intellectuals, enrolled in world-class universities or studying overseas. On the foreign affairs front, circumstances were more or less positive, and much more sanguine than in Taiwan, which was expelled from the United Nations during the 1970s. Geopolitically, Korea remained a key ally of the United States, despite the thawing Cold War, and an important strategic actor in maintaining East Asian regional stability. In other words, Korea's democratic transition and the introduction of free and fair elections occurred during relatively "good times" for the incumbent nondemocratic regime.[35] The DJP's crisis of legitimacy was, comparatively speaking, relatively mild.

Transitioning in good times affected the development – or nondevelopment, as it turns out – of salient political cleavages in Korea's political party system.

---

[33] Choi 1993; Koo 1993.
[34] Haggard and Kaufman 1995.
[35] See Slater and Wong 2012.

For one, the regime's opposition proved to be fragile, incapable of articulating or occupying issue space in ensuing electoral contests. Added to that, the incumbent ruling party was adept in taking away salient issue positions from the nascent opposition. The fact that the authoritarian party itself ushered in multiparty democracy was instrumental in dividing the opposition. As *minjung* expert and historian Nam-Hee Lee puts it, the early oppositional narrative of the *minjung* movement was framed "exclusively in the context of state repression and heroic resistance." She goes on to add that "narratives" of the *minjung*, animated by oppositional notions of patriotism (the *minjung* activists) and betrayal (the authoritarian state), were "unduly unifying and coherent, subsuming fissures and fractures under the larger narrative of minjung liberation."[36] As we now know, however, the simple dualism or dichotomous conceptualization of the *minjung* movement's cause – the repressive state versus the heroic resisters – was tenuous and the *minjung* coalition quickly disintegrated in the post-transition order.

Thus what might have provided the material for potentially enduring political cleavages to contest the ancient regime instead quickly gave way to contestation among opposition coalition members, fractionalizing the opposition. This was unlike what we saw with the *tangwai* movement in Taiwan, which formalized and organizationally crystallized into a political party at the time Taiwan began to democratize. The *minjung* movement, which many expected might become a potent electoral constituency for the opposition parties, fragmented soon after democracy was won. Students and workers, for instance, were seen to be too radical. Middle-class activists, meanwhile, sought to engage the formal political arena, with many again putting their electoral support behind the incumbent party.[37] From a strategic point of view, the authoritarian-turned-democratic DJP took advantage of the opposition's fragility and the legacies of weak opposition parties in Korean politics. The DJP, despite having faced tremendous opposition throughout the 1980s, nonetheless continued to enjoy considerable legitimacy among activists within the *minjung* movement; and as I have argued, the fact that the incumbent party initiated the democratic transition with Roh's historic declarations in 1987 actually regained the regime some popular legitimacy.

The DJP thus retained power after 1988. As the *minjung* coalition collapsed soon after the democratic breakthrough, opposition parties were unable to win their electoral support. To be sure, the opposition electoral coalition, centered on popular grassroots activists Kim Dae-Jung and Kim Young-Sam, who had together formed the New Korea Democratic Party (NKDP), fell apart in the run-up to the founding elections. Just as the *minjung* movement was ultimately weak and unstable, so too was the opposition party. The NKDP consequently fractured into two rival political parties: the Party for Peace and Democracy

[36] Lee 2007: 295.
[37] Mo 1996; Kim 1997.

(PPD) led by Kim Dae-Jung and the Reunification Democratic Party (RDP), headeded by Kim Young-Sam. The "two Kims" split the opposition vote in the 1987 presidential contest and in the 1988 legislative elections. Roh Tae-Woo narrowly won the presidential elections with a little more than one-third of the popular vote, and the DJP secured a plurality of legislative seats in 1988, winning just 34 percent of popular support. With the opposition divided and the DJP running on an incoherent mix of both elite concessions and populist promises, the political parties failed to generate any programmatic structure to the party system. Instead, the parties, especially the opposition parties, had to rely on the leaders' popular appeal and regional sentiments to garner electoral support.

Ideological Flexibility

Transitioning in good times not only allowed the authoritarian party to hold on to power and hasten the split in what was a fragile and internally contested opposition coalition, further weakening already weak opposition parties, but transitioning in good times also permitted a sort of ideological fluidity and flexibility in the political system that undermined the potential deepening of partisan cleavages in the post-transition order. By having initiated political reform, the DJP neutralized the authoritarian-democracy cleavage that had unified the *minjung* opposition, if fleetingly, during the mid-1980s. Initiating democratic reform also allowed the DJP to undermine any potential ideological or programmatic coherence within the opposition and opposition parties. The *minjung* is often remembered as having been an ideologically committed leftist movement, which many expected would invigorate electoral support for political parties on the left.

The collapse of the opposition coalition, however, demonstrated that despite the successful mobilization of the *minjung* movement for broader political reforms, *minjung* in actuality was far from a triumph of the supposed left. Middle-class activists, we have since learned, were always uneasy with labor's tactics; the gulf between the student-radical and the worker was wider than it seemed originally; the church crosscut these socioeconomic cleavages; and hence the cross-class, cross-cleavage coalition fragmented soon after Roh's decision to initiate political reform.[38] The *minjung* was, in a sense, a marriage of political convenience among otherwise disparate actors and interests, not one of ideological or programmatic conviction, and once the authoritarian-democracy cleavage appeared to have been resolved, the alliance fell apart.[39] There was, in other words, tremendous ideological flexibility and openness in the immediate post-transition order, which, I assert, was significant with respect to the weak or non-formation of predictable and enduring social, economic, and political

---

[38] Wong 2004a.
[39] Lee 2007.

cleavages along partisan lines. In fact, opposition parties were left scrambling for salient cleavages with which to appeal to voters; meanwhile, the incumbent ruling party postured as a non-ideological, non-programmatic, catchall party.

My point is that the combination of transitioning in good times and the presence of historically weak parties meant that, at the time, no ideological or programmatic basis existed on which partisan cleavages could form and endure. Ideological flexibility – or better put, the absence of ideological rigidity among parties – allowed the ruling party to strategically take ownership of and thus effectively neutralize for the opposition potentially contestable cleavages. As intimated earlier, what we might have imagined to be the social basis of an emergent left (i.e., workers, students) in both the *minjung* movement and the opposition parties failed to take advantage or ownership of the social justice reform agenda. *Minjung* activists were unable to mobilize a leftist base and thus make salient and contestable a left-right cleavage in the political party system. Instead, it was the Roh administration that had earlier eschewed and blocked political efforts to deepen social welfare reform that strategically turned to policies of socioeconomic redistribution in order to appeal to voters. The nominally conservative DJP, for instance, universalized medical insurance coverage in 1988 and 1989. It was also Roh's supposed conservative administration that set in motion plans to create a national pension (old-age income security) system. My point is that the ruling party strategically used social welfare policy promises to capture and take ownership of the social democratic agenda *because it could*; no extant ideological cleavages or programmatic partisan lines precluded the Roh government from doing so.[40]

The opposition had been outmaneuvered early on in the democratization process in Korea. Opposition parties, which were nominally characterized as progressive, were without any salient cleavages on which to formulate a coherent, enduring, and winning programmatic party identity; as political parties, they were left fledgling. In the context of ideological fluidity and flexibility, the opposition seemed to not stand for anything, whereas the ruling party seemed to stand for everything. Their former oppositional positions – antiauthoritarianism or socioeconomic justice – had been lost to the preemptive maneuvering of the ideologically malleable ruling party. The opposition parties were forced to rely on personalist or regional appeals to voters and the continuation of entourage politics to organize and retain the loyalties of the party rank and file.

Issue space for the opposition diminished, not widened, over time. In an effort to consolidate the ruling party's hold on power – recall, the DJP controlled only a plurality of seats in the National Assembly (125 of 299 seats) after 1988 and President Roh won the presidency with a little more than one-third of the popular vote in 1987 – the DJP reached out in 1990 to Kim Young-Sam of the RDP and Kim Jong-Pil of Korea's fourth major party, the New Democratic Republican Party (NDRP), to create a new and formidable catchall coalition

---

[40] Wong 2004b.

party called the Democratic Liberal Party (DLP). As expected, the DLP won the 1992 legislative elections with 39 percent of the popular vote and a slim majority of seats (149 of 299) seats in what was a three-party contest. Later that year, Kim Young-Sam of the DLP won the presidency with 42 percent of the popular vote, defeating his main rival, Kim Dae-Jung, who won 34 percent of the vote. The strategic move by the ruling party further marginalized the opposition party led by Kim Dae-Jung. And as a dominant catchall coalition party composed of both former opposition and ruling parties, the formation of the DLP also neutralized again the possibility of deepening social, economic, and political cleavages along ideological or programmatic partisan lines in Korea's political party system.[41] Kim Dae-Jung, who had always enjoyed considerable regional sympathies from voters in Cholla province, was forced to appeal again to personalist and regional sentiments for votes. In sum, the non-programmatic nature of Korea's political party system was as much a result of missed opportunities by a fragmented opposition during the late 1980s, as it was a consequence of strategic and preemptive maneuvering on the part of the ruling party during the early 1990s.

CONCLUSION

Korea's political party system is weakly institutionalized. Party identification among voters is low. Party labels are ephemeral, and they carry little meaning beyond the personalist and regional ties attributed to the party boss. Electoral volatility is high. Parties suffer from a legitimacy problem among citizens. And unlike the two-party system in Taiwan, the political party system in Korea is unstable, and the lines of electoral competition are inconsistent, unpredictable, and not enduring. This chapter has endeavored to explain why.

The political explanation offered in this chapter is composed of two parts. First, I argue that unlike in Taiwan, the ruling party in Korea's authoritarian period was firmly entrenched in the military. Whereas the KMT underwent a process of party reorganization during the early 1950s, followed by the party's professionalization and more inclusive membership, the ruling class in Korea continued to draw from the ranks of the military elite. Opposition parties remained weak throughout Korea's authoritarian period, as the military regime would periodically repress the opposition, as evidenced by the imposition of the highly repressive Yushin Constitution of 1972. Unlike in Taiwan, therefore, Korea did not have, on the eve of its democratic transition, a stable, organized and essentially institutionalized party system in place. Rather, parties in Korea were weak and unstable and had few institutional links to society. Whereas the democratic breakthrough in Taiwan was driven by the formation of a viable opposition party that developed from a long history of electoral competition, in Korea, democratization was pushed by a well-mobilized civil society that was quite detached from the opposition parties.

---

[41] Ibid.

The second part of my argument looks to the politics of democratic transition and consolidation, and how these processes constrained the development of programmatic parties in Korea. Again, the comparison with Taiwan's experience is useful. In Taiwan, as Cheng and Hsu point out in this volume (Chapter 5), the well-organized opposition party, the Democratic Progressive Party (DPP) quickly vied with the KMT for issue space and contestable cleavages soon after the democratic transition was initiated. The opposition party there defined itself along social, economic, and political cleavages. The DPP continued to evolve and refine its identity over time, but always in opposition to the ruling KMT along key issue areas. In Korea, on the other hand, from the time that democratic reforms were initiated during the late 1980s, the opposition failed to take credible ownership of potentially contestable cleavages in the formal political arena. As I have argued, the *minjung* movement quickly collapsed after 1987, and what was presumed to be the opposition's electoral base soon fragmented, leaving opposition parties scrambling to construct new winning platforms and programs. Meanwhile, the ruling party, the DJP, exploited the ideological vacuum left after the democratic breakthrough and adroitly took ownership of both progressive and conservative policy agendas. The formation of the catchall Democratic Liberal Party during the early 1990s further undermined the opposition's efforts to starkly draw and define programmatic differences between it and the ruling party.

My point is not to say that cleavages do not exist in Korean society and Korean electoral politics. Cleavages exist, and they provide the raw material for political contestation. They are, ideally, the bases on which ideologies are aligned, winning electoral platforms are articulated, and appealing choices and alternatives are constructed among contending political parties. Thus, while my point is not to say that such raw materials do not exist in Korea, the broader argument presented in this chapter asserts that parties have by and large failed to use these cleavages to define, sharpen, and thus institutionalize partisan differences among themselves.

The politics of the democratic reform during the 1980s and early 1990s revisited in this chapter continues to shape Korean democratic politics today. Notwithstanding some observations that partisan politics in contemporary Korea may be moving toward a more traditional left-right spectrum, as characterized by unofficial party labels such as "progressive" and "conservative,"[42] it is my view that when one looks carefully at the actual performance of political parties and their leaders, taking this trend seriously may be premature – that, in fact, left-right cleavages have not become deeply entrenched within the party system, and that parties and party leaders continue to hold inconsistent and often contradictory positions.

In the run-up to the most recent national elections in 2012, for instance, the Ministry of Finance released a report calculating that both the nominally

---

[42] Steinberg and Shin 2006; Moon 2009.

conservative and progressive parties' social welfare spending proposals would create fiscal deficits; in other words, both parties were competing by ratcheting up social welfare spending commitments, rather than differentiating themselves along conventional left-right, progressive-conservative lines. Incumbent President Lee Myung-Bak of the conservative ruling party, and not the progressive party, ran on an electoral platform of inclusive and shared economic growth. President Roh Moo-Hyun (2003–2008), considered a champion of progressive ideology and politics, fueled anti-American sentiment in Korea while he pursued a hotly contested free trade agreement with the United States. Roh's administration also legislated new social care programs (for the elderly and children), though the reforms were politically portrayed as active labor market policy measures to appeal to neoliberal voters and stakeholders.[43] Kim Dae-Jung (1998–2003) was at the same time the former grassroots activist with supposed leftist credentials and the neoliberal economic crusader under the tutelage of the International Monetary Fund. It was also President Kim Dae-Jung who further exposed Korea to global economic forces and whose administration centralized, rather than devolved, political power, even though the idea of "participatory democracy" first came about during his 1997 presidential campaign. And it was President Kim Young-Sam (1993–1998) who crushed labor during the mid-1990s, though his political rise was facilitated by his activist bona fides. Programmatic consistency and partisan predictability among parties and party leaders are weakly institutionalized in democratic Korea. Social, economic, or political cleavages, articulated in terms of ideology, party identity, and programmatic platforms to appeal to voters, have meant little in Korea's democratic politics.

REFERENCES

Amsden, Alice. 1989. *Asia's Next Giant: South Korea and Late Industrialization.* New York and Oxford: Oxford University Press.
Chao, Linda, and Ramon Myers. 1998. *The First Chinese Democracy: Political Life in the Republic of China on Taiwan.* Baltimore: The Johns Hopkins University Press.
Cheng, Tun-Jen. 2003. Political Institutions and the Malaise of East Asian New Democracies. *Journal of East Asian Studies* 3: 1–41.
Clifford, Mark. 1998. *Troubled Tiger: Businessmen, Bureaucrats and Generals in South Korea.* Armonk, NY: M.E. Sharpe.
Choi, Jang-Jip. 1993. Political Cleavages in South Korea. In Hagen Koo (Ed.), *State and Society in Contemporary Korea.* Ithaca: Cornell University Press.
Dickson, Bruce. 1996. The KMT before Democratization: Organizational Change and the Role of Elections. In Hung-Mao Tien (Ed.), *Taiwan's Electoral Politics and Democratic Transition: Riding the Third Wave.* Armonk, NY: M.E. Sharpe.
Dix, Robert. 1992. Democratization and the Institutionalization of Latin American Political Parties. *Comparative Political Studies* 24(4): 488–511.

---

[43] Peng and Wong 2008.

Haggard, Stephan, and Robert Kaufman. 1995. *The Political Economy of Democratic Transitions*. Princeton: Princeton University Press.

Hirschman, Albert. 1970. *Exit, Voice, and Loyalty: Responses to Decline in Firms, Organizations and States*. Cambridge, MA: Harvard University Press.

Im, Baeg-Im. 2011. The Origins of the Yushin Regime: Machiavelli Unveiled. In Byung-Kook Kim and Ezra Vogel (Eds.), *The Park Chung Hee Era: The Transformation of South Korea*. Cambridge, MA: Harvard University Press.

Kim, Byung-Kook. 2008. Defeat in Victory, Victory in Defeat. In Edward Friedman and Joseph Wong (Eds.), *Political Transitions in Dominant Party Systems: Learning to Lose*. London: Routledge.

Kim, Sunhyuk. 1997. State and Civil Society in South Korea's Democratic Consolidation: Is the Battle Really Over? *Asian Survey* 37(12): 1135–1144.

Koo, Hagen (Ed.). 1993. *State and Society in Contemporary Korea*. Ithaca: Cornell University Press.

Lee, Nam Hee. 2007. *The Making of Minjung: Democracy and the Politics of Representation in South Korea*. Ithaca: Cornell University Press.

Lee, Yoonkyung. 2006. Varieties of Labor Politics in Northeast Asian Democracies: Political Institutions and Activism in Korea and Taiwan. *Asian Survey* 46(5): 721–740.

Mo, Jongryn. 1996. Political Learning and Democratic Consolidation: Korean Industrial Relations, 1987–1992. *Comparative Political Studies* 29(3): 290–311.

Moon, Chung-In. 2009. South Korea in 2008: From Crisis to Crisis. *Asian Survey* 49(1): 120–128.

Moon, Chung-in and Byung-joon Jun. 2011. "Modernization Strategy: Ideas and Influences." In Byung-kook Kim and Ezra Vogel (Eds.), *The Park Chung Hee Era: The Transformation of South Korea*. Cambridge MA: Harvard University Press.

Park, Chong-Min, and Doh Chull Shin. 2006. Do Asian Values Deter Popular Support for Democracy in South Korea? *Asian Survey* 46(3): 341–361.

Peng, Ito, and Joseph Wong. 2008. Institutions and Institutional Purpose: Continuity and Change in East Asian Social Policy. *Politics and Society* 36(1): 61–88.

Rigger, Shelley. 1999. *Politics in Taiwan: Voting for Democracy*. London: Routledge.

Seong, Kyuong-Ryung. 2000. Civil Society and Democratic Consolidation in South Korea: Great Achievement and Remaining Problems. In Larry Diamond and Byung-Kook Kim (Eds.), *Consolidating Democracy in South Korea*. Boulder, CO: Lynne Rienner.

Shin, Doh Chull. 1999. *Mass Politics and Culture in Democratizing Korea*. New York: Cambridge University Press.

Shin, Eui Hang. 2003. The Role of NGOs in Political Elections in South Korea. *Asian Survey* 43(4): 697–715.

Slater, Dan, and Joseph Wong. 2012. The Strength to Concede: Ruling Parties and Democratization in Developmental Asia. Paper presented at the Annual Meeting of the Midwest Political Science Association, April, Chicago.

Steinberg, David. 1998. Korea: Triumph and Turmoil. *Journal of Democracy* 9(2): 76–90.

Steinberg, David, and Myung Shin. 2006. Tensions in South Korean Political Parties: From Entourage to Ideology? *Asian Survey* 46(4): 517–537.

Stockton, Hans. 2001. Political Parties, Party Systems and Democracy in East Asia: Lessons from Latin America. *Comparative Political Studies* 34(1): 94–119.

Tan, Alexander, Karl Ho, Kyung-Tae Kang, and Tsung-Chi Yu. 2000. What If We Don't Party? Political Partisanship in Taiwan and Korea in the 1990s. *Journal of Asian and African Studies* 35(1): 67–84.

Toka, Gabor. 1997. Political Parties in East Central Europe. In Larry Diamond et al. (Eds.), *Consolidating the Third Wave Democracies: Themes and Perspectives.* Baltimore: The Johns Hopkins University Press.

Wong, Joseph. 2004a. Democratization and the Left: Comparing East Asia and Latin America. *Comparative Political Studies* 37(10): 1213–1237.

Wong, Joseph. 2004b. *Healthy Democracies: Welfare Politics in Taiwan and South Korea.* Ithaca: Cornell University Press.

Wong, Joseph. 2012. Transitioning from a Dominant Party System to a Multi-Party System: The Case of South Korea. In Nicola De Jager and Pierre Du Toit (Eds.), *Friend or Foe? Dominant Party Systems in South Africa: Insights from the Developing World.* Tokyo: UN University Press.

Thailand's Feckless Parties and Party System: A Path-Dependent Analysis

Erik Martinez Kuhonta

INTRODUCTION

> Where the instrumentalities of popular control are, if not absent, at least weak or embryonic, as they are in Thailand, national politics becomes more simply a struggle for power as an end in itself among competing cliques and factions.   –Fred Riggs[1]

It will be useful to begin looking at the Thai party system by referring to a classic work on Thai politics – that of Fred Riggs. If we think of the "instrumentalities of popular control" as political parties, one is struck by the validity of Riggs's observation that politics is largely "a struggle for power as an end in itself among competing cliques and factions." Since the birth of its parties in 1932, Thailand's party system has been devoid of real programmatic differences. Instead, the system has largely been consumed by elites running empty political shells in the pursuit of spoils for their factions. Only in recent years has the party system begun to exhibit programmatic differences among its main contenders. Overall, however, the historical tendency of Thailand's party system has been one of institutional fecklessness and ideological vacuousness.

Thailand's party system is notorious for its low level of institutionalization. Underscoring this assessment, James Ockey writes: "There is widespread agreement that parties are too weak while their factions are too strong ... The importance of this consensus in the literature cannot be overstated."[2] Using three of the components of Mainwaring and Scully's definition of party system institutionalization – stability in the rules and nature of interparty competition, stable roots in society, and organizational autonomy and strength – it is clear that on all these attributes the Thai party system scores

---

[1] Riggs 1966: 212.
[2] Ockey 2003: 665.

low.[3] The party system is extremely fluid in terms of interparty competition. Most political parties can be defined in negative terms: they lack organizational depth; ideological goals; committed followers; and, above all, institutional value that supersedes the individual leader's grip over the party. Parties are especially vulnerable to the power of factions (*phuak*)[4] that have little interest in the party qua party, but rather look at parties simply as convenient shells through which to gain access to spoils. As a consequence, parties in Thailand tend to come and go from one election to the next. The main exception to this rule is the Democrat Party (Phak Prachathipat), the oldest party in Thailand that has developed significant institutional value as a party, established organizational procedures for internal party elections and decision making, and maintained a loyal social base.

What explains the weak institutionalization of the Thai party system? Some have argued that an uneven pattern of economic development has created the conditions for a weak party system.[5] In this explanation, the rift between the urban and rural sectors is particularly important. A largely uneducated, rural sector votes consistently for clientelist parties, giving little thought to whether these parties actually advance programmatic policies, whereas the heavily outnumbered urban, middle class favors programmatic parties. More generally, the shifting power of class structures, such as the rise of provincial businessmen or metropolitan business elites heavily influences the direction of the party system.[6] A second explanation is that factions tend to be the lifeline of parties, thereby weakening any possibility for a broader structure to set the political agenda. Patron-client relations based on kinship, friendship, or financial ties form the basis for these factions.[7] A third explanation is that a cycle of military coups has hindered parties' abilities to develop organizational capacities.[8] Since 1932, Thailand has experienced 19 attempted or successful coups that have interrupted periods of democratic rule and prospects for party development. Finally, a fourth explanation is that electoral rules shape institutional outcomes. In particular, rules that create incentives for the proliferation of parties or that reduce the need for cohesiveness are detrimental to party system institutionalization.[9]

---

[3] I do not include a fourth component from Mainwaring and Scully: legitimacy accorded to the electoral process. This component, in the way that it is formulated, relates more to a democratic party system, rather than to the concept of institutionalization. Note, also, that the component of "party organization" subsumes the party institutionalization attributes defined by Huntington. See Mainwaring and Scully 1995: 4–5.

[4] *Phuak* literally means "group." This can be interpreted as faction, or political grouping. For a detailed analysis, see Nelson 2005.

[5] See, e.g., Anusorn 1998: 443–444.

[6] Siripan 2006.

[7] Ockey 1994; Chambers 2005.

[8] Kramol 1982; Somsakdi 1987; Chai-Anan 1990; Suchit 1996.

[9] Chambers 2005; Hicken 2006. These articles generated a stimulating debate in the *Journal of East Asian Studies*. See Nelson 2007 and the responses by Hicken and Chambers in the same issue. See also Kuhonta 2008.

These arguments are all important and valid. However, while not denying the validity of explanations based on economic development, factions, military coups, and electoral rules, I argue that the core issue underlying Thailand's weak party system institutionalization has to do with the failure of social cleavages to become articulated in the party system. Without social cleavages, the party system has no real basis for institutional differentiation and organization. I claim that the failure of social cleavages to become entrenched in the party system has deep historical origins. Specifically, one must examine two historical periods – the 1932 revolution and its aftermath and the 1946 postwar period – in which opportunities for a programmatic and institutionalized party system were present but never fulfilled. These two periods should be seen as critical junctures: periods in history that shaped the long-term institutional trajectory of a nation.

Thus, what this chapter seeks to do is provide an argument for Thailand's weak party system that is ontologically distinct from prevailing explanations. That is to say, the argument advanced here will be a historicist one rather than one based on constant causes.[10] The central analytical idea of this chapter is that initial, institutional patterns get reinforced through time and can have a long-term impact on current configurations.[11] Thus, the early failure of cleavages to get articulated into the party system and for the system to gain some institutional structure has increased the odds that Thailand's party system would remain institutionally feckless in the contemporary period. It will be clear from the narrative of the two critical junctures and of the overall chapter that the role of military coups and of rivaling factions has played an important role in the structuring of the party system. Yet, what I want to emphasize is that the Thai party system demonstrates significant reproduction of early historical patterns.

In 1932, a military-civilian clique called the People's Party (Khana Ratsadorn) launched a coup d'état that established a constitutional regime. The People's Party was the first political party to emerge in Thailand but functioned primarily as a vehicle for uniting enemies of the monarchy. It acted in an authoritarian, top-down, elitist manner and failed to create a social base. Yet, in calling itself a political party and in advancing the idea of political representation, the People's Party did set a new basis for political engagement in Thailand. Its failure to move beyond a clique-like structure meant, however, that the party did not make any progress in terms of institutionalization. Most crucially, the fact that the party did not seek to completely oust the ancient regime, but simply to push it in a more legal, rational direction, reduced its need to mobilize social forces against its opponent. Had the party mobilized social forces against the monarchy, it would have created linkages with society and built up a strong, organizational structure.

In 1946, political parties competed in elections for the first time. A number of parties emerged representing distinct ideologies. These included leftist, regional,

---

[10] Stinchcombe 1968.
[11] Ibid.; Pierson 2004.

royalist, and military parties. During this period, there was significant ideological debate among parties and groups in society. In particular, a vibrant left was active in parliament and in civil society with the Communist Party of Thailand (CPT) also represented in the lower house. But while the parties did have competing agendas, they did not have much institutional depth. Most parties still remained largely elite based, with quite shallow roots in society. Thus, when the party system encountered a sharp challenge from reactionary, nondemocratic forces, it was unable to mobilize any real resistance. Most crucial at this stage of party development was that social cleavages were beginning to shape the party system, albeit in a very rudimentary manner, but because democracy was aborted, in the long run, the party system did not become based on social cleavages.

These two critical junctures – the 1932 revolution and the immediate postwar period – were important moments for party development. Both periods presented an opportunity for political parties to become central actors in the polity; in the first case, through a dominant party, in the second case, through a cleavage-based party system. But on each occasion, parties did not develop deeper organizational structures and social roots and consolidate their initial positions. In the first juncture, this was because the People's Party did not move beyond its initial basis as a revolutionary clique. In the second juncture, political parties did articulate interests but still did not have enough time to move beyond elitist structures. The failure of parties to consolidate their social interests into a more long-lasting party system then made it difficult for the party system to become institutionalized when democratic governments began to gain some traction, first in the turbulent mid-1970s, then in the cautious 1980s, and then in the more substantively democratic period of the 1990s.

The concluding section of this chapter discusses the most recent development in terms of party system institutionalization: the conflict between the lower classes, mobilized by Thaksin Shinawatra, and the Bangkok elite. Since the rise of Thaksin's Thai Rak Thai Party (TRT), the party system has experienced some institutional change driven in part by Thaksin's desire to create a powerful organization, as well as by the 1997 Constitution that sought to strengthen parties. The rise of TRT and the dominance of Thaksin led to significant social polarization, evidenced by the September 2006 coup, the violence of April–May 2010, and the May 2014 coup. This has, in turn, reinforced the potential for party system institutionalization precisely because social cleavages are now becoming manifest in the party system. But at this stage, it is still too early to tell how far the Thai party system will move from its historical mooring in personalism, factionalism, and feckless organizations.

THE STATE OF THE PARTY SYSTEM

Numerical data provide an aggregate picture of the dismal state of the Thai party system. High volatility and high effective number of parties indicate that the party system lacks institutional stability. The vote share of parties between elections

TABLE 12.1. *Effective Number of Parliamentary Parties (1979–2011)*

1979	6.07
1983	5.42
1986	6.14
1988	7.71
1992 March	6.01
1992 September	6.12
1995	6.43
1996	4.32
2001	3.04
2005	1.65
2007	2.76
2011	2.57

Source: Author's calculations.

registers sharp shifts, while new parties continuously enter and exit the system. The average volatility of the Thai party system (for 1992–2011) at 38.1 is one of the highest in Asia, and in the higher range in the developing world. If one treats all of Thaksin's parties (TRT, People Power Party [PPP], and Phua Thai [PT]) as one party, the volatility score is 34.2 – still very high.[12] The effective number of parliamentary parties is also one of the highest in Asia. From 1979 to 2011, the average effective number of parliamentary parties was 4.85. However, as will be discussed in the conclusion, the period post-2001 does show some difference. From 1979 to 1996, the effective number of parliamentary parties was 6.03, but from 2001 to 2011, the number dropped to 2.51 (see Table 12.1).[13]

If we look at more qualitative indicators, we find further evidence of the weak institutional character of the party system. Parties have generally lacked discipline and cohesion. They have been based largely on factions, rather than as parties qua parties. Most parties have been built from the top down, have been devoid of a mass base, and have been driven by personalities rather than by ideology or programmatic policies. Most of the personalities leading parties have come from a business background, whether from Bangkok or the provinces. This has led to parties being primarily concerned with spoils that can be generated through the acquisition of cabinet portfolios and the advancement of capitalist projects. Four problems in particular should thus be highlighted: the dominance of factions, the absence of ideology, feeble roots in society, and shallow organizational structures.

One of the central problems in the party system has to do with the power of factions. Instead of parties aggregating social interests, they tend to emerge based on the aggregation of factions, whose cohering bond is based on personal

---

[12] See the Introduction to this volume (Chapter 1).

[13] Note that "independents" in the 1979 and 1983 elections are classified as one party, which artificially lowers the effective number of parties. The effective number of parliamentary *factions* was calculated at 21.17 for the period 1979 to 2005 (Chambers 2005).

ties, whether family or friends, and financial or political benefits (such as a shared vote canvasser, or *hua khanaen*). The party system, in effect, has long been made up more of factional units rather than parties. "It is worth noting that the Thai people are closely tied to their primary organization, i.e., family, kin-group, classmate and clique," wrote a Thai political scientist in the 1960s, "Without resort to big organization or party machinery, the power holders of Thai politics concentrate their efforts on holding power through small groups, composed of members who know each other very well for years."[14]

The rise and fall of the government party has often more to do with a powerful faction, rather than the strength of party identity and organization.[15] From 1979 to 2001, factional conflict led to the downfall of six governments (see Table 12.2).[16] One study has calculated the statistical effect of factions on the durability of government, specifically of parliaments, coalitions, and cabinets.[17] It finds that factions tend to diminish the longevity of parliaments

TABLE 12.2. *Effect of Factional Infighting on Change in Government Party (1976–2001)*

Political Party	Number of Seats in Back-to-Back Election	Change in Seats between Elections
Democrat	1976: 114[a]	−82
	1979: 32	
Social Action	1983: 92	−41
	1986: 51	
Democrat	1986: 100	−52
	1988: 48	
Chart Thai	1988: 87 (96)[b]	−22
	1992 (March): 74	
Chart Thai	1995: 92	−54
	1996: 38	
New Aspiration	1996: 125	−89
	2001: 36	

[a] Although factional infighting weakened the Democrat Party, the government was ousted by a coup.
[b] Following the 1988 polls, Chart Thai increased from 87 to 96 seats. I have calculated the difference based on the increased number of MPs.
Source: Author's calculations based on Siripan (2006: 63); *Southeast Asian Affairs 1997*.

[14] Amara 1965. Cited in Darling 1971: 232.
[15] Some analysts have noted that the size of factions can affect their viability. Beyond a certain number, factions may no longer be able to share spoils, particularly the cabinet seats, among their key members. For Ockey, that threshold is 100; for Chambers, it lies around 80 to 90. Korn Dabbaransi, former leader of Chart Pattana Party, admitted that: "Once you have more than 80 MPs in your party, your party is sure to be destroyed because over time you cannot reward over 80 people." See Chambers (2005: 502). See also Ockey 1994: 262 (n. 27).
[16] Chambers 2005: 501.
[17] Chambers 2008.

and cabinets but extend the life of coalitions.[18] Furthermore, factions tend to have a more significant effect than parties on the longevity of government.

The reason factions are deeply problematic for the institutionalization of the party system is because they are primarily interested in using public office for personal gain. The goal of factions is not to advance a particular policy agenda, but simply to gain a cabinet seat as a means for patronage that will then benefit faction members. The strategy of virtually every faction in the party system is to seek a means of joining the governing coalition in order to maneuver for a cabinet post. Holding a cabinet portfolio provides a spigot for resources that can then be used to pay off debts from elections and to fund future elections.[19]

The most notable case of factional power and its effect on the life and death of government is that of Sanoh Tientong's Wang Nam Yen (Cold Water Basin) faction. In the 1990s, the Wang Nam Yen faction played virtual kingmaker in the Thai party system. In the 1995 election, Sanoh's faction propelled Banharn Silpa-archa's Chart Thai Party to victory. A dispute with Banharn led Sanoh's Wang Nam Yen to decamp and join the up-and-coming New Aspiration Party (NAP) of General Chavalit Yongchaiyudh, which then won the 1996 polls by a margin of two seats against the Democrat Party. Subsequently, the TRT jugger-naut absorbed many powerful factions, including Wang Nam Yen.[20] In the 2001 election, it had pulled in 117 incumbent MPs.[21] With most of the critical factions in its camp, TRT almost secured a majority of parliamentary seats and through more maneuvers easily established a grand coalition.

As factions are based largely on personalities, rather than ideology, program-matic goals are virtually absent. Factions can, of course, be centered on ideolo-gies or programmatic agendas, but in the Thai party system, this is generally not the case.[22] Therefore, factions arise largely to advance the interests of a partic-ular leader and his following. Only in the late 1940s and the mid-1970s did political parties uphold sharp ideological differences. The collapse of the party system in the late 1940s and the violent reaction to ideological unrest in the mid-1970s led in the long run to the complete marginalization of ideology. During these two periods, the Cooperative (Sahachip) Party in the 1940s and the United Socialist Front, the Socialist Party, and the New Force (Palang Mai) in the 1970s all espoused leftist ideals. But all of these parties were crushed by military force.

---

[18] Each additional faction in the cabinet diminishes parliamentary longevity by 99 days and cabinet durability by 14 days, whereas each additional faction in a coalition will lead to a coalition lasting 64 more days. This counterintuitive finding – that more factions increase coalitional longevity – is explained by the fact that factions that have not been granted cabinet portfolios are willing to hang on until they are granted a ministership. See Chambers 2008: 312–313.

[19] A useful case study of factional warfare over cabinet seats can be found in Ockey 1994: 268–272.

[20] For a good summary of the Wang Nam Yen's traveling exploits, see Chambers 2005: 508–514.

[21] Siripan 2012: 148.

[22] A few exceptions include a loosely based network of "Octobrists" – leaders from the October 14, 1973, revolution that overthrew the military regime. See Ockey 1994: 256.

The Democrat Party, the most institutionalized and longest-standing party in Thailand, has maintained a free market, centrist, and royalist leaning. It has also generally been perceived to be a supporter of liberal democracy, but its record in this regard is quite uneven.[23] The Democrat Party was initially not a stalwart of democracy, having supported the royalists and military forces in ousting Pridi Banomyong's government in 1947. But by the mid-1950s, the party had increasingly become a defender of liberal democracy through its jostling with the military.[24] During the turbulent period of the mid-1970s, a faction within the Democrat Party, led by two southerners, Chuan Leekpai and Surin Masdit, supported democratic, reformist programs that were at the heart of student protests, and in the 1990s, the party also rejected military coups.[25] Yet, the Democrat Party has often shown less interest in maintaining a principled ideological stance than in a pragmatic position that serves the party's self-interest. With the exception of the 1986 crisis in the party, the Democrats were willing to support a non-elected general, Prem Tinsulanonda, as prime minister. In December 2008, the Democrats made a deal, brokered by the commander in chief of the army, to take in a number of MPs who had gotten loose of Thaksin's vise. This deal allowed the party to gain the prime ministership, but it has been criticized as a rather shady, and indeed undemocratic, move because it so blatantly went against the choice of the electorate. In 2006 and 2014, the members of the Democrat Party boycotted elections they knew they would lose, thereby showing a clear lack of commitment to democratic principles when they do not suit their interest.

The fact that ideology and programmatic goals are absent from the party system has also meant that parties have not sought to cultivate a mass base. Split constituency returns provide strong evidence that parties lack a social base, because this means that voters do not have an allegiance to a particular party.[26] From 1986 to 1996, more than 50 percent of constituencies had split returns.[27] With the exception of the Democrat Party and TRT, the membership base of parties is extremely shallow.[28] TRT's membership skyrocketed within a

---

[23] Sungsidh 1996; Askew 2008: 44.

[24] Darling notes that the Democrat Party's opposition to military rule has a class basis, with the members of the Democrat Party hailing from the ruling class, and those from the military coming from the lower middle class and the peasantry. See Darling 1971: 236.

[25] However, regarding Chuan Leekpai's behavior during the 1992 crisis, see McCargo 1997b.

[26] A split return means that in a constituency (or district) with more than one MP, and with voters allowed more than one vote, the voter chooses at least two different parties.

[27] Hicken 2009: 97. The low percentage of split returns in the south is further evidence that the Democrat Party has a solid following, whereas other parties do not.

[28] At the end of 2004, the membership base of the Democrat Party was 4,018,286, whereas that of the TRT was 14,077,711. Surprisingly, Chart Thai's membership base was ahead of the Democrat Party, at 4,041,232. It increased its base by 2.3 million members in the span of three years. See Siripan 2006: 139. However, as Siripan 2012: 156 notes, after the Election Commission of Thailand asked for verification of membership numbers, membership declined to 2.7 million for the Democrat Party and slightly more than 1 million for Chart Thai.

few years, but analysts noted that members did not engage in any credible party activity.[29] In general, the incentive for membership development lies less in genuine efforts to establish deep organizational structures, but more in terms of complying with laws on political parties as well as with receiving public subsidies. The shallow nature of membership development is especially apparent from the disjuncture between a party's membership numbers and its actual votes. In the 2001 election, Chart Pattana, New Aspiration, and Chart Thai all received significantly fewer votes than their membership numbers.[30] Parties have even been known to seek out members simply by sending application forms to factories that workers would then sign and return in exchange for some material reward.[31] Even more problematic is that parties have not linked up with any social groups, such as labor unions, women's groups, or ethnic communities. Indeed, the Political Party Act prevents this linkage from happening by prohibiting registered organizations including labor unions and trade and professional associations from supporting parties or campaigning.[32]

Only two parties can be said to have established a solid social base. The Democrat Party is the unequivocal choice in the south and has strong backing among the Bangkok middle class, although the latter tends to be much more ephemeral than the support in the south.[33] One survey in 2008 shows that the Democrat Party's supporters are generally better educated than those of other parties and hail from government and state enterprise sectors.[34] The other party that has a social base is TRT, and its successor parties, the People Power Party and Phua Thai (PT [For Thais]). Emulating the strategy of the Social Action Party (SAP) in the mid-1970s,[35] TRT was able to gain the loyalty of rural villagers in the north and northeast primarily through its populist programs. TRT's supporters are generally less educated than those of the Democrat Party and tend to come from low-income occupations; they are workers, farmers, and small business owners.[36] However, the depth of the linkage between party and individual has occurred less through organizational penetration and active involvement of social groups than through the charisma of its leader and the popularity of the party's social reforms.

---

[29] Nelson 2002: 290–291.

[30] The opposite was the case for the Democrat and TRT parties. Chart Thai did not do as badly as NAP and Chart Pattana in terms of the ratio of votes to membership. Chart Thai received 86 percent of votes vis-à-vis membership numbers, NAP received 56 percent, and Chart Pattana received only 49 percent. Calculated from Siripan 2006: 73; see also Siripan 2012: 156.

[31] Kramol 1982: 33.

[32] Siripan 2012: 156.

[33] See Askew 2008.

[34] Siripan 2012: 155.

[35] Under the guidance of former banker Boonchu Rojanasthien, the SAP developed an innovative program, known as the *tambon* fund (subdistrict fund, or *ngen phan*) that would spur incomes in villages. Many of these programs were largely infrastructure related, such as building of bridges, wells, and dams, rather than skills enhancing or institution building.

[36] Siripan 2012: 155. The survey referred to PPP, but the PPP is a reincarnation of the TRT.

The shallowness of party roots in society is a function of the superficial nature of party organizations. Thai parties face a common dilemma shared among party builders in the developing world: how to build a party while still maintaining its organizational and ideological cohesiveness.[37] The attempt to create a deeper and more complex party with divisions and branches throughout a country is an extremely arduous endeavor because it requires a high level of organizational capacity to muster committed and disciplined members who will recruit new members and establish a basis for bonding party to social forces. As a consequence, Thai parties have often taken the easier route for party building: attracting factions and prominent leaders through material incentives.

Some parties, especially the Democrat Party, have made serious efforts to build a deeper organizational structure. In the mid-1970s, the party was riven between a conservative and a more progressive group. To counterbalance the conservative faction's ties to the military, the progressive group began building branches throughout the country to establish a powerful social base. From 1975 to 1976, the party established 66 branches in the central, northern, and northeastern regions.[38] This effort, led by Damrong Latthaphipart, was eventually overtaken by the 1976 coup and student massacre at Thammasat University, which led to the end of the brief three-year parliamentary period. Recurrent coups – 19 by 2014 – have been a significant factor in hindering organizational development. They prevent basic capacities of parties and legislatures to mature, such as the strengthening of parliamentary research units and the abilities of committee staff. In the 1980s, the Democrat Party sought a combination of both party expansion through organizational complexity and the absorption of politicians who already had a strong electoral base. The party was, therefore, able to deepen its base in Bangkok and the south, and it made efforts to bring in Islamic groups, students, intellectuals, traders, and former military personnel.[39] At the same time, however, it also elevated shady figures, such as Secretary-General Sanan Khachonprasart, who weakened its image as a clean, policy-oriented party.

The NAP, led by the former army commander in chief Chavalit Yongchaiyudh also made efforts in the 1990s to develop a complex organizational structure. The party moved quickly to establish branches throughout the country, particularly in the northeast. As Duncan McCargo notes,

During the early months at the NAP, more than 30 serving army officers worked full-time on establishing the party … Long before the NAP had a single MP, 80 full-time staff were working at the party's extensive Bangkok headquarters. The party produced large

---

[37] See Kohli 1987 for an example of how an institutionalized party, the Communist-Party Marxist in West Bengal (India), was able to expand its structure without diluting its ideology and social base.

[38] Chai-Anan (Undated), cited in Kramol 1982: 26–27.

[39] Noranit 1987, cited in McCargo 1997a: 123.

quantities of glossy literature, including a monthly newspaper replete with photographs of the leader.[40]

Yet, the NAP eventually relied more on absorbing factions from other parties in order to become a dominant force in the system. Its success at the polls in 1996 came largely through the recruitment of factions from Chart Thai, including the ever-mobile Wang Nam Yen faction. But this success was ephemeral, and its gain of 68 seats in the 1996 election eventually became a loss of 89 seats by the 2001 election, when TRT ransacked many of its MPs. The party was then merged into TRT in 2002.

These four key issues – the dominance of factions over parties, the dearth of ideology, feeble party roots in society, and low organizational complexity – all have historical origins. In the two critical junctures in which parties played an early role in Thai politics, they were riddled with these weaknesses. All of these deficiencies make it more difficult for social cleavages to become institutionalized in the party system. However, parties in 1932 and 1946 were not completely devoid of institutional and ideological strengths. The People's Party, particularly through the efforts of Pridi, did have some ideological goals and undertook some initial attempts at institution building. But in the end, the lack of cohesion within the party derailed any movement toward a stronger organization. In 1946, ideology was a fundamental ground of contention among the parties. Parties, however, did not have strong links with social groups and were not organizationally deep. Therefore, they were vulnerable to a military counter-reaction that received external support as the Cold War heated up in Asia.

It is important to underline that although parties did not develop the necessary attributes to become more effective actors in the polity, the political environment was also not in their favor. Two structural factors worked against party building during these critical junctures. In 1932, the absence of a colonial power to be overthrown diluted the imperatives for social mobilization and organizational deepening that aided other modernizing parties. Without an opponent to challenge, it becomes especially difficult to mobilize social forces for political action. In the late 1940s, the shifting geopolitical terrain, specifically the emerging Cold War, gave the military an edge against civilian parties, enabling it to consolidate its grip on power and crush radical and regionalist forces. The next two sections look at the problems of party building during these key nodes in modern Thai history.

THE 1932 REVOLUTION

On February 5, 1927, the People's Party (Khana Ratsadorn) was founded in Paris by a group of elite bureaucrats who were increasingly frustrated with the

---

[40] McCargo 1997a: 128. Quite notable in the NAP's ten-point statement was the comment that the party "was not based on the personality of any particular individual."

lack of mobility within the Thai state. Educated in Western cities, these military and civilian bureaucrats came together to plot a revolution that would break down the monarchy's grip on the state and establish a more rational-legal principle of governance (*lak wicha*). The party was made up of a number of factions: senior officials largely trained in Germany and younger officials mainly educated in France. This latter group was, in turn, divided among military and civilian factions. The younger civilian group possessed a more reformist inclination compared to the older bureaucrats and the military officers. But what united all party members was antagonism toward the monarchy.

On June 24, 1932, the People's Party executed a successful putsch. However, in the aftermath of the coup, the party found itself adrift, unsure of how deep it wanted its revolution to proceed. The central problem that continued to haunt the People's Party was that it did not begin as a social movement but as an elitist clique made up of various factions.[41] The consequences of this were manifold. First, lacking any social backing or institutional armature, the party ended up needing King Prajadhipok (Rama VII) to shore up its legitimacy out of fear of external intervention or internal uprising. Therefore, the party ironically allowed the king to hold on to a number of prerogatives, which weakened the party's capacity to pursue sweeping structural reform. Ultimately, Prajadhipok even managed to issue a decree banning all political parties. This was significant not just because it undermined the People's Party, but because it also brought to an end another incipient party, the Khana Chart (Nationalist Party), that had emerged to challenge the People's Party from a somewhat more right-wing position. The banning of parties prevented social cleavages from emerging in the party system. Second, the People's Party lacked ideological commitment. Its central protagonist and intellectual, Pridi Banomyong, possessed a strong leftist vision and he sought to inculcate this vision into the party, but many other principals, especially older elites, were anathema to any socialist pursuit. As a result, the party eventually dropped its socialist agenda. Third, the party was unable to deepen its organizational structure in part because it could not rouse and mobilize the masses to see much value in a revolutionary party. The party remained a vehicle of bureaucratic elites and failed to deepen its roots in society.

Organizationally, the People's Party had begun its coup with sophisticated plans for party building. On the day of the coup, the party started recruiting supporters to use as spies against its opponents. By early July, the party was accepting military personnel and organizing a branch in Bangkok. In August, it established the People's Party Association (Samakhom Khana Ratsadorn), whose goal was to broaden the party's social base. The association then created provincial branches in all provinces as a means of bringing state officials, including local government officials, provincial governors, provincial court chief justices, and provincial military and police leaders, into the fold of the

---

[41] This argument is drawn from, and expanded in, Kuhonta 2011: 134–143.

party.[42] In six weeks, the association had grown to 10,000 members and by 1933 had increased to 100,000 throughout the country.[43]

Though in some ways quite vague, the ideology of the People's Party advanced some substantive principles: the importance of people's representation albeit not necessarily in a fully liberal democratic form, as well as a socialist credo.[44] The party's six main principles included freedom and equality in politics, law, and business; internal peace and order; economic planning to provide economic well-being and work for all; equality of privileges; liberty and freedom; and education for all. The concern for work for all, equality of privileges, and education for all was the idea of Pridi, who had a clear sense of the kind of social revolution the party should achieve. Educated in law at the Sorbonne, Pridi was influenced by world historical currents in the late 1920s, particularly the Chinese and Russian revolutions that had successfully overthrown decadent monarchies.[45]

The party's socialist agenda was best articulated in Pridi's Economic Plan, known as the Samud Pokleuang (yellow-covered book). The plan sought to transform the Thai political economy into a socialist economy based on cooperatives, with land, labor, and capital under the direction of the state. Other elements of the plan included an estate duty tax to be levied on the royalist class and a social insurance scheme to protect invalids, the disabled, and pregnant women.[46] The left wing of the People's Party published two newspapers to propagate its agenda: 24 *Mithuna* and *Sajjang*.[47] Sanguan Tularaks, founder of 24 *Mithuna*, also translated and published a pamphlet by J. W. Kneeshaw entitled *Latthi Sochialism Mai Khwam Wa Arai* ("What is the meaning of socialism?"). Ten thousand copies of the pamphlet were distributed to raise awareness of socialism ahead of elections.[48]

However, efforts by Pridi and his younger civilian colleagues to push for a socialist agenda were constrained by the fact that many members of the party did not share this vision. Pridi clearly aspired to build some form of a mass-based, socialist party, but few of his fellow revolutionaries shared the same leftist enthusiasm. Many were conservatives who were concerned less with social revolution than with legal-rational reform of the existing system. Pridi's Economic Plan was debated fiercely but ultimately lacked organizational support to see it through. Its radicalism was deeply opposed by the king and other conservative figures who had been given key cabinet positions. But the crucial

---

[42] Murashima, Nakharin, and Somkiat 1991: 11–12.

[43] *Bangkok Times Weekly Mail*, August 22, 1932, cited in Copeland 1993: 7.

[44] The ideal of representing people, although ideologically rather vague, was, in fact, revolutionary "because the conception of man as an autonomous individual was something that no one in Thailand could have previously envisioned." Yano 1978: 134.

[45] Pridi 1978: 52. See also Pridi 1974; Baker and Pasuk 2000.

[46] See Pridi 2000. For further details and analysis of the plan, see Kuhonta 2011: 136–140.

[47] Kasian 2001: 35. "24 *Mithuna*" means June 24, the date of the revolution.

[48] Kasian 2001.

problem was again a lack of party organization and mass base. Without institutional armature and a mass movement to provide support, the Economic Plan had no basis for implementation. As one scholar put it: "What machinery could have been devised to carry out these schemes?"[49]

Born as an elitist organization, the People's Party remained deeply divided among different cliques and factions, which were all angling for power in a fluid political landscape. Constant rivalries among the senior members, the civilian junior members, and the military junior members and efforts by conservative forces from outside the party to sharpen these divisions prevented the party from operating as a collective body.[50] Thus, the dilemma of factional infighting that plagues the contemporary Thai party system was evident early on. In the absence of a clear ideological purpose, other than that of challenging the monarchy, the People's Party could not develop its organizational structure. Pridi's model for party building was China's revolutionary Kuomintang Party (KMT), but in fact the People's Party was nowhere close to resembling the institutional apparatus of the KMT.[51]

A central dilemma for Pridi was that the initial impetus for putting together the party – the desire to oust the monarchy – was not shared universally by the populace nor was it a goal that some of his conservative colleagues were interested in seeing completed to its full extent. When the king acceded to some of the party's agenda, the stimulus for change lost momentum, with the party not ready to create a republican system. Given the party elites' ambivalence of how far to take the revolution, the largely rural countryside responded with minimal excitement to the party. Despite early efforts at social penetration and mobilization through the People's Association, the People's Party could not mobilize social groups to pursue its agenda. The lack of mobilization meant that it had no basis for organizational development. Absent a major opponent with which to struggle, the People's Party could not gain any institutional and popular momentum. As the *Bangkok Times* reported:

The leaders of the People's Party have been able to study the reaction of the people as a whole to their movement. They have been helped by several itinerant commissions sent out from Bangkok to preach the revolution even in remote villages. These emissaries have probably been themselves taught and slightly saddened in the process. It is not easy to teach those whose energies are spent in the mud of the rice fields and in the thickness of the jungle that liberty and equality are things to which it is worthwhile to sweep kings from their thrones.[52]

If we place the People's Party in comparative perspective, it is notable that it faced a different structural environment compared to other modernizing parties. For parties that became dominant institutionalized forces, such as the Congress

---

[49] Coast 1953: 6.
[50] Details of every single factional tussle from 1932 to 1958 is provided in Riggs 1966: ch. 8.
[51] Thawatt 1962.
[52] "Democracy in Siam," *Bangkok Times*, February 6, 1933.

Party in India, the Vietnamese Communist Party, or the United Malays National Organization in Malaysia, colonialism was an important oppositional force that had the effect of strengthening them by reinforcing their ideological position and compelling them to develop organizational capacities so as to surmount the imperialist forces.[53] Although the degree of opposition to colonialism may have varied across these parties, the fact that they were engaged in a struggle against an alien force provided them with a greater incentive to join with social groups and mobilize society against the dominant regime. In effect, a structural cleavage emerged in these countries, wherein nationalist groups challenged entrenched colonial forces. By contrast, the initial, quick success of the 1932 coup and the lack of a need to mobilize society to uproot and challenge an occupying colonial power ultimately worked against the imperatives of party building at a critical juncture in modern Thai history. The People's Party was therefore unable to avail itself of a social revolution to restructure society because the presence of the monarchy had removed the impetus for complete social transformation. The ultimate consequence was that the party system did not mature and crucially did not lead to any social cleavages becoming articulated.

THE POSTWAR PERIOD

At the end of World War II, the military government run by Phibul Songhkram, one of the original plotters of the 1932 revolution and a military rival of Pridi, was completely discredited because of its support of Japan. An opportunity for a multiparty democracy thus emerged. Although parties were technically still banned, competing groups banded together into parties to contest the first postwar election. Pridi led a coalition made up of the Constitutional Front (liberal members of the former People's Party) and the northeastern-based Cooperative Party (Sahachip); members of the Seri Thai (Free Thai) Movement (resistance fighters during the war); and grassroots support from students, intellectuals, and labor groups, including the Central Labor Union (CLU). The CLU was an umbrella group that brought together various labor welfare associations. It sought an active political role in society by supporting the Cooperative Party and by giving an executive position in the union to the secretary-general of the party.[54]

Arrayed against Pridi's coalition were two main rivals: a royalist group, led by Khuang Apaiwongse of the Democrat Party and Seni Pramoj, the Seri Thai representative in Washington, DC, during the war, and the military, running under the façade of the Tharmathipat Party. These parties were not mass based,

---

[53] The KMT was not battling colonialism, but its attack on the Chinese emperor was purposeful and sustained, in effect serving as the functional equivalent of a colonial alien force.

[54] At its peak, the CLU had 60 member organizations and 75,000 members. See Pasuk and Baker 1995: 183.

but they did have sharp ideological differences compared to the other parties. Pridi's coalition, however, could boast some linkages with social groups. Northeastern members of parliament represented their region's call for greater autonomy from Bangkok. Leftist members of the Cooperative Party and of the Constitutional Front had some ties to labor groups. Labor groups were extremely active during this period, and they made their influence felt with Pridi's coalition.

After several parliamentary maneuverings, Pridi's coalition came to power in March 1946. Pridi quickly sought to consolidate democracy by writing a new constitution. This constitution was the most democratic one Thailand had seen. It made parliament completely elective, created a senate that was elected by members of the parliament, and made political parties legal for the first time. The new constitution also prohibited bureaucrats and soldiers from sitting in the senate, the lower house, or the cabinet.

This period also witnessed a rising leftist tide. To appease the Soviet Union and facilitate Thailand's entry into the United Nations, Pridi repealed the anti-communist law. In the August 1946 elections, a candidate from the Communist Party of Thailand (CPT) won a seat in Bangkok. The CPT actively championed student and labor organizations and published a weekly newspaper.[55] Throughout Southeast Asia, this was a period when the left was making head-way within the framework of a democratic system. For the first time, the left had a serious chance to gain political footing in a democratic polity.

However, the dire straits of the economy conspired to make it difficult for democracy to take hold. A shortage of consumer goods had led to rising inflation, in which retail prices stood at eight times their prewar level.[56] Furthermore, rampant corruption within the government and the bureaucracy hurt the legiti-macy of Pridi's rule, even if he himself was not tainted by corruption. What severely undermined Pridi was the death of the young King Ananda Mahidol. On June 9, 1946, the king was found shot in bed. Rumors spread that Pridi as the former regent had conspired to assassinate the king. Although the evidence pointed to an accidental death, Pridi's opponents, including the Democrat Party, continued to fan these rumors. Unable to manage this crisis, Pridi resigned the premiership.

With his resignation, the two parties that had supported him began to flounder. Without Pridi at the helm, they lacked the discipline to stay united. In the August 1946 elections, which were colored by the death of the king, Pridi's two parties barely held their majority. Throughout the year, the party system began to unravel. In May 1947, a faction split off from the Democrat Party, terming itself the People's Party (Phak Prachachon) and joined Pridi's coalition. Meanwhile, Phibul had created the Tharmathipat Party to reestablish his position in civilian politics. The Democrat Party stood staunchly with the

---

[55] Ibid.: 266.
[56] Darling 1965: 55.

Tharmathipat Party against Pridi's parties. The volatility in the party system, along with a stagnating economy, made the polity ripe for a coup.

On November 8, 1947, the military struck back and overthrew the civilian government. Brewing discontent within the armed forces and political instability throughout the country had created the opportunity for a successful coup. The Northern Army, whose mission during World War II was to regain territories lost to the British, was particularly unhappy with Pridi and the civilian government. Its mission in the Shan states had ended ingloriously; as they were demobilized and forced to give up territories in the north, they were obliged to follow orders from members of the Seri Thai movement. Army leaders believed that Pridi's Seri Thai was being rewarded against the army's own merit and interests.

Whereas Khuang and the Democrat Party were initially allowed to run the government, in April 1948 the military finally edged Khuang out and re-elevated Phibul to the prime minister's office. Another coup on November 29, 1951, firmly stamped the power of the military over the state. The struggle between civilian and military forces was now over. After this coup, Phibul restored the 1932 Constitution that allowed civil servants or active military officers to hold seats in the cabinet or the parliament. Phibul's cabinet was thus composed of individuals with bureaucratic offices.[57] Following this coup, the military was in complete command of all levers of power.

The collapse of democracy in this postwar period was the result of a number of crises. The death of the king was perhaps the nail in the coffin that sealed the fate of Pridi's government. But the inability of the government to deal with dismal economic conditions was equally critical. The inflationary conditions of the economy were particularly burdensome for the military. Already angered by the course of the war and their demobilization, many army officers found that they had no welfare benefits to tide them through a dire economy.

Democracy in Thailand was weakened especially by institutional feebleness. The lack of organizational coherence within Pridi's coalition severely reduced his government's ability to implement badly needed economic reforms. As Frank Darling put it: "Perhaps most serious was their [liberals'] lack of discipline and their inability to develop themselves into a cohesive political force. Unlike the military leaders who relied on the highly-disciplined armed forces, the liberals failed to build a national party organization on which they could gain political support."[58]

Ideology – beyond simply being pro- or anti-democracy – did matter in the postwar period, and the parties reflected a division between leftists and north-easterners on one side, and royalists and the aristocracy on the other side. Yet, even if parties were rooted in an ideological field, they did not have a social base. With the partial exception of the Sahachip Party representing the northeast,

---

[57] Thak 1979: 74.
[58] Darling 1965: 59.

parties did not have roots in society; therefore, they lacked the ability to mobilize their followers. Without a mass base, there was little foundation on which to maintain the organizational structure of the party. This was especially true once Pridi was forced to flee the country. By contrast, the military forces arrayed against Pridi were united against the civilian government. The military's inherent discipline easily provided it with greater organizational strength when competing with newly formed civilian parties. Given these shaky democratic foundations, it is not surprising that social cleavages could not become institutionalized into the party system.

The reemergence and consolidation of military power in postwar Thailand was a result not only of domestic struggles but just as much of external geopolitical support as the Cold War began to heat up in Asia. After World War II, the British had sought to punish Thailand for its alliance with Japan. In drawing up an extremely punitive proposal, known as the Twenty-One Demands, the British not only called for the return of territories they had colonized in Burma and Malaya but also demanded a monopoly over foreign trade, the right to station troops in the country, the right to reorganize military forces, and a monopoly over commercial airlines in Bangkok. The United States, siding with the new democratic government of Pridi, blocked most of the British proposal, deeming it excessive. But by the time that Phibul had ousted Khuang in April 1948, the global situation had been radically transformed and in the process, so had U.S. foreign policy. As the map in Asia looked increasingly red, with the relentless drive of the communists in China and the outburst of communist revolts throughout Southeast Asia, the United States began to reassess its alliances, becoming increasingly friendly with Phibul. In this emerging Cold War chessboard, Thailand appeared to be a stable beachhead in the war against communism, but one that had to be further solidified.

The economic and political benefits began to fall like manna from heaven for Phibul's staunchly anti-communist regime. In May 1949, Thailand joined the International Monetary Fund and the World Bank. A Thai military mission was then invited to join a tour of army and air force bases in the United States. Subsequently, the Supreme Commander for the Allied Powers (SCAP) in Japan provided $43.7 million in gold as payment for goods and services that Thailand had given to Japan during the war.

The Economic Cooperation Administration (ECA), run by the United States, provided significant economic and technical assistance through an initial grant of $8 million. A Special Technical and Economic Mission was subsequently established in Bangkok composed of about 50 technical experts who assisted in improving the country's agriculture, irrigation, transportation, communications, harbor facilities, commerce, education, and public health.[59] At the end of 1951, the Mutual Security Agency replaced the ECA, advancing a global program of military, economic, and technical assistance to deter communist

[59] Ibid.: 79.

aggression. From this program, Thailand was granted $7 million for economic and technical aid.[60] In October 1950, Thailand became the first country in Southeast Asia to receive a loan from the World Bank: $25.4 million for the purpose of building large-scale infrastructure projects.[61]

Phibul's stranglehold on power was thus greatly amplified by American geopolitical interests. With benefits flowing so rapidly from the United States, the Thai military had little difficulty repressing civilian politics. Social cleavages could not reemerge or get grafted onto the party system during this period because the right wing was firmly in control. Its mission to rule Thailand autocratically was fully supported by the United States, whose concern was to prevent communism from spreading into Asia.

INSTITUTIONAL REPRODUCTION: 1970S–1990S

It took 26 years for democracy to return and for parties to have a meaningful role in the polity. In October 1973, hundreds of thousands of university students flooded Rachadamnoen Avenue, Bangkok's most elegant thoroughfare, following a series of egregious acts of corruption by the ruling generals. Violent clashes on the streets of Bangkok eventually compelled the king to intervene and to drive the generals into exile, ushering in a brief, democratic period.[62] The democratic floodgates led to a chaotic proliferation of parties. In 1975, when democratic elections were held, more than 42 parties and 2,199 candidates ran for 269 seats in parliament. Most of these parties were simply aggregations of military generals and metropolitan businessmen who had no real programmatic goals except the attainment of political power through democratic means. There were, nonetheless, a few parties that, although elite-centered, did bring political programs to the table. These included the Democrat Party and the Social Action Party (SAP). The SAP was an offshoot of the Democrat Party, notable for the presence of executives from the Bangkok Bank who had ambitious goals of social reform. On the left, three parties – the New Force Party (Palang Mai), United Socialist Front, and the Socialist Party of Thailand – represented the country's vast majority of rural peasantry and urban workers. Although ideology mattered during this parliamentary period, no party had any significant mass base.

Social forces were extensively active during this open period. Students, workers, and farmers joined together in an alliance (*sam prasarn*) to persistently pressure the government and parliament to enact sweeping social reforms. They called for extensive land reform, sharp wage increases, and better conditions for laborers. In these years, Bangkok was a cauldron of recurrent protests and strikes. Between 1973 and 1976, there were 1,233 strikes, with an average

---

[60] Ibid.: 80.
[61] Ibid.
[62] The most insightful analyses of this turbulent period include Anderson 1977; Girling 1981; Morell and Chai-Anan 1981.

of 25.7 per month.[63] The democratic governments made real efforts to address the demands of the social groups, but a fundamental problem was that the parties and social forces were not united. Even though the Democrat Party and the Social Action Party made sustained efforts to advance some reforms, they were handicapped by their inability to follow through on policy, particularly given their weak capacity in the periphery, where conservative local bureaucratic elites resisted change. Crucially, parties did not ally with social groups and, therefore, lacked a mass base with which to back up legal directives.[64]

Democracy lasted only three years, collapsing in a furious bloodbath when thousands of university students, protesting the return of the generals from exile, were surrounded and attacked by thugs and paramilitary groups at Thammasat University on October 6, 1976. But even before this brutal denouement, democracy was already dying a death from a thousand cuts. One of the central problems was that the parties in parliament could not govern effectively. The SAP had first taken charge of the government and was able to hold its 13-party coalition together for barely more than a year. As the coalition began to fall apart over issues of patronage, the Democrats seized power with an equally shaky coalition. The dilemma of the Democrat Party was that it was deeply split down the middle. The right-wing camp was working with another party to undermine its own colleagues, while the left wing went on its own to build branches to strengthen its position. The party was working at cross-purposes despite holding the same institutional label. From 1975 to 1976, the left wing of the party had formed 66 branches in the central, northern, and northeastern regions. Furthermore, an alliance with General Krit Sivara, the former army commander in chief, who had sided with the university students at the height of the 1973 revolution was crucial to the progressives' hopes of institutional growth and survival. However, events moved beyond the control of the Democrat progressive faction as General Krit died just at the moment when tensions spiked. The attack at Thammasat ended all possibilities that parties would play any role in the near future of Thailand's governance.

After a one-year rule by an ultra-right-wing supreme court justice appointed by the king, the military sought to normalize relations; by 1978, a semi-democratic system was in operation with a general as prime minister at the head of a coalition of civilian political parties. This lasted until 1988 when parties and civil society groups increasingly pushed for a democratically elected head of state. In 1988, the Chart Thai Party under Chatichai Choonhavan finally gained the upper hand in parliament. With the exception of the 1991 coup that briefly interrupted this latest democratic period, the party system continued its trajectory of institutional fecklessness. In the March 1992, October 1992,[65]

---

[63] Nikom 1978: 283.

[64] For more details, see Kuhonta 2011: 151–163.

[65] There were two elections in 1992. The first was won by the military party, Sammakitham; the second followed the May 1992 popular uprising that ousted General Suchinda Kraprayoon from the prime ministership.

1995, and 1996 elections, different parties came to power and on each occasion a broad but unstable coalition was formed. As Table 12.1 has shown, the government party has consistently lost a huge share of its seats primarily because of factions bolting to join other parties that stood a better chance of cobbling together a winning coalition.

By the mid-1990s, a group of influential academics and civil society activists had begun calling for major constitutional reforms to address the vices of the party system.[66] The large number of parties,[67] the lack of organizational coherence and discipline, the excessive freedom of factions, and the general instability of governing parties and their coalitions finally led to a sweeping change in electoral and institutional rules that were reflected in the 1997 Constitution – known as the "People's Constitution" because of its extensive popular consultation. These changes included the creation of a mixed electoral system with single member districts and a party list, rules that increased the threshold to censor the prime minister or cabinet members, constraints on factions breaking away from parties, and incentives to choose cabinet members from the party list rather than from the constituency seats.[68] In the aggregate, these institutional changes were intended to create the conditions for the rise of a few national, programmatic parties, the long-term stability of governing coalitions, and the demise of clientelistic parties and powerful factions. Indeed, the 2001 elections reflected the hopes of the constitution drafters with the emergence of two major parties, the TRT and the Democrat, and a few middle-sized parties that became increasingly inconsequential.

CODA: HAS THAKSIN SHINAWATRA CHANGED THE CHARACTER OF THE PARTY SYSTEM?

The aftermath of the 2001 elections brought about a changed institutional landscape. After TRT absorbed a few other parties, it became the first party in Thailand's democratic history to hold a parliamentary majority. It then went on to become the only party to complete a full parliamentary term. TRT's electoral dominance, further ratified in the 2005 polls in which it gained an outright majority following the elections, and its general institutional development point to significant structural changes in the party system. An immediate outcome of this period was the sharp decline in the effective number of parties; in 2001, this was 3.04; in 2005, it was 1.65. By contrast, in 1996, the score was 4.32 (see Table 12.1).

Equally important, the party system *appeared* to have gained a dominant party with many attributes of institutionalization.[69] TRT was centered on a

---

[66] See Prawase 2002.
[67] In particular, the effective number of parliamentary parties.
[68] For details on the specific effect of each rule, see Kuhonta 2008: 380–382.
[69] McCargo and Ukrist 2005: ch. 3.

large membership base, extensive branches, policy-oriented platforms, and internal discipline. On the level of programmatic policies, Thaksin decisively shook up the party system. For the first time since the 1970s, a party's identity and electoral campaign pivoted on a social agenda that was populist and heavily pro-poor. Given the resounding success of TRT's platform (and of its successor parties, including the People Power Party and Phua Thai), all other parties have been forced to appear as programmatic, even as populist, as TRT.[70] But on other levels, such as the cohesiveness, discipline, complexity, and depth of the party, TRT ultimately does not seem to have been able to create a completely distinctive organization. The party's early growth was heavily dependent on factions made up of provincial elites recruited prior to the 2001 polls; the substantive role of the branches and memberships was rather superficial; and discipline and cohesiveness were less a function of party rules and procedures than of the financial and personal influence of Thaksin, as well as the effects of the 1997 Constitution. The party did create a strong sense of identity and it did establish a bond with society. But this was a result of both party programs and Thaksin's charisma. The overbearing influence of Thaksin on the party and the absence of procedural mechanisms for new leadership to emerge point to a party that had the trappings of institutionalization but ultimately fell back heavily on personalistic power for much of its identity and direction.[71] The difficulty of conceiving of TRT and its successor parties without Thaksin suggests that party institutionalization has not been very deep.

Despite the mixed record of TRT in terms of institutionalization, its programmatic vision earned it a unique prize in the party system: a loyal mass base that spans extensive regions of the country. With the exception of the Democrat Party's limited base in the south and parts of Bangkok, no other party has gained such an extensive mass following. After the 2001 and 2005 elections, a pattern began to emerge: TRT was clearly dominant in the northeast and the upper north, along with significant gains in the Bangkok area. More crucially, the 2006 military coup that ousted the TRT government and further elite machinations that undermined TRT successor parties spurred the formation of a social movement that has become the mass base of the party. This movement, known as the Red Shirts, is made up primarily of rural villagers but also includes workers in the informal economy, numerous intellectuals, and left-leaning professionals.[72] The Red Shirts rallied against the coup and against the elites' ability to put their preferred party, the Democrat, in power in December 2008 through questionable parliamentary

---

[70] Aim and Kuhonta 2012: 393–395; Siripan 2012.

[71] Note, e.g., the difficulty of Chaturon Chaisaeng in running the TRT after it was dissolved by the 2007 ruling from the Constitutional Tribunal.

[72] There is a growing literature on the social base of the Red Shirts. One study sees the Red Shirts as primarily lower middle class (Nithi 2010); another as "an emerging class of urbanized villagers who straddle both urban and rural society" (Thabchumpon and McCargo 2011); and one as a political movement rather than a class movement (Apichart 2010).

maneuvers. Therefore, even if TRT may have a mixed record in terms of institutionalization, it subsequently (under the guise of its successors, the PPP and PT), has decisively earned one key indicator of institutionalization: roots in society.

The heightened tensions between the Red Shirts and the government and army led to the deadliest violence in Thailand's history in April and May 2010, when 94 people were killed and more than 2,000 injured. Most of the casualties were Red Shirts. In May 2011, the Democrat Party announced that elections would be held in July and for the first time in Thailand's democratic history, mass mobilization played a key role in the fate of a party. The Red Shirts converted their discontent on the streets into fervent campaigning for Phua Thai. Although the Red Shirts remained an autonomous organization, they, in effect, acted as the party's grassroots base. Red Shirts flooded Phua Thai rallies, turning campaign events into a sea of bright red. They also set up educational programs for their supporters regarding electoral laws. As new rules were passed just before the House dissolution, new electoral laws came into effect, which included redistricting, ballot structure, and even changes in electoral formula.[73] The Red Shirt headquarters disseminated information to various provincial and local chapters to educate their own groups about the new changes.[74]

The mass mobilization of supporters of a Thai political party marks a change in the party system. Never before has a party had a mass base that actively attended rallies, joined campaign activities, and monitored polling stations. Never before have individuals from a specific social group identified so strongly with a political party. Does this development potentially presage a new era of mass-based institutionalized parties rooted in social cleavages? It is hard to say whether this will have far-reaching implications because – just like TRT – Phua Thai remains tightly controlled by Thaksin and because the Red Shirts remain an autonomous organization. Although there is some overlap in terms of MPs joining Phua Thai coming from the Red Shirt movement, the leadership and structure of the Red Shirts have matured independently of the party – albeit with the explicit purpose of supporting the party. Thus, Phua Thai may be considered a mass-based party, but with a mass that has its own organizational identity beyond the party. Recent events regarding the campaign to reform the *lese majeste* law as well as the issue of political prisoners furthermore suggest that some groups in the Red Shirts may be distancing themselves from Phua Thai

[73] Aim 2011.

[74] On election day, the Red Shirts set up a special unit to monitor the polls, which consisted of some 40 volunteers working around the clock to coordinate efforts to monitor both the campaign and the electoral process to prevent fraud. The end result was a minimum of one Red Shirt representative stationed at each of the 92,200 voting units across the country on election day. Such a level of monitoring by units other than governments or political parties to monitor elections is unprecedented in Thailand. Fieldwork observation, July 3, 2011.

given the two organizations' diverging views regarding Article 112, the law on *lese majeste*.[75]

Returning to the big picture, we have then a pattern of political development that is heavily constrained by its initial conditions – yet not fully determined. Since 1932, when the first modern party appeared, parties have lived checkered lives as shallow institutions with minimal organizational complexity, ideological coherence, and social linkages. Parties returned to govern democratically briefly in 1946, more significantly in the mid-1970s, and then decisively in the late 1980s and 1990s. Throughout these years, interrupted often by military interventions, there has been little institutional advancement. The central problem lies in the fact that Thailand was never faced with a systemic crisis that necessitated the growth of a mass movement. The 1932 revolution was a major opening for reform, but the monarchy was not considered a threat, unlike colonial authorities in Vietnam, Indonesia, and even to a lesser extent Malaysia. Therefore, the People's Party could not build momentum to deepen its roots and build its armature. In 1946, Thailand held its first multiparty elections with parties competing on distinct ideological cleavages. Yet, a tanking economy, a resurgent military, and a geopolitical context supportive of anti-communist autocrats conspired to undermine the party system and severely weaken the left. During these two critical junctures – the 1932 revolution and the 1946 postwar period – the lack of cohesiveness, ideology, and social linkages undermined the party system and lessened its chance for institutionalization.

Since Riggs's observation about the weakness of "instrumentalities of popular control," Thai politics has undergone significant change, yet the party system does not seem to have been able to move in step with other transformations. Only the recent polarization that has engulfed Thailand and created sharp cleavages in society appears to bring with it some real possibilities for institutional change, in large part because the structural fissures that are emerging are powerful and have the potential to solidify cleavages into the party system. Notably, these recent events also share some similarities with the 1932 revolution. However, where all this will lead is unclear, as much of the fissures and elite divisions remain in great flux. Whether Phua Thai will ultimately be tightly linked with the Red Shirts is a crucial piece of the puzzle of Thailand's party system institutionalization. And at the heart of this is the question of whether

---

[75] On January 29, 2013, the Yingluck Shinawatra government found itself in the awkward position of being forcefully challenged at a rally by a section of the Red Shirts called the "January 29 Front – Free Political Prisoners." The group, numbering in the thousands at the rally, accused the Phua Thai government as well as the leadership of the Red Shirts of not doing enough for political prisoners. It called for the release of all political prisoners: those arrested for the events of April–May 2010 and those charged with *lese majeste*. See "Red Shirt Group's Rally Puts Government in Tricky Spot," *The Nation*, January 30, 2013. See also http://thairedshirts.org/2013/01/30/red-shirts-pressure-government-to-grant-amnesty/.

elite figures will continue to dominate parties or whether parties will subsume elites in a broader institutional configuration.

REFERENCES (THAI NAMES LISTED IN ORDER OF FIRST NAME)

Aim Sinpeng. 2011. Thailand's Electoral Rule, *New Mandala*, May 30. Available at http://asiapacific.anu.edu.au/newmandala/2011/05/30/thailands-electoral-rules/.

Aim Sinpeng, and Erik Martinez Kuhonta. 2012. From the Street to the Ballot Box: The July 2011 Elections and the Rise of Social Movements in Thailand. *Contemporary Southeast Asia* 34(3): 389–415.

Amara Raksasataya. 1965. Trends and Problems of Thai Politics. Paper presented at the Jubilee Celebration of the University of the Philippines.

Anderson, Benedict R. 1977. Withdrawal Symptoms: Social and Cultural Aspects of the October 6 Coup. *Bulletin of Concerned Asian Scholars* 9(1): 13–40.

Anusorn Limanee. 1998. Thailand. In Wolfgang Sachsenroder and Ulrike E. Frings (Eds.), *Political Party Systems and Democratic Development in East and Southeast Asia*, Vol. 1, pp. 403–448. Aldershot, UK: Ashgate.

Apichart Sathitniranai. 2010. Krai kue sua daeng: mob wa jang prai rue klum chonchan klang mai. [Who Are the Red Shirts? Mob-Hungry Mob, Prai, or the New Middle Class]. In *Daeng Tammai: sangkhom Thai panha lae kanma khong sua daeng* [Red Why: Thai Society, Problems, and the Emergence of the Red Shirts], pp. 14–35. Bangkok: Openbooks.

Askew, Marc. 2008. *Performing Political Identity: The Democrat Party in Southern Thailand*. Chiang Mai: Silkworm Books.

Baker, Chris, and Pasuk Phongpaichit (Eds.). 2000. *Pridi by Pridi: Selected Writings on Life, Politics, and Economy*. Chiang Mai: Silkworm Books.

Chai-Anan Samudavanija. 1990. Thailand: A Stable Semi-Democracy. In Larry Diamond, Juan Linz, and Seymour Martin Lipset (Eds.), *Politics in Developing Countries: Comparing Experiences with Democracy*, pp. 271–312. Boulder: Lynne Rienner.

Chai-Anan Samudavanija. Undated Kan Pathana Khong Pak Karn Muang Thai: Suksa Chapoa Korani Khong Phak Prachathipat, 1975–1976 [Development of Thai Political Parties: A Case Study of the Democrat Party's Expansion]. 12–13.

Chambers, Paul. 2005. Evolving toward What? Parties, Faction, and Coalition Behavior in Thailand Today. *Journal of East Asian Studies* 5: 495–520.

Chambers, Paul. 2008. Factions, Parties and the Durability of Parliaments, Coalitions and Cabinets: The Case of Thailand (1979–2001). *Party Politics* 14(3): 299–323.

Coast, John. 1953. *Some Aspects of Siamese Politics*. New York: Institute of Pacific Relations.

Copeland, Matthew Phillip. 1993. Contested Nationalism and the 1932 Overthrow of the Absolute Monarchy in Siam. Ph.D. Dissertation, Australian National University.

Darling, Frank. 1965. *Thailand and the United States*. Washington, DC: Public Affairs Press.

Darling, Frank. 1971. Political Parties in Thailand. *Pacific Affairs* 44(2): 228–241.

Girling, John. L. S. 1981. *Thailand: Society and Politics*. Ithaca: Cornell University Press.

Hicken, Allen. 2006. Party Fabrication: Constitutional Reform and the Rise of Thai Rak Thai. *Journal of East Asian Studies* 6: 381–407.

Hicken, Allen. 2009. *Building Party Systems in Developing Countries*. Cambridge: Cambridge University Press.

Kasian Tejapira. 2001. *Commodifying Marxism: The Formation of Modern Thai Radical Culture.* Kyoto: Kyoto University Press.

Kohli, Atul. 1987. *The State and Poverty in India: The Politics of Reform.* Cambridge: Cambridge University Press.

Kramol Tongdhamachart. 1982. *Toward a Political Party Theory in Thai Perspective.* Singapore: Institute of Southeast Asian Studies.

Kuhonta, Erik Martinez. 2008. The Paradox of Thailand's 1997 "People's Constitution": Be Careful What You Wish For. *Asian Survey* 48(3): 373–392.

Kuhonta, Erik Martinez. 2011. *The Institutional Imperative: The Politics of Equitable Development in Southeast Asia.* Stanford: Stanford University Press.

Mainwaring, Scott, and Timothy Scully. 1995. Introduction: Party Systems in Latin America. In Scott Mainwaring and Timothy Scully (Eds.), *Building Democratic Institutions: Party Systems in Latin America*, pp. 1–34. Stanford: Stanford University Press.

McCargo, Duncan. 1997a. Thailand's Political Parties: Real, Authentic and Actual. In Kevin Hewison (Ed.), *Political Change in Thailand: Democracy and Participation*, pp. 114–131. London: Routledge.

McCargo, Duncan. 1997b. *Chamlong Srimuang and the New Thai Politics.* London: Hurst and Co.

McCargo, Duncan, and Ukrist Pathmanand. 2005. *The Thaksinization of Thailand.* Copenhagen: NIAS Press.

Morell, David, and Chai-Anan Samudavanija. 1981. *Political Conflict in Thailand: Reform, Reaction, Revolution.* Cambridge, MA: Oelgeschlager, Gunn, and Hain.

Murashima, Eiji, Nakharin Mektrairat, and Somkiat Wantana. 1991. *The Making of Modern Thai Political Parties.* Tokyo: Institute of Developing Economies.

Naruemon Thabchumpon and Duncan McCargo. 2011. Urbanized Villagers of the 2010 Redshirt Protests. *Asian Survey* 51(6): 993–1018.

Nelson, Michael. 2002. Thailand's House Elections of 6 January 2001: Thaksin's Landslide Victory and Subsequent Narrow Escape. In Michael Nelson (Ed.), *Thailand's New Politics: KPI 2001 Yearbook.* Bangkok: White Lotus.

Nelson, Michael. 2005. Analyzing Provincial Political Structures in Thailand: Phuak, Trakun, and Hua Khanaen. *SEARC Working Paper.*

Nelson, Michael. 2007. Institutional Incentives and Informal Local Political Groups (*Phuak*) in Thailand: Comments on Allen Hicken and Paul Chambers. *Journal of East Asian Studies* 7: 125–147.

Nikom Chandravithum. 1978. Labor Relations: Thailand's Experience. In Vichitvong Na Pombhejara (Ed.), *Readings in Thailand's Political Economy.* Bangkok: Bangkok Printing.

Nithi Aeosriwong. 2010. Karn muang khong sua daeng. [The politics of the Red Shirts]. In *Aan karn muang Thai 3: karn muang khong sua daeng* [Reading Thai Politics 3: The Politics of the Red Shirts], pp. 10–15. Bangkok: Openbooks.

Noranit Setthabut. 1987. *Phak Prachatiphat* [Democrat Party]. Bangkok: Thammasat University.

Ockey, James. 1994. Political Parties, Factions, and Corruption in Thailand. *Modern Asian Studies* 28(2): 251–277.

Ockey, James. 2003. Change and Continuity in the Thai Political Party System. *Asian Survey* 43(4): 663–680.

Pasuk Phongpaichit, and Chris Baker. 1995. *Thailand: Economy and Politics.* Kuala Lumpur: Oxford University Press.

Pierson, Paul. 2004. *Politics in Time: History, Institutions, and Social Analysis.* Princeton: Princeton University Press.

Prawase Wasi. 2002. An Overview of Political Reform. In Duncan McCargo (Ed.), *Reforming Thai Politics*, pp. 21–27. Copenhagen: NIAS Press.

Pridi Banomyong. 1974. *Ma Vie Mouvementée Et Mes 21 Ans D'exil En Chine Populaire.* Paris: UNESCON.

Pridi Banomyong. 1978. Some Stories Concerning the Formation of the People's Party and Democracy. In Thak Chaloemtiarana (Ed.), *Thai Politics: Extracts and Documents, 1932–1957.* Bangkok: Social Science Association of Thailand.

Pridi Banomyong. 2000. Economic Plan. In Chris Baker and Pasuk Phongpaichit (Eds.), *Pridi by Pridi: Selected Writings on Life, Politics, and Economy.* Chiang Mai: Silkworm Books.

Riggs, Fred. 1966. *Thailand: The Modernization of a Bureaucratic Polity.* Honolulu: East-West Center Press.

Siripan Nogsuan Sawasdee. 2006. *Thai Political Parties in the Age of Reform.* Bangkok: Institute of Public Policy Studies.

Siripan Nogsuan Sawasdee. 2012. Thailand. In Takashi Inoguchi and Jean Blondel (Eds.), *Political Parties and Democracy: Contemporary Western Europe and Asia*, pp. 143–164. New York: Palgrave Macmillan.

Somsakdi Xuto (Ed.). 1987. *Government and Politics of Thailand.* Singapore: Oxford University Press.

Southeast Asian Affairs. 1987. Singapore: Institute of Southeast Asian Studies.

Suchit Bunbongkarn. 1996. *State of the Nation: Thailand.* Singapore: Institute of Southeast Asian Studies.

Sungsidh Piriyarangsan. 1996. *Phak Prachatiphat: Jaak anurakniyom sulath seriniyom mai* [The Democrat Party: From conservatism to neoliberalism]. In Sungsidh Piriyarangsan and Pasuk Phongpaichit (Eds.), *Jodsamneuk lae udomkarn khong kabuankan prachathipatai ruan samai* [Political ideology and the current democratic movement]. Bangkok: Department of Economics and Friedrich Ebert Foundation.

Stinchcombe, Arthur L. 1968. *Constructing Social Theories.* New York: Harcourt, Brace & World.

Stowe, Judith. *Siam Becomes Thailand.* London: Hurst and Co., 1991.

Thak Chaloemtiarana. 1979. *Thailand: The Politics of Despotic Paternalism.* Bangkok: Thai Khadi Institute, Thammasat University.

Thawatt Mokarapong. 1962. The June Revolution of 1932 in Thailand. Ph.D. Dissertation, Indiana University.

Yano, Toru. 1978. Political Structure of a "Rice-Growing State." In Yoneo Ishii (Ed.), *Thailand: A Rice-Growing Society*, pp. 115–158. Honolulu: University of Hawai'i Press.

13

Party and Party System Institutionalization in the Philippines

Allen Hicken*

No country in Asia has a longer experience with democracy and democratic institutions than does the Philippines. The first national political party, Partido Federal, was founded in 1900. Direct local elections were held under U.S. colonial auspices in 1906 followed by national legislative elections in 1907. And yet, despite its long history the Philippine party system remains stubbornly under-institutionalized – regardless of how we choose to define and operationalize the concept. The chronic weaknesses of the party system are the source of a variety of ills, according to scholars, including an acute "democratic deficit,"[1] a lack of political accountability,[2] an under-provision of public goods,[3] and disillusionment with democracy among Filipino citizens.[4] In short, the party system is one of the biggest obstacles to democratic stability and good governance in the Philippines.

In this chapter, I examine characteristics and causal factors related to the Philippine party system. Using Mainwaring and Scully's institutionalization framework as a point of departure, I first demonstrate that the Philippines is indeed under-institutionalized (inchoate). I note and discuss apparent changes in the degree of institutionalization over time. Finally, I present an explanation for why the party system has developed as it has in the Philippines, an explanation that also accounts for the changes we observe over time. Specifically, like Hutchroft and Rocomora (2003), I argue that the development of the Philippine party system is inextricably linked to the manner in which democracy unfolded in the Philippines. Early decisions by colonial administrators and Philippine elite had the unintended consequence of entrenching a particular

* I want to thank workshop participants and the two reviewers for their helpful feedback.
[1] Hutchcroft and Rocomora 2003.
[2] Montinola 1999.
[3] Hicken 2008a, 2008b.
[4] Hicken 2011.

style of political party that has dominated the Philippine polity ever since. I argue that when the question of institutional reform has arisen in the decades since, the Filipino elite has consistently and sometimes strategically opted for institutions that were inimical to greater party institutionalization.

DEFINING INSTITUTIONALIZATION: WHAT IS IT AND HOW DO WE KNOW IT WHEN WE SEE IT?

The existing literature defines institutionalization in a variety of ways (see the Introduction to this volume [Chapter 1] in addition to Huntington 1968; Welfing 1973; Panebianco 1988; Mainwaring and Scully 1995; Levitsky 1998; Randall and Svasand 2002). One way to bring these disparate definitions together is to think of institutionalization as consisting of an external/ systemic dimension and an internal/organizational dimension.[5] Starting with the external/systemic dimension, party systems that are more institutionalized share two characteristics. First, there is stability in the rules and pattern of interparty competition. Second, political actors view parties as a legitimate and necessary part of the democratic process.[6] By contrast, in weakly institutionalized party systems, we see a high degree of instability in the pattern of party competition. There are both high birth and high death rates – new political parties regularly enter the system, while existing parties exit. There is also a high degree of electoral volatility – the fortunes of individual parties vary greatly from election to election. Finally, political actors in weakly institutionalized systems

---

[5] The discussion of these two dimensions draws on Hicken 2011.

[6] Some might argue that this second characteristic by necessity limits our analysis of institutionalization to democratic settings – in effect, it is a characteristic of modern democracy as much as it is a measure of institutionalization. With the exception of the martial law period, this limitation is not a problem for the Philippines. However, this characteristic can also be extended to nondemocratic/ semi-democratic settings with only slight modification. Even in nondemocracies, a minimal characteristic of institutionalization would be that the major power centers view the party/parties as a legitimate and necessary part of the political system. If the ruling elite views any party with distrust, even a dominant ruling party, then it seems safe to conclude that institutionalization is low. Likewise, where the powerful actors accept that parties are a legitimate and necessary part of the political system, even if that system is less than democratic, it is possible that that system is institutionalized (e.g., Singapore). Where a country scores on the other dimensions determines just how institutionalized it is. See Chapters 2, 3, 6, 7, and 9 in this volume for a discussion of institutionalization in nondemocratic contexts. See also Slater 2003; Brownlee 2008; Hicken and Kuhonta 2011.

This is not to say that studying institutionalization in nondemocratic contexts is unproblematic. I see two basic challenges. First, how do we weigh factors in systems where the ruling party is clearly viewed as legitimate and necessary by the ruling elite, but opposition parties are not (e.g., Vietnam and China)? Second, and more fundamentally, how do we assess concepts such as legitimacy and value infusion in settings where political actors, including voters, lack a choice between two or more meaningful alternatives? Where a meaningful choice is absent, whether because of the unequal playing field, voter intimidation, and so on, a vote may not be a reflection of a voter's true preference.

TABLE 13.1. *Party System Institutionalization*

External/Systemic Dimension
Stable pattern of interparty competition
Parties viewed as legitimate and necessary
Internal/Organizational Dimension
High degree of value infusion
High degree of organizational routinization

view parties as at best superfluous, and at worse a threat. It is this external/systemic dimension that corresponds most closely with the concept of *party system* institutionalization.

The second internal/organizational dimension concerns the nature of the party organization itself, and the parties' links with the broader society – what we might term the level of *party* institutionalization. To begin with, where parties are institutionalized they exhibit a high degree of what Levitsky calls value infusion (Levitsky 1998). There are strong links between parties and identifiable societal interests and groups of voters. Parties are rooted in society to the extent that "[m]ost voters identify with a party and vote for it most of the time, and some interest associations are closely linked to parties."[7] Party membership is valuable in and of itself and not just as a means to an end, and we can differentiate one party from another on the basis of its constituency and policy platform. Where parties are not institutionalized, political parties have weak roots in society, voters and politicians have few lasting attachments to particular parties, there are no enduring links between parties and interest groups, and parties have no distinct policy or ideological identities.

A second characteristic falling under the internal/organizational dimension is organizational routinization.[8] Institutionalized parties have entrenched organizations and established patterns of interactions. Parties are relatively cohesive and disciplined and are independent and autonomous from any charismatic leaders or particular financiers.[9] Put simply, parties have developed party organizations that "matter."[10] Where parties are weakly institutionalized, they tend to be thinly organized temporary alliances of convenience and are often extensions of or subservient to powerful party leaders. Table 13.1 summarizes these dimensions and characteristics.

So how institutionalized is the Philippine party system? Let's consider each of the dimensions in turn.

---

[7] Mainwaring and Torcal 2006: 7.
[8] Compare with Levitsky's 1998 discussion of behavioral routinization.
[9] Levistky 1998.
[10] Mainwaring and Scully 1995.

External/Systemic Dimension: Stability of Interparty Competition

One common indicator of the stability or volatility of the party system from election to election is the measure of electoral volatility. Electoral volatility captures the degree to which there is variation in aggregate party vote shares from one election to another. With a stable pattern of interparty competition, we expect to see a low volatility score, indicating that the same set of parties receives consistent levels of support from election to election. High levels of electoral volatility reflect instability in voters' preferences from election to election and/or elite-driven changes to the party system such as the demise of existing parties, the birth of new parties, party mergers, party splits, and so on.[11] Electoral volatility is not a perfect measure by any means – tracing party vote shares can prove extremely complicated when numerous party mergers or splits occur, or when a candidate's party affiliation is difficult to assess.[12] The latter is particularly a challenge in the Philippines, where candidates will often claim multiple party affiliations and candidate switching (turncoatism) is common. The very fact that party labels are so fluid in the Philippines is telling, but it makes calculating volatility challenging, so much so that some scholars eschew the attempt altogether.[13] Nonetheless, I believe it is possible to come up with reasonable estimates of volatility using some simple assumptions.[14] It is also important to note that electoral volatility does not allow the differentiation between the sources of instability – whether fickle voters or ephemeral parties.[15]

Electoral volatility is calculated by taking the sum of the net change in the percentage of votes gained or lost by each party from one election to the next, divided by two: $(\Sigma\ |v_{it} - v_{it+1}|)\ /\ 2)$. A score of 100 signifies that the set of parties winning votes is completely different from one election to the next. A score of 0 means the same parties receive exactly the same percentage of votes across two elections. The higher the volatility score, the less stable the pattern of party competition.

Table 13.2 is taken from the introduction to this volume (Chapter 1) and displays the volatility scores for the Philippines alongside those of other countries in Asia for comparative purposes. I divide the Philippines into two

---

[11] Mainwaring and Zoco 2007.

[12] Where possible, I follow Mainwaring and Zoco's 2007 rules about how to treat such situations.

[13] For example, Ufen 2008.

[14] Specifically, where candidates claimed multiple party affiliations, I use the largest party of which they were a member to calculate volatility. To the extent that the largest parties are those that are likely to be around over several elections, any bias is likely to be in the direction of understating the level of volatility. I also include independents and "other" minor parties as single categories for the purposes of calculating volatility. The average percentage for each category is less than 5 percent in any given election. Excluding the independents and "other" categories from the volatility calculation would have the effect of lowering the volatility score by an average of 2 points per election.

[15] Hicken and Kuhonta 2011.

TABLE 13.2. *Electoral Volatility in Asia*

	Years	Number of Elections	Volatility: 1st and 2nd Elections	Volatility: Last Election	Average Volatility
Malaysia II	1974–2013	10	8.6	4	10.1
Singapore	1968–2011	11	24.6	20.4	15.4
Taiwan	1992–2012	7	8.6	11.5	16.5
Sri Lanka	1947–2010	14	27.7	9.0	16.6
Japan	1947–2012	24	27.4	16.3	16.8
Philippines I	1946–1969	7	20.4	43.6	18.5
India	1951–2009	15	25.1	11.3	19.2
Cambodia	1993–2013	5	27.9	22.9	24
Indonesia	1999–2009	3	25.2	29.8	27.5
Malaysia I	1955–1968	4	38.8	36.4	30.6
Timor Leste	2001–2012	3	49.0	22.5	35.8
South Korea	1988–2012	7	41.9	35.2	36.5
Philippines II	1992–2013	8	57.0	42.9	38.3
Thailand I	1979–1991	4	40.8	32.1	38.4
Thailand II	1992–2011	8	48.7	58.2	42.0

Note: If the political parties linked to former prime minister Thaksin Shinawtra (Thai Rak Thai, Palang Prachachon, and Phua Thai) are treated as the same party, then the average volatility score for Thailand II falls to 32.6.
Sources: Authors' calculations; Hicken 2008.

periods corresponding to the pre– and post–martial law eras. The Philippines I period covers the seven elections between independence and martial law. The post-Marcos sample (Philippines II) covers the 1992 to 2013 elections.

Two things stand out in Table 13.2. First, the party system of post–martial law Philippines is very fluid. The fortunes of the individual parties tend to vary greatly from election to election. In other words, the results of past elections by and large are not a good predictor of future election results. In the case of the Philippines II, the result of a past election can be used to predict the result of the next election with less than 62 percent accuracy. Second, the Philippine party system appears to be much more volatile after martial law than it was before. Average volatility pre–martial law was 18.5. Post-Marcos, the average is 38.3. Figure 13.1 displays the electoral volatility scores over time.

If the argument that voters' ties to political parties develop gradually over time, bringing greater stability to electoral competition, is valid, we would expect electoral volatility to improve (decrease) over time in the Philippines. In pre–martial law elections, no clear pattern is evident. Electoral volatility did decline steadily for the first few post-independence elections but increased substantially in the two elections prior to martial

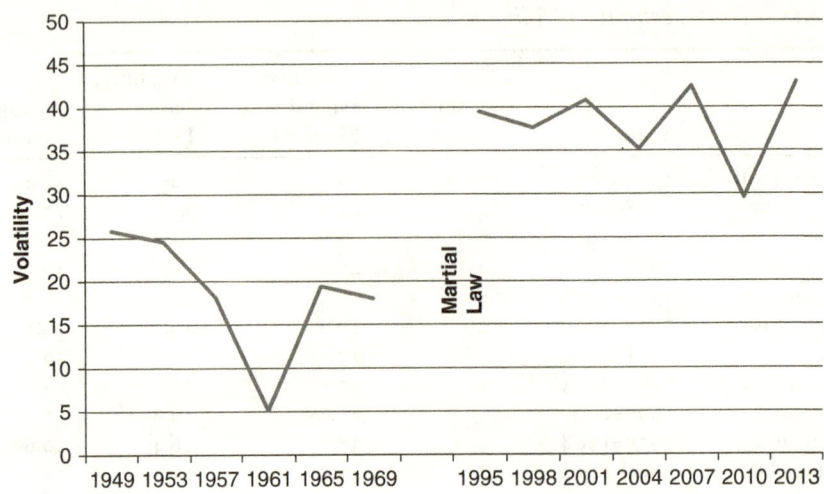

FIGURE 13.1 Electoral Volatility Pre– and Post–Martial Law
Source: Author's calculations from Hartman et al. (2001); COMELEC.

law. Since the fall of Marcos, there still does not appear to be any stabilization of the party system underway. Overall, the average volatility score for the post–martial law period is higher than before martial law (38 vs. 18) but both periods experienced relatively high degrees of instability in the pattern of interparty competition.

Another indication of the instability of the party system is the high rate at which parties enter and depart the party system. Table 13.3 displays the birth and death rates alongside the total number of parties for each election, all calculated using the parties that gain seats in the legislature. A birthrate of .33 means that 33 percent of the parties in a given year did not gain any seats in the prior election. A death rate of .33 means that 33 percent of the parties that won seats in the previous election did not capture any seats in the current election. Prior to martial law, it is clear that the Philippine party system had become a two-party system helmed by the Liberal and Nacionalista Parties. Combining this information with the volatility information from Figure 13.1, we observe that the rise in seat volatility in the 1960s was driven entirely by the shifting fortunes of the Nacionalistas and Liberals, and not by party entries and exits from the system.

Contrast this with the post-Marcos era. A couple of observations are immediately apparent from the table. First, it is clear that martial law marked the demise of the two-party system. Unlike the earlier period, the party system post-Marcos has not tended toward two parties. In fact, quite the opposite is true. During the past several elections, we have seen a large increase in the

TABLE 13.3. *Party Birth and Death Rates during House Elections (Seats)*

	Birthrate	Death Rate	Number of Parties
1946	NA	NA	7
1949	0.33	0.71	3
1953	0.33	0.33	3
1957	0.33	0.33	3
1961	0	0	2
1965	0	0	2
1969	0	0	2
	MARTIAL LAW		
1987	NA	NA	8
1992	0.43	0.50	7
1995	0.13	0	8
1998	0.50	0.50	8
2001	0.33	0.25	9
2004	0.73	0.11	30
2007	0.33	0.40	27
2010	0.67	0.12	60
2013	0.32	0.41	56

Source: Author's calculations from Hartman et al. (2001); COMELEC.

number of parties winning seats. This jump is driven mainly by an increase in the number of small parties taking advantage of the peculiar party list system used in the Philippines. This system is discussed in more detail later. Second, the party birth and death rates start high in the post-Marcos era and stay that way. Not only do we not see stabilization around two parties, we do not observe stabilization of any sort. A substantial number of parties continue to enter and exit the system each election, and it is these births and deaths that are the main drivers of electoral volatility. Figure 13.2 charts the birth and death rates along with the number of parties over time. The greater instability in the post–martial law era is clearly evident.

EXTERNAL/SYSTEMIC DIMENSION: LEGITIMACY

One of the most telling indications of a lack of institutionalization is the lingering doubt about whether the major actors view political parties as a legitimate and necessary part of political life. The disconnect between the ideal of democracy and the reality of Filipino democracy comes out again and again in surveys. In a 2001 World Values Survey, for example, 82 percent of respondents expressed support for democracy – a number comparable to what we observe in established democracies. However, a majority of Filipinos (55 percent) also report being dissatisfied with the way democracy works in their country, compared to

Allen Hicken

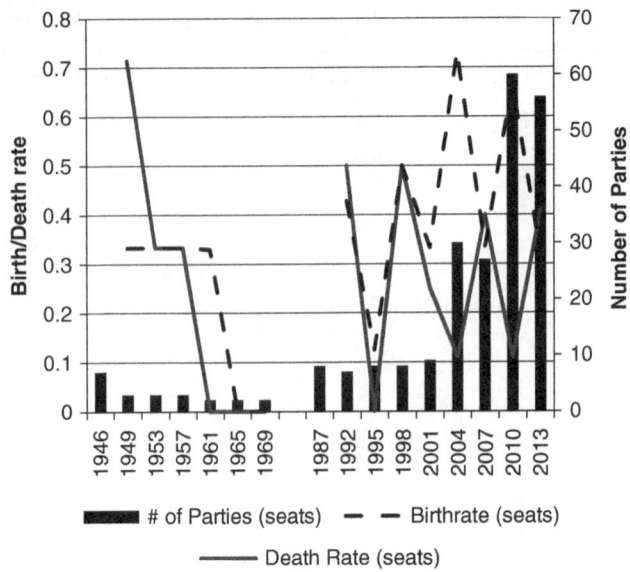

FIGURE 13.2 Party Birth and Death Rates during House Elections (Seats)

an average of only 24 percent in established democracies.[16] That dissatisfaction is strongly correlated with a distrust of the country's political parties. Only 45 percent of respondents report some confidence in Filipino political parties.[17]

Clearly, parties are viewed with some suspicion by the masses, but what about other major political actors? Do these power centers see party government as the only legitimate means to political power? Unfortunately, military intervention and coup threats continue to be prominent features of Filipino politics, with regular rumors of coup plots and actual military interventions in 1986 and 2001 to resolve political stalemates.

INTERNAL/ORGANIZATIONAL DIMENSION: VALUE INFUSION AND ORGANIZATIONAL ROUTINIZATION

How deeply rooted and organizationally strong are parties in the Philippines? One indication of the weak links between parties and cohesive societal interests in the Philippines is the high volatility scores discussed previously. Another indication of the low degree of value infusion within most parties is the lack of party loyalty manifest by large numbers of voters, even within a single election.

[16] WVS 2001; Hicken 2011.
[17] Ibid.

Filipino voters frequently split their votes between candidates from different parties. For example, Filipino voters cast two votes, one for a presidential candidate and one for a vice-presidential candidate. These votes need not be for candidates from the same political party. Taking advantage of this rule, voters frequently split their votes between two parties. As a result, the 1992, 1998, and 2010 presidential elections returned a president and vice-president from different political parties. In 1992, 2004, and 2010, the average difference between the top presidential contenders and their running mates was as much as 10 percentage points. In the 1998 election, the vote shares of the top presidential and vice-presidential running mates differed by an average of 26 percentage points.

Voter behavior during Senate elections is another indicator of the weakness of party labels. The Philippines uses a block vote (or MNTV) system to elect Senators; 12 of the 24 senators are elected every three years to six-year terms. Voters can cast up to 12 votes but are limited to one vote per candidate. The top 12 vote-getters are awarded the seats. To the extent that voters are motivated by party considerations, we would expect to see candidates from the same party receiving roughly the same number of votes. Large differences between candidates are an indication that voters have weak ties to particular parties.

The 2007 Senate election produced two large multiparty alliances: TEAM[18] Unity, a coalition of supporters of President Gloria Macapagal-Arroyo, and Genuine Opposition (GO), made up of anti-Arroyo politicians. During this election, the division between the pro- and anti-Arroyo forces was arguably the most prominent division in the electorate. And yet, when it came to their Senate votes, voters readily crossed alliance lines and/or failed to cast all of their available votes. GO candidates collectively received 50.9 percent of the total votes and 7 of the 12 seats, while TEAM Unity received 36.8 percent of the votes and 3 seats. Had voters been primarily motivated by party loyalty, we would expect one party alliance to sweep the Senate as each voter would simply vote a straight party ticket. Within each alliance, the difference between the largest and smallest vote-getters was wide. For the GO alliance, the candidate with the most votes received 3.5 times the number of votes as the last-place GO candidate. Within TEAM Unity, the gap was even larger, with the strongest candidate receiving more than five times the number of votes as the weakest candidate.

In 2013, we see a similar pattern.[19] Two large multiparty alliances formed: one centered on the sitting president Benigno Aquino III (Team PNoy) and the other on sitting vice-president Jejomar Binay and former president Joseph Estrada (the United Nationalist Alliance [UNA]). Voters once again showed little party loyalty – nine seats were filled by Team PNoy and three by the UNA.[20] For Team

---

[18] Together Everyone Achieves More.
[19] There were no large multiparty alliances for the Senate elections in 2010.
[20] Candidates were not paragons of partisan loyalty either. Three candidates appeared on the slate of both party alliances.

TABLE 13.4. *Vote Differentials between First- and Last-Place Candidates*

	1992	1995	1998	2001	2004	2007	2010	2013
Party Alliance 1	NA	1.9	4.1	2.4	6.9	3.5	NA	3.0
Party Alliance 2	NA	3.9	NA	4.6	6.1	5.1	NA	5.5
Largest Party	3.3	1.4	3.4	1.7	5.6	2.5	16.9	2.3
Second Largest party	2.2	3.5	4.1	3.1	1.8	4.2	8.4	1.6

Source: Author's calculations from election returns. The party alliances are as follows: 1995: Lakas-Laban and NPC; 1998: LAMMP; 2001: PPC and PnM; 2004: K-4 and KNP; 2007: Genuine Opposition and TEAM Unity; 2013: Team PNoy and UNA. The parties are as follows: 1992: LDP and Lakas-NUCD; 1995: Lakas-NUCD and NPC; 1998: Lakas-NUCD and LDP (the LDP was actually the fourth largest party, but the second and third largest parties ran only one or two Senate candidates in 2004); 2004: Lakas-CMD and the Liberal Party (the Liberal Party was actually the third largest party, but the second largest party, the NPC, ran only one Senate candidate in 2004); 2007: Lakas-CMD and NPC (the NPC was actually the third largest party, but the second largest party, KAMPI, ran only one Senate candidate in 2007); 2010: Lakas-Kampi and Liberal; 2013: Liberal and NPC.

PNoy, the first place vote-getter received more than three times the number of votes than the team's last-place candidate. For the UNA, the first-place finisher received 5.5 times the number of votes as the weakest candidate.

Perhaps the voters felt little attachment to these alliances – created solely for the purpose of this election. Did they exhibit more loyalty to parties within that coalition? The answer is no. The two largest parties in the 2007 election, in terms of seats in the House of Representatives, were Lakas-CMD and the Nationalist People's Coalition (NPC). The gap between the largest and smallest vote-getters for each party in the Senate elections was 2.5 times and 4.4 times the number of votes respectively. The numbers are similar for other Senate elections, as displayed in Table 13.4. For each election, I list the vote differentials between the largest and smallest vote-getters for the two largest party alliances and for the two largest parties (according to seats in the House) that ran more than two candidates in the Senate election. Similar to presidential contests voters, once again, exhibit little attachment to a particular party.

Another indication of the degree of value inclusion is politicians' loyalty to their party. Like voters, politicians in the Philippines are politically promiscuous. Party switching is a common occurrence and politicians often claim affiliation with multiple parties simultaneously. This party switching, or turncoatism, as it is called in the Philippines, occurs at all levels of elected office from president (Magsaysay, Marcos, and Ramos each switched parties prior to winning the presidency) to local officials. Below the level of president and vice-president, the vast majority of turncoats switch from the opposition to the president's party in an effort to secure some of the many resources and favors the president possesses. In fact, within the House of Representatives, enough party switching can occur to change the status of the president's party from the minority to the majority party, as happened after the election of Presidents Macapagal, Marcos, Aquino, and Ramos.[21]

Other indications show that party labels mean little to candidates. For example, a significant number of candidates regularly run as independents. Other candidates accept guest candidatures – an offer to run under a party's banner without formally switching parties. Still others run under more than one party banner – sometimes opting to run as a standard carrier for both the government and one of the opposition parties.[22]

Another indicator of value infusion is the extent to which political parties are clearly associated with particular societal interests. Two questions are especially germane: (1) To what extent do parties rely on different/distinct constituencies? (2) Can we differentiate one party from another on the basis of its policy platform? Traditionally, the ties between Philippine parties and identifiable societal interests and voter groups have been weak. Few voters, for example, identify with any political party. In one survey, two-thirds of respondents reported that no party truly promoted their welfare.[23] The broadest support any one party received in the survey was 8 percent. Philippine parties are generally ephemeral alliances of locally focused politicians, as opposed to cohesive political parties with distinct policy visions. In fact, one of the defining characteristics of the party system is the enduring lack of policy or ideological vision among most political parties.[24] When asked to describe the difference between political parties, a Filipino high school student tellingly quipped, "I do not believe one species of mud can be very different from another."[25]

There are, of course, some exceptions to this pattern. A few parties on the left and parties that run for party list seats tend to have clearer ties to identifiable constituencies and party platforms that are programmatically distinct. However, these parties have performed poorly at the polls (in the case of the left) or are constitutionally prohibited from having more than three seats in the House (in the case of party list parties).

In terms of organizational routinization, parties in the Philippines have yet to develop party organizations that matter.[26] Parties function almost entirely as electoral vehicles for powerful individuals. Parties are highly factionalized and noticeably devoid of any lasting autonomous organizational structures. In between elections parties cease to operate for all intents and purposes, with very little in the way of active connections to party "members." The internal governance structure of parties is also notoriously weak. Members who deviate from the party line (when there is one) are rarely sanctioned. Finally,

---

[21] Liang 1970; Banlaoi and Carlos 1996; Landé 1996; Hicken 2009.
[22] Hicken 2009.
[23] SWS 2006.
[24] Hicken 2011.
[25] Quoted in Sicat 1973: 97.
[26] Mainwaring and Scully 1995.

responsibility for and control of financing is decentralized, usually completely bypassing the formal party organization.[27] Philippines scholar Nathan Quimpo (2005) summarizes the state of Philippine parties in this way: "Far from being stable, programmatic organizations, the country's main political parties are nebulous entities that can be set up, merged with others, split, resurrected, regurgitated, reconstituted, renamed, repackaged, recycled or flushed down the toilet anytime."

In short, by virtually every measure, political parties and the party system exhibit low levels of institutionalization. On the external/systemic dimension, the pattern of interparty competition remains fluid, while it is not at all clear that the major actors in society, including voters, accept parties as legitimate and necessary. On the internal/organizational dimension, little evidence of value infusion exists – parties are not strongly rooted in society and do not have well-defined and distinct party platforms. Organizationally, parties tend to be feeble, factionalized, and fleeting.

EXPLAINING INSTITUTIONALIZATION

Sociohistorical Roots

A growing body of work examines how the political system in the Philippines (including the party system) was shaped by the manner in which democracy unfolded.[28] This is consistent with Mainwaring and Zoco's (2007) emphasis on the link between the timing of democratic transition and institutionalization, As discussed in the Introduction, they argue that there is a distinct difference between early and late democratizers. In early democratizers, political parties were mobilizing institutions – incorporating new citizens into the political system and pushing for an expansion of suffrage and other rights for those citizens. This helped forge strong links between parties and the citizens they helped mobilize. By contrast, in later democratizers, the move to competitive elections and the formation of new parties formation were preceded by, or occurred in conjunction with, the adoption of universal suffrage. As a result, parties did not have to become mobilizing institutions, and, consequently, the kinds of links and networks that characterized early democratizers never developed.[29]

On the surface, one might expect the Philippines to bear characteristics of an early democratizer. After all, democratic elections were introduced as early as 1906. However, the manner in which those elections were introduced is crucial. They were not the result of a victory of newly mobilized social forces over an entrenched elite, nor did they reflect a compromise between social forces and the

---

[27] de Castro 1992; Carlos 1997.
[28] This section draws on chapter 5 of Hicken 2009.
[29] Ibid.

elite. In either scenario, mobilization in pursuit of democracy might have laid the groundwork for institutionalized parties. Instead, democratic elections with universal male suffrage were imposed by the American colonial administration after it had defeated an indigenous independence movement and prior to the development of other mass mobilization efforts. In addition, early elections, the relatively benign colonial administration, and the promise of independence combined to undermine the development of a strong independence movement that might have formed the basis for strong, institutionalized political parties. So, despite the early arrival of elections, the Philippines looks a lot like a late democratizer – democratic elections being introduced prior to the development of the tradition or institutions of mass politics.

Several of the U.S. colonial government's decisions had the unintended consequence of hampering the development of a more institutionalized, cohesive, nationally oriented party system.[30] First, while the United States installed democratic institutions in the Philippines, it did very little to build up a strong central administrative bureaucracy.[31] As a result, political and economic power remained spread among a large land-owning elite throughout the country. This land-owning elite, known as the oligarchs, became the patrons atop numerous patron-client networks spread throughout the Philippines.[32]

Second, the early introduction of elections in the Philippines reproduced the decentralized and fragmented nature of political life at the national level.[33] As the political system was thrown open to electoral competition, those in the best position to compete for elected office were the oligarchs. They were able to use elections as a means of acquiring and strengthening political power, first locally, then nationally via congressional elections.[34] Political parties and Congress quickly became the domain of these powerful locally based interests, rather than a forum in which mass interests could be articulated and national policies debated.[35] In sum, the parties that came to dominate the political system were not cohesive parties with national constituencies, but internally mobilized,[36] highly fragmented parties with narrow, particularistic constituencies.

The interaction of the Philippine social structure, colonial administration, and early elections made the early institutionalization unlikely. However, this cannot completely explain why key features of the party system have endured in the Philippines for more than a century. Much has changed in the intervening hundred years, and many of these changes would seemingly auger well for the emergence of a more institutionalized party system. For example, by the 1960s,

[30] Hutchcroft and Rocamora 2003.
[31] Hutchcroft 2000.
[32] Tancango 1992.
[33] Hutchcroft and Rocamora 2003.
[34] Landé 1965; Anderson 1988; Wurfel 1988; Hutchcroft and Rocamora 2003.
[35] For an analysis of the policy consequences of this arrangement, see Sidel 1996 and Hutchcroft 1998.
[36] Shefter 1994.

traditional patron-client networks were breaking down, beginning first in and around Manila and then spreading to other areas of the Philippines.[37] Likewise, a new class of business elites had emerged to challenge the power of the oligarchs. This business elite (largely Manila based) had interests that were far different from those of the traditional landed elite.[38]

One could argue that path dependence might account for the stickiness of the party system in the face of these and other changes. However, given the political, economic, and social upheaval of the Marcos era, it is not difficult to imagine that new paths were at least possible following his fall from power. First, under Marcos, the relative decline of the oligarchs accelerated as he sought to centralize political and economic authority while empowering a new class of cronies.[39] Second, in their attempt to oust Marcos, opposition political parties joined together to back Corazon Aquino for president. They were supported by a large, mobilized segment of the Filipino populace. Yet, this mass mobilization and relative decline of the oligarchs did not lead to the creation of large, mass-based parties after the fall. Nor did the coming together of different opposition groups to overthrow Marcos translate into more cohesive parties post-Marcos. Instead, as discussed earlier, the party system that emerged was similar in most respects to the pre-1972 party system. One explanation for the continuity of the party system, despite the significant changes that occurred before and during the Marcos era, is the continuity of key features of the Philippine institutional environment, along with the strategic use of institutional reforms designed to keep the level of institutionalization low.[40]

Institutional Obstacles – Continuities

Alongside the historical and sociological factors discussed earlier, certain features of the Philippine electoral environment have discouraged the development of greater institutionalization.[41] This environment has remained relatively

---

[37] Wurfel 1988.

[38] Hawes 1992.

[39] Ibid. For an opposing view (i.e., that the reports of oligarchs' deaths were highly exaggerated), see Putzel 1993.

[40] The unwillingness of Aquino to capitalize on her popularity to form her own political party or take over the leadership of an existing party also likely contributed to the return of an under-institutionalized party system.

[41] A number of Philippines scholars blame the state of the party system on the establishment of a strong president (see, e.g., Grossholtz 1964; Wurfel 1988; Banlaoi and Carlos 1996). A powerful presidency, so the argument goes, undermines party cohesiveness, frees legislators and parties to focus on particularistic concerns (leaving national policies in the hands of the president), and generally discourages the development of an institutionalized party system. This observation is not unique to the Philippines – presidentialism is often associated with weak and non-cohesive legislative parties (Lijphart et al. 1993: 322; Samuels and Shugart 2010). However, I discount a powerful president as a significant causal variable for two reasons. First, Mainwaring and Zoco (2007) find no relationship between presidentialism and institutionalization once they control for

constant across the pre- and post-authoritarian periods and reinforced, and in some cases amplified, the effects of sociological and historical factors. Specifically, the electoral systems for both the House and Senate give voters strong incentives to place person before party and candidates an incentive to pursue a personal strategy while discounting the value of a party label. I have already discussed the method for electing the Senate. This method encourages senatorial candidates to eschew party strategies in favor of personal strategies. Senate elections are first and foremost personality contests, and senators generally possess little party loyalty. Multiple votes allow voters to split their votes among senatorial candidates from different parties – something that Filipino voters frequently take advantage of.

Elections for the House of Representatives are only slightly better. In House elections, single-seat districts – by themselves often associated with weak parties – are combined with a system that gives party leaders little control over their members' behavior and even over who runs under the party banner. For example, candidates are not required to obtain the nomination or endorsement of a political party to run for office. Candidates may run as independents or under the banner of more than one party.[42] Party officials often lack strong control over nominations and endorsements within their own party. Strong candidates can usually run under the label of their choosing. In some cases, strong/wealthy candidates will use a party's label with or without the party's official endorsement.[43] Some districts even feature multiple candidates claiming to represent the same party, giving rise to intraparty competition.[44] Finally, candidates and politicians are free to switch parties at virtually any time without penalty. All in all, the system is one in which there are few payoffs to either voters or candidates for investing in, or even paying attention to, political parties.

Institutional Obstacles – Interventions

In addition to the unfavorable electoral incentives – a constant throughout the democratic periods – a few key institutional interventions have had the effect of arresting any incipient institutionalization. Two of these interventions were not direct attempts to shape the party system and institutionalization, but the consequences were nonetheless profound. Two other interventions were strategically calculated to prevent the development of a stronger party system, and they have been fairly successful at doing so.

> other factors. Second, if there is a relationship, then some uncertainty exists about which way the arrows run. A strong presidency may hinder the rise of an institutionalized party system, but it may also be employed as an institutional antidote in polities with under-institutionalized party systems (Shugart 1999). In fact, the effort of the Philippines' first president, Manuel Quezon, to guarantee a powerful presidency was, in part, a reaction to the perceived shortcomings of the party system (Quezon 1940).

[42] See the earlier discussion of guest and joint candidacies.
[43] Wurfel 1988: 96
[44] Kasuya 2001.

The first two interventions that indirectly affected the party system were Marcos's actions under martial law and the introduction of a single term limit for the president after the fall of Marcos. As discussed in the Introduction, we know that the types of strategies adopted by dictators during authoritarian interludes have important consequences for post-authoritarian party system.[45] Had Marcos simply banned or repressed the Liberal and Nacionalista Parties during his rule, experience elsewhere in the world suggests that voter loyalties might have remained more or less intact, and the Liberals and Nacionalistas would have reemerged as strong parties when democratic elections returned. Instead, Marcos eventually coupled the banning of existing parties with the creation of his own electoral vehicle – the Kilusang Bagong Lipunan (KBL). Past experience predicts that such parties will tend to attract supporters and candidates at the expense of the traditional parties, but once democratic elections return, the party system tends to fragment as the artificially created new party falls apart. Indeed, this is precisely what happened in the Philippines. After the fall of Marcos, the former two-party system fragmented, the Liberals and Nacionalistas never fully regained their former strength, and the KBL quickly lost most of its support.

After the excesses of the Marcos years, it is not surprising that reformers put in place a number of constitutional provisions designed to limit the power of future presidents and would-be dictators. Key among these reforms was the introduction of a ban on reelection.[46] This had two (unintended) effects on the party system.[47] First, it undermined the incentives of sitting presidents to invest in party building. Why build an organization from which you are not going to be able to directly benefit? Second, it led to an increase in the number of presidential candidates and a corresponding increase in the number, birth rate, and death rate of political parties. Prior to martial law, the presence of a presidential incumbent with control of government resources encouraged coalescence around two large parties. Would-be challengers from within the government ranks had incentives to stay put, while the opposition faced strong incentives to back a single challenger to maximize its chances of defeating the incumbent. With the end of presidential incumbency, the incentives have greatly diminished, contributing to less party discipline, more factionalism, and a larger number of short-lived parties, as demonstrated earlier.

Finally, two reforms seem to have been specifically designed to thwart progress toward greater institutionalization. Shortly after independence, the election code was revised to allow for party voting. Rather than writing individual candidates' names, as had been the norm in the past, voters could write in the name of a party, and the ballot would be "deemed as a vote for each and every one of the official candidates of such party for the respective offices"

---

[45] Geddes and Franz 2007.
[46] Prior to martial law, presidents were limited to two terms.
[47] Choi 2001; Hicken 2009.

(Revised Election Code of 1947, Article XI, Section 149, No. 19). Had this option remained in effect, it is intriguing to consider whether voters might have developed stronger ties to particular parties, and whether parties might not have increased their efforts to win those party votes. However, politicians acted quickly to return to the status quo, amending the Election Code in 1951 to eliminate the party voting option.[48] Voters were once again required to write in the name of each of their chosen candidates for every elected office. Given that local and national elections are synchronized, this can mean that voters must write in up to 40 names on election day.[49] This cumbersome ballot structure provided voters with ample opportunities to split their votes between many parties, thus undermining the value of a party label. The introduction of electronic voting in 2010 meant that voters no longer had to write in names by hand, but they still lacked the option of casting a single vote for a party slate.

Finally, the adoption of a mixed member system, ostensibly to provide for better representation of marginalized voters and stronger ties between parties and their supporters, has arguably arrested progress toward greater institutionalization. A provision for a mixed member system was included in the 1987 Constitution. This was, in part, a response to the unprecedented level of mass mobilization and civil society activity in the wake of the People Power revolution. Reformers proposed the adoption of a German-style mixed member system that would allow new interests to be heard in the House of Representatives. However, the law fully implementing the measure was not passed until 1995 and not used in an election until 1998. In the intervening 11 years, much of the mass/civil society fervor had understandably waned.

In addition, opponents of the reforms were able to water down the provision substantially and minimize the impact on the existing party system. Rather than a German-style legislature with one-half of the seats allocated on the basis of party lists using proportional representation (PR), the Philippines reserves only 20 percent of the total House seats for the party list. Both political parties and sectoral organizations can compete for the seats. However, the five largest parties from the previous election are barred from competing. To obtain a seat, parties (or sectoral organizations) must receive at least 2 percent of the PR votes. For every 2 percent of the vote, a party is awarded a seat. No party or group can receive more than three seats via the list tier. The limit on the number of seats and the ban on mainstream parties competing has effectively kept the impact of these changes to a minimum. Whereas the party list provision has probably resulted in more diverse interests being elected to Congress, it has also

---

[48] Wurfel 1988: 94.

[49] For this reason, the distribution of sample ballots to voters becomes extremely important. Prior to elections, most candidates distribute sample ballots containing their name and the names of candidates for other offices. Tellingly, it is not uncommon for these sample ballots to contain the names of candidates from more than one party. Candidates often include popular candidates from other parties running in other races on their sample ballot in a bid to bolster their own electoral prospects.

partially ghettoized those interests. Mainstream political parties and politicians seem largely content to leave programmatic campaigning and the representation of marginalized interests to party list groups. At the same time, the low 2 percent threshold and 3-seat limit has led to an explosion of new, small parties in recent years.

CONCLUSION

One of the goals of this chapter was to demonstrate that the Philippine party system is relatively under-institutionalized. The data assembled here all point in the same direction – toward a low level of institutionalization. What is harder to do, particularly in the context of a single case, is to parse out the reasons for the lack of institutionalization. I have argued that the introduction of early elections in an environment rich in oligarchic elite but lacking a mobilized citizenry or mass organizations hindered institutionalization. The adoption of a particular set of electoral institutions reinforced this tendency. And finally, a few institutional interventions at key times undermined incentives toward further institutionalization. Three of these interventions, namely the creation of the KBL, the ban on presidential reelection, and the peculiarities of the party list system, also help explain why the pre– and post–martial law party systems differ in some respects.

So, in conclusion, why should we care about the level of institutionalization? We can observe differences in the level of institutionalization from country to country, but does it really matter for things we ultimately care about? Elsewhere I have argued that the level of institutionalization might affect democratic governance.[50] Specifically, I argue that under-institutionalized party systems are generally a hindrance to democratic consolidation and good governance in at least three ways. First, where parties and party systems are under-institutionalized, politicians will tend to have narrow constituencies and short time horizons – both of which are problematic for the provision of needed public goods. Second, a lack of party system institutionalization undermines the ability of voters to hold politicians individually and collectively accountable.[51] Finally, where party institutionalization is low, the disillusionment with the extant system might eventually produce ambivalence among some voters about the relative merits of the democratic status quo versus strong, decisive, albeit less democratic, leadership. This ambivalence, combined with weak party loyalties, may provide opportunities for antidemocratic/anti-party politicians to rise to power (e.g., Thaksin and Marcos).[52]

---

[50] Hicken 2008a, 2009.
[51] See also Mainwaring and Torcal 2006.
[52] Ibid.

REFERENCES

Anderson, Benedict. 1988. Cacique Democracy in the Philippines: Origins and Dreams. *New Left Review* 169: 3–33.

Banlaoi, Rommel C., and Clarita R. Carlos. 1996. *Political Parties in the Philippines: From 1900 to the Present*. Makati: Konrad Adenauer Foundation.

Brownlee, Jason. 2008. Bound to Rule: Party Institutions and Regime Trajectories in Malaysia and the Philippines. *Journal of Southeast Asian Studies* 8(1): 89–118.

Carlos, Clarita R. 1997. *Dynamics of Political Parties in the Philippines*. Makati: Konrad Adenauer Foundation.

Choi, Jungug. 2001. Philippine Democracies Old and New: Elections, Term Limits, and Party Systems. *Asian Survey* 41: 488–501.

Commission on Elections (COMELEC). 1992. *Report of the Commission on Elections to the President and Congress of the Republic of the Philippines on the Conduct of the Synchronized National and Local Elections of May 11, 1992*. Manila: Commission on Elections.

Commission on Elections (COMELEC). 1995. *Report of the Commission on Elections to His Excellency President Fidel V. Ramos and to Congress of the Republic of the Philippines on the Conduct of the National and Local Elections of May 8, 1992*. Manila: Commission on Elections.

Commission on Elections (COMELEC). 1998. *Election Results from the 1998 National and Local Elections. Data on Diskette*. Manila: Commission on Elections.

Commission on Elections (COMELEC). 2001. Election Results from the 2001 National and Local Elections. http://www.comelec.gov.ph/results_main.html.

Commission on Elections (COMELEC). 2004. Election Results from the 2004 National and Local Elections. http://www.comelec.gov.ph/results_main.html.

de Castro, Isagani, Jr. 1992. Money and Moguls: Oiling the Campaign Machinery. In Lornal Kalaw-Tirol and Sheila S. Colonel (Eds.), *1992 & Beyond: Forces and Issues in Philippine Elections*, pp. 36–78. Quezon City: Philippine Center for Investigative Journalism and Ateneo Center for Social Policy and Public Affairs.

Geddes, Barbara, and Erica Frantz. 2007. The Effect of Dictatorships on Party Systems in Latin America. Unpublished manuscript, UCLA.

Grossholtz, Jean. 1964. *Politics in the Philippines: A Country Study*. Boston: Little, Brown and Company.

Hartmann, Christof, Graham Hassall, and Soliman M. Santos Jr. 2001. Philippines. In Dieter Nohlen et al. (Eds.), *Elections in Asia and the Pacific: A Data Handbook. Volume II South East Asia, East*, pp. 185–238. Oxford: Oxford University Press.

Hawes, Gary. 1992. Marcos, His Cronies and the Philippines Failure to Develop. In Ruth McVey (Ed.), *Southeast Asian Capitalists*, pp. 145–160. Ithaca: Cornell Southeast Asia Program.

Hicken, Allen. 2008a. The Politics of Economic Recovery in Thailand and the Philippines. In Andrew MacIntyre, T. J. Pempel, and John Ravenhill (Eds.), *Crisis as Catalyst Asia's Dynamic Political Economy*, pp. 206–230. Ithaca: Cornell University Press.

Hicken, Allen. 2008b. Political Engineering and Party Regulation in Southeast Asia. In Benjamin Reilly et al. (Eds.), *Political Parties in Conflict-Prone Societies: Regulation, Engineering and Democratic Development*, pp. 69–94. New York: United Nations University Press.

Hicken, Allen. 2009. *Building Party Systems in Developing Democracies*. New York: Cambridge University Press.

Hicken, Allen. 2011. Political Parties and Party Systems in Southeast Asia. In Aurel Croissant and Marco Bunte (Eds.), *The Crisis of Democratic Governance in Southeast Asia*,pp. 151–170. New York: Palgrave Macmillan.

Hicken, Allen, and Erik Kuhonta. 2011. Reexamining Party Institutionalization through Asian Lenses. *Comparative Political Studies* 44(5): 572–597.

Huntington, Samuel P. 1968. *Political Order in Changing Societies*. New Haven: Yale University Press.

Hutchcroft, Paul D. 1998. *Booty Capitalism: The Politics of Banking in the Philippines*. Ithaca: Cornell University Press.

Hutchcroft, Paul D. 2000. Colonial Masters, National Politicos, and Provincial Lords: Central Authority and Local Autonomy in the American Philippines, 1900–1913. *Journal of Asian Studies* 59(2): 277–306.

Hutchcroft, Paul, and Joel Rocamora. 2003. Strong Demands and Weak Institutions: The Origins and Evolution of the Democratic Deficit in the Philippines. *Journal of East Asian Studies* 3(2): 259–292.

Kasuya, Yuko. 2001. Presidential Connection: Parties and Party Systems in the Philippines. Presented at the Annual Meeting of the Association for Asian Studies, Chicago, March 23–25.

Landé, Carl H. 1965. *Leaders, Factions, and Parties*. New Haven: Southeast Asian Studies, Yale University.

Landé, Carl H.1996. *Post-Marcos Politics: A Geographic and Statistical Analysis of the 1992 Philippine Elections*. Singapore: Institute of Southeast Asian Studies.

Levitsky, Steven. 1998. Institutionalization and Peronism: The Concept, The Case and the Case for Unpacking the Concept. *Party Politics* 4(1): 77–92.

Liang, Dapen. 1970. *Philippine Parties and Politics: A Historical Study of National Experience in Democracy*. San Francisco: The Gladstone Company.

Lijphart, Arend, Ronald Rogowski, and Kent Weaver. 1993. Separation of Powers and Cleavage Management. In R. Kent Weaver and Bert A. Rockman (Eds.), *Do Institutions Matter: Government in the United States and Abroad*, pp. 302–344. Washington, DC: The Brookings Institution.

Mainwaring, Scott, and Timothy Scully. 1995. Introduction. In Scott Mainwaring and Timothy Scully (Eds.), *Building Democratic Institutions: Party Systems in Latin America*, pp. 1–36. Stanford: Stanford University Press.

Mainwaring, Scott, and Mariano Torcal. 2006. Party System Institutionalization and Party System Theory after the Third Wave of Democratization. In Richard S. Katz and William Crotty (Eds.), *Handbook of Political Parties*, pp. 204–227. London: Sage Publications.

Mainwaring, Scott, and Edurne Zoco. 2007. Historical Sequences and the Stabilization of Interparty Competition: Electoral Volatility in Old and New Democracies. *Party Politics* 13(2): 155–178.

Montinola, Gabriella. 1999. Parties and Accountability in the Philippines. *Journal of Democracy* 10(1): 126–140.

Panebianco, Angelo. 1988. *Political Parties: Organization and Power*. Cambridge: Cambridge University Press.

Putzel, James. 1993. Democratisation and Clan Politics: The 1992 Philippine Elections. Mimeo.

Quezon, Manuel L. 1940. *Addresses of His Excellency Manuel L. Quezon on the Theory of a Partyless Democracy.* Manila: Bureau of Print.

Quimpo, Nathan Gilbert. 2005. Yellow Pad: Trapo Parties and Corruption. *BusinessWorld*, October 10, page S1/5. Accessed at http://aer.ph/trapo-parties-and-corruption/.

Randall, Vicky, and Lars Svasand,. 2002. Party Institutionalization in New Democracies. *Party Politics* 8(1): 5–29.

Samuels, David J., and Matthew S. Shugart. 2010. *Presidents, Parties, Prime Ministers: How the Separation of Powers Affects Party Organization and Behavior.* New York: Cambridge University Press.

Shefter, Martin. 1994. *Political Parties and the State: The American Historical Experience.* Princeton: Princeton University Press.

Shugart, Matthew Soberg. 1999. Presidentialism, Parliamentarism, and Provision of Public Goods in Less-Developed Countries. *Constitutional Political Economy* 10(1): 53–88.

Sicat, Loreta M. 1973. The "Fair Hope of the Fatherland." *Philippine Journal of Public Administration* 17 (October): 437.

Sidel, John T. 1996. *Capital Coercion and Crime: Bossism in the Philippines.* Stanford: Stanford University Press.

Slater, Dan. 2003. Iron Cage in an Iron Fist: Authoritarian Institutions and the Personalization of Power in Malaysia. *Comparative Politics* 36(1): 81–101.

SWS. 2006. *Attitudes towards Political Parties in the Philippines.* A joint production of Social Weather Stations, Ateneo School of Government, with the Support of the Konrad Adenauer Stiftung. Available from www.kas.de/wf/doc/kas_10415-544-2-30.pdf. Accessed May 8, 2008.

Tancangco, Luzviminda. 1992. *The Anatomy of Electoral Fraud.* Manila: MLAGM.

Ufen, Andreas. 2008. Political Party and Party System Institutionalization in Southeast Asia: Lessons for Democratic Consolidation in Indonesia, the Philippines and Thailand. *The Pacific Review* 21(3): 327–350.

Welfling, Mary B. 1973. *Political Institutionalization: Comparative Analyses of African Party Systems.* Beverly Hills: Sage Publications,

Wurfel, David. 1988. *Filipino Politics: Development and Decay.* Ithaca: Cornell University Press.

WVS (World Values Survey). 2001. http://www.worldvaluessurvey.org/.

14

Party System Institutionalization: Reflections Based on the Asian Cases

Scott Mainwaring*

In this concluding chapter, I offer some reflections on party system institutionalization based on the Asian cases examined in this volume. I take up four themes that are central to the book. First, I analyze why party system institutionalization remains an important theme for political scientists. In democracies and semi-democracies, some of the most important differences among party systems revolve around variance in institutionalization. Differences in party system institutionalization have important consequences both in competitive and authoritarian regimes.

Second, I argue that the most fundamental distinction among the cases analyzed in this volume is among competitive party systems, hegemonic party systems, and party-state systems. Competitive party systems are anchored in semi-democratic or democratic regimes. Elections are the route to executive and legislative power, and they are organized primarily around parties. Parties also structure legislatures in these systems. Hence, they are key to gaining access to power and to governing. Hegemonic party systems and party-state systems function within authoritarian regimes. Parties are important in these systems, but elections are not the primary route to executive or legislative power. Parties perform different functions in these nondemocratic regimes. Failure to observe a distinction among these three kinds of systems can lead to conceptual confusion and measurement problems, and to difficulty in understanding the relationship between party system institutionalization and democracy.

* I am grateful to Allen Hicken and Erik Kuhonta for very helpful suggestions and for encouraging me to write this chapter. Thanks also to T. J. Cheng, Victoria Hui, Benjamin Smith, Netina Tan, and Meredith Weiss for helpful comments and to María Victoria De Negri for research assistance. Six paragraphs in this chapter are slightly revised versions of material in Mainwaring 1999: 22–39, which in turn leaned on Mainwaring and Scully 1995. Mainwaring and Torcal 2006 also developed the themes discussed here.

Third, I define institutionalization and briefly discuss four dimensions of the institutionalization of competitive party systems: (1) the level of stability in interparty competition, (2) the strength of linkages binding voters to parties, (3) the degree to which voters perceive parties as necessary elements of democracy, and (4) the solidity of party organizations. These four dimensions are not equally valid measures for hegemonic party systems or party-state systems. For example, low electoral volatility in a democracy shows that in the aggregate, voters choose election after election to support the same parties. It is a clear measure of the stability of interparty competition. In an authoritarian regime, low electoral volatility may register voters' lack of choice, and it does not consistently indicate the distribution of voters' sincere preferences or stability of such preferences.

Finally, I examine the relationship between the level of institutionalization and democracy. I agree with Hicken and Kuhonta (in the Introduction to this volume) that it is a mistake to conflate democracy and party system institutionalization. The institutionalization of a party system is not necessarily good for democracy. The institutionalization of a hegemonic or a party-state system in the short to medium term precludes the possibility of democratization.

WHY STUDY PARTY SYSTEM INSTITUTIONALIZATION?

Work on party system institutionalization has burgeoned in the past two decades. The concept gave scholars a new way to draw distinctions among and to compare party systems.

Before the Third Wave of democratization, Sartori's (1976) classic typology based on the number of parties and ideological polarization arguably covered the most important dimensions for comparing competitive party systems. The world's set of democracies was limited in number,[1] and all of them had fairly highly institutionalized party systems, as was suggested by Lipset and Rokkan's (1967) notion of "frozen" party systems. Because variance in institutionalization was limited, the concept did not capture important cross-country differences among competitive party systems.

This situation changed with the Third Wave of democratization. Sartori's two axes for comparing party systems neglected a highly important difference among the greatly expanded set of the world's competitive party systems. Italy, France, Spain, and Portugal,[2] on the one hand, and Brazil and Peru in the late 1980s, on the other, all had polarized multiparty systems and hence by Sartori's criteria were all cases of polarized pluralism. But the dynamics of the party systems were very different. Italy, France, Spain, and Portugal had stable systems with moderate electoral volatility. The same main parties competed election after election.

---

[1] Dahl 1971: 248 listed only 28 democracies (he called them "polyarchies") in the world as of 1969.
[2] See Sani and Sartori 1983 on polarization in Italy, France, Spain, and Portugal.

In contrast, Brazil and Peru in the 1980s had unstable party systems with very high electoral volatility. Political outsiders running on new party labels won the presidency in Brazil in 1989 and in Peru in 1990, reflecting the deep discrediting of the existing parties. Major parties suffered huge electoral losses. For example, after winning an absolute majority of seats in both chambers of the national congress in the 1986 elections, Brazil's largest party, the Party of the Brazilian Democratic Movement (PMDB) won only 4.7 percent of the vote in the 1989 presidential election. In Peru, the instability of the system in the 1980s presaged its collapse in the 1990s, as the major parties of the 1980s became irrelevant contenders. A comparison of the Brazilian and Peruvian party systems with the aforementioned four European systems based on the number of parties and the level of polarization would have missed these radical differences in institutionalization. These differences produced very different political dynamics including the breakdown of democracy in Peru in 1992.[3]

It is not only as a way of comparing and conceptualizing differences across party systems that institutionalization became a useful concept. It is also helpful for explaining differences in some important outcomes. In Chapter 13 on the Philippines, Hicken argues that weak party systems under democracy narrow politicians' time horizons with adverse consequences for the provision of public goods; make it more difficult for voters to hold politicians accountable; and in cases of poor governance, can open the doors to anti-democratic populists. Flores Macías (2012) argued that party system institutionalization is central to understanding important differences in leftist governments' economic policies across contemporary Latin America. Institutionalized party systems constrain presidents, make it difficult for radical outsiders to come to power, and favor more moderate policies.[4] Smith (2005) argued that institutionalization of the ruling party enables authoritarian regimes to withstand crises. Moser and Scheiner (2012) showed that the effects of electoral systems vary considerably according to how institutionalized the party system is.

Because it has been a useful concept both for comparing and classifying and for explanation, many scholars who studied Latin America, Africa, and the post-Soviet region have analyzed party system institutionalization. However, as Hicken and Kuhonta note in Chapter 1, until recently, scholars of Asia had not joined this debate as much as scholars of other developing regions.[5]

While following an established research tradition on this subject, *Party System Institutionalization in Asia* breaks new ground. It extends the geographic

---

[3] Weak institutionalization of the Peruvian party system did not directly lead to the democratic breakdown. It did, however, enable the election of political outsider Alberto Fujimori in 1990. Fujimori presided over and was directly responsible for the breakdown of democracy.

[4] Institutionalized party systems blocked the road to radical populist left politics in Brazil, Chile, and Uruguay. In contrast, weakly institutionalized systems enabled leftist populists to come to power and implement more radical economic policies in Bolivia, Ecuador, and Venezuela in the 2000s.

[5] See Stockton 2001; Johnson 2002; Hicken 2006; Tan 2006; Ufen 2008; Croissant and Völkel 2012 for earlier works on party system institutionalization in Asia.

scope of work on this subject to many of Asia's important countries. In addition, this is the first volume that examines party system institutionalization across competitive and hegemonic party systems and party-state systems. This broad inclusion of cases across competitive, hegemonic, and party state systems suggests important new questions for the political science research agenda. How well do the concept and measurement of institutionalization travel across these different cases? How should we measure institutionalization in hegemonic and party-state systems? Does the institutionalization of a hegemonic party system or a party-state system favor or hinder the subsequent institutionalization of a competitive party system? This volume does not resolve these questions, but it has the great merit of opening a debate on them.

COMPETITIVE AND HEGEMONIC PARTY SYSTEMS AND PARTY-STATE SYSTEMS

In the Introduction, Hicken and Kuhonta argue for comparing institutionalization across different party systems in Asia. There is much to be gained from this endeavor, but we risk conceptual confusion, measurement problems, and misunderstanding causal relationships if we do not at the same time distinguish among competitive party systems, hegemonic party systems, and party-state systems. The most fundamental distinction among the cases analyzed in this volume is among these three basic types of systems. If we do not distinguish among them, we will not be able to understand the relationship between party or party system institutionalization and democracy. Nor will we properly conceptualize and measure institutionalization in hegemonic party systems and party-state systems.

The differences revolve around the fairness and competitiveness of elections and, by implication, around the political regime. As conceptualized here, a competitive party system means much more than the existence of some electoral competition. In competitive systems, elections determine who governs. Competitive party systems function in what Mainwaring et al. (2007) call democratic and semi-democratic regimes.[6]

In competitive systems, at least two parties compete in reasonably free and fair elections. These systems afford a real possibility of alternation in power, and they have a history of alternation.[7] Opposition victories are respected, and the

---

[6] The four defining characteristics of a democracy are that (1) free and fair elections determine who wins executive and legislative power; (2) the suffrage includes almost all of the citizen adult population; (3) there is solid protection of civil liberties and political rights, and the institutions designed to protect these rights are relatively unfettered; and (4) the military is under civilian control. Semi-democratic regimes involve some partial violations of at least one of these four principles of democracy, but elections are still truly competitive. Nondemocratic regimes involve a major violation of at least one of those four principles of democracy. See Mainwaring et al. 2007 for an extended discussion.

[7] Japan from 1955 until 1993 was an exception, but the LDP eventually lost power. On the long-term dominance of Japan's LDP, see Chapter 4 of this volume.

playing field is reasonably level. Parties other than the governing party almost always have at a minimum a substantial minority of seats in the national legislature, and they govern some important subnational jurisdictions (e.g., states, large cities). Among the countries covered in this volume, Japan (Chapter 4), Taiwan (Chapter 5), India (Chapter 8), Indonesia (Chapter 10), South Korea (Chapter 11), Thailand (Chapter 12), and the Philippines (Chapter 13) have competitive party systems.

The second basic category analyzed in this volume is a hegemonic party system. Sartori (1976: 230) defined hegemonic party systems as "one-party centered and yet display[ing] a periphery of secondary and indeed second-class minor parties ... The hegemonic party neither allows for formal nor de facto competition for power. Other parties are permitted to exist, but as second class, licensed parties." I modify one part of his definition: hegemonic parties allow for formal competition for power. Minor parties compete, and they win some seats. If there is no formal competition for power or if the minor parties are mere shams, then we have a party-state system, not a hegemonic party system. But in hegemonic party systems, the formal competition for power occurs within limits well described by Sartori: "Not only does alternation not occur in fact; it cannot occur, since the possibility of a rotation in power is not even envisaged ... The hegemonic party will remain in power whether it is liked or not" (1976: 230).

Hegemonic party systems function within authoritarian regimes. The winner is known ex-ante, and there are limits to competition. As Meredith L. Weiss writes in Chapter 2 on Malaysia, "We can be reasonably confident that the BN [Barisan National Front] will win at the federal level ... Elections have developed ... to pacify and depoliticize the population." There is more than one party, but the governing party benefits from a highly uneven playing field. Weiss adds, "Elections in Malaysia serve more to legitimate the existing government's continued rule than to offer a chance to change the government." This is a characteristic trademark of hegemonic party systems.

Elections in hegemonic party systems sometimes become more competitive. This happened in South Korea in 1988,[8] Taiwan in the 1980s,[9] Mexico from 1988 on,[10] and Brazil between 1974 and 1982. When the playing field is still uneven but the opposition is able to win a sizeable minority of seats in the national congress and perhaps some governorships, a hegemonic party system functions within a competitive authoritarian regime.[11] Competitive authoritarian regimes are not a subset of competitive regimes (democracies and semi-democracies), and hence they do not correspond to competitive party systems.

The conceptual boundary between a hegemonic and a competitive party system does not imply the impossibility of transformation from one category

---

[8] See Chapter 11 by Joseph Wong.
[9] See Chapter 5 by Tun-jen Cheng and Yung-ming Hsu.
[10] Loaeza 1999; Magaloni 2006; Greene 2007.
[11] See Levitsky and Way 2010 on competitive authoritarianism.

to the other. If a previously hegemonic system becomes so competitive that informed citizens, politicians, and parties believe that there is a chance of electoral victory for the opposition, and if there is a free and fair vote with a reasonably level playing field, it transforms into a competitive system. Just as hegemonic systems can transform into competitive ones, the reverse can also occur, as Chapter 9 by Sorpong Peou on Cambodia shows: a competitive system can devolve into a hegemonic one.

Among the cases in this volume, Malaysia (Chapter 2), Singapore (Chapter 3), and Cambodia (Chapter 9) have hegemonic party systems. The ruling parties in these countries dominate elections, capturing 60 percent, 93 percent and 56 percent of the seats in the lower chamber in the latest elections (2013, 2011, and 2013, respectively). Malaysia is an unusual case because a coalition, the Barisan National Front (BN), rather than a single party is hegemonic. But as Weiss observes in Chapter 2, the BN effectively functions like a hegemonic party, and it is registered as a party.

Competitive and hegemonic party systems exhibit a range in electoral competitiveness. Therefore, the boundaries between hegemonic systems and the other two categories are not absolute. At the low end of the spectrum of competition, hegemonic systems differ only modestly from less repressive party-state systems. Conversely, the most competitive hegemonic systems approximate competitive systems. Of the three hegemonic cases analyzed in this volume, only the Malaysian has come close to developing into a competitive system.

Party-state systems are the third fundamental category analyzed in this volume. In these systems, for all practical purposes there is just one official party. No meaningful competition occurs even if there are elections. The elections tend toward shams. Some party-state systems function within authoritarian regimes; others function under totalitarian or post-totalitarian regimes, as is the case with China and Vietnam.[12] These regimes have less space for opposition parties than regimes with hegemonic party systems, and the elections have no consequences for which party holds power. The actors are the governing party and the state, not parties that compete freely and fairly for votes.[13] The fact that the Vietnamese and Chinese Communist Parties controlled 93 percent and 100 percent, respectively, of the seats in the national assembly is illustrative. The political regimes in which party-state systems are embedded are usually more closed than those of hegemonic party systems.

China and Vietnam have party-state systems rather than party systems. A *system* is "a regularly interacting or interdependent group of *items* forming a unified whole."[14] As Sartori argued, because a system consists of more than

---

[12] For the distinction between authoritarian and totalitarian regimes, see Linz and Stepan 1996: 38–54; Linz 2000.

[13] Sartori 1976: 42–47.

[14] *Webster's Seventh New Collegiate Dictionary* 1963: 895, emphasis added.

a single element, a party system must consist of more than one party. Hence, a party system is a set of at least two electorally meaningful parties that regularly interact in patterned ways.

As Tuong Vu on Vietnam (Chapter 6) and Yongnian Zheng on China (Chapter 7) write, the idea of a party-state system does not imply a complete fusion of the two. The party and state "are two separable political entities" (quoting Yongnian Zheng).

To synthetically capture some of these differences across the three kinds of systems analyzed in this volume, Table 14.1 shows six indicators about the political regime and the party system. The first five underscore systematic differences among competitive, hegemonic, and party-state systems.

Column 1 provides a summary judgment of the regime-type as of 2013, following the three categories and the coding rules of Mainwaring et al. (2007): democratic, semi-democratic, and authoritarian. I subdivided the latter category by incorporating Levitsky and Way's (2010) notion of competitive authoritarian regimes. The coding is based primarily on the country chapters in this volume and secondarily on other sources listed in the references and Freedom House's narrative reports.

Freedom House scores have been widely used as a measure of political democracy. The scores in Column 2 combine the measures for civil liberties and political rights. Two, the lowest possible score, reflects a high-level democracy; fourteen, the highest possible score, indicates a very closed authoritarian regime.

Column 3 shows the kind of party system using the simple classification established in this section: competitive, hegemonic, and party-state systems. Because hegemonic and party-state systems function in authoritarian regimes, Freedom House scores should be higher in countries with these systems. In line with this expectation, according to Freedom House scores, the three countries with hegemonic party systems are less democratic than six of the seven countries with competitive party systems. The exception is Thailand, which according to Freedom House scores for 2012 was about as democratic or nondemocratic as Malaysia and Singapore. However, the country chapters in this volume and Croissant and Völkel (2012) suggest that Thailand after the restoration of a competitive system was a fragile semi-democratic regime until the May 2014 coup, whereas Malaysia and Singapore are cases of electoral authoritarianism. Before the 2006 coup, Thailand consistently registered better Freedom House scores than Malaysia and Singapore.

Column 4 shows that the seat share of the largest party is generally lower in the competitive systems, ranging from 26.4 percent in Indonesia to 61.3 percent in Taiwan, than in the hegemonic party systems, which ranged from 56.3 percent to 93.1 percent, and in the party state systems (91.6 percent for Vietnam and 100.0 percent for China).

The fifth column highlights one other feature that differentiates competitive party systems from hegemonic and party-state systems. Competitive systems

TABLE 14.1. *Regime and Party System Indicators in 12 Asian Countries, 2013*

	Regime-type	Freedom House score, 2013	Kind of party system	Percentage of seats of largest party in the lower chamber (year)	Last alternation in power through elections	Mean electoral volatility
Japan	Democracy	3	Competitive	61.3 (2012)	2012	16.8
Taiwan	Democracy	3	Competitive	56.6 (2012)	2008	16.5
South Korea	Democracy	3	Competitive	50.7 (2012)	2008	36.5
India	Democracy	5	Competitive	38.0 (2009)	2004	19.2
Indonesia	Democracy	5	Competitive	26.4 (2009)	2004	27.5
Philippines	Democracy	6	Competitive	47.4 (2010)	2010	37.0
Thailand	Semi-democracy	8	Competitive	53.0 (2011)	2011	42.0
Malaysia	Competitive authoritarian	8	Hegemonic	60.0 (2013)	never	10.1
Singapore	Authoritarian	8	Hegemonic	93.1 (2011)	1959	15.4
Cambodia	Authoritarian	11	Hegemonic	56.3 (2013)	never	24.0
Vietnam	Authoritarian	12	Party-state	91.6 (2011)	never	no competitive elections for national assembly
China	Authoritarian	13	Party-state	100.0 (2007–2008)	never	no competitive elections for national assembly

Source for Column 2: Freedom House, *Freedom in the World 2013.* Available at http://www.freedomhouse.org/sites/default/files/FIW%20202013%20Charts%20and%20Graphs%20for%20Web_0.pdf. For electoral volatility, Table 1.2 in Chapter 1 of this volume.

allow for the possibility of alternation in power through elections. Party-state and hegemonic party systems do not.

The final column, with data on electoral volatility, is useful for understanding differences in institutionalization within the family of competitive party systems. The range in institutionalization across the seven competitive cases is great. Taiwan quickly developed an institutionalized party system with low electoral volatility (16.8 from 1992 to 2012). With a mean electoral volatility of 16.5, Japan also has a stable party system, and India (19.2) is not far behind. In contrast, South Korea (36.5), the Philippines (37.0), and Thailand (42.0) have inchoate systems and high electoral volatility. Based on electoral volatility, Indonesia (27.5 percent) is an intermediate case.[15]

Most hegemonic party systems have low electoral volatility. Authoritarian regimes limit competition, and hence hegemonic parties should ensure fairly consistent aggregate electoral results over time. Volatility in Malaysia and Singapore is fully consistent with this expectation.[16]

A party-state system can evolve toward a hegemonic party system. Notwithstanding the possibility of such transformations, it is better to begin with conceptual clarity about these three systems and recognize fuzziness at the boundaries than to obscure these fundamental differences.

CONCEPTUALIZING AND MEASURING PARTY SYSTEM INSTITUTIONALIZATION

Institutionalization is a process by which a practice or organization becomes well established and widely known. Actors develop expectations, orientations, and behaviors based on the premise that this practice or organization will prevail into the foreseeable future. In politics, institutionalization means that political actors have clear and stable expectations about the behavior of other actors. In Huntington's (1968: 12) words, "Institutionalization is the process by which organizations and procedures acquire value and stability."[17] An

---

[15] See Croissant and Völkel 2012 for an analysis of party system institutionalization in five of the competitive party systems analyzed in this volume – Taiwan, Indonesia, South Korea, Thailand, and the Philippines – plus Mongolia and East Timor. See Hicken 2006 and Ufen 2008 on party system institutionalization in Indonesia, Thailand, and the Philippines; and Tan 2006 on Indonesia. The judgments of these scholars about the level of institutionalization in these five cases closely parallel mine and informed it. All four articles are useful complements to this chapter. For more in-depth assessments of institutionalization of the seven competitive party systems analyzed in this volume, see these four articles.

[16] The hegemonic party systems of Mexico and Brazil 1966–1982 were also characterized by low electoral volatility. Volatility in the Brazilian lower chamber averaged 8.2 from 1966 to 1978, the last election of unquestionable hegemonic party dominance, and 9.3 from 1966 until 1982. In Mexico, from 1970 until 1985 (again, the last election of indisputable hegemonic party dominance), it averaged 8.8 for the lower chamber. .

[17] Although I follow Huntington's 1968 definition of institutionalization, I do not share his conceptualization of it (pp. 12–24). His first of four criteria is that institutionalized organizations are

institutionalized party system is one in which politicians, citizens, and organized groups develop expectations and behavior based on the premise that the fundamental contours and rules of party competition and behavior will prevail into the foreseeable future. In an institutionalized system, there is stability in who the main parties are and how they behave.

Institutionalization is neither teleological nor linear.[18] There is no necessary progression from lesser to greater institutionalization, as the chapters on the Philippines (Chapter 13), Thailand (Chapter 12), Cambodia (Chapter 9), and Vietnam (Chapter 6) show. Formerly institutionalized party systems can deinstitutionalize and even collapse, as the Italian and Venezuelan cases in the 1990s showed.[19]

Mainwaring and Scully (1995) sketched four dimensions of the institutionalization of competitive party systems.[20] First, they manifest stability in patterns of party competition. This is the easiest dimension to measure, through electoral volatility.

This dimension is less relevant for assessing the institutionalization of hegemonic party and party-state systems. Low electoral volatility in a democracy signals aggregate stability in voters' electoral choices. In contrast, low volatility in an authoritarian regime reflects the absence of real choice for voters. It does not necessarily indicate anything about what voters' sincere preferences would be in an open electoral market. Hence, it does not necessarily reflect the bonding of voters to parties.

Because authoritarian regimes limit competition, electoral results tend to be stable, and they conceal a gap between sincere support for the official party and voting results. Some authoritarian regimes that stand on weak foundations are capable of manufacturing stable electoral results. Because there is no meaningful electoral competition, party-state systems usually have low volatility. The very concept of stability in interparty competition ceases to be meaningful in party-state systems because there is none. Even party-state regimes that are weakly

---

adaptable; less institutionalized ones are rigid. But this cuts against the grain of his own definition and most others. Highly institutionalized organizations are more stable and embedded in society. This stability and embeddedness make them more likely to be rigid. See Levitsky 2003: 15–24 for an excellent discussion of this point. Huntington's third criterion of institutionalization is greater organizational autonomy with respect to social organizations. Strong connections between organized interests and parties, however, show more, not less, institutionalization. They create more party rootedness in society. In addition, I disagree with Huntington's claims about the intrinsic normative desideratum of institutionalization (pp. 24–25) – for example, his tendency to conflate the "public interest" with strong institutionalization. The Soviet Communist Party was highly institutionalized, but it is questionable how much it advanced the "public interest." I agree with Huntington's second and fourth criteria of institutionalization: more complex organizations and more unified and coherent organizations indicate greater institutionalization.

[18] Lindberg 2007 makes a converging argument.

[19] Morgan 2011; Seawright 2012.

[20] See Jones 2010: 20–26 for an operationalization of the four dimensions of institutionalization.

institutionalized on other grounds might appear to be highly institutionalized on the basis of the stability of election results.

If elections are not competitive, low volatility does not necessarily indicate anything about institutionalization. As Sorpong Peou demonstrates in Chapter 9 on Cambodia, low volatility under authoritarian rule "can occur when authoritarian leaders personalize power without institutionalizing it."

Stability in the membership of a competitive party system shows that voters are sufficiently attached to the existing electoral options that they continue to cast their ballots for the same set of parties. In less institutionalized competitive systems, formerly major parties fade and new contenders occasionally capture a sizeable share of the vote. In contrast, under a hegemonic or a party-state system, stability in the membership of the party system (if there is one) primarily reflects the suppression of the opposition and a highly uneven playing field.

Whereas the first dimension of party system institutionalization looks at system dynamics, the others look at the individual and organizational underpinnings of those dynamics. The second is that in institutionalized competitive systems, parties have strong roots in society, and many voters have attachments to parties. Many voters identify with a party, cast their ballot for it across different levels of elections (e.g., president, governor, mayor, federal and state deputy), and prefer the same party over time. Some interest associations are closely linked to parties. Strong party roots in society help provide the regularity in electoral competition that system-level institutionalization entails.[21] Significant levels of party identification, although not a necessary condition for aggregate-level stabilization, facilitate it.[22] Party identification captures Huntington's idea that institutionalization is a process by which organizations and procedures acquire value. Conversely, where parties have weak roots in society, more voters are likely to shift electoral allegiances from one election to the next, thus bringing about greater potential for high volatility.

This second dimension applies only partly to hegemonic and party-state systems. The institutionalization of hegemonic and (especially) party-state systems hinges less on their capacity to win allegiances from citizens than it does in democracies. It depends critically on state capacity, repressive capacity, governing performance, and the regime's internal cohesion and capacity to mollify some powerful organized actors such as the military and different factions of the governing party.[23] Depending on how closed or open the authoritarian regime is, it can be difficult to evaluate the depth of the governing party's rootedness in society because of the challenges of undertaking valid public opinion surveys and the lack of free and fair elections.

Party rootedness in society is also relevant to governing parties in hegemonic and party-state systems. The capacity to win support in society is an asset to the

---

[21] Green et al. 2002; Dalton and Weldon 2007.
[22] If party identification is a relatively durable partisan identity that strongly influences voting behavior, high levels of party identification sharply limit aggregate volatility.
[23] See Bellin 2012 on the institutionalization of authoritarian regimes in the Middle East.

institutionalization of these governing parties, and it is relevant to analyzing institutionalization. Many hegemonic parties including the United Malays National Organisation (UMNO) and the People's Action Party (PAP) of Singapore care deeply about popular support, and some have deep roots in society. Elections are strongly contested because these hegemonic parties desire electoral legitimacy and a reliable, credible social base. They invest many resources to develop and cultivate those linkages.[24] The same was true of the PRI in Mexico (1940–2000) and to some degree ARENA/PDS in Brazil (1966–1985) – although the Brazilian system during its heyday revolved less on electoral legitimacy and more on repression than the PRI did.

Third, in institutionalized competitive systems, voters and organized political actors accord legitimacy to parties. They see parties as a necessary part of democratic politics even if they are critical of specific parties and express skepticism about parties in general. In most contemporary democracies, citizens voice low confidence in parties, but there is still a wide range in how much citizens value parties as necessary agents of democratic representation. The legitimacy of parties helps stabilize party systems and hence is a meaningful attitudinal dimension of institutionalization. A party system could stabilize at the aggregate level even if voters do not view parties as essential parts of democracy, but the legitimacy of parties facilitates aggregate-level stability.

This third dimension again is somewhat less relevant for conceptualizing and measuring institutionalization in hegemonic and especially party-state systems. These systems do not legitimize their rule primarily on the basis of free and fair popular votes or public opinion. Governing parties usually attempt to win legitimacy, but primarily on bases other than votes: effectiveness, a divine mandate, the ability to maintain order, the leader's charisma, and so on. The relationship between the legitimacy of parties and regime stability is not clear in authoritarian regimes. If they have a cohesive repressive apparatus, authoritarian regimes can be stable even if citizens do not view the hegemonic party as a legitimate agent of representation. If they open up to more competition, what appeared to have been a high level of legitimacy of the ruling party might turn out to have been a mirage created by the distorted filters of authoritarian rule.

Hicken persuasively argues (Chapter 13) that in nondemocratic settings, the legitimacy that powerful organized actors accord to the governing party is a measure of that party's institutionalization. However, this is a somewhat different criterion than the legitimacy parties have among voters in a democratic context.

These first three dimensions revolve around elections and representation. Elections are critical in the institutionalization of competitive party systems because parties' first and foremost function is organizing to compete in and win elections. They determine who governs. In contrast, in hegemonic party

---

[24] Thanks to Allen Hicken and Erik Kuhonta for this observation.

systems and state-party systems, elections do not determine who governs.[25] The process of constituting and institutionalizing a regime and a hegemonic or a party-state system hinges primarily on other dynamics. Therefore, we need to measure institutionalization in somewhat different ways in hegemonic and especially party-state systems. In the latter, elections have a symbolic function but are not critical in how the regime functions.

Finally, in more institutionalized systems, party organizations are not subordinated to the interests of a few ambitious leaders; they acquire an independent status and value of their own.[26] The institutionalization of a party is limited as long as it is the personal instrument of a leader or a small coterie.[27] When the electorally successful parties are personalistic vehicles, system-level institutionalization is low on this fourth dimension.

Solid organizations reflect and reinforce parties' penetration in society. The solidity of party organizations is multifaceted. It includes their financial resources, their personnel and the professionalization of the party bureaucracy, their organizational penetration beyond capital cities, the routinization of procedures for selecting candidates for public office and party leadership posts, and an assessment of whether the organization is a personalistic vehicle of a dominant leader.[28] Extensive party switching such as is found in Thailand and the Philippines shows weak attachment of politicians to party labels.[29]

This final dimension shifts the focus from system-level dynamics and features to individual parties. This is not an unwitting theoretical elision in the unit of analysis. The organizational solidity of parties is an element of systemic institutionalization.[30] This final dimension is the only one of the four that works seamlessly for assessing the institutionalization of hegemonic and party-state systems. Otherwise, institutionalization cannot be conceptualized and measured in exactly the same way for hegemonic and party-state systems as for competitive party systems.

In competitive party systems, these four dimensions usually work together; they usually reinforce one another and covary positively. For example, strong party roots in society (the second dimension) make voters less available to

---

[25] This is not to say that elections in hegemonic party systems and (to a lesser degree) party-state systems are irrelevant. They can help legitimate the regime; they can offer a minor pressure valve to channel muted opposition; they can demonstrate the power of incumbents. And in some cases, including Taiwan, South Korea, Mexico, and Brazil, these elections ultimately became highly contested and paved the way to a regime transition. See Hermet et al. 1978; Loaeza 1999; Lindberg 2006; Magaloni 2006; Schedler 2006; Brownlee 2007; Greene 2007; and Hicken 2008 on elections under hegemonic party systems and other forms of authoritarian rule.

[26] Huntington 1968: 15; McGuire 1997: 7–12.

[27] Janda 1980; McGuire 1997; Basedau and Stroh 2008.

[28] Basedau and Stroh 2008.

[29] Hicken 2006.

[30] On the institutionalization of individual parties, see Janda 1980; Panebianco 1988: 53–65; Dix 1992; McGuire 1997; Randall and Svasand 2002; Levitsky 2003: 15–24; Basedau and Stroh 2008.

change electoral choice from one election to the next and hence tend to limit volatility (the first dimension).[31] A widespread view that parties are not essential to democracy (the third dimension) limits voter linkages to parties (the second dimension). Solid organizations (the fourth dimension) make it easier for parties to build strong connections to voters (the second dimension). However, there is no theoretical or empirical reason to always expect high correlations across the four dimensions. In some cases, a party system might be highly institutionalized on one dimension but less so on another.[32]

PARTY SYSTEM INSTITUTIONALIZATION AND DEMOCRACY

This volume raises important questions about the relationship between party system institutionalization and democracy. In this section, I make three points about this relationship. First, institutionalization per se is value neutral, and it has nothing to do with democracy (see also Hicken and Kuhonta's Introduction). In the short to medium term, the institutionalization of a governing authoritarian party diminishes prospects for democracy and is an asset to regime stability.[33] Without deinstitutionalizing some aspects of the hegemonic party regime or the party-state system, democracy is unattainable. Hence, it is a mistake to conflate institutionalization and democracy. This point reinforces my earlier argument about the need to distinguish among competitive party systems, hegemonic party systems, and party state systems *before* comparing institutionalization across these different kinds of systems.[34]

Several chapters in *Party System Institutionalization in Asia* show that institutionalization per se is not intrinsically good for democracy and that the institutionalization of hegemonic party systems or party-state systems works against democracy. Weiss (Chapter 2) notes that the Malaysian case shows "the potential incompatibility of a strongly institutionalized party system with democracy, if that system is institutionalized prior to democratic consolidation." Writing on Singapore's hegemonic party system, Tan (Chapter 3) notes that "party institutionalization fosters the 'iron law of oligarchy,' limits internal dissent, and constrains electoral competition." Singapore's hegemonic party system and political regime are both highly institutionalized, and yet the regime is authoritarian. Writing on the Vietnamese Communist Party, Tuong Vu (Chapter 6) asserts that "institutionalization means the establishment of a totalitarian system, while deinstitutionalization is now opening up opportunities for democratization." In Chapter 9 on Cambodia, Sorpong Peou makes a converging argument.

---

[31] Dalton and Weldon 2007.
[32] Zucco forthcoming.
[33] Smith 2005.
[34] Lindberg 2007 forcefully makes the same argument.

Second, the volume raises interesting questions about whether having an institutionalized party that ruled under an authoritarian regime is an asset for party system institutionalization under a subsequent democracy. Hicken and Kuhonta in this volume note this possibility, and elsewhere (2011) they suggest that "to get a highly institutionalized party system it may be necessary to have some form of an authoritarian party in power at an earlier point in time." Along related lines, Riedl (2014) argues that where authoritarian incumbents in Africa were stronger, a more institutionalized party system resulted after transitions to competitive regimes. The solidity of the authoritarian ruling party is part of her measure of the strength of the authoritarian incumbents.

Hicken and Kuhonta's effort to understand connections between past regimes and parties and the present is a valuable contribution. A "strong" form of their argument (i.e., that an earlier institutionalized authoritarian might be necessary for an institutionalized contemporary party system), however, does not travel in time to the early European and U.S. cases or India, or in space to contemporary Latin America. In many nineteenth- and early-twentieth-century cases of democratization (including the United States and the United Kingdom), it was not necessary to have an authoritarian party in power at an earlier point in time in order to develop a highly institutionalized party system. The Brazilian case indicates that even in the Third Wave of democratization, it is possible to develop an institutionalized system that does not rest on the shoulders of the prior governing authoritarian party.[35] Two of the highly institutionalized Latin American party systems today (Chile and Uruguay) are in countries that did not have governing parties during the dictatorships of 1973–1990 and 1973–1984, respectively. Among the countries included in this volume, India is also an exception to the idea that an earlier authoritarian party is a necessary condition for the development of a moderately institutionalized democratic party system. India fairly quickly developed a moderately institutionalized party system after 1952 (see Chapter 8 by Csaba Nikolenyi).

In some Third and Fourth Wave cases of democratization, an authoritarian ruling party can facilitate building an institutionalized party system under democracy. Building a solid party system has been challenging in most cases of Third and Fourth Wave democratization, except for countries such as Chile and Uruguay that had long-established democracies with solid parties in earlier periods. The chapters in this volume on South Korea (Chapter 11), Thailand (Chapter 12), the Philippines (Chapter 13), and Indonesia (Chapter 10) add to the evidence that party system development in late democratizing countries is

---

[35] After governing all of Brazil's states except one continuously from 1966 through 1982 under military rule, the official party became a minor competitor by 1994. It was unable to field a competitive presidential candidate in any election since the transition to democracy in 1985. Because the formerly hegemonic party was relegated to the dustbin of history, it is doubtful that its earlier institutionalization under authoritarian rule helped institutionalize the post-1985 democratic party system.

difficult. Even South Korea, which enjoyed many positive conditions for the institutionalization of a democratic party system, has not done so. As Joseph Wong shows (Chapter 11), a somewhat institutionalized hegemonic party, the Democratic Justice Party (DJP) from 1980 to 1987 gave rise to a fluid system in the post-1987 democracy, characterized by high electoral volatility, especially for a country with its standard of living. In important respects, South Korea should have been a most likely case of institutionalizing a democratic party system in the aftermath of a transition. Its level of development, its solid state, and its history of sustained economic success were very favorable conditions.

Among the late democratizing countries analyzed in this volume, Taiwan is the only one that has developed an institutionalized party system. In Chapter 5, Tun-jen Cheng and Yung-ming Hsu argue convincingly that the institutionalization of a hegemonic party system under authoritarian rule proved to be an asset in subsequent democratization. An institutionalized democratic party system emerged during the transition, building on the foundation provided by competition between the hegemonic party (the Kuomintang [KMT]) and the partisan opposition during decades of authoritarian rule: "Age-old partisan competition between the two sides ... largely laid the foundation for the party system in democratic Taiwan." This is consistent with Hicken and Kuhonta's argument that an earlier solid authoritarian party is an advantage for subsequent institutionalization under democracy.

In Taiwan and Mexico, the combination of an institutionalized ruling party and an institutionalized opposition party (or parties, in Mexico) before the transition to democracy, and of regular competition between them, helped pave the way for building democratic party systems. If the combination of an institutionalized governing party and an institutionalized opposition party or parties is key, then the cases of Taiwan and Mexico do not offer clear lessons for cases such as China, Vietnam, and Singapore, in which opposition parties are extremely weak.

In other Asian cases, as the chapters on Malaysia (Chapter 2), Singapore (Chapter 3), Vietnam (Chapter 6), and China (Chapter 7) note, the institutionalization of hegemonic party systems or of party-state systems has facilitated their longevity without so far having any advantage for democratization. Moreover, as the Russian and many post-Soviet cases show, the transition from an institutionalized party-state system to an institutionalized competitive party system is fraught with challenges. The Soviet Communist Party was highly institutionalized, and yet the post-transition Russian party system was weakly institutionalized.[36] In the post-Soviet cases, democratic party system institutionalization is generally most advanced where the communist parties quickly became minor contenders.

Party System Institutionalization in Asia does not resolve the balance between the positive and negative legacies of an institutionalized hegemonic

[36] Moser 2001.

party system for subsequent democratic politics, but it has the merit of directly posing this important question. Although I applaud the fact that they have raised this important issue, I am less sanguine than Hicken and Kuhonta (2011) that the institutionalization of the ruling party under authoritarian regimes is generally an advantage for the institutionalization of a subsequent competitive party system. Party institutionalization under authoritarian rule can have pernicious as well as positive effects on building a subsequent democratic party system. If the authoritarian party relied extensively on patronage networks to build support for the regime – as usually occurs – the effects on party building under democracy are not unequivocally salutary. If it engaged in vote buying and does not forgo that practice in the new democracy, it would directly weaken the level of democracy. In addition, regime transitions can be disruptive. Parties that ruled under authoritarianism do not always fare well under democracy, as several post-communist and the Brazilian examples show.

The impact of an earlier governing authoritarian party on the institutionalization of a subsequent competitive party system seems to depend on the characteristics of that governing party and on the relationship between the party and the state. In some Asian cases including Taiwan, South Korea, and Singapore, the governing autocratic parties built effective states.[37] These parties were not predatory or patrimonial to the same degree as many ruling authoritarian parties,[38] and their social and economic achievements should make it easier for them to win votes in a new democratic era and should presumably facilitate institutionalizing a democratic party system. Patrimonial (in Max Weber's sense) ruling authoritarian parties can be quite institutionalized on some dimensions, but they are likely to be more of a hindrance than an asset to building a democratic party system.

The third and final point is that an institutionalized party system is functional for democracy. It does not ensure good democratic outcomes, but over the medium and long terms, it is difficult to have good outcomes under democracy without a reasonably institutionalized system.[39] In Chapter 13 on the Philippines, Hicken makes a similar argument.

An institutionalized party system helps promote better outcomes under democracy for several reasons. It helps organize the legislature along programmatic lines.[40] Where politicians are less attached to parties, as is true in many less institutionalized systems, patronage is the glue that binds legislative coalitions –

---

[37] On state capacity in South Korea, see Evans 1995. The World Bank Governance Indicators register the perception that Singapore has achieved strong state capacity as measured by its high scores for government effectiveness (2.41 standard deviations above the world mean in 2007), regulatory quality (1.87 standard deviations above the mean), rule of law (1.79 standard deviations above the mean), and control of corruption (2.20 standard deviations above the mean). See Kaufmann, Kray, and Mastruzzi 2008.

[38] An extreme example is ruling parties in sultanistic regimes.

[39] Ufen 2008.

[40] Aldrich 1995.

and it has a cost in terms of efficient provision of public goods. In an institutionalized party system, political outsiders face great barriers to becoming head of government – and many political outsiders have governed poorly. As Hicken notes in Chapter 13, an institutionalized party system provides longer time horizons, which is useful for effective governance.[41]

It is not coincidental that the least two institutionalized competitive party systems studied in this volume, the Philippines (Chapter 13) and Thailand (Chapter 12), have experienced persistent difficulties in democratic governance. Thailand had military coups and democratic breakdowns in 2006 and 2014. The Philippines has also endured frequent political violence and turmoil including a declaration of martial law in December 2009, widespread corruption and cases of notorious electoral fraud, and powerful influences of political clans of dubious democratic credentials. Weakly institutionalized party systems do not directly cause these negative political outcomes, but they provide an underpinning for such practices.[42]

Pérez-Liñán and Mainwaring (2013) provide systematic evidence based on Latin American cases about the positive effects of party system institutionalization on the level of democracy. The past (prior to 1978) level of competitive party system institutionalization helps explain the level of democracy (measured by Freedom House scores) in the Third Wave of democratization. This finding meshes with the argument by Hicken and Kuhonta (Introduction to this volume and 2011) that early patterns often have long-lasting effects.

Even among competitive party systems, however, the relationship between institutionalization and healthy democracy is far from linear. Hyperinstitutionalization might imply a stultified party system and could be consistent with an anemic democracy.[43] A clear relationship between party system institutionalization and good democratic governance probably holds only at the low end of the spectrum; that is, weak party system institutionalization tends to impede good democratic governance.

FINAL WORDS

This volume has advanced the debate about party system institutionalization in several ways. By analyzing competitive, hegemonic, and party-state systems, it opened important new research questions. I argued that it is essential to consider differences across these three kinds of systems before we analyze the level of institutionalization because institutionalization involves somewhat different processes according to the kind of system that exists. But analyzing them together has enabled the authors to advance knowledge of how

---

[41] See also O'Donnell 1994.

[42] O'Donnell 1994; Ufen 2008; Croissant and Völkel 2012: 257–258; Flores-Macias 2012; Hicken, Chapter 13.

[43] Coppedge 1994; Schedler 1995.

institutionalization occurs in different systems; of why institutionalization of a hegemonic party system or a party-state system is sometimes inimical to democracy yet how it can in others cases help foster the subsequent institutionalization of a democratic party system; and of what measures of institutionalization travel seamlessly from one kind of system to another, which do not, and why. The volume has also brought Asia into the broader conversation about party system institutionalization, and it has advanced the knowledge comparative political scientists have of the Asian cases.

REFERENCES

Aldrich, J. H. 1995. *Why Parties? The Origin and Transformation of Political Parties in America*. Chicago: University of Chicago Press.

Basedau, M., and A. Stroh. 2008. Measuring Party Institutionalization in Developing Countries: A New Research Instrument Applied to 28 African Political Parties. German Institute of Global and Area Studies Working Paper No. 69 (February). Available at http://www.giga-hamburg.de/dl/download.php?d=/content/publikationen/pdf/wp69_basedau-stroh.pdf.

Bellin, E. 2012. Reconsidering the Robustness of Authoritarianism in the Middle East. *Comparative Politics* 44(2): 127–149.

Brownlee, J. 2007. *Authoritarianism in an Age of Democratization*. Cambridge and New York: Cambridge University Press.

Coppedge, M. 1994. *Strong Parties and Lame Ducks: Presidential Partyarchy and Factionalism in Venezuela*. Stanford: Stanford University Press.

Croissant, A. and P. Völkel. 2012. Party System Types and Party System Institutionalization: Comparing New Democracies in East and Southeast Asia. *Party Politics* 18(2): 235–265.

Dahl, R. A. 1971. *Polyarchy: Participation and Opposition*. New Haven: Yale University Press.

Dalton, R. J., and S. Weldon. 2007. Partisanship and Party System Institutionalization. *Party Politics* 13(2): 179–196.

Dix, R. H. 1992. Democratization and the Institutionalization of Latin American Political Parties. *Comparative Political Studies* 24(4): 488–511.

Evans, P. 1995. *Embedded Autonomy: States and Industrial Transformation*. Princeton: Princeton University Press.

Flores Macías, G. A. 2012. *After Neoliberalism? The Left and Economic Reforms in Latin America*. Oxford and New York: Oxford University Press.

Green, D. P., B. Palmquist, and E. Schickler. 2002. *Partisan Hearts and Minds: Political Parties and the Social Identities of Voters*. New Haven: Yale University Press.

Greene, K. F. 2007. *Why Dominant Parties Lose: Mexico's Democratization in Comparative Perspective*. Cambridge: Cambridge University Press.

Hermet, G., R. Rose, and A. Rouquié (Eds.). 1978. *Elections without Choice*. New York: Wiley.

Hicken, A. 2006. Stuck in the Mud: Parties and Party Systems in Democratic Southeast Asia. *The Taiwan Journal of Democracy* 2(2): 23–46.

Hicken, A. 2008. *Building Party Systems in Developing Democracies*. New York: Cambridge University Press.

Hicken, A., and E. Kuhonta. 2011. Shadows from the Past: Party System Institutionalization in Asia. *Comparative Political Studies* 44(5): 572–597.

Huntington, S. P. 1968. *Political Order in Changing Societies.* New Haven: Yale University Press.

Janda, K. 1980. *Political Parties: A Cross National Survey.* New York: Free Press.

Johnson, E. P. 2002. Streams of Least Resistance: The Institutionalization of Political Parties and Democracy in Indonesia. Ph.D. dissertation, University of Virginia.

Jones, M. P. 2010. Political Parties and Party Systems in Latin America. In C. Scartascini, E. Stein, and M. Tomassi (Eds.), *How Democracy Works: Political Institutions, Actors, and Arenas in Latin American Policymaking*, pp. 19–46. Washington, DC: Inter-American Development Bank and David Rockefeller Center for Latin American Studies, Harvard University.

Kaufmann, D., A. Kraay, and M. Mastruzzi. 2008. Governance Matters VII: Aggregate and Individual Governance Indicators, 1996–2007. The World Bank (June). Available at http://info.worldbank.org/governance/wgi/pdf/GovernanceMattersVII.pdf.

Levitsky, S. 2003. *Transforming Labor-Based Parties in Latin America: Argentine Peronism in Comparative Perspective.* Cambridge: Cambridge University Press.

Levitsky, S., and L. Way. 2010. *Competitive Authoritarianism: Hybrid Regimes after the Cold War.* Cambridge: Cambridge University Press.

Lindberg, S. I. 2006. *Democracy and Elections in Africa.* Baltimore: Johns Hopkins University Press.

Lindberg, S. I. 2007. Institutionalization of Party Systems? Stability and Fluidity among Legislative Parties in Africa's Democracies. *Government and Opposition* 42(2): 215–241.

Linz, J. J. 2000. *Totalitarian and Authoritarian Regimes.* Boulder, CO: Lynne Rienner.

Linz, J. J., and A. Stepan. 1996. *Problems of Democratic Transition and Consolidation.* Baltimore: The Johns Hopkins University Press.

Lipset, S. M., and S. Rokkan (Eds.). 1967. Cleavage Structures, Party Systems, and Voter Alignments: An Introduction. In *Party Systems and Voter Alignments: Cross-National Perspectives*, pp. 1–64. New York: Free Press.

Loaeza, S. 1999. *El Partido Acción Nacional: La larga marcha, 1939–1994. Oposición leal y partido de protesta.* Mexico City: Fondo de Cultura Económica.

Magaloni, B. 2006. *Voting for Autocracy: Hegemonic Party Survival and Its Demise in Mexico.* Cambridge: Cambridge University Press.

Mainwaring, S. P. 1999. *Rethinking Party Systems in the Third Wave of Democratization: The Case of Brazil.* Stanford: Stanford University Press.

Mainwaring, S. P., D. Brinks, and A. Pérez-Liñán. 2007. Classifying Political Regimes in Latin America, 1945–2004. In G. L. Munck (Ed.), *Regimes and Democracy in Latin America: Theories and Methods*, pp. 123–160. Oxford: Oxford University Press.

Mainwaring, S. P., and T. R. Scully (Eds.). 1995. Party Systems in Latin America. In *Building Democratic Institutions: Party Systems in Latin America*, pp. 1–34. Stanford: Stanford University Press.

Mainwaring, S. P., and M. Torcal. 2006. Party System Institutionalization and Party System Theory after the Third Wave of Democratization. In R. S. Katz and W. Crotty (Eds.), *Handbook of Political Parties*, pp. 204–227. London: Sage.

McGuire, J. W. 1997. *Peronism without Perón: Unions, Parties, and Democracy in Argentina.* Stanford: Stanford University Press.

Morgan, J. 2011. *Bankrupt Representation and Party System Collapse.* University Park: Pennsylvania State University Press.

Moser, R. G. 2001. *Unexpected Outcomes: Electoral Systems, Political Parties, and Representation in Russia*. Pittsburgh: University of Pittsburgh Press.

Moser, R. G., and E. Scheiner. 2012. *Electoral Systems and Political Context: How the Effects of Rules Vary across New and Established Democracies*. New York: Cambridge University Press.

O'Donnell, G. 1994. Delegative Democracy. *Journal of Democracy* 5(1): 55–69.

Panebianco, A. 1988. *Political Parties: Organization and Power*. Cambridge: Cambridge University Press.

Pérez-Liñán, A., and S. P. Mainwaring. 2013. Regime Legacies and Levels of Democracy: Evidence from Latin America. *Comparative Politics* 45: 379–397.

Randall, V., and L. Svåsand. 2002. Party Institutionalization in New Democracies. *Party Politics* 8: 5–29.

Riedl, R. B. 2014. *Authoritarian Origins of Democratic Party Systems in Africa: A Comparative Study of Ghana, Senegal, Gambia, and Benin*. New York: Cambridge University Press.

Sani, G., and G. Sartori. 1983. Polarization, Fragmentation, and Competition in Western Democracies. In H. Daalder and P. Mair (Eds.), *Western European Party Systems: Continuity and Change*, pp. 307–340. London: Sage Publications.

Sartori, G. 1976. *Parties and Party Systems: A Framework for Analysis*. New York and Cambridge: Cambridge University Press.

Schedler, A. 1995. Under- and Overinstitutionalization: Some Ideal Typical Propositions Concerning Old and New Party Systems. University of Notre Dame, Kellogg Institute for International Studies Working Paper #213 (March).

Schedler, A. (Ed.). 2006. *Electoral Authoritarianism: The Dynamics of Unfree Competition*. Boulder, CO: Lynne Rienner.

Seawright, J. 2012. *Party-System Collapse: The Roots of Crisis in Peru and Venezuela*. Stanford: Stanford University Press.

Smith, B. 2005. Life of the Party: The Origins of Regime Breakdown and Persistence under Single-Party Rule. *World Politics* 57 (April): 421–451.

Stockton, H. 2001. Political Parties, Party Systems, and Democracy in East Asia: Lessons from Latin America. *Comparative Political Studies* 34(1): 94–119.

Tan, P. J. 2006. Indonesia Seven Years after Soeharto: Party System Institutionalization in a New Democracy. *Contemporary Southeast Asia* 28(1): 88–114.

Ufen, A. 2008. Political Party and Party System Institutionalization in South East Asia: Lessons for Democratic Consolidation in Indonesia, the Philippines, and Thailand. *The Pacific Review* i 327–350.

Zucco, C. (Forthcoming). Estabilidad sin raíces: la institucionalización del sistema de partidos brasileño. In M. Torcal (Ed.), *Los problemas de la institucionalización de los sistemas de partidos en América Latina*. Barcelona: CIDOB.

Index